FRANKFORT
TUCKY
BIG SANDY RIVER
VIRGINIA
Winston Salem
KNOXVILLE
RALEIGH
Asheville
CHARLOTTE
NORTH
CAROLINA
Chatsworth
Fairmouth JASPER
Liberty
SOUTH
Anderson
Athens
COLUMBIA
CAROLINA
Madison
Monticello
SANTEE RIVER
Griffin
UMBUS
MACON
SWANNAH RIVER
ALTAMAHA RIVER
GEORGIA
TALLAHASSEE
Jackson-ville
FLORIDA

The Atlantic Ocean!

SCALE

DECORATIONS and TEXT
BY PVT. BOYD C. MUTSCHLER
MAP DRAWN AND PUBLISHED
BY 16th ENGRS. REPRODUCTION UNIT
1st ARMORED DIVISION FORT KNOX KY.

NEUVERS OF 1941

ORTANT PROBLEMS PERTAINING TO WAR
nd sundry delineations of an
to the capacity of Soldiers

THE RISE
OF THE
G.I. ARMY
1940–1941

Also by Paul Dickson

Think Tanks

The Electronic Battlefield

Chow: A Cook's Tour of Military Food

The Dickson Baseball Dictionary

*War Slang: American Fighting Words and Phrases
from the Civil War to the Gulf War*

The Official Rules

Sputnik: The Shock of the Century

The Bonus Army: An American Epic (with Thomas B. Allen)

A Dictionary of the Space Age

Bill Veeck: Baseball's Greatest Maverick

Courage in the Moment: The Civil Rights Struggle, 1961–1964

Leo Durocher: Baseball's Prodigal Son

THE RISE OF THE G.I. ARMY 1940–1941

THE FORGOTTEN STORY OF
HOW AMERICA FORGED
A POWERFUL ARMY
BEFORE PEARL HARBOR

PAUL DICKSON

Atlantic Monthly Press
New York

FIRST EDITION

Published simultaneously in Canada
Printed in Canada

This book was set in 11-pt. Janson Text LT by Alpha Design & Composition of Pittsfield, NH.

First Grove Atlantic hardcover edition: July 2020

Library of Congress Cataloging-in-Publication data is available for this title.

ISBN 978-0-8021-4767-7
eISBN 978-0-8021-4768-4

Atlantic Monthly Press
an imprint of Grove Atlantic
154 West 14th Street
New York, NY 10011

Distributed by Publishers Group West

groveatlantic.com

20 21 22 23   10 9 8 7 6 5 4   3 2 1

To the memory of Thomas B. Allen and James Srodes—great, good friends and accomplished fellow writers—both of whom were constantly at my elbow helping and encouraging me with this book but who would not live to see it published.

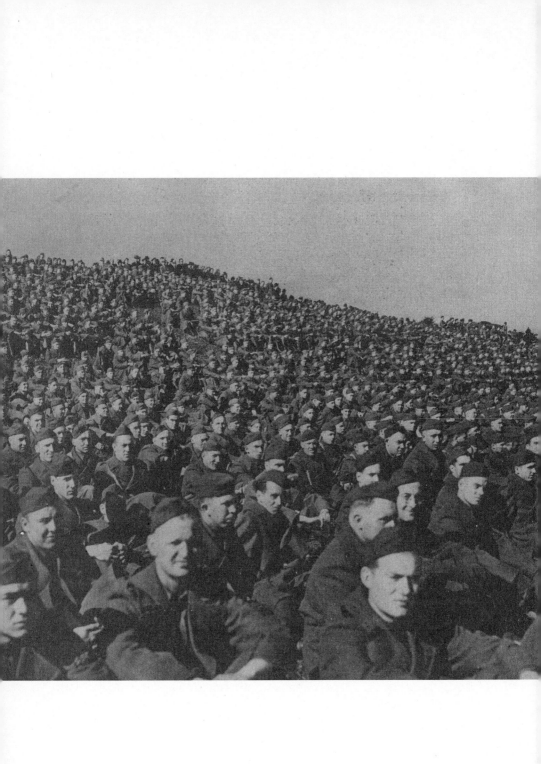

So sorry was the state of the U.S. Army in 1939 that had Pancho Villa been alive to raid the southwestern United States it would have been as ill-prepared to repulse or punish him as it had been in 1916.

—Carlo D'Este, *Patton: A Genius for War*

World War II was the largest and most violent armed conflict in the history of mankind. However, the half century that now separates us from that conflict has exacted its toll on our collective knowledge. While World War II continues to absorb the interest of military scholars and historians, as well as its veterans, a generation of Americans has grown to maturity largely unaware of the political, social, and military implications of a war that, more than any other, united us as a people with a common purpose.

—Michael P. Stone, Secretary of the Army, 1992

Far-flung ordinary men, unspectacular but free, rousing out of their habits and their homes, got up early one morning, flexed their muscles, learned (as amateurs) the manual of arms, and set out across perilous plains and oceans to whop the bejesus out of the professionals.

—Norman Corwin, *On a Note of Triumph*,
his hour-long CBS Radio broadcast
after victory in Europe, May 8, 1945

CONTENTS

Prologue   *xi*

Chapter 1   A Rude Awakening   1

Chapter 2   The Tree Army to the Rescue   23

Chapter 3   A "Phoney" War Abroad and   43
a Mock War at Home

Chapter 4   For the Want of a Nail   72

Chapter 5   "Your Number Came Up":   100
The 1940 Peacetime Draft

Chapter 6   Assembling the New Army: 122
"The Blind Leading the Blind"

Chapter 7   The Battle of Tennessee and   148
the "Yoo-Hoo" Incident

Chapter 8   "Over the Hill in October":   168
Treason, Sabotage, and the Vote

Chapter 9   Stagecraft: The Extraordinary Preparations   190
for the War in Louisiana

Chapter 10   The Battle of the Bayous   209

Chapter 11   Promotion and Purge   241

Chapter 12   The Carolinas: The Final Scrimmage   251

Chapter 13   December 7, 1941   279

Chapter 14   "Little Libya," Irish Maneuvers, and   293
      Operation Torch

Chapter 15   Victory Laps: V-E, V-J, and—Later—   317
      the Double V

     Acknowledgments   *351*

     Picture Credits   *354*

     Bibliography   *355*

     Notes   *369*

     Index   *415*

PROLOGUE

The United States of America had let down its defenses. In contrast to the four million Americans armed by the end of World War I, by 1935 the United States Regular Army had declined to 118,750 men, which, as Army Chief of Staff Douglas MacArthur noted, "could be crowded into Yankee Stadium" and he added that it would be "relatively helpless" in the event of a foreign invasion.

The situation was little improved on September 1, 1939, the day on which Germany invaded Poland and a day when the United States Army was smaller than that of Portugal, with fewer than 200,000 men. American troops were still learning obsolete skills and preparing for defensive warfare on a small scale rather than for a two-ocean war overseas. Most of the Army's divisions were staffed at half-strength and scattered across numerous posts. Their equipment was also obsolete, and their reliance on horses and mules was anachronistic. The Army officer corps harbored many not suited to lead troops into combat.

In the latter part of the 20th century, many Americans either never knew or forgot that a vast American citizen army had been created prior to the attack on Pearl Harbor. Also largely forgotten was that during those 828 days between the beginning of the war in 1939 and the "day of infamy," December 7, 1941, a fully functioning peacetime military draft system had been put in place and that after a purge of senior officers, a new cohort of senior officers was rising through the ranks, which would eventually lead the nation and its allies to victory. What is more, this new peacetime army was given a dress rehearsal for the war ahead in the form of three massive military maneuvers in the spring, summer, and fall of 1941, which ended just a few days before the attack on Pearl Harbor.

Heading into the third decade of the 21st century, this element in the narrative of the Second World War has moved farther in the margins of history. I base the assertion that all this has been lost or forgotten in recalling the World War II narrative on personal experience. Here is but one example: when first I began researching the extraordinary but largely untold story of the 1940 military draft and the 1941 maneuvers, I mentioned the prewar draft to several people at a Fourth of July party and was corrected by a well-read man who had served in the U.S. Air Force and fancied himself a student of American military history. He was convinced I was wrong and insisted that the nation in 1940 was still mired in a deep period of isolation and could not possibly have mobilized before the war. He advised me to check my facts.

The primary question I wanted to research was how the United States had been able to create a well-led, mobile army that was in place by the time of the attack on Pearl Harbor. Beyond that, I wondered how the U.S. Army could have been ready to field infantry and armored divisions, made up in large part with draftees and volunteers, to stand up to Adolf Hitler's Storm Troopers and Panzer divisions on the ground, first in North Africa and then Europe.

The roots of the answers could be traced to events a decade before Pearl Harbor. Henry L. Stimson was a leading member of what was once referred to as the Establishment. Born into a wealthy New York family in 1867, he graduated from Yale and then Harvard Law School. A Republican, Stimson's career in public service began in 1906, when President Theodore Roosevelt appointed him to the position of U.S. attorney for the Southern District of New York, where he became known for his vigorous prosecution of antitrust cases. Stimson served as secretary of war for President William Howard Taft in 1911, served as an artillery officer in the U.S. Army during the First World War, and in 1929, President Herbert Hoover made him his secretary of state.

In May 1931, Secretary Stimson, now 64, met with his old friend and fellow New York attorney Grenville Clark, 49. The two men had worked together in the period before the First World War. In 1915, Stimson had assisted Clark in creating the Plattsburg Plan, under which some 16,000 business and other professional men were trained at their own expense to be Army officers at the Plattsburg Barracks in New York State and other locations. Because of the success of the officer training program, which was in full operation well before the United States entered the war, Clark was seen as an apostle of military preparedness and, by extension, universal military service.*

During their 1931 meeting, Stimson made a bold prediction: that within ten years, Germany and Japan would join hands in an alliance and ignite a second world war. He thought that this time Germany would run all over France and the rest of Europe, Japan would run over much of China, and then Germany would attack Russia. He foresaw a ten-year war in which the United States would bear the brunt of the fight, unless a coalition of nations—namely Great Britain, Russia, and the United States—could be formed, in which case the war could be ended in five. He then asked Clark if he would undertake a secret mission, monitoring the situation through intelligence-gathering trips overseas, mainly into China and Russia.[1]

Clark turned down the assignment but did not forget Stimson's prediction. After the Nazi invasion of Norway in April 1940, Clark believed Stimson's prediction was about to come true and proposed that the United States establish its first-ever peacetime military draft.

After a long battle for approval, a bill was passed and made into law on September 16, 1940, calling for the registration of all American men between the ages of 21 and 34; they would be given a registration number based on a number assigned by their local draft board, where

---

* In 1940, the accepted spelling of the municipality in Upstate New York was Plattsburg. It was later changed to Plattsburgh, which is how it is commonly referred to today. Earlier, the Pennsylvania city known as Pittsburg had been given the official spelling of Pittsburgh.

registration cards had been shuffled and numbered sequentially from one to the number of the last man registered by that unit. After the assignment of numbers was over, the numbers were printed on slips of paper, which were put into capsules that were then dumped into a ten-gallon fishbowl, to be drawn one at a time to establish the draft order. On October 29, 1940, Henry Stimson put on a blindfold, reached into the fishbowl, and pulled out the first capsule. Stimson was now President Franklin D. Roosevelt's new secretary of war, appointed to that position at Clark's suggestion. President Roosevelt then announced the number that had been drawn: 158. Across the nation, 6,175 young men who had been the 158th man to register at their local draft board held that number; many of them would be in uniform within a matter of weeks.

Many people believe that the United States built an army with volunteers and draftees *after* the Japanese attack on Pearl Harbor. But in fact, it was the controversial peacetime draft before Pearl Harbor that put the nation in a position to fight so quickly and effectively.

Beyond the draft itself, a key element of the transformation was a series of large-scale maneuvers. The most famous were the Louisiana Maneuvers of 1941, which allowed the United States to test itself and learn by the mistakes it made in mock warfare, in which the infantry fired blanks instead of bullets and warplanes dropped flour bags rather than bombs. Not only did the maneuvers train the men in crucial new weapons and methods of warfare, but they also helped create a new and unique "G.I." culture that was invaluable in boosting morale and bonding men from all backgrounds into a cohesive group before they set off to fight around the world. These boys of the Great Depression brought with them skills and attitudes their fathers and uncles had not had during the First World War. To cite one small but significant example, these youngsters could read maps, having been brought up reading gas station road maps. They also knew engines and having seen their first jeep or Piper Cub light aircraft, within minutes would be under the hood trying to figure out how they could make the engine work better.

But key members of Congress vowed not to extend the original draft legislation, which had called for only one year of active duty. A political battle erupted between those supporting the extension and the continued training of the new army of draftees and those who wanted to bring them home and effectively isolate the United States from global conflict. The battle reached its zenith only weeks before Pearl Harbor, when the House of Representatives came within a single vote of dismantling the draft and sending hundreds of thousands of men home, which would have all but destroyed the United States Army. The isolationists were led by the charismatic, pro-Nazi American hero Charles Lindbergh, who pitted himself against President Franklin D. Roosevelt. The two came to despise one another after the Nazi invasion of Poland, when Lindbergh pleaded for the United States to look the other way as Hitler conquered Europe. Besides key members of Congress, other advocates of isolation included automaker Henry Ford, a young Walt Disney, and Teddy Roosevelt Jr., son of the 26th president.

As the political battle raged, the Army's chief of staff, General George Catlett Marshall, with Franklin Roosevelt's support and authority, created a new army, purging from it more than a thousand officers he deemed unfit. Men whose names would become famous in the war in Europe would emerge as stars during the training of the draftees in the 1941 maneuvers.

Atop the list was the brilliant but arrogant George S. Patton, a veteran of the First World War, who called the draftees "civilians in khaki pants." Much has been written about Patton during the two world wars, but little has been written about his role as a prime catalyst in preparing the nation for combat and victory. Patton, born to a wealthy California couple, grew from a colonel stationed at Fort Myer in Virginia, where he was deeply involved in society horse shows, into an audacious and brilliant tank commander. Dwight David Eisenhower would also emerge from these exercises. After the war, Eisenhower credited the war games in Louisiana as the "grand maneuver" that proved of incalculable value in winning the war.

Marshall's challenges were many. A lot of the draftees were malnourished and otherwise suffering under the difficult circumstances common in the Great Depression. Many were not happy about their new status, especially when posted to remote bases, where they were bored and homesick. Some threatened to desert if the original one-year period of service was extended.

But attitudes changed with the three realistic war games staged in 1941, in which more than 820,000 new soldiers participated. Conducted in Tennessee, Louisiana, and the Carolinas, the exercises transformed the way Americans would wage war and paved the way for the highly disciplined, fast-moving units, including armored cavalry units led by bold and resourceful officers that led to victory in North Africa and Europe. The maneuvers themselves tell a dramatic story filled with colorful characters and monumental (sometimes comic) missteps, taken as the Army learned by its mistakes. But the maneuvers—largely unchronicled—are also essential to understanding the United States' involvement in World War II and the ultimate outcome of the war. The Louisiana games, held in the late summer and early fall of 1941, were among the most watched and carefully reported events of 1941—but they were largely forgotten when real war ensued with Japan's attack on Pearl Harbor on December 7 and Germany's declaration of war on the United States on December 11.

This is the story of how hundreds of thousands of young men were drafted and transformed into an organized, effective fighting force able to invade North Africa ten months after Pearl Harbor, many critical months ahead of the time Hitler's planners had predicted for a significant American intervention. After heavy losses in North Africa, the U.S. Army learned quickly and ultimately prevailed there, jumped into Sicily, and moved up through Italy into Europe, which eventually led to victory in Europe. The counter-narrative to this book will be the battle fought against the power of Jim Crow and the establishment of racial integration of the Armed Forces. The battle for integration would be fought at the highest level, pitting a reluctant Franklin D. Roosevelt against A. Philip Randolph, who with other civil rights leaders threatened a massive march on Washington.

CHAPTER 1

A RUDE AWAKENING

At 2:50 a.m. on Friday, September 1, 1939, President Franklin D. Roosevelt was awakened by a telephone call from the U.S. ambassador to France, William Bullitt, who reported that Nazi Germany had just invaded Poland and was bombing her cities.

"Well, Bill," the president said. "It has come at last. God help us all."[1]

At 4:30 a.m., Roosevelt issued a futile plea to Germany and other European nations to refrain from bombing civilian populations or unfortified cities from the air. He requested "an immediate reply," which he knew would not be forthcoming.

Later that morning, FDR formally appointed General George C. Marshall chief of staff of the United States Army, a job that officially made Marshall the president's top military adviser. Marshall replaced General Malin Craig, who had reached the mandatory retirement age of 64 the previous day. A graduate of the Virginia Military Institute, Marshall had been a highly regarded staff officer for General John J. "Black Jack" Pershing, the commander of the American Expeditionary Force on the Western Front in Europe during World War I. Marshall had later become assistant commandant at the Army Infantry School and had served as deputy chief of staff in Washington since 1938.

Roosevelt had actually selected Marshall on July 1, when Marshall was appointed acting chief of staff and had begun assuming the full responsibilities of the job. At the time, some noted that Roosevelt had jumped over 20 major generals (two-star generals) and 14 brigadier generals (one-star generals) to get to Brigadier General Marshall, though a majority of those men were within four years of retirement age.

The appointment came as something of a surprise to many in the military, who thought FDR's new chief of staff would be General Hugh Drum, the next man in line for the position and the logical choice; but Drum, who wanted the job, had self-promoted himself out of it. He had been pushing for the job for a decade and had lobbied heavily to get it—for example, exhorting Colonel George S. Patton to visit then retired general Pershing to persuade him to recommend Drum to the president. Roosevelt had been lobbied so fiercely by Drum supporters that it was rumored he could be heard wandering about the White House muttering, "*Drum, Drum,* I wish he'd stop beating his *drum.*"[2]

Three other men wanted the job badly enough to lobby for it, and through their friends and political allies had bombarded the White House with arguments in their favor. Marshall, who clearly was interested in the job, was appalled by the other candidates' lobbying and chose to remain silent. Marshall's biographer, Leonard Mosley, later observed: "All the other hopefuls were making such a noise about themselves, and so many big drums were being beaten on their behalf, that it was his silence that would make him most audible to the President."[3]

Roosevelt had summoned Marshall to his study in the White House the previous April to announce the decision to consider him for the job. Marshall let the president know quite directly that he always "wanted to be able to speak his mind."

"Is that all right?" Marshall asked.

"Yes," the commander in chief replied, smiling slightly.

"You said 'yes' pleasantly, but it may be unpleasant," Marshall responded.[4,5]

This was what Roosevelt wanted to hear: he wanted someone who could stand up to him on military matters, as Marshall had done twice previously as deputy chief of staff, when he had respectfully but forcefully dissented. With perilous days ahead, the last thing FDR wanted was a yes-man as his chief military adviser. Marshall also had the support of Harry Hopkins, the president's closest adviser, who admired Marshall and lobbied for him on his own, without Marshall's knowledge or blessing.

From the outset, Marshall made it clear that he would not run the Army for the benefit of its senior officers. He informed Roosevelt that he was ready to get rid of those who did not measure up. In a real war, he later wrote, the needs of the enlisted men came first. He believed that the Army owed its soldiers competent leadership above all.

Marshall came to the job with a mission to prevent the errors of 1917–18, when he had planned offensive operations as a member of Pershing's staff. Not only had Marshall's position allowed him to witness the brutality and waste of war, but he had seen firsthand the limitations of a poorly prepared force. In September 1918, he helped orchestrate two U.S. operations in France—an attack on Saint-Mihiel and an offensive in the Meuse-Argonne region—both of which, though successful, resulted in the massive loss of American lives. According to Marshall, "the young officers did not know how to regroup their men after the initial advance . . . and when the time came to push on, they were unable to carry out their mission."[6]

Marshall was a man of strong opinion based on that wartime experience. While still an aide to Pershing, he had published an article entitled "Profiting by War Experiences" that addressed the matter of orders issued in combat. Marshall took the position that a "hastily prepared order" was often better than a "model" one, particularly if the model order failed to reach frontline commanders in a timely fashion. According to Marshall, "Our troops suffered much from the delays involved in preparing long and complicated orders due to the failure of the staff concerned to recognize that speed was more important than technique."[7]

Initially, the personal relationship between Roosevelt and Marshall was a cool one. Before the formal appointment, when FDR called him George, Marshall took it as a show of disrespect and insisted on being addressed as General. Roosevelt would never make the same mistake again. For his part, Marshall worked hard to keep his distance from Roosevelt; he even made a point not to laugh at FDR's jokes.

Later in the day that he was formally given the job, the Washington, D.C., *Evening Star* reported that in the space of three minutes, Brigadier General Marshall had accepted two promotions and three additional stars—the first as a major general in the Regular Army and two more as he took the oath of chief of staff, an automatic promotion to the rank of four stars, normally the highest rank attainable in the U.S. Army in peacetime. Marshall made no statements in connection with the promotions and declined "for political reasons" a request from newsreel photographers to pose in front of a map of Europe. The last thing Marshall wanted at that moment was to give the impression that he and the president he served were scheming to get the nation involved in the conflict in Europe.[8]

"My day of induction was momentous," Marshall later wrote to a friend, "with the starting of what appears to be a world war."[9]

On September 3, two days after Marshall's swearing in and the Third Reich's invasion of Poland, France and Great Britain declared war on Germany and the Second World War was fully underway in Europe. That night, Roosevelt took to the radio waves in one of his customary fireside chats with the American people to lament the situation in Europe. He then added: "I hope the United States will keep out of this war. I believe that it will. And I give you assurance and reassurance that every effort of your Government will be directed toward that end." Roosevelt then uttered his oft-quoted thought about war: "I have said not once but many times that I have seen war and that I hate war. I say that again and again."[10]

What Roosevelt did not say that night was that if and when the nation was drawn into this war, the United States Army was not even prepared to wage a defensive battle to protect North America, let alone stage an offensive campaign on the other side of the Atlantic. But of this both he and Marshall were fully aware.

In France and Great Britain, the few days between Germany's invasion of Poland and the declaration of war had been spent preparing for the hostilities to come. This was most dramatic in London, where more than 1.5 million people, mostly children, had been moved to the countryside in four days, and all schools located in areas felt to be prime targets for Nazi bombers were closed for the duration of the war. London-based CBS Radio reporter Edward R. Murrow told his American audience that he found it difficult to describe a city in which there were no youngsters shouting on their way home from school or playing in the parks. Responding to the belief that the bombs were about to rain down, London veterinarians opened their offices so that people could come in to have their dogs put to sleep. "Outside the vets' surgeries," said one eyewitness, "the slain lay in heaps."[11]

As the Nazi conquest of Poland played out, the world absorbed the lesson that Hitler had violated Western rules of warfare that had stood for centuries. "There had been no time allowed to redress the grievances before the invasion, no declaration of war by the aggressor, no will to honor commitments on the part of the Allies, no time for the ponderous machinery of the democracies' military might, no refusal to hurt civilians, and no courteous treatment of a vanquished enemy," as one historian summed it up.[12]

At the time of the invasion of Poland, the German army had 1.7 million men divided into 98 infantry divisions, including nine Panzer divisions, each of which had 328 tanks, eight support battalions, and six artillery batteries.

In stark contrast, the U.S. Army, comprising 189,839 regular troops and officers, in 1939 was ranked 17th in the world, behind the army of Portugal. Furthermore, the Regular Army was dispersed to 130 camps, posts, and stations. Some 50,000 of the troops were stationed outside the United States, including the forces that occupied the Philippines and guarded the Panama Canal. The Army was, as one observer described it, "all bone and no muscle." The United States Marine Corps stood at a mere 19,432 officers and men, fewer than the number of people employed by the New York City Police Department.[13]

The United States did have Reserve officers and the National Guard, which required its members to attend 48 training nights and two weeks of field duty per year to fulfill their obligation, but this was hardly enough to prepare them for combat without sustained additional training. Making matters worse, an attempt to get former soldiers to sign up for the Army Reserve, begun in 1938, was failing. Fewer than 5,000 men signed up within the first year, despite the fact they did not have to go to camps or drill but only to agree to be ready in an emergency. The pay was meager but not insignificant during the Depression: $24 a month. The Army even issued special recruiting posters for these soldiers, calling them Modern Minute Men.[14]

At the end of World War I, the Army had contained more than two million men; since then it had been neglected and allowed to shrink in both size and stature. General Peyton C. March, the Army's chief of staff at the end of that war, was of the opinion that the United States had rendered itself "weaker voluntarily than the Treaty of Versailles had made Germany." He concluded that the country had made itself "militarily impotent."[15]

The meager budget needed to run the Army dwindled as the Great Depression deepened. In 1935, the Army's annual budget bottomed out at $250 million, and the force had declined to 118,750, at which point Douglas MacArthur, then Army Chief of Staff, observed that the entire Regular Army could be placed inside Yankee Stadium.[16]

"Let me give you a specific example of the effect of these reductions upon the efficiency of the Army," George C. Marshall later observed. "During this period I commanded a post which had for its garrison a battalion of infantry, the basic fighting unit of every army. It was a battalion only in name, for it could muster barely 200 men in ranks when every available man, including cooks, clerks, and kitchen police, [was] present for the little field training that could be accomplished with available funds. The normal strength of a battalion in most armies of the world varies from 800 to 1,000 men."[17]

American troops were learning obsolete skills and preparing for defensive warfare on a small scale. As military historian Carlo D'Este wrote: "So sorry was the state of the U.S. Army in 1939 that had Pancho Villa been alive to raid the southwestern United States it would have been as ill prepared to repulse or punish him as it had been in 1916."[18]

The Army had only a few hundred light tanks and maintained a horse cavalry as an elite mobile force; it was no match for the heavily armored German divisions. Those who had advocated replacing horses with tanks and other armored vehicles during the period between the wars had actually been threatened with punishment. As a young officer, Dwight D. Eisenhower later recalled, when he began arguing for greater reliance on armored divisions, "I was told that my ideas were not only wrong but dangerous and that henceforth I would keep them to myself. Particularly, I was not to publish anything incompatible with solid infantry doctrine. If I did, I would be hauled before a court-martial."[19]

In the late 1930s, a significant number of cavalry officers were becoming increasingly vocal in their opposition to mechanization in general and to any attempt to replace the horse with new combat vehicles, especially armored cars. In 1938, Major General John Herr became the chief of cavalry, and his position was that "mechanization should not come at the expense of a single mounted regiment."[20]

Organizationally, the Army was divided into small sections that hardly ever trained together as larger coherent units because of a lack of funds. The paucity of travel money was underscored in 1938 when Marshall, stationed in the Vancouver Barracks in Washington State near Portland, Oregon, got orders to report for duty in Washington, D.C., as deputy chief of staff. The move precipitated a flow of letters back and forth between Marshall and then chief of staff Craig, discussing whether the funds could be raised to bring Marshall and his family east by train rather than sending them to Washington by military transport and through the Panama Canal. The funds were found, but the point was made that budgetary considerations were debilitating. Commanders billeted with larger units visited smaller units under their command only once a year—and then only if travel money could be found.[21]

The officer corps was demoralized because promotions were rare and based primarily on seniority. Army captains, for instance tended to be in their late 30s or early 40s. Many of the better-qualified younger officers had long before left the service.

Some soldiers wore the flat-brimmed steel doughboy helmets from World War I and carried bolt-action rifles from as far back as the Spanish-American War of the late 1890s. In 1939, supply wagons were still commonly pulled by teams of mules, and heavy artillery was moved by teams of horses. Soldiers' pay was abysmal—$21 a month for a private, just as it had been in 1922. And expenses were high; if an infantryman wanted a calibrated rifle, he had to buy one from the Army for $35. Men who did not like the Army or the command to which they were assigned could buy their way out for $135 after a year. Transfers from one unit to another were unheard of, and the only way to make a move to another command was to pay the $135 and then reenlist with the unit one wanted.

The option to purchase one's discharge coupled with the technical schooling the Army provided was also frustrating the Army's efforts. Much of its recruiting was based on the premise that an enlistee could learn while he served. Men were joining the Army, acquiring skills, and then buying their way out. Between 1934 and 1938, 30,360 men bought their discharges; approximately 15 percent of them were technical school graduates.[22]

Making matters worse, in the early years of Roosevelt's New Deal policies, all troops were forced to take a mandatory "month without pay," a flat cut that reduced soldiers' monthly basic take from $21 to $17.85. Marshall himself defended the troops in a letter posted on April 13, 1934, to Brigadier General Thomas S. Hammond, then commander of the Illinois National Guard's 66th Infantry Brigade. Marshall wrote of his men:

> They cannot resign; they must present a certain standard of appearance no matter how closely pressed they may be finan- cially; they must accept the added expenses of moves and special service; they constitute the government's final backing in the event of grave emergencies; they must hazard their lives in the

government service, with no choice of resigning if they do not care to serve. Yet on these servants the Federal government imposed its most drastic program of economy, and at a time when it was demanding more of the Army to meet the special requirements of the New Deal, than of any other branch of the government.[23]

The month without pay was a temporary measure and later lifted, but to many in the Regular Army the pay cut was a scar that remained. For those paying attention, Marshall had become the voice defending the average Joe who stuck with the Army through thick and thin.

Some units had better athletic teams and occasionally better food, but there were budgetary limitations. From 1922 until 1927, the government allocated 30 cents per day per man for food, and by 1938 the allocation had inched upward to 43 cents. For most men, potatoes were a staple of the evening meal, along with corn bread, beans, coffee, and a gloppy stew of meat and vegetables known as "slumgullion" or "slum" for short.

The desertion rate from the Army was not generally made public, but it was not significant; if a soldier went AWOL (absent without leave) and was not found after 90 days, the Army removed him from the rolls, convened an *in absentia* court-martial, and awarded him a dishonorable discharge. During the period from 1920 to 1932, any civilian law enforcement officer who returned a deserter to the Army was awarded $50; the bounty was reduced to $25 in 1933. Once returned, the offenders served their "bad time" at hard labor on work details, often making "little ones out of big ones"—smashing rocks with a sledgehammer. When they returned to normal duty, the bounty money was deducted from their pay in small amounts each payday until it was paid off.[24]

Despite the low pay and limited benefits, the job was a secure one, while work on the outside was often insecure and scarce. By 1932, approximately 13 million Americans were out of work, which amounted to one of every four able and willing workers in the country. Since the infantryman was the civilian labor-market equivalent of an unskilled laborer, not surprisingly the desertion rate reached a low point of 2 percent during these years, despite the reality that most of the Regular Army was housed in flimsy structures erected during the First World War and designed for temporary occupancy.

The Army that General Marshall inherited in 1939 was one that did not like to enlist married men. If a private or corporal wanted to marry, he had to get permission from his commanding officer, and it was granted only on rare occasions. As Victor Vogel pointed out in *Soldiers of the Old Army*, his memoir of the prewar Army, "This eliminated a great deal of trouble for the Army and saved the United States a lot of money, because few professional soldiers would give up military service for a wife."[25]

Soldiers were officially discouraged from marrying until they had reached the rank of sergeant. That could easily mean waiting for a decade, because an enlistee served his first three-year enlistment as a private and his second hitch as a private first class, and then he often remained at that rank. Many men who enlisted with an eye to raising a family were long gone from the service before they made sergeant.

Vogel observed that the pay of the lower ranks was too meager to support a family, and no special benefits covered the expenses incurred by dependents. During the years between the wars, married enlisted men below the rank of sergeant were often forced to live in poverty. "They *exist* in squalid surroundings, dingy dark, overcrowded rooms where the simplest rules of sanitation and hygiene are difficult if not impossible of accomplishment," wrote Brigadier General William P. Jackson, commander of Madison Barracks at Sackets Harbor, New York, in a 1931 report on men under his command. He added, about his married men: "Their health, morale, vitality and efficiency is bound to suffer." Jackson concluded his report by pointing out that his married men became objects of charity, providing this example: "Recently a donation of $19 was made by officers to provide fuel and milk for a new mother and her baby."[26]

This Army of primarily single men lived in barracks on outposts surrounded by honky-tonks, where beer sold for a dime a bottle and "sporting houses" were populated by women who, in Vogel's words, were "out to fleece as many men as possible in as short a time as possible." Prostitutes would arrive from the nearby cities on payday and be gone a few days later when the men's money ran out. Many of the smaller western Army posts of the time were isolated relics of the Indian Wars, held open for political rather than military reasons, that had in some cases devolved into slums in the middle of nowhere.[27]

The men entering the Army in the years before the Second World War were generally poorly educated; high school graduates who showed up in camp as privates were rare. In terms of society at large, the men of the Regular Army were often regarded as outcasts.

In addition to all this, the weapons provided to Regulars and Reservists were for the most part obsolete and inadequate. The basic anti-aircraft gun was a .50-caliber machine gun, entirely insufficient for its intended purpose. The 37 mm gun developed by the U.S. Army Ordnance Department was then considered an excellent anti-tank weapon, but when Marshall was testifying before the Senate Committee on Military Affairs in February 1939, he reported that the Army had only one of these weapons in its arsenal.[28]

If conditions were bad on the ground, they were worse in the air. In the fall of 1939, at the moment Hitler's Luftwaffe warplanes were destroying Kraków and Warsaw, the United States' air forces ranked 20th in the world and possessed only a few modern combat aircraft. German airmen, who had visited the United States before the Polish invasion, often as guests of aviator Charles Lindbergh, concluded that American airpower was an oxymoron. Lindbergh, a bona fide American hero for his 1927 pathbreaking solo transatlantic flight, had become sympathetic to the Nazi cause.

Earlier in 1939, in asking for more money for the air forces, Roosevelt himself had termed their strength as "totally inadequate."

Following up on Roosevelt's assessment, General Frank Andrews, who headed the air forces, then known as the U.S. Army Air Corps, described the United States as a "sixth-rate airpower," with only a handful of planes equal to those being flown by the Germans or the British.[29]

Historian Russell Weigley later wrote that during the 1920s and 1930s the U.S. Army "may have been less ready to function as a fighting force than at any time in its history." As George Marshall himself wrote in his first biennial report on the armed forces: "During the post-war period, continuous paring of appropriations has reduced the Army virtually to the status of that of a third rate power."[30]

Framing this grim overall picture, war-related industries in 1939 were minor, marginal operations doing little to improve the quality or quantity of military equipment and munitions. This was most distressful to Marshall, who told a writer from the *New York Times* in May 1939, when it became apparent that he was in line to become Army chief of staff: "A billion dollars the day war is declared will not buy ten cents worth of such material for quick delivery." In 1957, Marshall would tell an interviewer of the "tragic feeling" that a prompt, forceful rearmament program in 1939–40 would have shortened the war that was surely coming to the United States, perhaps saving billions of dollars and countless casualties.[31]

If the Army's deficiencies were not already apparent to Marshall, they were on full display beginning on August 5, 1939, less than a month before he was formally sworn in as chief of staff, when more than 1,200 trucks carrying 17,000 members of the National Guard passed through Washington, D.C. If Marshall needed a firsthand reminder of the challenges he faced, all he had to do was look out his office window in the sprawling Munitions Building on Constitution Avenue and watch as the convoy passed through on its way to field exercises on the Civil War battlefield at Bull Run, in nearby Manassas, Virginia. The men were ill equipped, many carrying dummy arms, and poorly trained for real warfare, as many had never fired a weapon—even an ancient one—in training. Some of the men rode into their mock battle packed into station wagons, giving one writer the impression he was watching troops heading out for a picnic.[32]

The Manassas exercises were staged as a theatrical event, harking back to a 1904 maneuver reenacting the Battles of Bull Run. In 1904, members of Congress, foreign dignitaries, and much of the capital's social elite sat under an enormous circus tent to watch the mock battle unfold. These 1939 maneuvers, dubbed "the third battle of Manassas"— essentially restaged the original Civil War battles, albeit with aircraft and trucks, to discover the strengths and shortcomings of the 1939 Army.[33]

One army, the Blue, composed of National Guardsmen, aimed to attack Washington, which was defended by the Black Army, represented by the Regular Army. All told, the exercise involved 23,000 troops brought in from three states and the District of Columbia. As in 1904, it was staged as a highly visible event meant to be viewed by the public.

During the same period in August, the Army staged a second series of exercises in the piney landscape around Plattsburg, New York, located across Lake Champlain from Vermont. It involved 52,000 troops from 11 states. Both operations were designed to test the strengths and weaknesses of the Regular Army as well as National Guard units. As was the case in Virginia, the invaders in northeastern New York were the National Guard and Reservists, while the defenders were Regular Army.

The Manassas exercises ended with the Regular Army defenders of the capital driving back the mechanized National Guard invaders to a line two miles short of Manassas, at which point a cease-fire was called. "The battle of Washington was over. Washington was safe from attack, with invaders in stubborn retreat," declared a reporter for the *Washington Post*. What seemed most evident here was that the Guardsmen and Reservists were not ready for war, even with the assistance of an array of tanks and trucks. The Regular Army was still viewed as the winner when it came to land warfare.[34]

The man in charge of the maneuvers in Upstate New York was Lieutenant General Hugh Drum, commander of the First Army, who on the night before the first phase of the mock battle declared that the army taking the field was "in fact not an army at all, but rather a collection of individual units . . . partially equipped, and woefully short in manpower, weapons, motors." Drum's First Army, a portion of which was in the exercise, was supposed to have 320,000; instead a mere 75,000 were under his command.[35]

But the main conflict of the Plattsburg exercises ended early, with a cease-fire called after two days of torrential rain and thunderstorms that left three men dead from a single lightning strike and 15 others injured from the effects of the storm. Many of the men on the field—soaked, demoralized, and mired in mud—left much of their personal equipment behind when the event was called off, and they were immediately herded into trucks and trains to take them home. The men on the field had been defeated by the weather.[36]

The problems brought to light were many and were not restricted to the Guardsmen. Although the spirit of the rank-and-file troops was praised, their ability as warriors was not. More than half the 52,000 men mobilized in Plattsburg had never fired their weapons in a combat course of instruction. Training had been utterly and totally inadequate. As one senior officer put it, the men and many of their officers were totally unprepared for "the mechanism of battle—the conduct of the fight." The list of specific failures was nothing short of appalling. Cover and concealment on the battlefield was neglected, as was liaison and support between units. Serious delays had occurred in the distribution of orders, and many officers and men were unable to properly read maps. Men were led into battle in close formation, and scouts had to work too close to the columns they were supposed to protect. Food supplies to the men in the field were delayed or broke down completely. All these failures made clear the deep logistical problems the Army faced.[37]

Nor was either maneuver well planned in terms of the field of play. "Troop movements were ludicrously held up at roadside fences, not because of the barbed wire," observed *Newsweek*, "but because, in the absence of a suitable field for maneuvers in the area, the nation's defenders could not trample a farmer's corn." Perhaps the most stunning omission from the mock battlefields was the conspicuous absence of aircraft. A small item in one newspaper explained the omission: "The airmen are too busy with expansion to put on a show."[38]

Using both named and unnamed sources from both maneuvers, the newspaper criticism rose to a crescendo. ARMY ADMITS WAR SHOWED DEFICIENCY read a headline in the *Baltimore Sun* above an article arguing that the maneuvers showed the Army was relatively less prepared than it had been in 1917 and that there had been a deplorable lack of training, especially among the Guardsmen and Reservists. "It must be remembered as far as the National Guard is concerned," one general told the *Sun* reporter, "that they are civilian soldiers who get only a small amount of training each year and with other things to do than learn soldiering."[39]

Finally, the man in charge of these war games, General Drum, labeled the performances of all those involved "deplorable and inexcusable." The Army simply did not know how to fight. Plattsburg showed Drum and others that the nation's armed forces needed to learn the mechanism of war—just how, under complex modern conditions, to advance, hold ground, and maintain liaison, supply, and command. Drum would later say that for the Army the Plattsburg revelations ended the old era and began a new one.[40]

On August 31, Senator Henry Cabot Lodge Jr. of Massachusetts, who had participated in the Plattsburg maneuvers as a uniformed Army Reserve Cavalry officer, spoke before the annual convention of the Veterans of Foreign Wars; he pointed out how poorly things seemed on the ground during those maneuvers and decried the state of the Army in general. "In the mechanization of the army we are surpassed in quantity by every first-class European power." Within a few hours of Lodge's speech one of the powers, Poland, was attacked by a highly mechanized Nazi army.[41]

Even though the 1939 maneuvers had been staged before he became chief of staff, Marshall was bothered by their poor outcome, and he renewed his efforts to plan improved maneuvers for 1940 and 1941.[42]

The deficiencies spotted in Plattsburg and Manassas tended to be magnified after Germany's invasion of Poland and were cited by newspaper editorialists in arguments for greater preparedness. The Army needed an overhaul—but not the enlisted men, who in the words of an editorial in the *Brooklyn Eagle* showed "splendid spirit and morale," despite their inability to fight.[43]

The treatment of African American soldiers in the American Revolution provided a sad prism for the future. Although black men served with honor at the Battles of Lexington and Bunker Hill in 1775, the Continental Congress voted then to keep black people—both enslaved and free—from serving in the Continental Army. To train black men for armed warfare, the delegates believed, might lead to slave insurrections. The ban was a sop to slaveholders in both the South and North. But early in the war, the royal governor of Virginia offered to emancipate slaves who joined the British Army, which led Congress to reverse its decision, fearing that those emancipated men might become part of the army it was fighting.

Race remained a major issue for the Army in the decades that followed. As had been true during World War I, black soldiers in 1939 were required to join black units whose commissioned officers were white. In that earlier war, black Americans had been quick to enlist, not only to serve their country but also to demonstrate to their fellow Americans that they were entitled to the full rights of citizenship and an end to the discriminatory laws and practices known as Jim Crow. By the First World War's end, 2.3 million black men had registered for the draft; 367,000 eventually served in uniform.[44]

In retelling the story of the black military experience, important figures in the traditional narrative emerge as men of duplicity and dishonor. A most notable example of this was President Woodrow Wilson who, in June 1917, was aware of the transfer and ultimate discharge from the Army's highest-ranked black officer and a West Point graduate named Charles Young. An outstanding officer, Young had advanced to the rank of colonel, where he now outranked both white junior officers and all enlisted men, who were required to salute him. Making him more of a liability to those protecting the Jim Crow Army was the fact that his next promotion would make him a brigadier general and more disruptive to a hierarchy that depended on exclusion based on race.[45]

In World War I, General John Pershing denied black Americans the right to go into combat under the American flag, placing them instead under the French flag. In France they fought with spirit and valor and became an inspiration to the war-weary French. Soon after their reassignment, Pershing issued a directive to the French commanders, instructing them to "treat black Americans as white Americans did" and went on to say that "we must not eat with them, must not shake hands or seek to talk or meet with them outside the requirements of military service. We must not commend too highly the black American troops, particularly in the presence of Americans. We must prevent the rise of any pronounced degree of intimacy between French officers and black." The French dismissed the order, which had no bearing on the reality of a war being waged in foul, rat-infested trenches, but this same American military attitude toward black people was still in place when Marshall took command of the Army in 1939.

The Army had no interest in recruiting black Americans, and the proof was in the numbers. The editorial page of the *Pittsburgh Courier*, one of the leading black newspapers of the time, began arguing in 1938 for an American army that mirrored the general population and was at least 10 percent black. The *Courier* reported at the end of 1939 that the Regular Army of the United States "contained only 4,451 black enlisted men and five black officers, as compared with 229,636 white enlisted men and 1,359 white officers."[46]

The fact that black men were totally excluded from the Army Air Corps was particularly irksome, especially to African American leadership. The cover of the July 1940 issue of the *Crisis*, the official magazine of the National Association for the Advancement of Colored People (NAACP), graphically summed up this grievance by depicting military aircraft flying over an airfield, with the words FOR WHITES

ONLY splashed across the image and a caption at the bottom reading: "WARPLANES—NEGRO AMERICANS MAY NOT BUILD THEM, REPAIR THEM, OR FLY THEM, BUT THEY MUST HELP PAY FOR THEM." Focusing on the same issue, the magazine's December 1940 cover showed an Army aircraft over a well-appointed airfield. This time the caption read: "FOR WHITES ONLY—A U.S. ARMY AIR CORPS TRAINING PLANE OVER THE 'WEST POINT OF THE AIR'—RANDOLPH FIELD, TEXAS. NEGROES ARE NOT BEING ACCEPTED AND TRAINED BY THE ARMY AIR CORPS AT *ANY* FIELD IN THE NATION, DESPITE ALL THE TALK OF NATIONAL UNITY AND OF THE URGENCY OF EVERY GROUP SERVING IN NATIONAL DEFENSE." On the same cover, the magazine previewed two other articles on race and the Army: "When Do *We* Fly?" by James L. H. Peck, and "Jim Crow in the Army Camps," by "A Negro Soldier."[47]

The 1939 attack on Poland gave the world its first look at a devastating new form of brutal mechanized warfare. Within a matter of hours, huge columns of tanks working in close cooperation with the German air force attacked and quickly penetrated the Polish defenses. The speed and violence of the attack paralyzed the Polish defenders. The climax of these armored drives came far behind the frontlines, as the Nazi spearheads linked up, trapping the bewildered Polish formations in a series of isolated pockets.[48]

The skill of the Nazi propaganda machine added to the feeling of dread and despair in much of the Western world. One of the lies that stunned at first and lived on was the false assertion that the Polish cavalry had charged mindlessly into the face of Panzer tanks—a lie constructed to display the stupidity of the Poles and the futility of trying to fight the Nazis by conventional means. On September 1, 1939, just as Roosevelt was appointing Marshall as chief of staff, a Polish cavalry regiment operating on Poland's northwestern border attacked a column of German infantry, scattering the invaders. Before the Polish horsemen had a chance to regroup, a squad of Nazi armored vehicles attacked them with cannons and machine guns, inflicting heavy casualties. Reporters were later brought to the battlefield, shown some of the dead horses, and told that the horses had been killed in a frontal attack on the German tanks. The manufactured myth took immediate root.

A *Paris Soir* account of the event, translated and syndicated to American newspapers, had the Polish general ordering his men to draw their sabers and charge the Panzer machine guns and flamethrowers. The battle lasted a mere ten minutes: "The cavalrymen were mowed down, the horses seared by fire. The general was killed. The few survivors rode into a near-by forest and, it was said killed themselves." The headline for the story as it ran in the *Miami Herald* was POLISH CAVALRY COMMITTED SUICIDE IN HOPELESS CHARGE. The story was repeated again and again. Among others, Winston Churchill would mention it in his history of the Second World War. Yet the Nazis had staged the event.[49]

Many now began to see the Nazi attack as a trap that would lead to the inextricable involvement of more nations, a point underscored on September 10, 1939, as Canada, still a dominion of the British Empire, announced that it was now in the war and that it planned to quickly supply men for the British Armed Forces. As Canada joined the fight in the days after the fall of Poland, the U.S. Department of War stood by with no declared interest in enlarging its Army. Secretary of War Harry Hines Woodring was a strong advocate of neutrality and unwilling to push for significant troop increases. A Roosevelt appointee and once a close friend of the president, Woodring was a popular figure in Washington, but Roosevelt viewed him as an increasing liability. In December 1938, Roosevelt had tried to convince the secretary to resign and become ambassador to Canada, but Woodring chose to hang on.

Woodring had strong support from the isolationists, and to remove him forcibly would have exposed Roosevelt to charges that he intended to enlist the United States in some kind of European entanglement. Making things even worse, Woodring was also engaged in a public feud with his own assistant secretary of war, Louis A. Johnson, an advocate of universal military training and the expansion of military aviation.

One of the few things these two men agreed on was that there was no immediate need to expand the Army.

By maintaining his neutrality during this period of internal discord, Marshall kept the Army and the War Department functioning—a feat helped by his good personal relations with both Roosevelt and Woodring. A strong Marshall supporter when he was appointed Chief of Staff, Woodring would later brag that helping George Marshall get the job was the most important thing he had ever done to serve his country.[50]

Woodring's isolationism was not at all unusual in Washington in 1939. A powerful isolationist, or anti-interventionist, movement emerged and grew in strength in the United States during the 1930s. Between 1935 and 1937, led by a strong isolationist bloc, Congress enacted three neutrality acts that banned Americans from giving loans to nations engaged in war, from shipping munitions to them, from traveling on their vessels, and from arming American merchant ships—effectively, an arms embargo against those countries at war with or trying to resist Nazi Germany. In September 1939, after the German invasion of Poland, President Roosevelt asked for an end to the arms embargo created by the neutrality laws. Fierce battle ensued in both houses of Congress, ending in a win by the interventionists—but the 243–181 vote in the House of Representatives showed that isolationism was still a factor to be reckoned with.

Upon taking office, Chief of Staff Marshall immediately began to reshape the standard Army division by transforming its four large but undermanned regiments into three smaller and more effective regiments with full manpower and greater mobility. Marshall considered the old standard divisions, known as square divisions, to be too unwieldy for maneuvering, controlling, and supplying. By transitioning from square divisions to the new triangular ones, Marshall radically changed the way the infantry would fight in the future. He eliminated the brigade commander of the old division and sped up communications through the division so that an order could go from top to bottom in two hours or less, compared to the five hours it took the square division. Trucks would replace horses and be used to shuttle men and equipment, permitting forces to move 45 miles a day for many days at a time. The old divisions could move only 15 miles a day, which was only as long as the soldiers' feet held up.

The square division had been created for trench warfare. It was composed of regiments in columns that could hurl themselves against enemy defenses in successive waves—becoming in effect cannon fodder. As military historian Christopher Gabel has noted, "Such tactics, obsolescent by 1918, were totally anachronistic by 1939, as was the square division itself."[51]

These three new divisions, made up of infantry-artillery combat regiments, could operate separately or as a group. Marshall saw the triangular division as a flexible, faster, and more efficient way to wage war.[52]

In 1939, Marshall began training three streamlined infantry divisions* and one cavalry division for a series of war games that would be staged in an area somewhere in the arc extending from Georgia to Texas. Marshall let it be known that these would be the largest peacetime maneuvers in the history of the United States. He was keenly aware of the need to prepare American infantrymen for a new kind of brutal, fast, and merciless warfare—*blitzkrieg*, German for "lightning war." There was nothing abstract about this German invention; what happened in Poland defined *blitzkrieg*.[53]

The Polish army was defeated before the end of September as 1.5 million Nazi troops, supported by more than 2,000 tanks and more than 1,000 aircraft, broke through Polish defenses along the border and advanced on Warsaw, which, after heavy shelling and bombing, surrendered to the Nazis on September 27, 1939, with some 140,000 Polish soldiers taken prisoner.

---

* At some point early in the process, the new divisions were given the description *streamlined*, which made the change more quickly understood by the public and members of Congress. The word *streamline* had been coined in 1868 as an element of hydrodynamics (defined as the path of a particle in a fluid, moving in smooth flow without turbulence, relative to a solid object past which the fluid is moving). It soon came to have popular meanings (free from turbulence; shaped so that the flow around it is smooth) and by the 1930s had its modern extended meaning of "simplify and organize," which is exactly what Marshall was doing.

As Germany had invaded from the west, the Soviet Union attacked Poland from the east on September 17. Soviet foreign minister Vyacheslav Molotov declared that the Polish government had ceased to exist and that the Soviet Union was exercising the "fine print" of the Hitler-Stalin non-aggression pact—the conquest and occupation of eastern Poland. On September 29, Germany and the Soviet Union agreed to divide control of Poland roughly along the Bug River, with the Germans occupying everything to the west, the Soviets taking all territory to the east.

On September 4, the day after Roosevelt had delivered his fireside chat on the world situation, he met with Marshall to discuss the expansion of the nation's military. This was the moment the administration took its first significant step in the mobilization the U.S. Army for the next world war. The invasion of Poland had triggered hopes of Marshall and other Army leaders for substantial increases in U.S. Army manpower, but those hopes were short-lived. On September 8, a week after the invasion, Roosevelt declared what he termed a "limited state of emergency" and allowed a modest increase of 17,000 troops in the Regular Army and 35,000 in the National Guard. Roosevelt had actually reduced new strength levels recommended by Marshall from 280,000 to 227,000 for the Regular Army and 435,000 to 235,000 for the National Guard. Roosevelt's position was that it "was all the public would be ready to accept without undue excitement." FDR's fear was that a larger increase would further mobilize those who favored isolation in favor of intervention.[54]

Marshall then ordered his Army staff officers to begin planning for the increases in manpower. He said that "the initial figures were only the first increment" and that "future expansions would result in a larger number of officers." This action was accompanied by an executive order that called up members of the Organized Reserve Corps to active duty. The War Department was also ordered to correct certain deficiencies in resources; this included the purchase of $12 million worth of motor transportation.[55]

The American public at this moment was still largely isolationist, and while Marshall and Roosevelt could see the potential for American involvement in a European war, they had to continue to move carefully and slowly.

CHAPTER 2

THE TREE ARMY
TO THE RESCUE

In fiscal year 1939, the funds earmarked for training the Army amounted to $12 million or 2.7 percent of the Army's meager appropriations—about $65 per man. The Army's appropriations totaled $646 million, but of this, $192 million, or close to 30 percent, was earmarked for non-military purposes such as the cost of operating the Panama Canal, river and harbor work conducted by the Army Corps of Engineers, and work with the Civilian Conservation Corps (CCC). A New Deal relief program that first went into operation in 1933 to provide work for unemployed, unmarried men ages 18 to 25, the CCC was established to help impoverished families during the Depression by requiring the men to send the larger portion of their monthly pay home.[1]

Little understood at the time—and largely forgotten in the intervening decades—was the Army's major role in creating and maintaining the Civilian Conservation Corps. The CCC became a driving force for improving the Army and facilitating the education and professional development of key officers, including Omar Bradley, George Marshall, and Roosevelt's inherited Army chief of staff, Douglas MacArthur.

On March 21, 1933, less than three weeks after he was elected, President Roosevelt proposed the formation of the CCC; it was established by an act of law on March 31. Within a week after enactment, the first camp opened near Luray, Virginia, with an enrollment of 2,500 men.

A stated goal of the CCC was to conserve, protect, and enhance the nation's natural resources, and it was given tasks ranging from combating soil erosion in the Dust Bowl to increasing the nation's recreational assets by building vacation lodges and laying out mountain trails. By the time the program ended in 1942, its cadre of young men had planted nearly three billion trees, constructed more than 800 new parks, and upgraded most existing state parks. They built trails and roads in remote areas of the country, improved beaches on both coasts, and created golf courses and softball fields close to urban areas. The CCC was known far and wide—by both its admirers and detractors—as FDR's Tree Army.[2]

The other goal of the CCC was to enlist young, unmarried men and get them into a disciplined environment in which they could serve the nation while helping their families. The target recruits included the unemployed, troubled city kids, and menacing young hoboes who roamed the nation and were often referred to as the "wild boys of the road," after the title of a 1933 movie.

In order to be successful, the CCC needed the deep commitment of the leaders of the U.S. Army. It was born at a time when the image of the Army was suffering because of the recent use of Regular and National Guard troops to quell strikes and subdue other domestic disturbances. The most dramatic, distressing, and photogenic of these incidents was the Army's role in the expulsion of the so-called Bonus Army from its camp at the Anacostia Flats in Washington, D.C., in July 1932.

Five and a half years after the armistice ending World War I, in May 1924 Congress finally reacted to the increasingly loud and public demands of veterans that the Congress fulfill its earlier promises to compensate them for their wartime service by passing a bill granting a bonus payment to those veterans that the legislation termed "adjusted service compensation."

The intent of the bill was to make up for the vast difference between what a man in uniform was paid and what was paid to a war worker at home. A man working in a shipyard building warships could easily earn six or seven times as much as a man in uniform. The legislation was passed but only after overriding the veto of President Calvin Coolidge, who had declared in his veto message that the nation owed nothing to able-bodied veterans and "patriotism which is bought and paid for is not patriotism."

Under the terms of the new legislation, any man who had served in the Armed Forces during the war was due compensation at the rate of $1 a day for time served in the United States and $1.25 for every day spent abroad—exactly the same basic pay given them when they were in uniform. But there was a stunning catch to this bonus: any man entitled to a bonus of $50 or less was to be paid immediately, but all the others were to be issued certificates that could not be converted to cash until 1945 when they would receive full payment. It was cynically nicknamed the "Tombstone Bonus" by disappointed veterans because the only way to get cash payment before 1945 was for the veteran to die.

Nothing happened until May 1929, when Congressman Wright Patman of Texas, a fellow veteran of the war who had suffered its privations, proposed a bill calling for the immediate cash payment of the bonus. The bill, however, did not make it out of committee, and any momentum in Congress for early payment died as the stock market crashed in October. Then came the Great Depression, and at the beginning of the bleak new year of 1932—when unemployment had reached 25 percent of the workforce and hundreds of thousands of Americans were homeless—Patman resurrected the legislation, but it again landed in committee with little hope of getting out, let alone being passed.

On March 15, 1932, Walter W. Waters, an unemployed former Army sergeant, stood up at a meeting of war veterans in Portland, Oregon, and proposed that all present join him by hopping a freight train and traveling to Washington to lobby for the money that rightfully belonged to them. Nobody took him up on his offer that night, but he kept working on the idea and by early May, when a revised version of Patman's bill was introduced and quickly shelved in the House of Representatives, Waters had pulled together a group of about 250 followers who had to show evidence of war service, pledge to uphold the Constitution, and to submit to the discipline of Waters and other elected officers. Waters and his small band departed Portland with $300 between them, riding in empty freight cars, and headed to Washington to demand payment. These men saw themselves as lobbyists behaving in much the same manner as lobbyists for the large corporations had in demanding—and receiving—reparations for their war work.[3]

This defining moment of the Great Depression took shape as word of Waters's group spread and, following their lead, some 20,000 World War I war veterans and their families converged on Washington, D.C., in May to demand that Congress and President Herbert Hoover pass legislation to allow them to immediately turn their bonus certificates into cash.

The House of Representatives passed Patman's bonus bill by a 211–176 vote on June 15, which was cause for great rejoicing among the individuals and families in Washington whose numbers had been increasing by the thousands. The Senate was to vote two days later, and during that day more than 8,000 members of what was now known as the Bonus Army assembled in front of the Capitol. Another group of more than 10,000 headed for the Capitol from the main camp in Anacostia but were stopped by a drawbridge that the District of Columbia police had raised, anticipating trouble. Senate floor debate on the bill continued beyond dark. Finally, about nine thirty, Waters was brought inside by a Senate aide. Moments later he reappeared to deliver the bad news: the bill had gone down to defeat. At that moment, when it looked like the veterans might attack the Capitol, Elsie Robinson, a reporter for the Hearst newspaper chain, whispered something in Waters's ear. Apparently taking her advice, Waters shouted out to his men: "Sing 'America.'" When the song was over, the anger seemed to have become less fierce, and most of the assembled veterans headed back to their camp.[4]

After the Senate defeat, a large portion of the Bonus Army elected to stay and continue its struggle. Observers who visited the veterans' main camp were impressed by the high degree of self-discipline and the good humor that prevailed among those encamped there, but what was most astonishing to those observers was that white veterans, from the Deep South as well as the rest of the country, shared rations, chores, and lodging in complete amity with the 2,000 or so black vets of the Bonus

Expeditionary Force (the name the bonus marchers gave themselves). Historian Constance McLaughlin Green commented, "Not a trace of Jim Crow in the entire Bonus Army during the days of waiting, or the evening when the Senate defeated the bill, or in the weeks thereafter during which some 10,000 dejected 'bonuseers' stayed on in stubborn belief that Congress would still come to their rescue."[5]

When it appeared that the bonus would not be paid and the marchers refused to leave, Hoover ordered the Army to evict them. Employing infantrymen of the Regular Army, tanks, tear gas, and a detachment of saber-wielding cavalrymen on horseback commanded by Major George S. Patton, Army Chief of Staff General Douglas MacArthur drove the marchers out of Washington across the Anacostia River Bridge. Later that night the Army set fire to the main camp on the Anacostia Flats, across from Capitol Hill.

Eyewitnesses, including MacArthur's own chief of staff, Dwight D. Eisenhower, would insist that Secretary of War Patrick J. Hurley, speaking for the president, had forbidden the Army to cross the river into the Anacostia camp and that Hurley had dispatched two high-ranking officers to bring this order directly to MacArthur. Eisenhower wrote later: "He said he was too busy and did not want either himself or his staff bothered by people coming down and pretending to bring orders."[*,6]

Young Eisenhower escaped being tainted by the episode, as he had been the voice of reason in a chaotic situation. At first he had argued with his superior, MacArthur, that the Army should stay out of what was essentially a local police matter and later attempted to convince MacArthur not to cross the bridge into Anacostia. "The whole scene was pitiful" is how Eisenhower later described that night. It was assumed later that George Marshall considered himself fortunate that he had had other duties to perform during the period and had not been ordered

---

* It is apparent from their writings that MacArthur and Eisenhower did not like each other. All MacArthur says in his memoir, *Reminiscences*, about their prewar association was that in confronting the Bonus Army, "I . . . brought with me two officers who later wrote their names on world history, Majors Eisenhower and Patton."

onto the streets of Washington to superintend the dirty work of expel-
ling the veterans and their families.[7]

In the days following the expulsion, newspapers, magazines, and
newsreels showed graphic images of what had taken place in front of
the Capitol dome, which was obscured by clouds of smoke and tear gas.
Tanks rolled through a battle zone located between the White House
and the Capitol as cavalrymen waved their swords at veterans, and infantrymen bearing fixed bayonets and wearing gas masks marched against
them, forcing them out of downtown. "It's war," the voice on a newsreel
narrated as images of the expulsion played across the screens in movie
theaters from coast to coast, "the greatest concentration of fighting troops
in Washington since 1865 ... They are being forced out of their shacks
by the troops who have been called out by the president of the United
States." Reports came back to Washington that in many of these movie
houses, the Regular Army troops were booed along with MacArthur
and Patton. To many Americans, those being gassed and driven from the
Capitol were the heroes, not the infantrymen used to disperse them.[8]

Franklin D. Roosevelt, then Democratic nominee for the upcoming presidential election, was on the record stating his opposition to the
immediate payment of the bonus because he felt that it would favor one
specific group of Americans at a time when the whole nation was suffering. But after seeing pictures and reading the first newspaper reports of
the eviction, he reportedly turned to an adviser and said, "This will elect
me." In fact, Roosevelt would win the election three months later by a
landslide seven million votes. Laying aside the impact of the Depression
on voters, Patton later posited that the Army's "act[ing] against a crowd
rather than against a mob" had "insured the election of a Democrat."
Hoover biographer David Burner felt that the incident "dealt a fatal
blow to the re-election of the incumbent. In the minds of most analysts,
whatever doubt had remained about the outcome of the presidential
election was now gone: Hoover was going to lose. The Bonus Army
was his final failure, his symbolic end."[9]

The expulsion of the Bonus Army cast a long shadow over MacArthur and Hoover and helped pave the way for Roosevelt and his New

Deal. When FDR took office, he began looking to reallocate funds for his new programs and initially demanded that the Army cut its budget by $50 million, or a full 33 percent. The number of infantrymen would be retained, by order of Army chief of staff MacArthur, but deep cuts would be made to normal field-training exercises, including target practice. Cuts were also proposed to flight training for the Army Air Corps, research and development, and a host of other activities deemed superfluous by the incoming administration. As part of this scheme, the number of junior officers would also be reduced substantially.[10]

After Congress authorized the formation of the CCC in March 1933, Roosevelt said that he wanted to enroll 250,000 men by July 1, a goal that quickly proved to be unattainable. When the CCC failed to meet Roosevelt's early expectations, signing up only 100,000 men in its first two months, its director suggested that the War Department and MacArthur take over the program. Roosevelt and his top advisers reluctantly agreed when the president realized that the Army was his only viable option. On May 10, the CCC was placed under War Department control. After spending an initial few days on organization, MacArthur described CCC planning as "the greatest peacetime demand ever made upon the Army," adding that it "constitutes a task of character and proportions equivalent to the emergencies of war."[11]

MacArthur mobilized those under his command, despite the opposition of some military men who felt the assignment could have a bad effect on the nation's ability to wage war. He understood that Roosevelt was fighting the effects of the Depression rather than preparing for a foreign war and realized that it gave him added leverage in holding on to his officer corps, which Roosevelt and Congress wanted to substantially reduce in size.

MacArthur did everything possible to provide the CCC with Army officers for proper supervision and administration. Officers detailed to train the National Guard, the Reserve Officers' Training Corps (ROTC), and the Citizens' Military Training Camps (CMTC) were sent back to their units to be reassigned to the CCC. Most of the Army's schools were closed, their personnel now given teaching assignments with the CCC.

Overnight, the Army was forced to change. "We were en route to Fort Benning [from Fort Screven, Georgia] for Corps Area Maneuvers when the concentration was called off . . . because of the President's emergency employment proposal for 250,000 men," then major George C. Marshall wrote to an acquaintance.[12]

Officers had already seen a reduction in pay and travel and subsistence allowances under Hoover. But, as one historian wrote, "It was left to Franklin D. Roosevelt to bring the depression home to the soldier." In order to reduce government expenses, Roosevelt dispensed with the reenlistment bonus for the men of the Regular Army. This amounted to a loss of $75 in the lowest pay grades and $150 above the rank of corporal. He cut the Army pay scale so that a private's monthly pay of $21 was now cut to $17.85.[13]

The CCC created other challenges for the Army, not the least of which was caused by its pay grade, as a CCC enlistee would earn $30 per month. Never mind that most of the CCC recruit's pay was sent home to help the man's family, the difference was still dramatic, $12.15 more per month than the Army private received.[14]

The Tree Army felt like a slap in the face to the men of the Bonus Army and to other veterans who were told they were too old to qualify for the CCC. The veterans felt they were the first casualty in Roosevelt's war on the Depression. During his election campaign, Roosevelt had promised a balanced budget. As soon as he became president, he started a quiet process that would achieve the balance by slicing $480 million from veterans' benefits. He began by appointing Lewis W. Douglas as his director of the budget. A Democratic congressman from Arizona, Douglas had advocated a slash in appropriations for benefits during the Hoover administration. Millionaire heir to a Phelps-Dodge copper-mining executive, Douglas resigned from Congress to take the budget job.

Douglas had been gassed in France during World War I and decorated for bravery, and he believed, as a veteran, that service in uniform did not guarantee special privileges, especially since veterans—including those dating back to the Civil War—garnered 24 percent of the federal budget while representing only 1 percent of the population. He sought to implement the $480 million in cuts through the Economy Act of 1933, Roosevelt's major budget proposal. The act was rushed through Congress and signed by Roosevelt so swiftly that veterans' organizations did not have time to mount a full-scale lobbying campaign against it.[15]

Too late to stop it, those representing veterans flooded congressional offices with heart-wrenching stories of vets hurt by the Economy Act. Arthur Krock, chief Washington correspondent for the *New York Times*, wrote: "Down many Main Streets go armless veterans who used to get $94 a month from the Government, and now get $36." Men who had lost two legs or two eyes would have their pensions reduced as well. Those with service-related illnesses would lose up to 80 percent of their pensions. Veterans with diseases such as tuberculosis and neurosis would lose their entire pensions if their conditions were not unequivocally connected with their service in uniform.[16]

"I know many, many veterans will soon be laid in there [sic] graves, death being brought on by the additional worry which is bound to come," an Ohio official of the Disabled American Veterans organization wrote to a member of Congress, who passed the letter on to the White House.[17] Death did indeed come to troubled veterans. A Philadelphia man killed himself and left a message to President Roosevelt, saying that because his benefits were gone, he had no way to provide for his family except through his death, which would give his wife the remaining $275 from his bonus. A patient in a Dayton, Ohio, veterans' hospital killed the chief of the medical staff after being told that because he no longer got a $60 benefit check, he had to leave the hospital. Veterans sometimes owned no civilian clothes, and those who were reclassified and evicted from soldiers' homes often ended up on the streets, wandering about in their old uniforms.[18]

Reports of suicides poured into congressional offices, and members of Congress began to regret their hasty endorsement of the Economy Act. Roosevelt held firm and appealed to the veterans' patriotism in a special message. "I do not want any veteran to feel that he and his comrades are being singled out to make sacrifices," he said. "On the contrary, I want them to know that the regulations issued are but an integral part of our economy program embracing every department and agency of the government to which every employee is making his or her contribution."[19]

In early May 1933, a new wave of Bonus Army marchers began to show up in Washington, again demanding their bonuses but also arguing for the restoration of benefits veterans had just lost. Unlike the first Bonus Army, this group came in with a list of grievances, including the lament that they were too old to be eligible for the nascent CCC. They seemed angrier than the 1932 marchers. Hoover's problem became Roosevelt's, as the trickle turned into a steady stream.

Soon some 3,000 veterans had arrived and were housed in a tent city, which the new president had ordered the Army to build on the grounds of an abandoned fort near Mount Vernon, on the Virginia side of the Potomac River. In an outing arranged by the White House, First Lady Eleanor Roosevelt withstood the rain and the mud to join the vets in a friendly get-together and sing-along. "Hoover sent the Army; Roosevelt sent his wife" became a new rallying cry among the vets.[20]

Opposed to paying the bonus, Roosevelt realized that he needed to get the marchers out of town by any means other than force. Although the Civilian Conservation Corps had been created for single young men, FDR unveiled a plan on May 11 to include war veterans, waiving age and marital requirements. Executive Order 6129 provided special camps for an initial placement of 25,000 veterans, including older men who had fought in the Spanish-American War.

About 2,500 of the vets in Washington signed up immediately; others rejected the proposal, likening the dollar-a-day wage to slavery. On May 19, about 400 of the men who had rejected the offer marched to the White House, chanting: "We want our back pay—not a dollar a day." But the edge had been taken off the demonstrations, and many of those who rejected the CCC accepted the government's offer of a free ride home. Eventually, 213,000 mostly middle-aged vets would spend time in the CCC during its nine years of operation.[21]

Under MacArthur's direction, all Army training programs were suspended and all resources of the Regular Army were made available to the CCC. For example, all the instructors and recently graduated officers from the Army's Command and General Staff College at Fort Leavenworth, Kansas, were ordered to report immediately to CCC camps throughout the country.

Ecstatic to have surpassed FDR's goal by mobilizing close to 300,000 recruits by the July 1, 1933, deadline, MacArthur sent out a personal congratulatory message to all members of the Army in which he deemed the mobilization an exercise that boded well for the actual preparation for war. "Such splendid results," MacArthur declared, "could have only been possible because of 'high morale' and 'devotion to duty' by the Army."[22]

By embracing FDR's plan, MacArthur had not only helped to reestablish his public reputation after the Bonus Army expulsion, but he had also gained strength in his battle to keep the Army from suffering even deeper budget cuts. Using the Army's dedication to making the CCC a success, MacArthur was able to convince the White House and Congress to revise the originally demanded 33 percent cuts in the Army's budget down to 11 percent. "Gen. MacA. finally won the most important phases of his fight against drastic cutting of National Defense," Dwight Eisenhower wrote in June 1933. "We will lose no officers or men (at least at this time) and this concession was won because of the great numbers we are using on the Civilian Conservation Corps work and of Gen. MacA's skill and determination in the fight."[23]

MacArthur also saw the CCC as a windfall to the Army. Although the demands of this massive new program brought to a sudden halt the Army's normal garrison routine, as officers and non-commissioned officers (NCOs) went off to establish and supervise the camps, these camps could be converted to military use and were populated with potential military recruits. The young men of the CCC were vaccinated, properly fed, subjected to basic discipline, and in many cases taught to read and write. Emergency dental care was widely given, and simple skin diseases were treated with drugs—including some that were too expensive for poor civilians. When a man left the CCC in good standing, he was given honorable discharge papers containing work experience and a health record that could be used in applying for a job.

In addition, anyone who wanted to sign up for a second hitch in the CCC had to rise to a leadership position. This meant that the CCC was, in effect, training its own cadre of disciplined non-commissioned officers— including that ofttimes rarest of wartime commodities: sergeants.[24]

However, the new administration feared that this welfare program would be seen as the American equivalent of the paramilitary Hitler Youth movement, which was making headlines in 1933. Roosevelt thus forbade military training as part of the CCC curriculum. American Socialist Norman Thomas was quick to remark that the CCC work camps seemed more like the product of a fascist state than a socialist one.

Furthermore, not all CCC recruits were comfortable with the relationship between the Tree Army and the real one. Oscar Baradinsky, a recruit from New York City, saw the CCC as nothing more than a propaganda and recruiting arm of the military. He made his case in an open letter to the president, which was published in the July 1934 edition of *Panorama: A Monthly Survey of People and Ideas*, an ephemeral periodical with a clear antiwar slant published in Boston. Baradinsky reported that at his camp in New Jersey, on the night of June 21, 1934, the Army was recruiting men from the camp for three-year hitches. "He painted a pretty picture of Army life, sunny Hawaii, glamorous Panama, etc.," Baradinsky wrote of the recruiter. The young Corpsman believed this was contrary to the president's promise that the camps would not be used to recruit.

Disturbed by the realization that the CCC had strong military ties, Baradinsky entered the mess hall a few nights later and recalled for his fellow Corpsmen accounts that he had read of shrapnel blowing away the faces of young soldiers in the previous war. He foresaw a terrible tragedy in the offing, fearing these faces were fated to be blown away in the next war. He then got up from the table, walked to headquarters, and told the Army captain in charge that he was quitting, which he was allowed to do without penalty.[25]

As if to bolster Baradinsky's case, in early 1935—in opposition to Roosevelt's stance—MacArthur proposed that two months of military training be added to service in the CCC. He suggested this before the

House Appropriations Committee, saying, "I think there would be nothing finer than the men in the CCC camps should be used as a nucleus for an enlisted reserve." He added: "These men are already fit for military training. I think the idea would be popular with them. I think if we had, for instance, 300,000 list reserves who could be called up to the colors immediately our military condition of preparation for defense would be immeasurably better." MacArthur argued that the program would be cost-effective and that the new Reservists could be paid as little as a dollar a month for their service as Reservists.[26] The proposal was rejected then and again later. Congress and the administration had no stomach for the inevitable photographs in the papers of CCC men drilling with rifles and bayonets rather than laboring with rakes and shovels.

Although forbidden by the president to recruit CCC prospects directly, MacArthur's recruiters resorted to a sly scheme to convince men who were on the fence. The CCC paid $30 a month, compared to only $21 a month in the Army (full pay had been restored in 1934). But clever recruiting officers quietly pointed out that $25 a month from the CCC was automatically sent home to help the man's family, while a private in the Army could keep the whole $21. "The sales talk is working," wrote Ray Tucker in his syndicated column, Washington Whirligig, of August 5, 1935. "Soldiers are signing up at the rate of 2,500 a week—faster than quartermaster and medical office accounts can handle them."[27]

The overall impact of the CCC on the military proved to be positive in that it made the Army stronger and better able to deal with a sudden influx of new men. At Fort Benning, Georgia, in 1933, Major Omar Bradley took command of six all-black CCC companies. These recruits he said were from the poorest farm areas of Georgia and Alabama, and some of the men had not had a square meal for at least a year. Bradley gave them food and physicals, set up a pay account, put them through a few weeks of training, and sent them on to replant the large deforested areas of the Deep South.

Bradley's enthusiasm for the CCC seemed boundless. "The Army's magnificent performance with the CCC in the summer of 1933, undertaken so reluctantly, was one of the highlights of its peacetime years," he later recalled. "It all ran with clockwork precision; the CCC itself was judged first rate. It was a good drill for us." To some in the Army, the CCC had been seen as a burden, but to Bradley and others it was a blessing.[28]

The CCC's impact on Marshall was even more significant and enduring. From his Eighth Infantry Regiment headquarters at Fort Moultrie, South Carolina, a large base on Sullivan's Island near Charleston, Marshall found himself the administrator of an enormous labor project involving 25,000 young men flooding 17 work camps across the southern United States. Marshall threw himself into the CCC assignment with great enthusiasm. As he was facing a shortage of officers, his wife, Katherine Tupper Marshall, volunteered to help. As she encountered these young Americans, she was appalled by the all-too-visible effects of the Great Depression on them and the price they were paying for it. The men were underfed, and sores and skin rashes were the norm. The general condition of their teeth was appalling. They fought for food, even when there was an abundance of it, and they snarled at one another like packs of feral dogs. Fully half of the men being processed were illiterate.[29]

During this period, George Marshall praised the CCC, saying it was "the greatest social experiment outside of Russia." He pointed out in a letter to a friend that he was "struggling to force [the recruits'] education, academic or vocational, to the point where they will be on the road to really useful citizenship by the time they return to their homes." Marshall saw his role in rebuilding these men's lives as helping to rebuild the country, noting that he considered the corps "a splendid experience for the War Department and the Army."[30]

Marshall was unforgiving when it came to officers who complained about their CCC duties. A major came into Marshall's office to announce that he was resigning. "I've put twelve years in the Army," he said. "I'm a graduate of West Point. I'm not going to come down here and deal with a whole lot of bums. Half-dead Southern crackers, that's what they are!"

"Major, I'm sorry you feel like that," Marshall responded. "But I'll tell you this—you can't resign quick enough to suit me. It suits me fine! Now get out of here!"[31]

Conversely, the officers who assumed leadership roles in the CCC under Marshall were often singled out for praise and ultimately promotion. When a national award was offered to the best camp in the country, Major Alex Starke's camp at Sumter, South Carolina, was named the winner. Starke later became a brigadier general during the Tunisian campaign in 1942.[32]

Marshall was also cognizant of the problems of his own soldiers, whose incomes had been slashed by the new administration, and he did much to alleviate their distress. "In order that the men could manage to feed their families on their small pay, my husband personally supervised the building of chicken yards, vegetable gardens, and hog pens," Katherine Marshall remembered. "He started a lunch pail system whereby the men could get a good hot dinner, cooked up at the mess to take home to their families at a very small cost."[33]

But the stress on the Regular Army went beyond hot meals. In April 1934, after leaving his southern post, Marshall wrote to a commander in the Illinois National Guard outlining the extent of the stress created by the CCC assignment coupled with Roosevelt's pay cuts: "Officers and men were suddenly scattered in 1,400 Camps throughout the United States, under the necessity of maintaining their families in one place and themselves in another. The wives and children of married soldiers were often without funds for food and rent." Marshall then pointed out that because of the pay cuts many soldiers struggled to keep up with a $10 a month allotment sent home to their parents, while the CCC man was able to send home a monthly allotment of between $25 and $40 depending on the circumstances back home. He then went on to compare the two situations: "While the soldier had no choice of post or duty. The CCC recruit was free to terminate his connection with the government at any time, and he could not be worked more than six hours a day. The regular soldier in the CCC camp was usually on duty twelve hours a day." Marshall concluded, "Despite the inequalities and injustice of this arrangement, the regular soldiers gave their earnest and most efficient services to make the CCC the success it has been."[34]

William Frye, Marshall's earliest biographer, believed that despite this situation Marshall refused to resent these recruits for the disparity in pay and chose to see them "as the bewildered victims of a depression which had broken them financially and shaken their spirits," adding that "they received from him the same sympathetic interest and close attention he gave to his troops."[35]

Marshall's greatest impact, however, was on the CCC recruits themselves, whom he taught to work together. He gave them a sense of discipline. "Most of all," his wife later commented, "he gave those boys back their self-respect. That was the first time those boys came to realize they weren't just nothing, that they were supposed to measure up to something."

Colonel Laurence Halstead, acting chief of the infantry, wrote to Marshall in May to comment on the Army's role in developing the CCC: "This work is onerous and probably distasteful to the Army as it is not exactly military work but I feel that it is the salvation of the Army. In fact, it is my opinion that the Army is the only Governmental agency that was able to handle this proposition. I have noticed a cessation of talk of reducing the Army by four thousand officers since we started in on the conservation work."[36]

When a French Navy cruiser, *D'Entrecastaux*, paid a courtesy call to Charleston, near Fort Moultrie, in mid-September 1933, Marshall entertained the officers and crew at a nearby CCC camp, which he dedicated as Camp Lafayette in honor of their visit. The Marquis de Lafayette, Marshall pointed out, had first landed near the site some 150 years earlier. The dedication was accepted by the French consul in the name of the Republic of France. After the band from Fort Moultrie played "The Star-Spangled Banner" and "La Marseillaise," the French officers and men were fed CCC fare at the camp, and the CCC recruits led the sailors from the ship on a tour of the facilities.[37]

The dedication at Camp Lafayette, which made headlines and was described in magazine features in France, illustrated the point that under Marshall's tutelage, the camps were points of pride and patriotism rather than objects of pity. During the same month that Marshall staged the events at Camp Lafayette, he was promoted to the rank of colonel.

As it became clear that Marshall's service to the CCC was both a triumph for the Army and the CCC, MacArthur began to see Marshall as a threat—"an enemy conspiring against him," in the words of William Manchester in *American Caesar*—and sidelined him by taking him out of a command role and making him an instructor in the Illinois National Guard, based in Chicago.[38] Marshall wrote to MacArthur begging to remain with his regiment, insisting that another instructor's job—away from his troops—would be fatal to his future in the Army. MacArthur chose not to respond, and the Marshalls headed north. One of his biographers, William Frye, termed the assignment "a savage blow" to Marshall. Later, Katherine Marshall recalled their early days in Chicago, describing her husband's "grey, drawn look which I had never seen before and is seldom seen since."[39]

Despite his initial dislike of the Illinois assignment, work with National Guard units gave Marshall exposure to men who saw themselves as civilians first and soldiers second as well as experience dealing with politicians—both uncommon connections for officers at this time. Unlike many officers, Marshall did not see the men of the National Guard as second-rate, and he worked hard to improve Reserve facilities and training and made good use of Reserve officers.

Marshall still wanted a full military command, complete with CCC responsibilities. Finally, in August 1936, after MacArthur had resigned as chief of staff, Marshall got his wish when the new chief, Malin Craig, assigned him to be commander of the Vancouver Barracks in Vancouver, Washington. While there, Marshall supervised 27 CCC camps in the Pacific Northwest. His assignment, from new secretary of war Woodring, said: "A large part of your time will be taken up with CCC inspections and activities . . . The success of that movement depends upon constant inspections and holding up standards."[40]

When Marshall arrived in the Northwest, he was in command of camps populated with young men from more than 20 states, including those from as far away as Boston and Providence. He again became fascinated by the potential of the Corpsmen, paying special attention to the educational programs of these camps. "He strove to have the best instructors it was possible to get," his wife recalled. "He wanted to prepare them as far as possible to take responsible jobs back home." The welfare of the 10,000 CCC men under his command was paramount. "If the boy's teeth were in bad condition, woe befell the CCC dentist who extracted when he could have filled!"[41]

Ever the idealist, Marshall worked hard to remake the lackluster educational system in his CCC district. He remarked to a friend: "I am struggling to force their education, academic or vocational, to the point where they will be on the road to really useful citizenship by the time they return to their homes. I have done over my corps of civilian educators, and their methods, until I think we really have something supremely practical."[42]

Marshall regarded his two years in Vancouver as among the happiest times of his life, and he lauded the experience as "the best antidote for mental stagnation that an Army officer in my position can have." He turned the Vancouver Barracks from a decaying mess into one of the most beautiful bases in the western United States. The reenlistment rate by the men in his command was one of the highest in the nation. He later observed: "I found the CCC the most instructive service I ever had, and the most interesting," adding that, because of the corps, the Army had "very much to learn about simplification and decentralization" during wartime. To General John J. Pershing, Marshall wrote that he regarded the CCC to be "a major mobilization exercise and a splendid experience for the War Department and the Army." Personally, it was important to Marshall's own career, as evidence suggests that Marshall first came to Roosevelt's attention as a leader and staunch supporter of the CCC.[43]

Unlike other Army officers who saw the men of the CCC as somehow inferior or lacking, Marshall respected them and held them in high regard. "As a whole," he wrote to an associate a few months after arriving in the Northwest of the men in the CCC, "they are a fine lot, hardworking, studious in following the educational courses we provide, and seeming to develop considerable ambition, along with the necessary energy and resolution." The letter, which was quoted in its entirety in William Frye's 1947 biography of Marshall, prompted this comment from Frye on Marshall's words on the men of the CCC: "His interest in those under his command or supervision [was] as individual human beings, not as units in a table of organization."[44]

Marshall, who had made a point of writing letters of recommendation for worthy Corpsmen seeking employment after their CCC time was up, had the favor returned in the form of a cartoon, published in the CCC district newspaper on his departure in 1938, when he was joining the Army general staff in Washington, D.C. The cartoon contained a "Letter of commendation" from the Corpsmen, reading: "Dear Gen. Marshall: We know you always placed our welfare first, signed enrollees of Vancouver CCC district."[45]

While both Marshall and Bradley would spend the rest of their lives alluding to their CCC experience, the outspoken conservative MacArthur never mentioned the experience in his memoirs or referred to it in his public speeches. As one MacArthur biographer remarked about the general's leadership at the CCC, "It was as if it never existed. And yet, he found an odd fulfillment in running the program, as he made clear in a letter to CCC Director Robert Fechner: 'it is the type of human reconstruction that has appealed to me more than I sometimes admit.'"[46]

The point that MacArthur was loath to admit but that Marshall, Bradley, and others embraced was that the CCC allowed the Regular Army to achieve in a time of peace something of what it was trained to do in wartime, namely "to mobilize, organize, and administer an army of citizen soldiers." The officers in charge of the CCC lacked the well-defined coercive power they had with Regular Army troops, so they had to turn to reason and the power of personality to lead the CCC. These skills would later be essential during a mass mobilization for war. Marshall biographer David L. Roll concluded that the CCC experience "buttressed Marshall's faith in the value and effectiveness of a citizen army."[47]

On April 5, 1937, FDR recommended to Congress that the CCC be made a permanent agency of the federal government. On June 28, 1937, Congress passed and the president signed an act extending the CCC for a period of three years, to begin on July 1, 1937. One of the arguments made for the extension was that the Tree Army could become the backbone of a new, expanded Army when it was needed. Two years later, when Germany invaded Poland, Marshall knew the time had come and that expansion would happen sooner rather than later.

After the Second World War, Bradley declared that the CCC had saved the Army and that without it the Army might have seen a massive cut in the officer corps and gone into the war without many important leaders, including himself, Joseph W. "Vinegar Joe" Stilwell, and many other officers. He added that those three million CCC workers who left their camps to go on active duty went on to "save the world."[48]

CHAPTER 3

A "PHONEY" WAR ABROAD AND A MOCK WAR AT HOME

At the time of the invasion of Poland, the United States was fiercely divided. A majority of Americans were firmly isolationist, their stance based on an increasing belief that America's involvement in World War I had been a terrible error, especially when viewed through the dim prism of the Great Depression. Many Americans were reminded of the old popular song "Don't Let the Same Bee Sting You Twice." A poll conducted by George Gallup at the end of 1938 found that 70 percent of American voters thought U.S. involvement in the earlier conflict had been an out-and-out mistake.[1]

Hating a war in which many of its members had fought, the American Legion was at the heart of the movement trying to push neutrality acts and other isolationist laws through Congress. The rhetoric of the legion was more pacifist than martial, and this attitude became stronger after the Polish surrender, even though one-third of the members of Congress were legionnaires themselves.[2]

Furthermore, many of the men still occupying beds in Veterans Administration hospitals were draftees from the previous war whose wounds were significant enough to keep them in need of perpetual care. A wounded soldier on the street, including amputees on crutches and victims of gas attacks carrying portable devices they needed to help them breathe, was still a common sight in the United States in 1939.

The most radical isolationists claimed that virtually all of the nation's current problems stemmed from the Great War. Senator Gerald Nye of North Dakota went so far as to blame America's Great Depression on the unbridled economic expansion created by the war.[3]

The Nazi invasion of Poland had energized congressional isolationists and attracted powerful new celebrity voices. The retired Marine Corps general Smedley Butler, a two-time Medal of Honor winner, became an ever-louder voice, declaring that "war is a racket." This maxim, also the title of his book, was shorthand for his belief that the only victors in any war were banks and large corporations. Butler's book had been published in 1935, and its message seemed to become louder over time.

On September 15, 1939, Charles Lindbergh delivered a nationwide radio address in which he strongly urged America to remain neutral— to "stand clear" of the squabble in Europe. Lindbergh envisioned a Nazi victory in Europe as a certainty and thought America's attention should be directed toward Asia and Japan. "These wars in Europe are not wars in which our civilization is defending itself against some Asiatic intruder," he intoned in the passage that seemed to gather the most attention. "There is no Genghis Khan marching against our Western nations. This is not a question of banding together to defend our White race against foreign invasion." Many newspapers carried long excerpts from the speech and some—including the *New York Times* and *Herald Tribune*—published the full text of the speech. Building on the theme of racial strength, Lindbergh would follow with an article in the November 1940 *Reader's Digest*, warning Americans to not allow themselves to be led into "a war which will reduce the strength and destroy the treasures of the White race, a war which may even lead to the end of our civilization." He also warned against "dilution by foreign races . . . and the infiltration of inferior blood."[4]

As a euphemism for *genes*, "blood" was very much an issue in 1939. A small but effective group was spreading the propaganda that humanity would be improved by encouraging the ablest and healthiest people to produce more children and the "deficient" to produce fewer or no children at all. Several states were officially sterilizing those deemed to be inferior. Hitler proudly pointed out that he was only observing the laws of several American states, including California, that allowed for the forced sterilization of the "unfit." The belief system, known as eugenics, held that certain good or bad genes were the monopoly of certain races and ethnicities, fueling the Nazis' claim that they were creating a superior race.[5]

In addition to the isolationist faction, antiwar movements on American college and university campuses grew along with pro-German sentiment, egged on by radio priest Father Charles Coughlin and the minister Gerald L. K. Smith, both of whom preached anti-Semitism and lauded American fascism. The America First Committee—founded by pacifist Yale students but eventually dominated by conservative isolationists—became the most significant of the organizations fighting to keep America out of the European war.

The autumn of 1939 was a period of anxiety as the world tried to anticipate when Hitler would pick his next victim. Aggression finally came on November 30, but the aggressor was the Soviet Union, not Germany, and Finland was the victim. The attack was a clear act of aggression aimed at acquiring more territory, and it resulted in the Soviet Union's expulsion from the League of Nations.

The ongoing reorganization of the United States Army made few headlines, and Roosevelt's modest increase in the size of the infantry made scant difference. As military reporter John G. Norris wrote in the *Washington Post* on October 8, "The United States will still have to be grouped with small nations of the world in the size of their military establishment. It will rank perhaps 14th or 15th, gaining a rung or two by its own enlargement and by the disappearance of the Polish army, which ranked way ahead of the United States."[6]

The invasion of Poland by the Nazis provided a stark reminder for the United States of its own weaknesses. Although popular attention seemed to be placed on the apparent superiority of the tanks of Hitler's Panzer divisions, an even greater concern to Marshall and other military planners was how the airplane had been used by the

Germans in the blitzkrieg that had razed Poland. As Donald M. Nelson, an American official later charged with the responsibility for arms production during the war, recalled: "Nothing like this technology for completely demolishing a modern nation had ever been seen before. Production centers had been smashed, communications completely disorganized. With their air force obliterated, the Poles might as well have been fighting with clubs. These reports were electrifying to the men who, sooner or later, would be responsible for American defense or war production."[7]

The year ended with Roosevelt and Marshall working with quiet determination to improve the Army in size and efficiency, despite Secretary of War Woodring's opposition. The situation was dire. "On New Year's Day of 1940, when the peril was beginning to close in on us, the United States Armed Forces might almost have been called our 'Disarmed Forces'" was Nelson's view of the situation.[8]

At the end of December, Woodring had presented his annual report on the state of the military to the president and asserted once again that national defense could not be defined in terms of manpower or money but rather in terms of the efficiency of new weaponry. He argued, "One million naked savages armed with 1,000,000 spears and 1,000,000 shields would be slaughtered by 100 men armed with 100 of the Army's new semiautomatic shoulder rifles and a baker's dozen of the Army's new tanks."

What Woodring did not point out was that these new weapons were in short supply, and many of the specific items existed only as prototypes. Only 15,000 of the Garand M-1 rifles he alluded to were then available, and only 300 new ones were being produced a week. Also, pitting "naked savages" against the United States Army displayed Woodring's unwillingness to confront the fact that the next war was not going to be fought with spears and shields but with arms, aircraft, and armored vehicles forged from German steel.[9]

In January 1940, Roosevelt tried once again to move Woodring out of the way, this time offering him the ambassadorship to Italy. Again Woodring declined, choosing to hold on to his office despite the fact that a large part of the United States Army now saw him as a road-block rather than a facilitator. Marshall, on the other hand, was letting Congress know in no uncertain terms that the Army was improperly trained and prepared. "We have been forced [by lack of funds] to build up our technique of command and control, and even our development of leadership, largely on a theoretical basis," he declared at one point.[10]

Congress listened but was slow to move, as the clouds of war seemed to be dissipating rather than gathering. Over the winter of 1939–40, a certain quiet fell over Europe, which led to a feeling of stalemate and inaction that lasted into the spring and past Easter. Some described the inactivity as a truce of sorts and the basis for a negotiated settlement. The situation became known as the Phoney War,* an odd, slangy phrase that came into use within days of Poland's defeat.[11] During this time, French and German troops eyed one another across Germany's Siegfried Line and France's Maginot Line, the latter a 280-mile-long defensive line of concrete fortifications, obstacles, and installed weapons built in the 1930s to deter invasion by Germany. Named for André Maginot, a former French minister of war, it ran along the entire length of the Franco-German border. The French believed it to be impregnable.

In the United States, the issue of the Phoney War became fodder for columnists and editorial writers, some of whom saw it as a hiatus in a larger period of aggression. "It is being said that this is a phoney war. But we shall understand the war better if we remember that it was preceded by eight years of phoney peace," wrote Walter Lippmann in his widely syndicated *New York Herald Tribune* column in late October. "From the Japanese invasion of Manchuria in 1931 until the Nazi invasion of Poland in 1939, the peace of the world was disintegrating under the demoralization of class war, the pressure of subversive propaganda and intrigue, and the intimidation of armed and ruthless conspirators." He concluded by calling the phoney peace an act of war.[12]

---

* The word *phony/phoney*, which first appeared in print in the early 20th century, was spelled with an *e* by the British and without one by Americans. But during the era of the Phoney War, the British spelling tended to be used on both sides of the Atlantic.

But Lippmann appeared to be in the minority, as others declared the Phoney War* to be the end of, or a long-term deferral of, hostilities. As journalist and Army historian Mark Skinner Watson later wrote about this period, it had "lulled the fears of only the uninformed, but the uninformed were numerous."[13]

Many of those who had fled Paris and London fearing a Nazi attack returned home reassured that the Nazi saturation bombing they had dreaded had not come to pass. By Christmas, Londoners were neglecting to carry the gas masks they had been issued, and many prefabricated bomb shelters lay unclaimed at distribution points. By the end of January, nearly 60 percent of Britain's 1.5 million evacuees had returned to their homes. And 43 percent of British schoolchildren had returned to their classes, often to schools that had been shut down in September 1939 because they were in areas considered dangerous and now needed to be reopened to accommodate the children who had returned to their homes.[14]

The Phoney War compromised the British public's dedication to fighting the war against Germany. There was widespread antipathy toward food and gasoline rationing, blackouts, and other wartime restrictions that now appeared to be unnecessary. Citizens of England and France had to be constantly reminded that their countries had already declared war on Germany.

Especially in the United States, odd opinions and prophecies were frequent, including those relentlessly spewing forth from the mouth of Charles Lindbergh. He now took to the pages of the *Atlantic* magazine to declare that it was time for Germany, France, and England to come together in common defense against the "Asiatic hordes" who would soon penetrate and devour Europe.

Because London and Paris were not being bombed at this moment, some even thought that it might be possible to restart peace talks with

---

* Equivalent labels were the *bore war* in English, *la drôle de guerre* (the strange war) in French, and *der Sitzkrieg* in German (the sitting war). *Time* magazine dubbed it the Lullablitz.

Hitler. The *Harvard Crimson* ran a series of hopeful editorials pleading for a negotiated settlement between Germany and the Allied powers. One of the *Crimson* editors, John Fitzgerald Kennedy, son of the American ambassador to England, wrote to his father in early 1940 to report: "Everyone is getting much more confident about our staying out of the war but that of course is probably because there is such a lull over there."[15]

As military activity reached a virtual standstill and the diplomatic front became quiet, the volume of press coverage shrank during the winter months. Foreign affairs had dominated front pages in the fall, but by February such articles were scarce. In their place were silly stories, such as "Real, Phoney War Finds George Snoring Peacefully," the tale of George, a toothless, 120-year-old alligator in the London Zoo, who had been asleep since the beginning of the Phoney War and not affected at all by food rationing.[16]

On February 23, 1940, as Marshall argued for funds before skeptical members of the House of Representatives Committee on Appropriations, he addressed the issue of the Phoney War: "If Europe blazes in the late spring or summer, we must put our house in order before the sparks reach the Western Hemisphere."[17] Marshall believed that the conflagration would come soon enough, and he told the committee he was doing all he could to get ready for it by obtaining the arms and equipment needed to outfit an Army of one million men.

At the time of this testimony, Marshall had already begun to inform Congress of his plans to test his new triangular divisions in large-scale maneuvers. During the course of the hearings, Marshall disclosed that in addition to maneuvers scheduled to take place in May somewhere along the Gulf Coast, which had already been revealed, three other exercises would be held in August 1940.[18]

To many members of Congress the concept of such maneuvers was new. Some knew about the "sham battles" or "sham wars" staged earlier in which two opposing forces in formation fired blanks at one another while civilians watched the show from a safe distance, as had been true of the 1939 Manassas maneuver, but this was an entirely different operation mounted on a large scale for a period of days or weeks.[19]

Under Marshall's direction, a maneuver was envisioned as a carefully prepared operation, undertaken for training soldiers in the field in large numbers, concentrated at great distances from their normal home stations. These maneuvers would have as much to do with troop movements, communication between units, and logistics as they would with the actual *faux* combat. Aircraft from both the Army Air Corps and the Navy would be involved. And unlike the 1939 exercises in Manassas and Plattsburg, which were straightforward, scripted attack-and-defend operations, these maneuvers would allow officers on the ground to operate as they would in a real war, without a script, and thus serve as a test of tactical leadership.

Marshall knew exactly what he was looking for as a stage for the maneuvers: a largely underpopulated area able to sustain the damage and destruction that the maneuvers would inevitably produce. Scouts went out all over the United States to locate ideal areas. After studying their reports, Marshall finally decided on the lower Sabine River area for the first exercise. The river formed a natural border between Texas and Louisiana, and the area long ago had been involved in boundary disputes between the United States and Mexico. The mock war zone selected was a sparsely populated, reptile-rich swampy area presenting its own set of challenges. The front for the staged warfare would extend along the river for 25 to 30 miles.

The exact location of the first of these events had been kept under wraps until February 7, 1940, when Senator John Holmes Overton Sr. (Democrat of Louisiana) announced to the press that he had gotten word directly from Marshall that the maneuvers would take place in Louisiana. Marshall had told the senator that the Army needed a large area with plenty of rivers as obstacles for a mobile infantry to overcome. Overton was pleased, as he saw the maneuvers as a boon to Louisiana's economy. He estimated that the cost of the exercise would be $28 million; Louisiana would receive a large slice of that amount.[20]

Gaining permission to trespass on private land was a process that moved rapidly once the mock war zone had been mapped out. Some

6,500 individual and mostly small landowners signed on granting access to 3,400 square miles. A mere three and a half square miles were denied outright, and there was an additional ten square miles where the owner could not be found. By the time the maneuvers were ready to start, more than two million acres had been set aside for the mock war. The area was almost three times the size of Rhode Island.[21,*]

As the Phoney War dragged on overseas, Marshall gradually brought other southern politicians into his plans. On March 21, Marshall told Representative William M. Colmer (Democrat of Mississippi) that in the early part of May, 36,000 troops would pass through his state as they traveled from Fort Benning, Georgia, to the Sabine River in Louisiana for the exercises, which would soon be known far and wide as the Louisiana Maneuvers. These maneuvers were scheduled to begin on May 5 and end on May 23.[22]

But war games were one thing and war another. One effect of the Phoney War on the United States was that in the spring of 1940, public opinion was strongly opposed to American involvement. One poll, taken in March, held that 96.4 percent of Americans were against going to war with Germany.[23]

To many, Marshall's requests for more troops and equipment were regarded as "mere warmongering," in the words of Marshall's wife, Katherine. As if to underscore the point, on April 3, 1940, the House Appropriations Committee—the same body that Marshall had warned about the coming blaze—cut the modest defense budget by 10 percent, more than $67 million below the amount requested by the president. Among the items cut was $12 million for a cold-weather air-training base in Alaska, which caused Marshall to be "very much concerned," as the base was needed to protect naval bases planned for the Aleutian Islands as well as the rest of Alaska—all of which would be a prime invasion point for Imperial Japan if it attacked North America. Without the new base, Alaska's defense would rest on the occupants of some wooden barracks constructed in Sitka about 40 years earlier.[24] The cuts were especially

* Rhode Island's area is 776,957 square acres.

damaging to the Army Air Corps, which had requested 496 new aircraft but was granted only 57.[25]

"One thing is certain," British Prime Minister Neville Chamberlain said of Hitler on April 4, 1940, in a speech delivered in Central Hall, Westminster. "He missed the bus." Five days later, Chamberlain was proven disastrously wrong when the Phoney War came to an abrupt end. Germany invaded Denmark, which surrendered in only six hours, and at the same time Nazi warships entered Norwegian waters, attacking ships and landing troops that began to occupy key cities by the end of the day.[26]

The next morning's eight-column headline in the *New York Times* read: GERMANS OCCUPY DENMARK, ATTACK OSLO. By the next day, as the Associated Press announced, a new Norwegian government had been formed under the leadership of Vidkun Quisling, the head of the Norwegian Nazi Party. Almost immediately, the name Quisling became a powerful eponym for *collaborator* and *traitor*. Despite the Nazi flag flying over Oslo and the flight of the royal family and much of the government to the north, the Norwegian resistance and the regular army continued to fight, along with expeditionary forces sent by the British and the French.[27]

The Louisiana Maneuvers of 1940 were billed as the greatest military maneuver in U.S. history. Seventy thousand uniformed army men from camps and bases in 33 states began assembling in two locations in the Deep South in March. Texas was sending the greatest number of men to the event, 12,000, and Georgia and New York State provided 7,000 apiece. The 70,000 troops represented about half the standing U.S. Army. In addition, the Army was sending almost all of its 400 or so working tanks, including several of experimental design, along with 340 armored vehicles and 3,000 trucks. One hundred and twenty-eight aircraft, including bombers and pursuit, attack, and observation aircraft, would take part in the games.

Units were assigned to one of two armies, which would assemble approximately 600 miles apart, a separation made more difficult by

swamps and muddy terrain. The troops of the Blue Army headed to
Fort Benning, Georgia, while the Red Army gathered around Natchitoches, Louisiana. As the ordered equipment arrived, the two armies
moved forward, the Red taking up positions along the Texas side of
the Sabine River and the Blue Army on the Louisiana side. Marshall
provided the two armies' commanders with the following information
on the countries at war:

> Blue (East) is a small nation with a common boundary at the
> Sabine River with another small nation, Red (West). Blue has a
> small army, normally scattered throughout the country. Red has
> an even smaller army. These troops, however, are highly trained
> and are concentrated along the border.
>
> Boundary disputes, local border incidents and alien minori-
> ties have resulted in increasing tension between the two nations.
> On April 20, the Red government provocatively announced it
> would hold its spring maneuvers just west of the Sabine River.
>
> The Blue government became alarmed, increased its gar-
> rison at its border town of Alexandria and announced that it
> would move its Army to the vicinity of Alexandria for large-scale
> maneuvers.

The Red Army was to be the aggressor nation, schooled in the
tactics of blitzkrieg, and the Blue, the defending force, protecting its
national border along the Sabine River from a foreign invader. The
Sabine, much of which marks the Texas-Louisiana line, was also regarded
by many as the border between the Old South and the Southwest, so
the sense of it as a national border was not far-fetched.

As the director of the maneuvers, Marshall was quick to point out
that these exercises would have importance far greater than that normally attributed to war games. These maneuvers would be unscripted
and, as in real war, based on "free play." Commanders would be tested
on the ground, where their errors and achievements would be boldly
displayed. The maneuvers were meant to be a test of man, machine, and

command. The maneuvers were to allow American troops to test tactics similar to those the Nazis were employing in Europe and to learn how to defend against them.[28]

The exercises would test not only the new triangular divisions but also the methods of marching men into battle. Gone were the close formations of 1917–18. Advancing or retreating troops would now move through the underbrush, spaced several yards apart in irregular patterns, an approach exemplifying the differences between the old square divisions and the new triangular ones.[29]

The stated premise of the maneuvers was that they were designed to test American forces in case of an invasion of North America, but this would be essentially a cover story, as Roosevelt, Marshall, and everyone else involved in the event knew they were also an early test of an expeditionary army.

Because the news of what was happening in Europe dominated the headlines and the front pages of newspapers in the United States, news of these maneuvers tended to fall on the back pages of news sections in papers outside the region. The events became a boon to the daily newspapers of the Deep South and the Gulf Coast, however, which often played the maneuvers as front-page news; BIG BATTLE EXPECTED IN MANEUVERS TODAY was the lead story on May 5 in a Columbus, Georgia, daily.[30]

Although members of Congress and the press were allowed to witness the maneuvers, foreign military attachés would not be invited for a number of reasons but especially to prevent the disclosure of tactics the Army was developing with regard to the use of its newest weapons and revised structure.[31] The United States was beginning to fully awaken to the reality that some were out to do it harm. Although details were scarce, at least one dispatch filed by Henry N. Dorris of the *New York Times* mentioned that he had been privately informed by several National Guard officers of "fifth column activities"—espionage and/or sabotage—in their units and that the Federal Bureau of Investigation had been called in to "uproot" such elements.[32]

* * *

Once assembled, for the remainder of March and April the two armies trained and prepared for the battle ahead. The Red Army recruited thousands of civilian volunteers from several states to act as spotters of enemy aircraft. The lion's share of the spotters were members of the American Legion, and the name of their unit was the Third Army Aircraft Warning Service. Volunteers clamored to join this force.[33]

Getting men and machines in place for the maneuvers showed that despite shortages, the Army had the ability to move motorized columns quickly over long distances, as 41,000 men of the Blue Army moved 600 miles in six days from Georgia through Alabama and Mississippi to converge on Alexandria, Louisiana. The feat—achieved thanks to the use of a large number of trucks to transport men and horses as well as weapons—was immediately termed the largest and fastest mass movement of armed troops ever witnessed in the United States during peacetime.[34]

On May 8, 1940, all but a few of the Army's 70 generals were present to observe the maneuvers in Louisiana. It was the greatest assemblage of American generals ever in one place. The Associated Press described the initial ground attack, which began at 4:30 a.m. on May 9 as the smaller Red Army drove east out of Texas toward the Blue Army: "Detouring, doubling back in sudden withdrawals and heavily camouflaged with green boughs, the big armored trucks roared down back roads and country lanes, awakening farmers, and setting their dogs to howling."[35]

The predawn attack by horse and mechanized units was halted only temporarily by the Blue Army, which was unable to summon its reserves in time.

Within a few hours, the Red Army had forded the shallow, murky Sabine River, and its First Cavalry had thundered into Leesville, 20 miles east of the river. Other Red units captured Slagle, DeRidder, Hornbeck, and Robeline. The Blue Army forces defending Louisiana suffered a stunning defeat under a battering attack by mechanized troops. The Red Air Corps then gained further ground, theoretically destroying Mississippi River bridges at Vicksburg and New Orleans, virtually isolating the Blues. One element of the Red Army moved quickly toward

Alexandria, the Blue capital, but just as it began to look like the objective was in sight it ran into a large Blue Army force that had dug in on the grounds of a local college. In New Orleans, the Red's Fifth Division rolled into the city in a 60-mile-long procession.

The Associated Press report called the defeat of the Blue Army "bewildering" and noted that in order to keep the maneuvers going, umpires ruled that Blue troops could move across certain bridges that had been "destroyed" by Red warplanes. A reporter embedded with the Blue Army declared it unprepared for war.[36]

The first of three planned phases of these maneuvers ended on May 9 with the apparent defeat of the Blue Army, although the generals running the operation reminded the press that this was not a contest and that keeping score was inappropriate. At this point in the maneuvers, it was up to the press to decide who had won and lost, which it did in dispatches that told of a quick, decisive, and bewildering Blue defeat.[37]

In Europe the next day, in excess of two million German troops invaded France, Luxembourg, Belgium, and the Netherlands, employing blitzkrieg tactics.* Reaction came in many forms and forums, including prophetically on Wall Street, where stocks hit the low point of the year the next day. By contrast, the stocks of steel, copper, and aircraft and munitions makers shot up. What Charles F. Speare of the North American Newspaper Alliance (NANA) described as the "peace stocks" took a beating. The market seemed to be betting on nothing less than total war for the United States.[38]

Word of the Nazi invasion of France and the Low Countries spread quickly among those participating in the maneuvers. An Associated Press dispatch filed from Louisiana described "a sobering atmosphere of grim reality" settling over the mock battlefields. The only official statement came from Lieutenant General Stanley D. Emrick, commander of the Third Army, who said at a press conference: "The Army is ready for any 'M' day to defend this country." *M day* in Army parlance then stood

---

* May 10 was also the day Neville Chamberlain resigned, replaced by Winston Churchill as British Prime Minister.

for general mobilization day, and despite Emrick's confidence, as the maneuvers continued they showed that the Army was ill prepared for such a mobilization.

While the maneuvers were still underway, Marshall testified before a Senate Appropriations subcommittee, pointing out that the armies involved had no reserves in terms of men or materiel: "In other words, if they were bombed actually instead of theoretically in the maneuvers today there is no duplicate truck to take the place of the one that is destroyed. If our pilots operating in the maneuvers today were shot down we do not have the actual pilots to take their places."[39]

That situation was beginning to change, slowly, in the early months of 1940, as more and more money was being laid out for arms and munitions, and the new factories to produce them were coming online. On May 16, six days after the Nazi attack on France and the Low Countries, President Roosevelt appeared personally before both houses of Congress and called for "arms to make our defenses invulnerable, our security absolute." He asked for new arms appropriations of $1.182 billion and then urged the aircraft industry to establish a production capacity of 50,000 warplanes per year.[40]

During the second phase of the exercises in Louisiana, the tide turned quickly. Now the Red Army was suddenly overwhelmed and unprepared for war; its only hope was to bring reinforcements to the front, with which it tried to repel a Blue attack. But the Blue Army was successful, driving the Reds back to the Sabine River and into Texas. The Red forces, outnumbered three to two, were simply unable to hold their positions against the highly mobile teams of the Blue Army.

The final phase of the maneuvers lined the two armies up along a 60-mile front. After two days of stalemate, the Blue Army defeated the Red Army. The final engagement was, however, based on imaginary numbers and assumptions, as the aircraft that actually attacked the other side were so small in number that the judges had to multiply their impact to get a score. Rather than display American airpower, the exercises were a display of its total inadequacy. One reporter, noting the reliance on imaginary aircraft to stage an attack, compared the simulation of war to nothing more than a penny firecracker.[41]

These maneuvers revealed how ill prepared the Army was for waging the kind of well-led mobile warfare being waged in Europe by the Germans. At one level, problems such as a shortage of reliable tanks and trucks and repair teams to keep these vehicles moving could be solved with money, but the greater problem was the failure of leadership. Commanders in Louisiana chose to lead from behind their lines rather than out in front with their troops. "Commanders and staffs mistakenly believed that they could run the war from headquarters," Army historian Christopher R. Gabel concluded, "relying on maps and telephones, much as they had in the static warfare of 1918." The result, on display in Louisiana, was that both offense and defense were poorly coordinated.[42]

The most severe early criticism came on May 27, in a room full of senior officers at Camp Beauregard, Louisiana. The bearer of bad news was Major General Herbert J. Brees, the chief control officer for the maneuvers. "If results would not have been so tragic," he said, "some of the so-called attacks without use of supporting weapons were so absurd as to be farcical."

Brees claimed that officers at all levels, showing a disinclination to move across country to engage the enemy, had failed to play the game. Because of poor or absent communication, there were instances of friendly troops firing into one another. He also cited the officers for not ordering the infantry out of their vehicles and into the field to engage the enemy. "You can't fight in a truck," he shouted.

As tough as he was on the officers, Brees praised the men under them: "My hat is off to our enlisted men, be they private, corporal or sergeant." His highest praise was reserved for the non-commissioned officers—enlisted men who had risen to the rank of sergeant and whom he termed the backbone of the Army—who "acted on their own, intelligently, with initiative, with a keen and complete understanding of what it was all about and what they were trying to do." Finally, Brees called for a major increase in the number of armored vehicles: "We need more tanks—light, medium and heavy."[43]

Good intelligence and airborne reconnaissance were lacking. To some, the exercises took on the aura of comic opera, complete with slapstick props. Trucks were dispatched with the word TANK written on their canvas covers. Stovepipes served as stand-ins for mortars, and broomsticks mounted on wood blocks acted as machine guns. As one of the supply officers later said, it was galling to see what should have been the most powerful army in the world "playing soldiers."[44]

Time pointed out the lack of Air Corps participation, practically no realistic antiaircraft practice, and no practice whatsoever with and against parachute troops—which the U.S. Army had not yet officially recognized as a functional element. The magazine too dismissed the exercises as kids playing soldiers: "Overnight, the pleasant doings in Louisiana became old-fashioned nonsense. Against Europe's total war, the U.S. Army looked like a few nice boys with BB guns."[45]

Noting the costs, more than 200 injuries, and the accidental deaths of a dozen men, several members of Congress questioned the validity of the exercises. One of the problems underscored by the maneuvers was the fact that any camaraderie and shared experience among the soldiers who had trained over the course of many weeks were lost when the exercises were over, as the men were dispersed to points as far away as Fort Lewis, Washington, 13 days away by truck under ideal conditions and precise planning.

Nationally syndicated columnist Westbrook Pegler listened to an unnamed general boast that action in Louisiana proved the U.S. Regular Army was as tough as the German army. Pegler took strong exception, pointing out that the Regular Army was badly scattered and could not possibly be assembled quickly in the continental United States during an emergency.[46]

One of the most direct critiques came from reporter T. A. Price of the *Dallas Morning News*, who began by pointing out the "alarming inadequacy" of the combat aircraft available, in both the exercises and the Army at large. But his strongest criticism concerned the fact that two armies—one highly mechanized and mobile (Blue) and the other preponderantly infantry (Red)—had been created at great expense and were now being sent home. Relying on comments from officers on the scene, Price insisted that the armies created for Louisiana should be held intact as a model for other armies that would be needed in the future. If allowed to disperse, he noted: "We not only will have no Army but will have torn up the only model we ever have made for an Army. Most of the sweat, toil and improvement in morale that have been won here will have been lost forever."[47]

One of the participants in the Maneuvers was Republican senator Henry Cabot Lodge Jr. of Massachusetts, who had also served in the 1939 exercises in Plattsburg, New York. Lodge was now a captain in the cavalry reserves assigned to Patton's Second Armored Division as a staff officer. The grandson of his namesake, Senator Henry Cabot Lodge, he was clearly the most important political figure in uniform in Louisiana. Speaking to an Associated Press reporter during the maneuvers, he noted shortages in manpower and tanks and called for the immediate creation of a Regular Army of 750,000 men, a demand he repeated on the Senate floor when he returned to Washington. Lodge told the Senate that the shortages were "very grave deficiencies." Money was needed to effect such changes, and Lodge immediately began to help Marshall convince Congress to increase Army appropriations to improve the nation's military readiness.

Lodge's strongest demand in terms of weaponry was for more tanks. Referring to his recent days in Louisiana he testified: "I have recently seen all the tanks in the United States, about 400 in number, or about one finger of the fanlike German advance about which we have read, or about the number destroyed in two days of fighting in the current European War. The Germans have a rough total of 3,000." Lodge went on to point out that all but a few of the tanks held by the United States were light tanks weighing in at 12 tons or less, whereas some of the Nazi tanks were 80-ton giants.[48]

Marshall, who had hoped to attend the maneuvers himself but was unable to because of the press of events in Washington, carefully reviewed the reports from Louisiana and expressed his dismay in "the ragged performance of officers and troops and the lack of realism." He immediately began thinking ahead to a second round of maneuvers, in 1941.[49]

In perspective, the 1940 Louisiana Maneuvers were in the words of military historian Mary Katherine Barbier: "significant because it was the first of its kind. Never before had the Army practiced for war on such a vast scale during peacetime."[50]

Only African American newspapers reported that a division of black troops in the Blue Army had taken part in the second and third phases of the maneuvers. A report in the *Chicago Defender*, with the headline NEW ORLEANS HOST TO 1,000 RACE SOLDIERS,* noted that the unit's commander was pleased these men had entered New Orleans as part of the victorious Red Army. If hostile racial incidents occurred in the 1940 maneuvers, they did not make news in the black press, which had an ear to the ground for overt incidents and would have reported them.[51]

The Blue forces had also field-tested the Army's new C rations (combat rations), billed as "the balanced meal in a can," which had been in development since 1938.** Along with tins of spaghetti and meatballs, Irish stew, or pork and beans, C rations included condiments, soluble coffee, chocolate bars, and a small can opener. The meal was the first designed to be heated in its own can. When the Blue Army was suddenly switched from fresh food (A rations) to what the soldiers then called battle rations, it came as a complete surprise, and the canned food was not well received. By all accounts, the ration was palatable when warmed but tasteless when served cold.[52]

---

* During this period it was common for the newspapers united under the banner of the black press to refer to African Americans with the word *race*, just as *race records* was the term used to describe 78-rpm phonograph records produced for the African American market between the 1920s and the early 1950s.

** With modifications—some major—the C ration would remain the military's combat meal until 1958.

An important aspect of the maneuvers was the testing of new equipment, including new portable two-way radios, which soldiers dubbed walkie-talkies. ("Soldiers are masters at nicknames," Ralph McGill commented in the *Atlanta Constitution*.) These wireless devices were used to keep commanders in touch with forces up to two miles away.[53]

One bit of good news to come out of the maneuvers was that no epidemics or large-scale infections occurred. The Army's "health defenses" had been tested and found to be working. This was no minor concern, as death due to infection and disease among U.S. forces in the Great War had occurred at a one-to-one ratio to combat deaths. (The 1918 influenza pandemic killed more than 657,000 Americans, including tens of thousands of military members.) The health report was delivered to the Army by Surgeon General Thomas Parran Jr., following an Emory University conference on malaria control and eradication. Parran said that the Army had a larger number and better quality of health-service units than it had had at the beginning of the previous war and that in the event of a draft, malaria, tuberculosis, and syphilis would be the main concerns regarding men coming into the service.[54,*]

Although the officer corps was sharply criticized for its actions during the exercises, certain officers and units had outperformed others, and Marshall could determine, through reports coming back to him, who might be part of his next generation of leaders. Perhaps the most outstanding young commander in these first maneuvers was Colonel Joseph "Vinegar Joe" Stilwell. During an important moment in the conflict between the Blue and Red Armies, Stilwell had led a Blue blitzkrieg-style invasion of northern Louisiana with a high-speed column of tanks—just the kind of bold initiative Marshall was looking for. Because of the enterprise and quick thinking Stilwell displayed, Marshall marked him for a major leadership position and would later choose him to lead Allied forces against the Japanese in Burma and China.

* Parran gained notoriety later in the century because of his role in overseeing the early period of the infamous Tuskegee syphilis experiment in which the government withheld treatment from poor black men suffering from syphilis in rural Alabama. The experiment lasted from 1932 to 1972.

Another officer who unexpectedly benefited indirectly from the maneuvers was 53-year-old colonel George S. Patton, who had been invited to participate in the exercises as a referee. Patton hated being relegated to the role of umpire, and his redemption began at a clandestine meeting at a high school in Alexandria, Louisiana, on May 25, the last day of the maneuvers. It was also the day the Germans took Boulogne, France, and British troops were ordered to retreat to Dunkirk.

The men at the meeting had individually come to the conclusion that the most important lesson driven home by the maneuvers was an immediate need for a unified armored force separated from both the infantry and the horse cavalry. Envisioned was a powerful American version of the German Panzer divisions now slicing through European defenses. Beloved by many, the cavalry was beginning to look like an anachronism during the exercises, as trucks were required to haul the horses on long marches.[55]

The group at the meeting, led by Brigadier General Adna R. Chaffee Jr., included Brigadier General Bruce Magruder, head of the Provisional Tank Brigade, who had been arguing for this transformation for years before the 1939 Nazi invasion of Poland; Alvan C. Gillem Jr., Magruder's executive officer; and other advocates of tank warfare. The group met with Brigadier General M. Frank Andrews, one of Marshall's closest advisers, in the Alexandria schoolhouse to discuss the future of mechanization. The goal of the meeting was to take tanks out of the hands of the horse cavalry and the infantry. What Chaffee and those who agreed with him faced was unyielding opposition from the chiefs of the cavalry and the infantry, who were in Louisiana but not invited to the schoolhouse session.

One of the men Chaffee did invite was Patton, who had been a standout tank commander during the Great War. Although he held a lower rank than most of the others in attendance, Patton seemed to be the ideal candidate to help bring this transformation to fruition.

At the end of World War I, the nation had had a tank corps of more than 20,000 officers and enlisted men, but it had been eliminated by Congress in 1920. At that point, Patton's focus had returned to the horse cavalry and the equine pursuits that went with it. He organized society horse shows from his base at Fort Myer, across the Potomac from Washington, D.C. In the early 1930s, Patton was regarded as one of the most accomplished polo players in the United States, and he was a driving force in creating enthusiasm for the sport within the Army.

But the interwar years had not been kind to Patton's public image. Many Americans knew him only as the man who had led Army troops against the Bonus Army marchers in 1932—presenting an image of the commander that was compelling, damaging, and photogenic. Patton's cavalry, followed by tanks and infantrymen carrying loaded rifles with fixed bayonets, had driven members of the Bonus Army and their families off the streets of Washington, D.C., along with curious bystanders and civil servants on their way home from work. His infantrymen, protected with gas masks, had thrown hundreds of tear gas grenades at the dispersing crowd; it was the same powerful tear gas that had been used as a weapon in World War I. One of the men Patton drove out of downtown and from his makeshift quarters, Joe Angelo, of Camden, New Jersey, had been decorated for saving Patton's life during the Meuse-Argonne offensive in 1918. The morning after the Bonus Army's camps were burned, Angelo had approached Patton, who curtly announced that he did not know him and instructed that he be taken away, a situation that produced most unflattering headlines.[56]

For a moment in 1932, thanks to reports in major news outlets, Angelo was the hero and Patton the goat. Between that unfortunate event in 1932 and his public reemergence in 1940, Patton's service had been pedestrian, especially to a man who saw himself as a warrior waiting for the next conflict in which to shine. What attracted Patton to Chaffee, whom he met for the first time during the maneuvers, was the firm belief that the United States needed large tank divisions—and men like Patton to lead them.[57]

The participants in the schoolhouse meeting agreed that Andrews should go back to Washington and suggest that two armored divisions be created, employing the mechanized Seventh Cavalry Brigade and the infantry's Provisional Tank Brigade as their basis. One division would be stationed at Fort Knox, Kentucky, and the other at Fort Benning, Georgia. The group assumed that Marshall would be receptive to the idea.

As if to underscore the importance of the schoolhouse meeting, before the end of the month, Nazi armored columns broke into France and shot through all the way to the English Channel, cutting off British and French units in Northern France and Belgium. The French army began to fall apart, and the British, who were in France as an allied force, evacuated 400,000 troops from Dunkirk and lost most of their heavy equipment between May 26 and June 4. France held on until June 14, when the Nazis invaded Paris, which fell easily and without a fight. France asked for an armistice three days later and surrendered on June 22. The grim reality was that Nazi Germany had successfully invaded and occupied six European nations in fewer than 100 days.[58]

With each wave of bad news from abroad came a new request for arms spending. As the British debacle was unfolding in Dunkirk, Roosevelt went back to Congress and asked for an additional $1.278 billion over and above the $1.82 billion he had asked for two weeks earlier. After the French collapse, the Navy requested an additional $4 billion to establish a two-ocean fleet of warships. Despite the power of the isolationists at this moment, these funds were easily obtained in the name of national defense, and the Navy's request passed the House, 316–0. The largest naval procurement bill to that point in U.S. history, it increased the size of the Navy by 70 percent, adding 257 new ships, including 18 aircraft carriers and a large fleet of aircraft to go with them. On August 19, the Senate Appropriations Committee bundled these requests together and unanimously approved a more than $5 billion supplemental national defense measure, designed to finance both the construction of an Atlantic and Pacific Navy and the establishment of a fully mechanized Army.[59]

On June 2, 1940, exactly a week after the end of the maneuvers and the schoolhouse meeting, George Gallup released the results of a national poll, which were widely reported in newspapers across the country. Gallup's American Institute of Public Opinion, which he had founded in 1935, commanded a high level of attention and respect in 1940, its reputation launched in 1936 when Gallup successfully predicted that Franklin Roosevelt would defeat Republican candidate Alf Landon and win re-election in a landslide.

The new poll concluded that Americans were well aware of what was going on in Western Europe. It also discovered that more than four voters in every five had concluded that the present Army and Navy were inadequate to protect the United States from foreign attack.

As had been shown in earlier surveys, two out of three Americans believed that if Germany should defeat England and France, she would sooner or later attack the United States. The survey also revealed that the greatest apprehension of Germany's intentions was among southerners, of whom 82 percent feared a German attack. By contrast, the Upper Midwest, where isolationism was strongest, showed less apprehension, though 61 percent expressed concern.

Gallup also discovered that one-half of the American people now believed the United States should follow the path of various European nations and "institute compulsory military training for all able-bodied young men of military age for a period of one year." By an overwhelming margin (85 percent to 15 percent), Gallup found that the public believed military training should be introduced into the hundreds of Civilian Conservation Corps camps.[60]

On June 24, General Chaffee was ordered to return to Washington, where he was made the first chief of the armored force. On June 30, the War Department announced the creation of an American tank force, headquartered at Fort Knox, Kentucky. It quickly attracted the nickname of the "American Panzer force," underscoring the belief that it would soon equal the German tank force. Command of the Second Armored Brigade, part of the Second Armored Division at Fort Benning, Georgia, was assigned to Patton, who arrived at his new post on July 29, 1940. In taking the assignment, Patton relinquished command of the Third Cavalry Regiment and Fort Myer.[61]

With the American tank force established, the need for more tanks was urgent. When Patton took his new assignment, the Army had only about 500 tanks, and some of these were not sufficiently armored for use in the kind of battle operations the Nazis were engaging in. More were being produced, but they were at first slow in coming, and only a few hundred were built in 1940. However, in 1941 production went into high gear, along with a search to find the men to operate them. Those in charge assumed volunteers and men eager to transfer from other units would step up but that ultimately, the force of proud, brave tankers would have to be recruited from the civilian population.[62]

The country not only had to manufacture tanks, aircraft, and other up-to-date tools of war, but it also had to create well-trained, well-equipped, highly mobile, motivated, and disciplined armed forces numbering in the millions. And at some point, these men had to be field-tested under battlefield conditions.

Many felt it was not feasible to simply attract a massive group of able volunteers and that the only way to create this force was through conscription. However, Marshall himself at least initially believed that an intensive recruiting program could attract the number of volunteers needed to populate a new army and was not convinced that conscription was necessary.

Roosevelt was up for re-election in November, and isolationist factions continued to stifle any talk of intervention in Europe. Roosevelt and his inner circle feared the Republicans would nominate a candidate who would campaign against any military expansion, including a peacetime military draft. The president had a second reason to be reluctant about a draft: Americans were historically resistant to compulsory military service of any type, let alone the peacetime variety.

Opposition to the idea that all able-bodied young men should be required to perform military service dated back to the early days of the republic, residing in the words of then vice president Elbridge Gerry in 1784: "Standing armies in time of peace are inconsistent with the principles of republican governments, dangerous to the liberties of a free people, and generally converted into destructive engines for establishing despotism." Instead, Gerry thought reliance should be placed on each state's "well regulated and disciplined militia."[63]

For this reason, the United States disbanded the Continental Army of 1783, after the Treaty of Paris brought an end to the Revolutionary War and the final British forces had departed New York City. The federal government then called up four state militias to provide some 700 men to confront any new threats from native tribes and the British. A newly organized version of his First American Regiment was all that President George Washington had under his command as commander in chief upon taking office in April 1789.

Later that year, Secretary of War Henry Knox proposed a plan for a system of defense that called for all free American men to perform military service as a means of countering the powerful standing armies of Europe. However, suspicions about a creating an American standing army, especially in view of the recent war and the despised British Quartering Act, which had required Americans to provide shelter for British military forces, prevented the enactment of the plan.

The first real test of the militia system came with the Whiskey Rebellion in 1794, which began when farmers in Western Pennsylvania, outraged by a federal excise tax on distilled spirits imposed to relieve the federal deficit, attacked and burned the home of a tax collector. With their ranks enlarged to 6,000, the men camped outside Pittsburgh and threatened to march on the city. One rebel, inspired by the French Revolution, pressed for the use of guillotines to dispatch tax collectors.

In response, President Washington, at the urging of Alexander Hamilton, under the provisions of the Militia Act of 1792, assembled 15,000 militiamen from eastern Pennsylvania and the surrounding states as a federal unit, commanded by Virginia's Henry Lee, and prepared them to march upon the Pittsburgh camp. Washington himself took command of the federal force as it reached Bedford, Pennsylvania.*

---

* This marked the first and last time a sitting president led armed troops.

"The soldiers even set up a dazzling light display in town to honor the president," wrote historian William Hogeland. "The blazing display read: 'Woe to anarchy.'"[64]

When it arrived, the federal militia found the rebels unwilling to fight. The mere threat of the federal force had stifled the rebellion and established once and for all the sovereignty of the federal government. The army configured for the Whiskey Rebellion was quickly disbanded, and the rebels who had been sentenced to be hanged were pardoned by Washington.

During the War of 1812, Congress repeated the experience of the Revolutionary War by encouraging voluntary enlistment, coupled with requests to the states for militia units. Thousands of militia units existed, but most had little military value; they met carrying guns only once a year, on an obligatory muster day, events that often turned into little more than drinking sprees. A paltry 20,000 men enlisted, and as the United States seemed headed for defeat, the secretary of war, James Monroe, proposed the nation's first serious attempt at national conscription by proposing a universal draft. A modified version of Monroe's plan was approved by Congress, but it came too late to have an effect on the outcome of the war. Reacting to this legislation, Congressman Daniel Webster declared that the United States was "not yet in a temper to submit to conscription. The people have too fresh and strong a feeling of the blessings of civil liberty to be willing thus to surrender it."[65,*]

The war with Mexico in 1846–48 did not require forces in sufficient numbers to raise the issue of conscription, but it did demonstrate that volunteers on short enlistment times created new problems. As General Winfield Scott led his troops on the approach to Mexico City, some 40 percent of his men had to be sent home because their one-year enlistment terms had expired. General Scott was forced to wait for reinforcements,

---

* It has been pointed out that Monroe's plan embodied the four basic principles of conscription later adopted in the 20th century: universal obligation, individual selection, local administration, and national control.

while the army of the Mexican president, General Antonio López de Santa Anna, defeated and dispersed, found time to recover.

The Union's conscription act of March 1863, put in force at the height of the Civil War, made all men of able body between ages 20 and 45 liable for military service, but a draftee who produced a human substitute or paid the government a flat $300 was excused. A defective and greatly unpopular piece of legislation, the act provoked nationwide disturbances, known as the draft riots. The uprisings were bloodiest in New York City, where for four days in July 1863, large, violent outbursts occurred, some of such intensity that they were deemed to be a war within a war. Not only unfair, the Civil War draft was ineffective—only 6 percent of the 2.5 million who served in the Union Army from 1861 to 1865 were inducted by conscription.[66]

Conscription in the South was far more demanding and inflexible than it was in in the North. The Confederacy's conscription law, which was enacted on April 16, 1862, not only subjected all men between the ages of 18 and 35 eligible to be drafted into military service but also voided existing voluntary enlistment contracts and required those men to serve for the remainder of the war. Of the million men who fought for the Confederacy, close to 80 percent were volunteers now forced to stay for the duration with the remainder who were drafted under the provisions of the law.

Initially, substitutes could be hired to replace draftees, but this practice was eventually outlawed along with almost all occupational exemptions. The one major exception came under the Twenty-Slave Law, which allowed a legal exemption for one overseer or slaveholder for every 20 enslaved people owned. The law was enacted October 11, 1862, in reaction to a preliminary version of the Emancipation Proclamation, issued by U.S. president Abraham Lincoln less than two weeks earlier. In the South, Lincoln's proclamation was seen as an attempt to inspire a slave rebellion. The law, which only benefited the large land-owner, contributed to the widespread belief that the war was fought by the poor—albeit poor whites—for the benefit of the rich and a negative factor for troop morale.[67]

In May 1917, the United States committed itself to a full mobilization of manpower and resources to support its allies in a European war that had assumed the slogan "the war to end war" (or "the war to end all wars"). At the time, an overwhelming majority in Congress passed the Selective Service Act, creating "local, district, state, and territorial civilian boards to register, induct, examine, classify and ship out men between the ages of twenty-one and thirty" for active duty for the war's duration. The boards could also issue deferrals.

Then secretary of war Newton Baker coined the term *selective service* to indicate that the Army would take only the men it wanted. Left out would be those who were essential to the wartime economy and those who were physically or mentally unfit for service. The system automatically exempted ministers, divinity students, and public officials from some of the higher categories. It also recognized that dependency could serve as a basis for exemptions.

The full military draft faced considerable opposition from southern and western Congressmen and their constituents. Some 300,000 men failed to respond to their draft notices, and 170,000 more deserted within weeks of reporting. In one dragnet staged in New York City in 1918 to catch those who had not reported, 16,000 men were arrested. Of the 3.5 million men who served during the war, 72 percent were conscripts.[68]

The draft was canceled abruptly at the end of World War I in November 1918. On March 31, 1919, all the local, district, and regional medical advisory units were dissolved, and on May 21, 1919, the last state draft headquarters office shut its doors. The U.S. Army's provost marshal general was relieved of all duties on July 15, 1919, thereby fully closing down all the elements of the Selective Service System of World War I and sidelining the giant goldfish bowl from which random numbers had been pulled.

CHAPTER 4

FOR THE WANT OF A NAIL

The degree to which America did not want to go to war again was exemplified by the attitude of college students who had come of age as the nation dealt with the plight of the veterans of the Great War. With the Selective Service System in mothballs and no great push for volunteers, these young Americans had little concern for military service, yet they sensed the inevitability of war and conceived of such service as a future folly.

They dealt with their fear of future war through satirical action. One such initiative was inspired by impending payment of the bonus owed to the veterans of World War I. While it would not come until June 15, 1936, three months earlier, Lewis J. Gorin Jr. and seven friends at Princeton University's Terrace Club founded the Veterans of Future Wars and issued an anticipatory call to arms in the *Daily Princetonian* on March 14, 1936, under the headline: FUTURE VETERANS, UNITE!

I. War is imminent.
It is high time that we openly, in the face of the world, admit that America shall be engaged in it.

To this end the Veterans of Future Wars have united to force upon the government and people of the United States the realization that common justice demands that all of us who will be engaged in the coming war deserve, as is customary, an adjusted service compensation, sometimes called a bonus. We demand that this bonus be one thousand dollars, payable June 1, 1965. Because it is customary to pay bonuses before they are due we demand immediate cash payment, plus three per cent compounded annually for thirty years back from June 1, 1965, to June 1, 1935. All those of military age, that is, from 18 to 36, are eligible to receive this bonus. It is but common right that this bonus be paid now, for many will be killed or wounded in the next war, and hence they, the most deserving, will not get the full benefit of their country's gratitude. For the realization of these just demands, we mutually pledge our undivided and supreme efforts.

Soldiers of America, Unite! You have nothing to lose.[1]

At the same moment at all-female Vassar College, the Association of Gold Star Mothers of Veterans of Future Wars was chartered to gain support for sending young women to Europe to view the future graves of their sons—a spin on the practice of sending boatloads of real Gold Star mothers to Europe to visit the burial grounds of their fallen sons. The name was so offensive to many, including the Gold Star mothers of World War I, that the collegians almost immediately changed it to the Home Fire Division—a play on the notion that women would remain behind to keep the "home fires" going.

The groups at Princeton and Vassar formed an immediate alliance and began working in concert to establish eight regional commanders for both groups and to set up chapters on all American campuses. The idea spread swiftly, thanks to the well-connected Princeton students, who among them harbored stringers for the *Philadelphia Inquirer*, the *New York Times*, and the Associated Press. Within ten days after the release of the Princeton group's manifesto, the movement had swelled across the country. By the end of March, 120 college chapters had been established from coast to coast, as well as many non-collegiate units, and the group had a paying membership of more than 6,000 that included a number of faculty members and a small number of politicians, including a former U.S. senator.[2]

In New Jersey, Drew University's chapter created a fabricated cemetery displaying the names of students who would fall in future conflicts and called for a Tomb for the Future Unknown Soldier. B. H. Berman, a student at Georgetown University in Washington, D.C., penned an anthem for the future warriors, sung to the tune of "Over There."

> *Fall in line—fall in line,*
> *Now's the time—now's the time.*
> *To collect our bonus*
> *That Franklin D. will loan us*
> *So we won't fight him over here,*
> *So raise your glasses and give three cheers*
> *For the war that's comin' to take us hummin'*
> *And we won't be there 'til it's over, over here.*

Satellite groups—such as the Chaplains of Future Wars, organized among divinity students, and the Correspondents of Future Wars, among aspiring journalists—were soon collecting dues and giving the official salute of the Veterans of Future Wars: the right arm held out, palm up, beggar style. The Correspondents of Future Wars, founded at City College of New York, demanded training in "the writing of atrocity stories and garbled war dispatches for patriotic purposes." The group offered honorary membership to anyone who could come up with a motto for the next war as misleading as "Make the World Safe for Democracy," President Woodrow Wilson's exhortation to Congress in 1917, when he sought a declaration of war against Germany.[3]

A major force spurring the movement's growth was the ire it invoked in its first days. A Texas Democrat, Representative William D. McFarlane, said the Princeton group "ought to be investigated," and the real VFW (Veterans of Foreign Wars) put out a statement in which it "wonder[ed] what Hobey Baker and Johnny Poe, as well as other alumni of Princeton who died in France, might say to this apparent insult to their service."[4] James E. Van Zandt, head of the VFW, said the students were "a bunch of monkeys . . . too yellow to go to war," who deserved a good spanking. Representative Claude Fuller of Arkansas said the group was "saturated with communism, foreign influence and a total disregard for American patriotism." The Red-baiters and sputtering patriots had a field day, and the college students responded: Gorin insisted that Van Zandt was himself a Red and offered to debate him on national radio.[5]

One of the few voices of assent was that of Representative Maury Maverick of Texas, a wounded and decorated veteran who thought the scheme was "swell" and asserted that if the United States paid for wars in advance, it wouldn't have any more wars. Maverick had spent a year in hospitals after sustaining a spine injury from a German bullet and, having lost parts of five vertebrae, was rarely free from pain. He had recently introduced legislation that would take the adoration of war (he called it "martial sex") out of ROTC by mandating the reading of antiwar material.[6]

Eleanor Roosevelt also came down on the side of the students: "I think it's just as funny as it can be! And—taken lightly, as it should be—a grand pricking of lots of bubbles." She thought the name Gold Star Mothers of Veterans of Future Wars had been ill advised but found the idea of a women's auxiliary in itself "very amusing."[7]

A reporter working for William Randolph Hearst's newspapers was sent to Princeton to "expose" the latest maneuver from Moscow. There was a growing tendency among many American leaders to take such movements as a serious threat, as the mood among students became increasingly antiwar, a category into which the Veterans of Future Wars fit. A poll of Columbia University seniors, published when the Veterans of Future Wars was only a few weeks old, revealed that a majority would refuse to fight in a war conducted outside the United States.[8]

Spring break occurred at the beginning of April for the Princetonians, and one of the founders, Thomas Riggs Jr., son of the former governor of Alaska, returned to his home in Washington, D.C. On April Fool's Day, he announced that he was going to register as a lobbyist and ask for $2.5 billion for his "pre-vets." Informed that he did not have to register, he met with a number of members of Congress and walked away with support from eight of them, including Maury Maverick, who said he was willing to give them $10 billion "any old day."[9]

Suddenly the movement, now 20,000 strong, was big enough to prompt a counter-movement of sorts. In late April, the American Legion opened up a "first aid station and supply depot" in Washington, staffed by World War I vets pretending to be members of the Gimme Bita Pi fraternity, who offered diapers and rubber pants to the students, whose behavior it regarded as infantile. The legion met its match in the students, who responded to an invitation to an open house at the mock first aid station by telegram: "Appreciate kind invitation STOP . . . Unfortunately pressure of real business prevents acceptance of any purely social engagements STOP When we get our bonus we can play too."[10]

Members of the Princeton group appeared on the radio, wrote articles, and were interviewed by reporters. Their pictures ran, according to one account, in thousands of newspapers. When a *March of Time* newsreel crew arrived on the Princeton campus to document the movement, more than 400 students (hired by the newsreel company) made the movement look larger than it actually was.[11]

Less than a week after the American Legion held its annual convention that September, Lewis Gorin's book, *Patriotism Prepaid*, was published.* It was billed as the basis for "one of the most powerful youth movements America had ever witnessed!" Reviewers seemed split on whether the book, written in academic style, was satire or serious social criticism.[12] The *New York Times* thought it was satire, but the *Wall Street Journal* thought Gorin was arguing that the next war would be so colossally expensive that after adding the money being demanded for future wars to the amount necessary to pay veterans of past wars, nothing would be left in the national till. This, said the *Journal*, was nothing less than "superb financial idealism."[13]

The Veterans of Future Wars had one more arrow in its quiver: the fact that the actual World War I bonuses would be paid on June

---

* The full text of Gorin's book is online at: https://archive.org/details/patriotismprepai 031233mbp.

15. In late May, the Princeton group sent out invitations to a "Treasury Raid," which would feature dancing in the street on the day the bonuses would be paid. President Roosevelt and First Lady Eleanor Roosevelt, among other politicians and celebrities, were invited.

On May 31, with a membership of close to 50,000, the Veterans of Future Wars issued a "peace without pacifism plan" that called for no declaration of war by the United States without a popular referendum and a plurality akin to that needed to attaching a new amendment to the Constitution: "The United States shall not enter into a state of war with any nation except in self-defense, unless by the will of two-thirds of those voting in three-fourths of the States."[14]

Although press interest in the Princeton organization eventually dissipated, the generation that came of age in the late 1930s expressed true misgivings about fighting another overseas war. The fact that the movement's strongest outward manifestation took the form of parody did not diminish its message. Those who wrote it off as a joke or a prank were missing the point.

By the time of Germany's invasion of Poland in September 1939, the government increasingly feared that members of the Veterans of Future Wars would balk at voluntary or conscripted service in what the group's founders had called the "folly of war." Reinforcing the Veterans of Future Wars position, in October 1939 a new organization was formed at Princeton called the American Independence League, whose purpose was to keep the United States out of the European war. This new group caught on in the same manner as the Veterans of Future Wars: within a month, some 50 eastern colleges had or were in the process of establishing chapters.

In early November, *America*, a well-known Jesuit weekly magazine, completed a nationwide poll of 54,000 Roman Catholic college students at 182 educational institutions on the subject of the war. The results were stunning and consistent with the June Gallup poll: more than one-third of the students said they would become conscientious objectors in the event the United States government elected to send an army to fight in Europe, and an astonishing 97 percent of the students opposed U.S.

involvement in the European war. These and other findings pointed the magazine to its conclusion: "The collegians are against war and most of them choose not to fight."[15]

Some people felt that the invasion of Poland had made educated young people even more likely to choose pacifism, arguing that this generation of collegians had been unduly influenced by writers who generally detested war and felt that it could be avoided by negotiation. This view was given its loudest voice by the poet and Librarian of Congress Archibald MacLeish, who felt that post–World War I writers "had done more to weaken democracy in the face of fascism than any other group." MacLeish named several writers, including Ernest Hemingway, John Dos Passos, and Erich Maria Remarque.*

As a man of letters, MacLeish had nothing but praise for these writers, but as an anti-fascist, he saw them corrupting a generation unable to see the moral issue at hand. This moral blindness afflicting the young and well-read was, in his opinion, more concerning than even the lack of planes and antiaircraft guns, "for if the young generation is distrustful of all words and distrustful of all moral judgments of better and worse, then it is incapable of using the only weapon with which fascism can be fought—the moral conviction that fascism is evil and that a free society of free men is good and worth fighting for."

Stated forcefully in a speech on May 23, 1940, to an educational group at a convention in New York City, MacLeish's remarks were carried over network radio. The headlines reporting on the event went right to the point: MACLEISH ASSAILS THE CYNICS (*Baltimore Sun*); M'LEISH FINDS U.S. MORALLY UNREADY (*New York Times*).[16]

As if to underscore MacLeish's point, a petition signed by 1,486 Yale University students was sent to President Roosevelt, asserting that the United States should stay out of the European war and should give no credit, supplies, or manpower to Britain or any other nation fighting

---

* The books mentioned by name were John Dos Passos's *Three Soldiers*, Erich Maria Remarque's *All Quiet on the Western Front*, Ernest Hemingway's *A Farewell to Arms*, Richard Aldington's *Death of a Hero*, Andreas Latzko's *Men in War*, and Walter Millis's *Road to War*, which was published in 1935 and by 1940 was being called the isolationists' bible.

Hitler. Members of the group said that the idea for the petition was spontaneous and that with a little more time they could have gathered 2,000 signatures.[17] Increasingly, American observers and editorialists questioned whether an effective opposition to the peace-at-any-price mentality of American youth could be mounted. Millicent Taylor, editor of the *Christian Science Monitor*, in an editorial in early June 1940 suggested that older Americans needed to work hard to convince their sons and daughters that the danger ahead was real and not subject to a negotiated settlement. Taylor agreed with MacLeish that the writers of the Lost Generation were to blame. Others—including public intellectual Mortimer J. Adler of the University of Chicago—suggested the fault lay with a generation of young, cynical professors: "Whether they go to war or not, irreparable harm has been done to the young men of this generation."

Those in 1940 who understood that an army had to be raised realized the initiative had to come from outside the White House and Congress. New York attorney Grenville Clark, age 58, a wealthy and dynamic patriotic gadfly and advocate of a strong America, seized that initiative.

Before and during World War I, Clark had established a program to train business and professional men to be Army officers. Already successful in his own right and heir to banking and railroad fortunes, Clark had joined other businessmen to pay for these Civilian Military Training Camps, which produced some 40,000 officers for the American Expeditionary Force. Because the first and most famous camp was located near the town of Plattsburg, in Upstate New York, the effort became known as the Plattsburg Plan.

Clark, who never sought office himself, was interested in change through influence. To this end, he maintained strong friendships with both Republicans and Democrats, and his wealth and a powerful circle of friends made his bipartisan appeal all the stronger.

Like many others, Clark was convinced that the United States was ill prepared to fight a war in which its involvement was becoming increasingly likely. A former classmate of Roosevelt's at Harvard and a lieutenant colonel in the Army in World War I, Clark was a Republican, an interventionist, and a civil libertarian, who believed that fascism was the greatest single threat to America's freedoms.

On May 8, 1940, 24 hours before Germany invaded Belgium, the Netherlands, and Luxembourg, several members of the Civilian Military Training Camps Association met at a dinner in New York to plan a celebration of the 25th anniversary of the first Plattsburg camp. A pedestrian discussion soon gave way to a momentous recommendation from Clark, who urged that the "best observance of the anniversary" would be a powerful civilian-led campaign of preparedness in 1940, against "an emergency already as threatening as the one in 1915." He advocated for "a peacetime conscription act so that the U.S. could do its share promptly when inevitably drawn into the big war."[18]

This initial meeting led to an even larger dinner on May 22, to which leaders of the training camp initiative from all over the country were invited. In advance of the meeting, Clark wrote to Roosevelt to let him know what he was planning and asked for the president's comments. Roosevelt encouraged Clark's group to meet, noting: "I am inclined to think there is very strong public opinion for universal service so that every able-bodied man and woman would fit into his or her place. The difficulty of proposing a concrete set of measures 'short of war' is largely a political one—what one can get from Congress."[19]

The second dinner included several presidents of Ivy League universities, two Congressional Medal of Honor recipients, and Julius Ochs Adler, general manager of the *New York Times*. The group drew up a selective service plan that outlined who would control the draft, the size and scope of the new army to be created, and the need for specific deferments. The plan gave power to local draft boards staffed by volunteers, recognizing from the outset that the more decentralized the draft, the more easily Americans would accept it.[20]

Clark and colleagues argued that the nation would be the next one Germany attacked after France and Britain fell and that given America's military weakness, Nazi troopships could sail up the Potomac River, take

Washington, D.C., and then move north into Baltimore, Philadelphia, and New York City.[21]

Still lacking the public backing of Marshall or Roosevelt, Clark and other advocates for conscription met in Julius Adler's office on June 3 to formally create an organization and plan a campaign. By the end of the day, the National Emergency Committee, with Clark as its chairman, had 200 members; by the end of the week it had more than 1,000 across the country.

Using $250,000 raised from Clark and other wealthy members, the committee promoted the need for the draft, taking its message directly to newspapers, radio stations, American Legion posts, universities, and chambers of commerce. The committee hired Perley Boone, a former *New York Times* journalist and publicity director for the recently closed 1939 New York World's Fair, who developed a staff of writers and photographers to churn out press releases and other material supporting the draft.[22]

Roosevelt insisted that Clark and his ad hoc committee not use the words *draft* or *conscription*; he preferred the term *muster*, which implied something less than compulsory service. Unable to get Roosevelt to publicly support an actual draft, the Clark committee worked on Congress. A bill written by Clark,* which he had been working on since late May, was soon shown to members of both houses.[23]

Even on June 14, 1940, the day German soldiers entered Paris, and with his mail running 2–1 in favor of the draft, FDR insisted that it was not yet time for conscription. Army Chief of Staff George Marshall also believed that a draft instituted too quickly could create more problems than it solved. According to Clark's biographer, Marshall came close to losing his temper in an early meeting over Clark's brashness in demanding support for a draft. To Marshall, a civilian, even one with Clark's credentials, trying to instruct the chief of staff how to run the Army

---

* An essential line in the bill: "Congress declares that in a free society the obligation and privilege of military service should be shared generally in accordance with the fair and just system of compulsory military training and service."

and properly prepare for war was out of place. Others have described Marshall's reaction in even more dramatic terms. According to FDR biographer Kenneth S. Davis, after Clark told Marshall that he would be derelict in not pressing the president to accept conscription: "Marshall's face reddened. It was only through a terrific effort of self-control that he managed to end the interview politely, abruptly, and coldly, *very* coldly, instead of in a hot flare of wrath."[24]

While he gradually concluded that conscription was the only way to build the Armed Forces, Marshall was unwilling to speak out on the issue until he thought the time was right and would not do so unless he had Roosevelt's approval. Realizing that the political consequences of a draft could undermine FDR's re-election bid, Marshall felt that the Army was not yet prepared for a draft. He wanted an orderly increase in manpower and needed more time to create such a system, because, as he explained, "The training of young men in large training camps on the basis of compulsory training is something that we cannot manage at the present time. We do not have the trained officers and the instructors to spare."[25]

Having decided to support the Clark initiative, Marshall wanted to see the bill introduced as an initiative led by civilians while he stood quietly in the wings. He reasoned that if he was to lend public support to the bill before it was formally proposed, the public could regard it as his legislation, creating a potential backlash in Congress that could disrupt future mobilization efforts. Years later, he recalled, "I was much criticized because I didn't take the lead in the selective service legislation. I very pointedly did not take the lead. I wanted it to come from others . . . Then I could take the floor and do all the urging that was required."[26]

With FDR's blessing, Marshall privately sent key staff members to help draft the legislation, which at this point looked as if it lacked the proper support. The Democratic Senate majority leader, James Byrnes, told Clark that there was not "a Chinaman's chance" that compulsory military training would pass in Congress.[27]

Roosevelt and War Secretary Woodring were increasingly at odds, especially regarding aid to Britain. On June 17, Roosevelt ordered his treasury secretary, Henry Morgenthau Jr., to send the British a dozen B-17 bombers. Rather than comply, Woodring fired off a memo to Roosevelt, stating that he strongly opposed the proposed action. The president had no choice but to request Woodring's resignation, which he did by letter. On leaving the government, Woodring immediately became an active member of the America First Committee, an organization devoted to preventing the United States' entry into the war. Over time, Woodring had become a liability to Roosevelt, and now it was clear he would become an active force working against him.[28]

The War Department, led by acting secretary Louis A. Johnson, chose to abstain from supporting the draft as the debate heated up in June. As late as June 25, Johnson was urging Roosevelt to approve a plan that would encourage enlistments rather than rely on conscription. Under what was known as the Civilian Volunteer Effort (CVE), local patriotic service clubs such as the Kiwanis and Lions, as well as chambers of commerce and other organizations, would become active and aggressive in recruiting men for the Army.[29]

On June 19, with Woodring out of the way, Roosevelt asked Henry Stimson to be his new secretary of war. The selection of Stimson had been engineered by Grenville Clark, who saw Stimson as Roosevelt's best choice. Having previously served as governor general of the Philippines, secretary of state under President Herbert Hoover, and secretary of war under President William Howard Taft, Stimson was well qualified for the job. Roosevelt urged Stimson, a Republican, to accept the position, thinking he would become a stabilizing force in whom both the public and the Army would have confidence.

Pointing out that he was approaching his 73rd birthday, Stimson asked for time to consult with a few friends. He also wanted to make sure the president understood that he favored compulsory military service. In Washington, Stimson was a known quantity who had nothing but contempt for the isolationists, who he felt were playing into the hands of the Axis powers.[30]

Stimson had given two major speeches—the first at Yale University, the second broadcast on NBC Radio—about the need for compulsory military training. In the latter speech, entitled "America's Interest in Britain's Fleet," Stimson underscored his belief that the United States could not afford to let Britain follow France into defeat—not for sentimental or cultural reasons but because America would be the next to fall.

At the same time Roosevelt asked Stimson to join his cabinet, he asked Frank Knox, owner of the *Chicago Daily News*, to become his secretary of the Navy, replacing Charles Edison, the son of inventor Thomas Edison, who had resigned earlier in the year to run for governor of New Jersey. Knox was also a Republican and had previously run as the vice presidential candidate on Alf Landon's ticket, against Roosevelt, in 1936. Knox had served with Teddy Roosevelt's now-legendary Rough Riders in the Spanish-American War and had performed as an artillery officer in 1917. Clark felt that Knox was the perfect complement to Stimson.

Stimson's acceptance was conditional on two important points: that he retain the power to appoint his own subordinates in the War Department and that Knox accept FDR's nomination as secretary of the Navy. Roosevelt agreed to the first condition, and Knox took the job, so the stage was set for a rare era of bipartisanship on the issue of conscription. Both Stimson and Knox had been members of the Clark committee, and both had been brought to Roosevelt's attention by Clark, who saw them as key supporters of the draft and Republicans who would create the bipartisan alliance the nation needed to prepare for war. Historian and Marshall biographer David L. Roll termed this development "Clark's plan," adding that it enabled FDR to "pull off a shrewd political masterstroke—the appointment to his cabinet of two of the most prominent Republican foreign policy voices in the nation."[31]

On June 20, before the appointments of Stimson and Knox were made public, Senator Edward R. Burke, an anti–New Deal Democrat from Nebraska, and Representative James Wolcott Wadsworth, a Republican from New York, introduced Clark's bill for peacetime selective service in their respective houses of Congress. Formally titled the Selective Training and Service Act of 1940 (Public Law 76–783, 54 Stat. 885), it became known as the Burke-Wadsworth bill. Neither man had much to lose if the bill failed—Burke had already lost renomination in the Nebraska primary elections, and Wadsworth was from a Republican district considered safe regardless of his position on conscription.

This odd marriage had been brokered by Clark, who moved quickly to get the bill into the public arena. Publicist Perley Boone sent advance copies to major newspapers, and the moment the bill was introduced, the wire services sent it to thousands more. The White House deliberately withheld visible support for the bill, not wanting to be linked directly to a potential defeat in Congress, which Roosevelt felt would please Hitler, dishearten the British, and damage his own chances in an election year.

The major arguments for conscription were that the Army as constituted had not adequately prepared the United States against the possibility of invasion and that in the years since the enactment of the National Defense Act of 1920, the Army had been forced to work below the levels the legislation permitted. The isolationist counter-argument was that a volunteer army would suffice and that a draft would drag the United States into war.

On June 21, Roosevelt announced the appointments of Stimson and Knox. MASTERSTROKE BY ROOSEVELT STUNS THE GOP was the headline in the *Atlanta Constitution*. Roosevelt had not only moved, in his words, "to encourage national solidarity in a time of world crisis," but he had also driven a wedge between the Republican isolationists and the Republican interventionists in the days before the Republican National Convention. Choosing these two men was, as one historian would later describe it, "a masterful political move on the part of a masterful politician."[32]

When congressional hearings began on July 3, Perley Boone was on hand to distribute a letter to members of both houses from General John Pershing asserting that enforced military training was not un-American but rather would promote democracy by throwing different classes of people into close contact with the goal of preserving the American way of life. Pershing also pointed out that if the United States had adopted compulsory military training in 1914, it would not have been necessary in 1917 "to send partially trained boys into battle against the veteran troops of our adversary." Pershing then concluded: "Certainly we could have ended the conflict much sooner, with the saving of many thousands of lives and billions of treasure."[33]

The effect of the letter, widely distributed to the press, was felt the next day in many Fourth of July editorials across the country. Under the headline CONSCRIPTION IS AMERICAN, Washington, D.C.'s *Evening Star* used Pershing's letter to support peacetime military conscription as a way of ultimately avoiding war rather than fostering it. But the press was split along isolationist/interventionist lines and reacted to the Pershing letter accordingly.[34]

After its introduction, the Burke-Wadsworth bill made little headway in Congress, as many still worried about the public reaction to a peacetime draft. It clearly needed a push from the outside, which prompted Clark, Boone, and the others supporting the legislation to redouble their efforts and seek new allies. Corporations were solicited for support. Allen L. Lindley, vice president of the New York Stock Exchange and a member of Clark's committee, wrote to every member company listed on the exchange, asking for endorsements to help enact the bill. Clark himself set up temporary headquarters in the Carlton Hotel in Washington, where he managed the lobbying effort.[35]

The debate was carried out publicly in letters to the editors of newspapers, which at their most extreme had an apocalyptic tone. When one writer to the *Sacramento Bee* insisted the draft was in God's plan, another responded: "I do not think God wants any nation to toss its offspring onto the fiery altars of Moloch," referring to a Canaanite deity associated with child sacrifice.[36]

A leading Republican and likely presidential candidate, Senator Robert A. Taft, led the opposition and argued that a compulsory draft was more typical of totalitarian nations than of democracies. "The theory behind it leads directly to totalitarianism," Taft argued. "It is absolutely opposed to the principles of individual liberty which have always been considered a part of American democracy."

The loudest opponent of Clark, his committee, and the legislation under consideration was Senator Rush Dew Holt, a fiercely antiwar firebrand Democrat from West Virginia, who attacked those who backed the bill as "Wall Street lawyers, international bankers and directors in munitions enterprises," the very forces he claimed led America into the First World War. Holt stated that Clark and his allies had treasonous intent as they plotted to lead the nation into war to preserve its and their overseas investments. His attack on the floor of the Senate on August 6 made it seem as if the meetings in the Harvard Club were shady affairs held in secret. He termed the money that had been raised to promote conscription a "slush fund," which then as now referred to monies set aside for illicit purposes. *New York Times* General Manager Julius Ochs Adler, "a man who holds stock in corporations in countries now at war, was there." Holt then added: "Mr. Adler wants the American boy to protect his investments."

But as Holt was winding up his attack, he was openly challenged by Senator Sherman Minton of Indiana, the majority whip and a strong ally of the administration, who alleged that during World War I, Holt's father had opposed the war effort to the extent that he had advocated not raising food to be sent to the American troops in France, a group that had included Minton.

"A malicious lie," was Holt's response. "If the administration wants filth and gutter mud to be thrown they get the Senator from Indiana to throw it." Minton responded: "And when Hitler wants it thrown you throw it." Then Minton added that Holt's father had sent his eldest son to South America to hide from the draft. Minton then added: "I get a little impatient at being lectured to from a slacker family." Holt came back asserting that Minton's claims were untrue and these lies "like lice, continued to be carried by rats"—a line that occasioned what the *Chicago Tribune* reported as "uproarious laughter" from the Senate gallery packed with foes of the draft.[37]

The back-and-forth continued into the following day, when after a further round of insults and accusations the "debate" lost its steam with Minton getting the last word by stating that the rules of the Senate would not allow him to express the contempt he held for the senator from West Virginia.[38]

It was what the *Chicago Tribune* characterized as "one of the most vitriolic exchanges in recent history" and what the *San Francisco Chronicle* called a "barroom brawl." Although the isolationists and the newspapers that supported them saw justification in the attack, it was quickly rebutted. Adler, for example, pointed out that the only companies he held stock in were the *New York Times* itself and its printing company.[39]

As the draft bill was debated and discussed, the growing fear in the United States in the early summer of 1940 was that Great Britain would fall to Nazi Germany just as France, Holland, Belgium, Poland, Denmark, and Norway had fallen already. Beginning in July 1940, the fear intensified as Hitler's Luftwaffe relentlessly bombed England, and the German navy blockaded it in preparation for a planned Nazi invasion.

Fear was also growing that Imperial Japan was on its own path of conquest. During the summer of 1940, Japan's war in China was entering its fourth year with no end in sight. Some Americans feared Japan might actually attack North America by way of Hawaii or the Aleutians. Senator Rufus Holman of Oregon went a step further and claimed that he had learned from "authoritative military sources of imminent peril of an invasion" threatening the entire Pacific coast including Alaska.[40]

Finally, Roosevelt saw his opportunity to support the Clark plan when the Republicans nominated former Democrat Wendell Willkie as their candidate on June 28, whose support for the draft was expressed a month later and amplified in his formal acceptance speech. In a press conference on August 2, FDR felt he could now unequivocally endorse draft legislation and declare it essential to national defense, during which he also declared that the effort to create a new army with volunteers had failed.[41]

On August 7, in a letter to Senator Arthur Vandenberg of Michigan, former secretary of war Harry Hines Woodring argued, "I cannot see the need of compulsory military training at this time, and I should like to see the bill amended so that it does not become effective until, and after, the Chief of Staff of the United States Army has first advised the Senate in writing that the voluntary system has completely broken down." Woodring believed that voluntary service had not been given a chance by the Roosevelt administration, which had earlier refused his plan to raise Army pay to $30 a month for volunteers. Woodring also criticized conscription as smacking of "totalitarianism."[42]

Roosevelt stuck to his guns, insisting that the volunteer system had indeed failed just as Willkie's position became firmer. On August 17, in a campaign speech in front of a crowd of 20,000 in Indiana, Willkie said, "I cannot ask the American people to put their faith in me without recording my conviction that some form of selective service is the only democratic way to secure the trained and competent manpower we need for defense." Some isolationists claimed that Willkie was simply in favor of a future, not immediate, conscription—an interpretation Willkie scotched on August 26, when he told reporters that he was "unequivocally in favor of immediate conscription."[43]

When a group of isolationists led by Representative Hamilton Fish Jr.,* a Republican of New York and FDR's old Dutchess County antagonist, attempted to delay the implementation of the draft by 60 days in the final version of the bill, Willkie urged that the provision be eliminated. Fish and other Republicans, including Joseph W. Martin Jr. of Massachusetts, chairman of the Republican National Committee, hoped to delay the draft until after the election when, they hoped, Roosevelt would have been defeated and the chance to stop the draft would again present itself.[44]

It was a hot summer, rendered hotter by the ongoing sideshow on Capitol Hill. A group of black-veiled women dressed in mourning clothes and calling themselves the Congress of American Mothers staged

---

* Fish himself had been compromised: he and a handful of fellow members of Congress had used their franking privileges to distribute tens of thousands of pro-Nazi documents from fraudulent front groups postage-free. This was not known at the time but would become known before the war was over. Fish claimed to be unaware of the Nazi tie to these groups. Other members of Congress who knowingly or unknowingly lent their franks to the Nazis were Clare E. Hoffman, Henry C. Dworshak, Bartel J. Jonkman, Harold Knutson, John G. Alexander, James C. Oliver, Gerald P. Nye, and D. Worth Clark.

a death march against FDR's plan for conscription in peacetime. They constructed a papier-mâché dummy with a coconut for a head of pro-conscription senator Claude Pepper of Florida, which they strung from a tree on the Capitol grounds. "We're hanging Claude Pepper to a sour apple tree," the women chanted, "so our sons and husbands can live on and be free." Pepper, well known for his good sense of humor, took time to admire the mock lynching and declared it a splendid demonstration of free speech and the American way. The Capitol Police demanded that the women cut the effigy down, and it was delivered to Pepper's office by police escort.[45]

The protests then moved inside, as the women in black entered the Senate gallery and later shifted to the House when the debate over the draft bill moved there. On September 3, one of a 600-member delegation from a Communist group called the Peace Mobilization Society, which was vehemently opposed to the U.S. entry into the war, stood up in the House gallery and shouted, "American conscription is American fascism." As the protester was being ejected by Capitol Police, Representative Edward E. Cox of Georgia poked back by calling the protesters "lousy bums and bohunks" for trying to break in and influence Congress. *Bohunk* was a slur directed against eastern Europeans, especially Czechs, and was one more example that any hint of civility was melting in the late summer heat.[46]

The Peace Mobilization Society was a clear and immediate result of the German–Soviet Union non-aggression pact made earlier in the year, at which time the Communist Party USA became officially opposed to war with Germany. Its protest underscored the point that two factions—at opposing ends of the political spectrum and for different reasons—wanted to keep the nation out of the war and the draft.*

---

* One of the most famous members of the organization was African American writer Richard Wright, who made his views clear in "Not My People's War," published in the June 1940 issue of the *New Masses*. He argued that black Americans should not support the war effort and should work hard to keep the United States neutral. Jerry W. Ward and Robert J. Butler, *The Richard Wright Encyclopedia* (Westport, Conn.: Greenwood, 2008), 418.

Late on September 4, the debate boiled over as House majority leader Sam Rayburn urged representatives to reject the Fish amendment, saying: "It is bad psychology, it is bad business. To wait means more war." Tensions escalated during the night's debate, in which Representative Beverly M. Vincent (Democrat of Kentucky) called Representative Martin L. Sweeney (Democrat of Ohio) a traitor for opposing the selective service bill. The exchange culminated in what the Associated Press called "a free-swinging, hard-hitting fist fight on the House floor," in which several "vigorous blows landed on the face of each man." The doorkeeper of the House noted that he had not seen anything like it in his 50 years in the House.[47]

Not only did Willkie demand that the Fish amendment be eliminated, but he also insisted that the draft was not a party issue separating Republicans and Democrats. On hearing Willkie's statement, Fish accused him of having fallen for the propaganda of the interventionists and the eastern press and columnists.[48]

When the Senate and House held a conference committee to reconcile their versions of the bill, the Fish amendment was excluded, while the bill the Clark group originally submitted remained largely intact. Marshall had informed legislators that it would take two years for the draft to bear measurable results and that the Army would not be prepared to fight a war until then. He pushed lawmakers to conscript men for an 18-month tour of duty, but in his eagerness to get the bill passed, he settled for a year's service, unless a national emergency was declared by Congress after the 12-month term. In such a situation, the draftees could be retained. The compromise would come back to haunt Marshall the following year.

Since the Louisiana Maneuvers in May, other maneuvers had taken place in five locales—Upstate New York, Wisconsin, Minnesota, the state of Washington, and Louisiana again—in August. Almost 300,000 Regular, National Guard, and Reserve troops had been involved, from units representing all 48 states.

The largest of these August exercises involved 105,000 men in Plattsburg between August 5 and 25, once again under the command of General Hugh Drum. Because they were billed as an attempt to mimic the stress of a real national emergency, the 1940 Plattsburg exercises seemed important enough for President Roosevelt, Secretary of War Stimson, and Army Secretary Patterson to show up in the presidential railroad car and tour the maneuver area before the finale to the mock war got underway.[49]

But these maneuvers quickly proved to be an exercise in futility rather than a show of preparedness as the paucity of real weapons and the most basic equipment seemed to highlight all reports and observations. "The soldier trudging through the dust with a length of gutter pipe on his shoulder in lieu of a trench mortar got precious little training except for his legs," commented Marshall Andrews, who was covering the exercises for the *Washington Post*. But this was just the beginning, as Andrews noted that men lacked blankets, tents, mess gear, and even proper uniforms. Some men who had made the trip to Plattsburg were not allowed to participate because they did not have uniforms or as Andrews phrased it: "guns stayed silent . . . because their crews could not be uniformed."[50]

Unlike the spring maneuvers in Louisiana, Plattsburg and the other August exercises received little newspaper coverage while they were taking place but a great deal when the results from these exercises were evaluated in early September. The conclusion was reached that no single division of the National Guard was ready for combat. The most critical summary appeared on the front page of the *New York Times* on September 9: "Inadequate equipment, a high percentage of 'green' officers, and raw recruits in all units of the Regular Army and National Guard and serious deficiencies in staff and command work even in the elementary fundamentals of 'soldiering' were revealed by the unprecedented series of army maneuvers which were held last month." The article ended with all observers agreeing that the draft was needed to build up the Army's strength.[51]

The final official reports from these exercises were even worse. One of the most damning recounted the alarming frequency with which men, ill prepared for marching and living in the outdoors, collapsed in the field. Units wandered aimlessly, communications failed, and supply lines failed, often leaving Guardsmen without food. Few of these deficiencies were the fault of the National Guard; the blame for most, rather, lay with the War Department, which had neglected the service for years and had outfitted it with little more than materiel left over from the previous war. Ancient Springfield rifles were labeled "50 CALIBRE," and stovepipes standing in for guns were mounted on trucks masquerading as tanks.

"The 1940 summer encampments demonstrated beyond dispute, that in terms of ground forces the nation was virtually defenseless," Army historian Christopher R. Gabel later concluded. "The National Guard's make-believe guns spoke louder in Congress than they did on the maneuver field."[52]

While Clark and his band of civilians had taken charge of the draft movement, Marshall was allowed to distance himself from that battle. He was free to adopt a new strategy, based on his fear that the Regular Army lacked the manpower to train conscripted men while keeping intact for emergency duty on this side of the Atlantic—such as putting down a Nazi-backed revolution in Brazil. He concluded that the solution to this problem would be to activate the whole National Guard, which could absorb thousands of draftees and give them basic training. Roosevelt agreed and encouraged Marshall to go to Congress and testify in favor of the draft and calling up the National Guard. Marshall made these points and on August 27 was given congressional authority to bring men of the National Guard into the Regular Army for one year. On August 31, Roosevelt issued Executive Order 8530, calling up 60,000 men in units of the National Guard in 27 states to report on September 16. This first call amounted to about one-quarter of the National Guard. Guard officers below the rank of captain who had dependents were given 20 days to resign if they chose to, and all men under 18 were discharged.[53]

On September 16, a week after the *New York Times* critique was published, the Burke-Wadsworth bill establishing a military draft passed the Senate 47–25 and was subsequently approved in the House by a vote of 232–124 on the same morning.[54,55] Clark and his band of unpaid lobbyists "practically wore out shoe leather tracking down and button-holing Senators and Representatives," recalled General Lewis Hershey, who became the director of the Selective Service System after the bill was passed.

Thus ended what was later termed the most tumultuous summer in Congress in living memory. Under the final version of the act, all American males between 21 and 45 years of age were required to register for the draft. The government would select men through a lottery system under which "all drafted soldiers had to remain in the Western Hemisphere or in United States possessions or territories located in other parts of the world."

A group of about 1,000 opponents of the draft who had camped outside the Capitol during the final debates now moved to a position in front of the White House. Their anthem, "Down by the Riverside," contained the line: "Ain't gonna study war no more."

The same day the bill passed, the first 60,000 of 270,000 National Guardsmen who would be called between that moment and June 30, 1941, when the Army would be authorized to grow to 1.4 million, reported for active duty. The first divisions to arrive—the 30th from the South, the 41st from the West, the 44th from the Northeast, and the 45th from the Southwest—were distributed geographically to create minimal industrial disturbance to any one region of the country since the vast majority of Guardsmen held jobs.[56]

That evening, George Marshall delivered a special address on CBS Radio: "The next six months include the possibility of being the most critical period in the history of the nation . . . We must be prepared to stand alone," he warned. Marshall also went out of his way to express his faith in the American citizen-soldier:

I fear that we expect too much of machines. We fail to realize two things: First, that the finest plane or tank or gun in the world is literally worthless without technicians trained as soldiers—hardened, seasoned, and highly disciplined to maintain and operate it; and second, that success in combat depends primarily upon the development of the trained combat team composed of all arms. This battle team is the most difficult, the most complicated of all teams to create, because it must operate on unknown ground, in darkness, as well as in daylight, amid incredible confusion, danger, hardship, and discouragements. It is a team of many parts, the decisive element of which remains the same little-advertised, hard-bitten foot soldier with his artillery support.[57]

Marshall could celebrate, but the timing of this victory was far from ideal for Roosevelt. Samuel Rosenman, one of FDR's closest advisers, told the president: "From a political point of view, there couldn't have been a worse time for them to have passed this bill. The actual drawing of numbers will probably take place right smack in the middle of the campaign, and of course you are going to be blamed for it in a great many homes."[58]

However, a shift in attitude among young Americans of draft age strongly suggested that the draft would not bring the resistance many had predicted. The Gallup Poll had never done opinion sampling among those under 21, but when the draft issue surfaced in 1940, the editors of the *Reader's Digest*, then the most popular magazine in the world, commissioned a poll of Americans between the ages of 16 and 24. Some questions were directed at both sexes and others were asked only of males. The results, published in the October 1940 issue, were a pleasant surprise to those who worried about the state of American youth, which the magazine termed "tough-fibered, loyal and hopeful." It added: "They have faith in the future. They are not radical—in fact they are surprisingly conservative in their views."

The pollsters asked young men whether they objected personally to a year of military service, and 76 percent said they did not. Many of them requested proper training: "If I'm likely to fight, I'd rather know how." The fundamental acceptance of compulsory military service by this "slice" of the nation's manhood (some 10 million men) closely approximated acceptance by the general population, which Gallup polled several times on the issue.

In the commentary accompanying the poll results, Gallup pointed out that commentators and editors who had been telling America that its young were a flabby, pacifistic, yellow, cynical, and discouraged lot had now been handed a stinging rebuke from the very young people they were criticizing. Gallup named Walter Lippmann of the *New York Times*, Dorothy Thompson of the *New York Tribune*, and the president himself for advancing this negative point of view. Thompson was a woman of great influence; in 1939 she had been named the second-most influential woman in the country after Eleanor Roosevelt. Gallup suspected that many of those pushing the negative portrayal of American youth had been swayed by the "fulminations of such noisy groups as the American Youth Congress," a Far Left group with strong ties to the Communist Party that had demonstrated against the Burke-Wadsworth bill.[59]

As if to underscore the Gallup conclusion, on October 10, a poll taken at the University of Maryland by the student newspaper found that Maryland students favored compulsory military training by a 5–1 ratio. News like this was welcome, as the draft system was about to face its first test less than a week later.[60]

Section 4(a) of the new law stated that no discrimination be shown against any person on account of race or color. However, section 3(a) of the same act gave Army and Navy authorities unlimited discretion in deciding whom to accept into their ranks and how to employ those they accepted. In other words, discrimination was banned, but segregation was not. Jim Crow still ruled.

Because the military was segregated, race-specific draft calls more often than not limited the number of black recruits. In 1940, there were six black units in the Army. African American draftees could be assigned only to these units or to new ones being planned. Attempts to send African American draftees to the Army were rejected before segregated barracks and mess facilities could be put in place. In 1940 it was unthinkable that blacks and whites could eat or sleep under the same roof.[61]

With draft registration in mind, civil rights leaders went to the White House on September 27, 1940. A. Philip Randolph, head of the black Brotherhood of Sleeping Car Porters, was accompanied by Walter White, the head of the NAACP, and T. Arnold Hill, an administrator for the Urban League. They demanded the racial integration of the Armed Forces as well as changes in the hiring practices of the burgeoning defense industry. The president told the men that progress was actually being made: African Americans were going to be assigned to combat services in numbers proportional to their percentage of the overall population, "which is something," he added. The black leaders then pushed on the issue of integration. According to White's account of what happened next, Roosevelt at first thought about the formation of integrated divisions in the Army but after some additional thought seemed to accept the idea that the Army could place black combat units alongside white ones and over time "back into" desegregated units. Roosevelt made it clear that this idea would have to begin in the North. Progress it seemed had been made—that is, only if and when these first steps were taken.[62]

When the group of civil rights leaders then raised the question of desegregating the Navy, Secretary of the Navy Frank Knox quickly responded that such a move would be all but impossible. He explained: "We can't do a thing about it because men live in such intimacy aboard ship that we simply can't enlist Negroes above the rank of messman." Roosevelt jumped in at this point to say that the Navy "was organizing musical entertainments and new bands for ships" and putting "Negro bands" on ships could allow white sailors to come to accept sharing space with black sailors. As the meeting ended, FDR thanked the black leaders for their time and promised that he would talk with his cabinet and other top officials about the issue of racial integration in both military services.[63]

But the nation's military leaders—including Stimson, Marshall, and Knox, and almost all of FDR's cabinet—were totally opposed to any of the changes proposed by the president, especially as so many other pressing military issues were up for discussion. Marshall made the key argument: "There is no time for critical experiments which could have a highly destructive effect on morale."[64]

Unaware of debates taking place without their knowledge, Randolph and the other leaders had been encouraged by their meeting and were waiting anxiously to hear from the president. They did not hear from FDR himself, but on October 9, Stephen Early, the president's press secretary, issued a press release endorsed by the president saying that black troops would be used in combat roles, but the status quo would be maintained, and black and white enlistees would serve apart from each other in their own units. Early promised that African American units would be created in virtually every branch, including aviation, and endorsed a long-standing policy "not to intermingle colored and white enlisted personnel in the same regimental organizations." As if he had not been understood he added that "no experiments should be tried . . . at this critical time."

Unfortunately, the wording of the press release gave the firm impression that the policy of continued segregation had been endorsed by White and the other black leaders who immediately demanded that the president retract the "damaging impression" that they had endorsed Jim Crow policies. Press Secretary Early then issued a formal retraction, but the damage had been done.[65]

The impact of the press release, with an endorsement from the president in the form of the initials "OK, FDR" effectively turned it into a statement of racial policy that would remain in effect for years to come. Morris J. MacGregor, an official Army historian of racial integration of the military, observed that the press release was "immediately elevated in importance by War Department spokesmen, who made constant reference to it as a presidential directive" and that it was actually cited by "some Army officials as a presidential sanction for introducing seg-regation in new situations, as, for example, in the pilot training of black officers in the Army Air Corps."[66]

The reaction from the black press was loud and clear. As *Time* magazine framed the story in its October 28 issue: "From Memphis'

Beale Street to Harlem's Lenox Avenue, the U.S. Negro press last week suddenly took fire. It blazed up over the Army's No. 1 social problem: what to do with Negro officers and Negro enlisted men." *Time* then noted: "Even Harlem's pro-Roosevelt *Amsterdam News* joined in the outraged hubbub. JIM CROW ARMY HIT, ran its page one banner over a story denouncing the Army's policy."[67]

The outraged black press immediately began a crusade to integrate the Armed Forces, which would continue throughout the war and beyond. Individual black Americans also took note. Leon Hardwick's impassioned letter, published in the *Washington Post*, argued that the segregation of the Armed Forces worked against "ironclad national unity" and as such was "a threat to the security of the nation."[68]

Such criticism came at a particularly awkward time for Roosevelt, whose opponent in the upcoming election was a vocal advocate of civil rights and was becoming more and more popular among black voters. Willkie had a citizens' committee composed of a group of prominent black leaders, including the head of the Associated Negro Press, who backed him because they believed he offered the promise of "better conditions for the Negro people."[69]

In the weeks prior to the election, Roosevelt tried to offset the negative effect of the Army's announcement and appeal to black voters by promoting Colonel Benjamin O. Davis Sr. to the rank of brigadier general, making him the first person of color to hold that rank in the Regular Army. He also appointed Colonel Campbell C. Johnson, the commander of Reserve officers' training at Howard University, as a special aide to the director of the Selective Service System. Finally, he appointed Judge William H. Hastie, dean of the Howard University Law School, as a civilian aide to the secretary of war.[70]

In and of themselves, these appointments were welcomed, but they dodged the problem and were also seen as a clumsy attempt to appease the demands of those demanding full racial equality. As Walter White later wrote of the appointments: "Had they been twenty men each, the problem faced could be ameliorated only to a slight degree as long as the basic evil of segregation was not ended."[71]

CHAPTER 5

"YOUR NUMBER CAME UP":
THE 1940 PEACETIME DRAFT

To many mid-20th-century Americans, October 16, 1940, would forever be known as R-Day—the day all men between the ages of 21 and 45 were required to register for the draft. As long lines formed, Franklin Roosevelt addressed the nation on the radio: "On this day, more than 16 million young Americans are reviving the 300-year-old American custom of the muster. On this day, we Americans proclaim the vitality of our history, the singleness of our will and the unity of our nation."

In the District of Columbia, 47 registration centers accommodated the 113,371 men who lined up in a cold rain to register. Almost half a million registered in Chicago. Long lines were reported in many cities, and some started well before the registration centers opened at 7:00 a.m., even as early as 2:00 a.m. Handling the registration were more than 100,000 unpaid volunteers and civil servants assigned to the task. Stragglers were allowed an extra five days if they had a good excuse, so the number on the actual R-Day was probably less than 16 million; the number finally counted was 16,316,908 on the Monday following R-Day.*

The mechanism for this day had been carefully put in place well before the draft legislation was even discussed in Congress. In mid-June, weeks before the legislation was enacted, the *Providence Sunday*

---

* The total population of the United States according to the 1940 census was 132,164,569.

Journal revealed that a massive quantity of draft registration cards had been secretly printed by the Government Printing Office. The War Department denied this, but the Rhode Island newspaper was not only able to get unofficial confirmation that it was true, but it also learned that large sums of money were being authorized to set up the system.[1]

The level of cooperation achieved by a nation still split between isolation and intervention was remarkable. Newspapers set up special bureaus of draft information to answer questions about registration, and radio stations made sure their listeners knew how and where to register. The registration form itself was simple, its boxes filled in by examiners who asked a dozen basic questions. An examiner then needed to eyeball the registrant to determine whether his build was slender, medium, or stout. Under the column for race were five choices for the examiner to choose: "White, Negro, Oriental, Indian, or Filipino."

The wallet-size draft card handed back to the registrant contained basic information, including the registrant's date of birth and proof that he had registered. He was advised to keep it with him at all times, and it came into immediate use in establishing proof of age when buying alcoholic beverages.

Some had feared on R-Day the kind of armed resistance that had erupted in 1917 as small groups of men indicated that they would rather fight the draft than the Germans, but it did not materialize. Seminole Indians in Florida, who were still technically at war with the United States and had at first showed signs of resistance, agreed to register, though a later report indicated that some Seminole men hid deep in the Everglades to avoid complying. With one notable exception, congressional isolationists held their tongues and stood in line at their designated registration points. The exception was Senator Rush Holt, who demanded and got a special registrar to come to his office to sign him up, after which he denounced the draft as "silly and unnecessary."[2]

As George Gallup's poll indicated, college students and graduates had gone through a transformation from pacifism and isolationism to intervention and a willingness to register for the draft. There was no simple explanation for the change other than the impact of the news coming in from Europe. Mirroring campuses across the country, some 4,700 students and faculty members at Harvard University registered on R-Day, and the process went smoothly and without incident. Awareness had grown of the devastation occurring in Europe and the British Isles. The newspapers and radio broadcasts on the morning of R-Day carried news of massive Nazi bombing attacks on the coasts of England, Scotland, and Cardiff, Wales, as well as another night of saturation bombing of London.[3]

The newspapers collectively assembled under the banner of the Associated Negro Press treated R-Day as an opportunity rather than a burden. The *New York Amsterdam News* noted that in Harlem congestion at some registration centers was unlike anything ever seen in the history of the community. Long lines of men six deep appeared in various areas. Despite the lines and a bitter, cold wind, the newspaper reported there was "a marked air of joviality" in all the crowds.[4]

Many reports of R-Day noted glib and fatalistic remarks from men waiting in line. "See you in Flanders," said one cocky registrant in St. Louis, referring to the killing fields of the First World War. Adurm Oppenheimer of Portsmouth, Ohio, was identified as the only veteran of that war to be required to register for the 1940 draft. He had lied about his age and enlisted in the Marine Corps at the age of 13; he was now 35.[5]

Celebrities signed up across the country. John Wayne, there on location, registered in Big Bear Lake, California. A host of stars lined up in Hollywood and Beverly Hills, including Don Ameche, Lon Chaney Jr., and Robert Taylor. Henry Fonda and James Stewart, two of Hollywood's most popular stars, made a point of rising before dawn to be among the first in line at their Hollywood registration station. Bandleader Kay Kyser led his musicians in military formation from the RKO studio to a nearby precinct, where they signed up en masse, as did the Washington Redskins football team, which registered as a group, headed by quarterback "Slingin'" Sammy Baugh.[6]

In Chicago, heavyweight boxing champion Joe Louis, 26, signed up at a registration station for black men, accompanied by his brother and manager. He used his full name—Joseph Louis Barrow. Photographs of his registration appeared in newspapers throughout the country the following day with the caption on the AP image: HE'S A FIGHTER FOR YOU, UNCLE SAM. The *New York Amsterdam News* article on the Louis registration listed a host of other black sports stars who had registered, including Negro league slugger Josh Gibson of the Homestead Grays. Home-run king Hank Greenberg, on his way back from Detroit to his native Bronx, stopped in Geneva, New York, to register. Fireball pitcher Bob Feller, who signed up on his way to a hunting trip, bearing a shotgun, told a reporter: "I'll be all right. I've got more control with this shotgun than I have with the baseball." Yankee slugger Joe DiMaggio made the newspapers because he was momentarily unable to come up with the full legal name of his employer, which was the American League Baseball Club of New York.[7]

William McChesney Martin Jr., president of the New York Stock Exchange, spent more than six hours trying to find his proper registration station, only to wait in a long line, which inspired the *Wall Street Journal* to puckishly compare his travail to the wanderings of Ulysses in search of Ithaca. Four members of the Rockefeller family (Laurance, John D. III, Winthrop, and David) proudly stood in line, as did the student sons of Ambassador Joseph P. Kennedy (Joseph Jr., at Harvard, and John F., at Stanford) and two of Roosevelt's sons (John, in Nahant, Massachusetts, and Franklin Jr., in Indianapolis, where he was attending a Democratic Party luncheon).[8]

Newspaper readers learned about people who registered, even those who would never be able to bear arms. An article in the issue of the Washington, D.C., *Evening Star* that hit the streets of the nation's capital late in the afternoon of October 16 told of doctors and nurses who had been deputized to register 400 men in 11 local hospitals. Some of these men were too ill to move or were strapped into casts. One man, who had been wearing braces on his legs for a dozen years and had been operated on six times, told the *Star*: "I'm only 26 and I can shoot. I had a BB gun once." Patients in mental hospitals were registered in their wards, usually by the superintendent of the institution.[9]

The shock of it all was the order and apparent ease with which the task had been completed. The *New York Times* summed it up on the morning of October 17: "The young men of the nation registered yesterday for the first peacetime draft in history in conditions as peaceful as a prayer meeting." The *Times* and other major newspapers were unable to report a single incident of violence against the system. New York City mayor Fiorello La Guardia said there was only one reported disturbance in the city, and that was a fistfight between two men over who would be first in line to register. The following morning, the pro-conscription *Times* headlined a celebratory editorial: THE NEW ARMY IS BORN.[10]

Conscientious objectors and war resisters were few and far between, and most of them registered. The American Civil Liberties Union (ACLU) had been adamant in advising all conscientious objectors to register and warned that "those who do not even identify themselves on registration day are in precisely the same position as draft evaders and would doubtlessly be prosecuted when apprehended." The time to announce one's objection to the war was when called up for the draft, and the ACLU was on record saying that it would not defend men who refused to register but would be on the frontlines for men who had registered and declared their status.[11]

Eight students at Union Theological Seminary in New York City refused registration and were immediately served with summonses to appear before a grand jury. In Washington, D.C., the only conscientious objector to show up at a registration station and then refuse to register was a Jehovah's Witness preacher. One of three who refused to register in the state of Connecticut proclaimed his objection and apparent willingness to go to jail by simply making the statement: "A man does not rule his conscience: his conscience rules him."*

The one truly sad story of the day involved World War I veteran Samuel Miller, 43, chairman of the Atchison County, Kansas, draft board and head of the local American Legion post. He had watched men register all morning and then gone home, written a note, and shot himself,

---

* One of the theological students who had refused to register was David Dellinger, 25, who would be indicted on October 21. He became a leading antiwar advocate and achieved his greatest fame as one of the Chicago Seven defendants during the Vietnam War era.

as he feared consigning registrants to the same horrible experiences he had suffered two decades earlier at Verdun, Meuse-Argonne, and Saint-Mihiel, in France. His father was quoted as saying, "He took the soldier's way out."[12]

At the end of the registration process, the registrars' draft cards were immediately turned over to an appropriate local official, who checked them and passed them on to the local draft boards, where they were piled high and numbered serially, from one to the sequential number of the last man registered by that unit. The list of registrants, showing the serial number assigned to each man, was then published in special inserts to local newspapers, which were widely distributed. Everyone who registered now had a number from 1 to 8,994, the final number belonging to the last man registered at the local registration station with the largest number of men showing up.

The actual draft began at a ceremony in Washington, D.C., at the Departmental Auditorium on Constitution Avenue* on October 29, 1940. Wherever there were radios, Americans tuned in to what was about to happen. "The only time a teacher brought a radio into class was on the day they drew the numbers," recalled historian and World War II Marine Corps veteran Edwin C. Bearss, who was then attending a small country high school in Montana. "It was a very important event."[13]

"This is a most solemn ceremony. It is accompanied by no fanfare— no blowing of bugles or beating of drums. There should be none," Roosevelt intoned at the opening. "We are mustering** all our resources,

---

* The 750-seat auditorium is still located between 12th and 14th Streets NW (1301 Constitution Avenue) in Washington and is little changed since the day of the drawing except for the fact that it is now known as the Andrew W. Mellon Auditorium.

** Still wary of using the terms *draft* or *conscription*, which do not appear in this speech, Roosevelt continued to use the term *muster*, thus evoking memories of Lexington and Concord and flintlock muskets. The Army itself disliked the term *draft*—possibly because it associated the term with the draft riots of the Civil War and the draft dodgers of World War I—and preferred that Americans refer to it as *selective service*. Popular culture sided with *draft*. A frequent one-liner in the fall of 1940 told of parents who named their first

manhood, and industry and wealth to make our nation strong in defense. For recent history proves all too clearly, I am sorry to say, that only the strong may continue to live in freedom and in peace."[14]

Despite Roosevelt's claim of no fanfare, the event was conducted with, as one historian put it, all the "panache of a Hollywood award ceremony." Warplanes flew overhead as Roosevelt spoke. Small, blue-tinted celluloid capsules containing the lottery numbers, which had been escorted to the ceremony by an honor guard of 500 veterans of the Great War and then dumped into a ten-gallon fishbowl, were stirred with a large wooden spoon carved from a beam in Philadelphia's Independence Hall. The fishbowl itself was the same one used for the 1917 draft and had been moved from Philadelphia to Washington with a full military escort.[15]

A blindfolded secretary of war, Henry Stimson, drew the first capsules from the bowl to establish the draft order. The strip of yellow linen used as a blindfold was cut from the covering of the chair used at the signing of the Declaration of Independence. After Stimson pulled out the first capsule, he handed it to Roosevelt, who announced the first number drawn: 158. A woman in the large audience in the auditorium, Mildred C. Bell, screamed loudly enough to be heard over the radio; her son Robert Bell held the number 158. Across the nation, 6,175 men also held that number and now knew they were required to report immediately for a physical examination.

The publicity firm promoting selective service located Robert Bell and his fiancée and made them available to the press the next day. The couple was set to marry on November 8, but Bell insisted that he would not ask for deferment as a man with a dependent wife.[16]

Later that day in Boston, Roosevelt delivered a campaign speech in which he addressed the parents in the audience whose sons were now subject to the draft: "I have said this before, but I shall say it again and

---

born "Weather Strip" because he would keep his father out of the draft. Hollywood began signing its biggest comic stars for movies about conscription, including Bob Hope, for *Caught in the Draft*, and Harold Lloyd, for *My Favorite Spy*.

again and again: Your boys are not going to be sent into any foreign wars. They are going into training to form a force so strong that, by its very existence, it will keep the threat of war far away from our shores. The purpose of our defense is defense."[17]

In Washington, half the numbers had been drawn by midnight. By the wee hours of the morning, legionnaires, tourists, and anyone else who dropped by the auditorium were allowed to pull capsules containing random numbers from the fishbowl. The process of drawing numbers continued all night, ending at 5:00 a.m. One of the men, whose number came up 7,298 in the lottery, was the president's youngest son, John, which meant he was going to be called in the first year.[18]

After all the numbers had been drawn from the fishbowl in Washington, local boards sent out a questionnaire to each of the men that would be used to determine eligibility. Each man had five days to answer an eight-page series of questions, the responses to which would be confidential, seen only by his local draft board. Questionnaires filled out by conscientious objectors would be reviewed by the Justice Department and the Federal Bureau of Investigation. The first question focused on physical condition, to determine whether the person had a physical defect or disability or chronic poor health that would render him unable to serve.

Based on the sworn answers, draft boards then separated the men into four groups. The first, 1-A, contained those available for induction into the armed forces. Classes 2 and 3 deferred induction, respectively, because of the candidates' importance to the nation in his civilian occupation or because of persons dependent on him for support. "Obviously," according to a guide to conscription published in the *Washington Post*, "after John Doe writes 'foreman in an aircraft factory' in the occupation blank, he will never be sent any closer to the army than his own assembly line."[19]

Class 4 included those whose induction was prohibited by law (including state governors and sitting judges), and the special class 4-F was for those unfit for service for reasons of physical or mental health or because they were in prison, a mental hospital, or were otherwise removed from the larger society.[20]

Attached to each draft board was an appeals board, a physical examination board, and a medical appeals board. The rules given to the local boards were simply stated: "A man had to be at least five feet tall but no taller than six foot six, weigh at least 105 pounds, have vision correctable with glasses, have at least half his teeth, not have been convicted of a felony, and be able to read and write." Foreign men who had taken out their first citizenship papers were eligible; those who had not were ineligible. Membership in the Communist Party, the pro-Nazi German American Bund, or other political organizations did not disqualify a man from being classified 1-A.[21]

On October 22, officials of the Selective Service and the War Department held a press conference, during which they urged local draft boards to resist the temptation to use conscription to rid their local communities of young men looked upon as problems. The oft-expressed sentiment that the Army would make men of these bad boys had been challenged in World War I, when 88,000 such soldiers—described as men of mental and nervous instability—had broken down under the strains of military life and had in the intervening years cost the government a total of $33,000 per man, as many of them required extensive hospitalization.[22]

On November 2, the Associated Press ran a small story announcing that Lewis J. Gorin, founder and one-time leader of the Veterans of Future Wars, was now a second lieutenant in the Field Artillery Reserve Corps, a position he had held since the previous June. He said that the draft was a good thing and necessary. The story reported that after graduating from Princeton, Gorin had attended Harvard Law School and been admitted to the bar in Louisville in 1939. The story effectively served as an obituary for the Veterans of Future Wars and the impulse that started it.[23]

On November 5, Roosevelt won a comfortable re-election victory, with a plurality of almost five million votes, a feat accomplished by relying on strong support from trade unions, big-city political machines, and the traditionally Democratic South. Because his opponent, Wendell Willkie, had embraced the need for conscription, the power of the isolationists at the ballot box had been blunted. Hitler's ferocious conquests in Europe and the relentless bombing of London had also thinned the ranks of the isolationists, but they were still very much a factor in American political life when FDR won his unprecedented third term.

The continuing escalation of defense spending was a factor all through the election, and by the time Roosevelt was reelected, the nation was in the throes of a mass transformation from consumer products to the goods needed to fight a war. There were several catalysts for this beyond the additional funds granted by Congress and the constant pressure coming from Roosevelt, Stimson, and Marshall, including orders for aircraft and munitions from Great Britain; a five-year amortization plan, passed by Congress during the summer, that enabled industry to write off new plants and improvements; and action by a team of industrialists, led by William Knudsen, president of General Motors, to work out the problems and encourage the mass production of guns, artillery, tanks, ships, and other materiel. In early December 1940, a *Time* magazine reporter who traveled out of Washington, D.C., into the rest of the United States wrote that leaving that enclave "was like leaving the quiet of an office to walk into the crashing roar of the factory."[24]

On November 14, in a New York City courtroom, the eight theological students who had refused to register reiterated their refusal. After the judge gave them ample time to change their minds, they were sentenced to a year and a day in a federal penitentiary. Their defense had been that they were simply adhering to the teachings of Jesus Christ. The trial signaled the government's position that refusal to take part in the system was considered a felony. In the months to come, some 6,000 men who opposed the war as a matter of conscience or religious belief were imprisoned for failing to register or serve the nation in any form; these were mostly observant Jehovah's Witnesses who were not only opposed to service in the war in Europe as they had been in World War I but who also refused to accept the option of alternative service.*

* German Jehovah's Witnesses also refused military service in Nazi Germany, and more than 10,000 of them would die in Hitler's concentration camps.

Conscientious objectors (COs) who were inducted were given two alternatives. If they totally rejected military service, they were allowed to work on conservation projects in camps not unlike those of the CCC. The person whose beliefs allowed him to serve in the military but in a non-combatant capacity was assigned training or duties that included using weapons. A great number of these men ended up as medics or medical technicians, which meant they were willing to take the risks of combat without bearing arms.

As the draft came closer, the urge to marry had become stronger. On Saturday, August 31, extra police were called out to control crowds lined up to get into marriage-license bureaus in Manhattan and Brooklyn. Many denied that they were getting married to beat the draft, but others made no bones about why they were tying the knot at this particular moment. "Well, I'm going to beat the army now," said one bridegroom to a reporter from *Newsweek* magazine. Statistics collated and released later underscored the impact of the draft on marriage. In the Seattle area, for example, the number of marriages registered went up 25 percent from the previous quarter in the three months ending on October 31.[25]

One way the Army was able to absorb the great influx of draftees was through the widespread use of CCC graduates as leaders. The appeal of former CCC men was that they had been inoculated, had received dental care, and had been schooled in the basic regimentation and discipline required for the Army. The CCC Corpsmen were to be found everywhere in this new army, as 350,000 of them had graduated annually since 1933. Men from the Reserve Officers Corps, who ran the camps, also helped fill the Army's expanding leadership needs.[26]

Several attempts to add military training to CCC training in the wake of the draft legislation had previously been rejected. The addition did not come until August 1941, when military training was added to the syllabus for all 1,100 Civilian Conservation Corps camps then in operation. There would be 20 hours of "general defense training," beginning immediately for the 200,000 men in the camps. No weapons would be issued, but the clear intent of the program was to ready CCC recruits for the Army and to work in defense industries. Once this basic work was completed, selected CCC Corpsmen were trained in such fields as first aid, cooking, road construction, and two-way radio operation, including learning to use Morse Code. From this point forward, the CCC was part of the mechanism for creating a new army. The Corpsmen still had to be drafted or volunteer, but this prepared them for that day.[27]

In the days following R-Day, an oft-repeated thought—promoted by the government—was the upside potential of a conscripted year in the Army, during which volunteers and draftees would be assigned a specialty and be trained in that specialty. "The Army has changed a lot since the time your dad was taught to march across a parade ground without falling on his bayonet," penned a writer for the popular Sunday newspaper supplement *This Week*. "When the average draftee leaves the service today he will be far better equipped to earn a living than he was when he went in." The notion promoted and sold to young American men was that a year in the Army would be transformative rather than a burden. "Among other valuable things, he will have one terse answer to that thorny question of the prospective employer: 'What practical experience have you had?' That answer will be: '*Plenty!*'"[28]

Men who were drawn to such specialized training were invited to volunteer on induction day, with the idea that they would soften the impact of the draft and cut down on the numbers who would actually be conscripted. As a class, these men who chose to go to the front of the line were known as "volunteer draftees." This softened the blow of the conscription in the early months as some 71,000 volunteer draftees asked to have their names moved to the top of the list at their local boards. For this reason, the number of draftees to be called by December 1 was reduced substantially. In some areas, the number of volunteers was so high that few men were actually called in 1940. Forty percent of these volunteer draftees were unemployed, evidence that the Depression was still a fact of everyday life.

The first group of men to be called were the 6,175 men holding number 158. The next seven numbers were 192; 8,239; 6,620; 6,685;

4,779; 8,848; and 6,262. It was later discovered that the capsules had not been well mixed in the fishbowl, and an abundance of very high numbers had been pulled first. The men with early numbers received a letter with an order to report for induction. The order named the branch of service to which the man was assigned, giving the date, time, and place where he was to report, where the required paperwork would be taken care of, and the final medical examinations administered.[29]

On November 18, two months and two days after President Roosevelt signed the nation's first peacetime conscription bill, the first group of 984 volunteer draftees reported at 9:00 a.m. to induction centers in six New England states and were the first group to be officially recorded. These men were immediately subjected to a second physical examination. The process was simple but not subtle. It was a fast-moving assembly line, set up to accommodate about 25 men per hour. Stark naked men were assigned new numbers, written either on placards hung around their necks or on the backs of their hands. This gauntlet included a psychiatric exam, which led some examiners to conclude that nakedness made men more likely to shed their defenses.[30]

At the end of the examination, the men were told whether they had been approved; those who had failed were sent home. Those approved were fingerprinted, given a serial number, and sworn in. The serial number would identify that man from this point forward. From there, they were sent to an Army reception center, where they were given uniforms, vaccinated, and given a basic course of military training before being sent on to regular units. Only the early draftees experienced the jolt of waking up at home one morning and sleeping the next night at a military facility; this practice would eventually be abandoned, and later inductees were sworn in and sent home for two weeks to get their affairs in order.

The first man to be officially inducted was from Boston: John Edward Lawton, age 21, an unemployed plumber's helper whose position as number one was secured when the three men in front of him failed their physical examinations. He, like the other men in line, was a volunteer draftee. "You," said Captain Harold C. Linderman, the officer who swore him in, "are the first man in the United States to be inducted under this program. You've got a lot to live up to and we're expecting a lot from you."[31] Lawton became a symbol for the tens of thousands who followed. Few daily newspapers failed to carry his name the next morning.[32]

Prior to the draft, the government expected no more than 2 percent of the men called up or volunteering to be rejected because of physical deficiencies. Echoing Lawton's experience of moving up as the three men in front of him were rejected, the headline in the next morning's *Boston Herald* was about the percentage of volunteer draftees rejected for being physically unfit: 20 P.C. OF DRAFTEES SENT HOME. These men had already had a chance to declare disability on their questionnaires and had been examined by one doctor, yet they were still deemed unsuitable for induction.[33] The rejection rate among volunteer draftees rose to 25 percent: imperfect eyesight, unsound heart action, and lack of teeth were the leading causes.[34]

The rejections proved highly disruptive; the rejected men had already resigned from jobs, and some had given away much of their civilian clothing in anticipation of a year in the service. One induction official told the *Baltimore Sun* that many of these rejectees suffered considerable embarrassment because they had been given elaborate send-offs by their neighbors and fellow townspeople only to be put in the position of having to go back home. One volunteer draftee who had been given an elaborate going-away party begged to be kept and departed the induction center in tears.[35]

The problem of men quitting jobs to volunteer in the first call and then being rejected became so severe that the state of Georgia announced it would help them get their old jobs back or find new employment.[36]

For every man who tried to avoid induction by feigning a false ailment or going to the extreme of having teeth removed by a dentist, there seemed to be another who tried to hide a deficiency, as if to prove his manhood and/or patriotism. The term *negative malingering* was coined to describe concealing or minimizing existing symptoms. For example, examining physicians learned to spot epileptics trying to hide their condition by looking at their lips and tongue for the scars created by seizures.[37]

Virtually every draft board had stories of men who demanded they be reexamined after being rejected or who tried to enlist in another branch of service.

John Fitzgerald Kennedy, who had graduated from Harvard in June 1940, had enrolled at Stanford University in September under a "permit to attend," which allowed him to audit classes of his own choice without credit. Kennedy was already a minor celebrity, having turned his senior thesis on the failure of Great Britain to arm itself in its own defense into the best seller *While England Slept*, which had been published in July.

Kennedy's number, 2,748, was the 18th pulled from the fishbowl by Secretary of War Stimson; he became one of 22 Stanford students among the first prospective draftees. Although Kennedy had been selected, his status as a Stanford student qualified him for an automatic deferment until the final day of the academic year.[38]

In early 1941, as the situation in Europe continued to deteriorate, Kennedy decided not to wait until his period of deferment was up but instead enlisted in the Army as a potential officer candidate. However, he was turned down because of chronic back problems. He then applied to the Navy as an officer candidate and was again turned down for medical reasons.

In September 1941, with the assistance of the director of the Office of Naval Intelligence, Captain Alan Kirk (a former colleague of Kennedy's father) and a letter from a Boston doctor declaring him fit for service, John F. Kennedy was accepted into the United States Navy. After interviewing Kennedy, Commander E. M. Major wrote a summary, which read in part: "Subject's education, ability, unusually wide acquaintance and background, together with his personal qualifications fit him for commission as Ensign, IV(S). Subject appears qualified for service in OP-16F in the Office of Naval Intelligence." In October 1941, young Kennedy accepted his commission as an ensign in the U.S. Naval Reserve.[39]

Actor James Stewart was at the height of his fame in late 1940 when he was drafted—the first top film star to be called. His 1939 picture *Mr. Smith Goes to Washington* had been a tremendous hit, and *The Philadelphia*

Story had just been released. However, Army doctors rejected him as underweight by ten pounds based on a required height-to-weight ratio. He was six foot, three inches and weighed only 138 pounds. A private pilot, Stewart hoped to get into the Army Air Corps eventually and was determined to be inducted.

To get up to the required weight, Stewart sought the help of Don Loomis, Metro-Goldwyn-Mayer's trainer, who was legendary for helping stars add or subtract pounds in his studio gymnasium. When the actor was reexamined on March 21, 1941, he was deemed to be 1-A and was immediately sworn in and sent to Fort MacArthur in San Pedro, California.* "I'm sure tickled I got in," he told reporters, who noted that his salary immediately went from $12,000 a month at MGM to $21 a month as a private. A few days later, Stewart was transferred to the Army Air Corps, which had been his goal from the start.[40]

Almost immediately, a debate started over whether it would have been better for Stewart to remain a civilian and pay federal income taxes that would support the cost of 150 infantrymen, or to have him in uniform, fostering high morale among other draftees, who saw how willingly and happily Stewart served his country. Hollywood syndicated gossip columnist Jimmie Fidler debated both sides in his column and concluded: "The one final argument in favor of Jimmy being taken into the Army, of course, is that had he tried to escape by pulling political strings, there would have been the damnedest uproar this land has heard in many a day."[41]

What America was learning during this peacetime draft was that a person's reputation, surname, or income meant little to local draft boards. Winthrop Rockefeller, scion of the nation's richest family, became Private Rockefeller when his number was pulled out of the fishbowl. William McChesney Martin, the young president of the New York Stock Exchange, was pulled out of his high-paying job for basic training at

---

* Stewart later told journalist Starr Smith, author of *Jimmy Stewart: Bomber Pilot* (Saint Paul, Minn.: Zenith Press, 2005), that he had had a confederate operating the scales at the second weigh-in. Apparently, he was right on the edge of the proper weight and could take no chances.

Camp Croft, South Carolina. "Naturally," Martin said as he left Wall Street, "all of us were subject to this law and must expect inconveniences, but I'm sure many others have been more adversely affected than I."

The first sports celebrity called to arms was Hank Greenberg, the Detroit Tigers' slugger who was the highest-paid player in the game (earning $50,000 a year) and had been named the American League's most valuable player of 1940. Whether or not Greenberg would be drafted had been an open question for months because of his flat feet. A rumor also circulated that he would ask for a deferment based on his importance to the national game. However, Greenberg asked for no special treatment and was ordered to report for duty on May 7, 1941. He played his last game on May 6, slamming two home runs to beat the New York Yankees 7–4. The following morning, he was inducted into the Army at Fort Custer, Michigan, and assigned to the Fifth Division, Second Infantry Anti-Tank Company. As with Stewart, the press made much of Greenberg's new monthly salary of $21. More than any other celebrity, Greenberg became the face of the peacetime draftee whose life was changed by a number pulled out of a fishbowl.[42]

Others were called whose fame awaited them. Andy Rooney, a student at Colgate University in Hamilton, New York, did not apply for a deferment. He was drafted and whisked away to Fort Bragg, North Carolina, where a sergeant refused him space to store some books he had brought with him from college. Rooney later got assigned to a staff position on the military's daily newspaper, *Stars and Stripes*, where he began a long and distinguished career in journalism.

Bill Mauldin was born in 1921 on an apple farm in Mountain Park, a small community in southern New Mexico. He was a sickly child whose early years included contracting rickets that stunted his physical growth. Growing up, Mauldin loved to draw and continued to do so as a young private in the Arizona National Guard, which he joined on September 12, 1940. Mauldin weighed only 110 pounds, which made him ineligible for the Regular Army, but the National Guard had much looser physical requirements. The examining physician was more interested in whether he had hemorrhoids than in his weight because that affliction would have prevented a recruit from making the jarring 1,000-mile trek in the back of a truck to Fort Sill, Oklahoma, where his unit, the 45th Infantry Division, was sent upon being federalized. Once there, Mauldin volunteered to become the cartoonist for the *45th Division News*, a four-page tabloid weekly.[43]

On the last day of 1940, the *Journal of the American Medical Association* published a report asserting that the newly registered men were in far better health than those inducted in 1917, proof that the general health of the nation was good. The conclusion was based on 1,643 draft registrants examined by 120 draft boards in the City of New York. However, the sample was taken from a locale where poverty, access to medical care, and the devastation of the Depression were at totally different levels than they were in other parts of the country.[44]

Reality was quick to intrude, as the government learned the extent of malnutrition and other negative side effects of the Depression and the years of drought that created the Dust Bowl. Nearly half the men drafted in the first 12 months were sent home. More than 100,000 were rejected because they could neither read nor write. Another large group was toothless or lacked more than half their teeth. Men with punctured eardrums were turned back because the injury made them susceptible to poison gas attack, even while wearing gas masks. More than 30,000 of the first million were sent home because they had untreated, active cases of syphilis, gonorrhea, or other venereal diseases.

Most disturbing was the number of men who displayed the effects of poor nutrition. Of the first million men screened by draft boards in 1940, at least 130,000 were rejected for severe disabilities relating to malnutrition. This led to the decision to boost the most common items in American pantries with vitamins and minerals. Thiamin, niacin, iron, and eventually riboflavin were added to flour, enriching breads and breakfast cereals. Government-ordered food fortification was not new—iodine had been added to table salt since the 1920s to prevent goiter—but the rejection rate for the malnourished gave the movement new impetus.[45]

The creation of vitamin-enriched flour was accomplished by an agreement between representatives of the milling and baking industries, the American Medical Association, and the federal government. This was prompted not only by the situation in the United States but also by an earlier British move to add synthetic thiamin to bread to act as a counter-balance to deficiencies brought about by food shortages. American enriched bread was created by changes in the milling process as well as the addition of vitamin concentrates and cost less than two-tenths of a cent per one-pound loaf.* These changes were quietly and gradually instituted beginning in early 1941.[46]

Using food to create more efficient Armed Forces became a rallying cry. "If America is to be strong—strong enough to preserve the freedoms of civilized life in the modern world—we must hasten to build not only better bombing planes, but better human bodies," is how one writer put it in the March 1941 issue of *Harper's* magazine.[47]

Many of those who made it through their physical exams were still in no shape for the rigors of military life. General Omar Bradley, who received a large number of draftees, National Guardsmen, and Reservists at Fort Benning, wrote in his memoir: "The rude shock we experienced for the draftees was the discovery that they, the prime youth of America, were generally in appallingly poor physical condition. Only a very few were capable of the sustained physical exertion that they would experience in combat."[48]

Odd fears were generated by the draft, including those that men who married in haste to avoid the draft would create a wave of divorces when the threat was over and that the birth rate would decline as single men would be taken out of the marriage pool when they were assigned to remote military bases far from home. Eugenicists feared that the

---

* The companies that baked bread were quick to see this as an opportunity to boast that their enriched product had an effect on "building" healthy bodies. Wonder Bread was one of the earliest beneficiaries of the enrichment program.

nearsighted, the hard of hearing, and those with weak hearts would be turned down by the military and "left behind to marry, bear children and thus perpetuate hereditary weaknesses."[49]

By the end of 1940, with the system still in its early days, fewer than 20,000 men had been inducted into the Army. This was a drop in the bucket compared to the hundreds of thousands expected to be inducted in 1941, and the high rejection rate was still concerning. The problem of coming up with a sufficient number of men in the 1-A category was so great that one local board clerk in Washington, D.C., expressed her frustrations in a lament based on an American nursery rhyme.

Ten little registrants standing in a line
One joined the Navy, and then there were nine.
Nine little registrants sitting on a gate
One broke a vertebra, then there were eight.
Eight little registrants talking 'bout heaven
One went conscientious, then there were seven.
Seven little registrants, what a strange mix!
One became a pilot, then there were six.
Six little registrants very much alive
One went and drowned and then there were five.
Five little registrants full of canny lore
One stole a pig and then there were four.
Four little registrants, spry as could be
One became twenty-eight, then there were three.
Three little registrants, all alone and blue
One fed his relatives, then there were two.
Two little registrants, what can be done
One went to a psychiatrist, then there was one.
One little registrant, classified 1-A
Physically, mentally, morally okay.
One little registrant to tote a big gun
He got married and then there were NONE![50]

On the other hand, the American public believed that the U.S. Army and the local draft boards were off to a good—and equitable—start. In one of the more lopsided national polls Gallup ever conducted in its history, 92 percent of all Americans, including draftees and draft registrants, said that the draft was being handled fairly, and 91 percent felt that the Army was taking good care of the men drafted so far. An overwhelming majority of 89 percent said they thought the draft was a wise step and a "good thing," given the circumstances in Europe.[51]

In those early days, the draft got overwhelmingly positive coverage in the press, likely due to the strong affirmation given to Gallup. One draftee, who undoubtedly spoke for many in a letter to the *Washington Post* in early January 1941 complained about the newspaper's depiction of the draft as a lark. "The draft is necessary for national defense," he wrote. "But let us all respect it and not make the subject sound like a glorified Boy Scout hike."[52]

Some of the coverage seized on the humor of the situation, with cartoons depicting lawyers peeling potatoes and men being issued uniforms many sizes too big or too small. Not everybody was laughing. "So far, the Great American peacetime draft of 1940 has failed to strike its present and potential victims as particularly funny," wrote a feature writer for the *Baltimore Sun*. "They look morosely on the prospect of being wrenched from civilian life with its pleasant lack of rigors to spend a year of military training. The prospect is but fairly improved by the hard-working propagandists who, so far, have sought to dazzle prospective rookies with dreams of alluring hostesses, abundant, well cooked and provocatively varied meals and jolly good times with the interesting chaps who will be their camp mates."[53]

The end of the year 1940 also saw a new push for arms production, when on December 29, President Roosevelt declared that the United States must become the "great arsenal of democracy" and as such ensure that the Axis would be defeated. He made his case to the American people in a special radio address: "For us this is an emergency as serious as war itself. We must apply ourselves to our task with the same resolution, the same sense of urgency, the same spirit of patriotism and sacrifice as we would show were we at war." In a single moment Roosevelt put national defense first, and that meant creating the means by which to defend the nation and supply those fighting fascism. "The immediate need is a swift and driving increase in our armament production"—which meant the nation had to build "more ships, more guns, more planes—more of everything."[54]

Four days later the undersecretary of war, Robert Patterson, held a press conference to announce that arms production goals were expanding immediately in order to rapidly turn the nation into the arsenal Roosevelt had envisioned. The projects announced included contracts with a number of major corporations—among them General Electric, Buick Motor Company, and North American Aviation—to begin producing aircraft engines, aircraft frames, turbo superchargers, rifles, and chemicals needed for explosives. Patterson also promised that within the year there would be enough new Garand rifles to supply one for each man in the expanded U.S. Army.[55]

CHAPTER 6

ASSEMBLING THE NEW ARMY: "THE BLIND LEADING THE BLIND"

Even before the first group of conscripts had been sworn in, changes were taking place that would have a major effect on the Army into which these men would be inducted. Perhaps the most dramatic—if not the most important—was the new kind of offensive force George Patton was creating: an American Panzer division shaped and customized to Patton's vision and framed around correcting the mistakes he had witnessed as an umpire in the 1940 maneuvers as well as the mistakes he had witnessed in World War I. Patton had the backing of those in high places, including Secretary of War Henry Stimson, who considered him a friend and a born leader.

Promoted to brigadier general on October 2, Patton became acting commander of the Second Armored Division a few days after the November election, around the time he acquired the nickname "Blood and Guts." He had repeatedly told the young officers that soon they would be "up to their necks in blood and guts." Patton was also called "the Green Hornet," after a popular radio superhero, because of the pea-green, double-breasted jacket and green riding britches he had designed, which he hoped to have adopted for all of his troops. He also wore a football helmet painted gold, which is why his troops also called him "Flash Gordon," after the comic strip space warrior charged with the job of protecting the universe from evil forces.[1]

Above all, Patton was trying to instill a sense of purpose and a will to fight among his men, and these nicknames were in keeping with that spirit. Discipline was important to him, as was proper dress. His enemies were complacency and lack of order. Despite many shortages and a lack of proper housing for his men at Fort Benning, Georgia, he worked diligently to get them ready for his drills and maneuvers.

When he began to publicly display the power of the force he was assembling, Patton realized that a key to his success lay in his ability to appeal to the news media. He wanted public attention focused on the armored force that he believed he personified. His message was loud and clear: the United States had the highest-quality weapons, and the men possessed a great fighting spirit. Although he knew this was not yet be true—especially regarding the weapons—Patton knew it would be. He viewed his initiative as the future of warfare and spent every waking hour pushing his troops and building tank crews with high morale.[2]

Patton staged his first display for reporters on November 25, showing the visitors the power of 259 tanks engaged in mock combat. As the tanks fired blank shells, producing 15 "minutes of hell," Patton remarked that he would hate to be in front of that power in wartime. It was, by all accounts, a dazzling display.[3]

In December, Patton staged a high-profile mass exercise in which 6,500 men were quickly transported—in some 1,100 vehicles ranging in size from tanks to motorcycles—well over 400 miles from Columbus, Georgia, to Panama City, Florida, and then back. Patton believed that an armored division had to be able to move quickly and efficiently, and this exercise proved his point. To Patton, the maneuver was at once a test of discipline, supply procedures, types of formations, communication and control procedures, air-to-ground communications, and field maintenance.

Patton led the men out of camp riding in the open turret of a tank. Once the expedition was half over, he declared that his "Panzer addition" to Uncle Sam's Army was superior to anything in Europe, and in fact there was nothing in the world like it, despite the combat-tested German tank units. Several such statements of world superiority were made during the maneuver and appeared in scores of newspapers, under headlines such as: PANZER UNIT WINS PRAISE—BEST IN WORLD GENERAL DECLARES.[4]

Patton's advocacy for his troops, training methods, and logistics was relentless. He and his staff spread the word that his men, though far from restaurants, had nevertheless been served hot, chef-prepared breakfast and dinner—hot beef, two vegetables, fruit, and dessert—as well as box lunches containing three sandwiches and an apple; indeed he considered the men who prepared food to be chefs, not cooks. As part of morale building, motion-picture projection equipment was brought along for nighttime entertainment, as was football and baseball equipment for games during lunch breaks.[5]

The maneuver ended with a simulated night attack on Fort Benning. Only one of the 231 tanks in the exercise broke down and had to be towed home, a testimony to Patton's stress on maintenance and the ability to fix mechanical problems on the go.

Patton repeated the maneuver in January, as he prepared to fill his understaffed units with large numbers of recent draftees deemed suitable for an armored division. Patton knew he would be hard-pressed to get his men ready for war. He realized, as one of his biographers put it, "that in a none-too-distant future these raw levies would have to face some of the most highly professional, battle-hardened and blood-thirsty soldiers the world has ever known; men Spartan in outlook, united by a discipline of steel and with a fanatical faith in the Nazi creed for which they were ready to fight and if necessary to die."[6]

Patton was hardly the only one devoted to creating a high level of morale for the incoming troops. Before the first man was drafted, General Marshall announced the formation of the Morale Division to provide National Guardsmen, Reservists, and draftees with activities to keep them mentally, physically, and spiritually occupied during leisure hours. From the start, the Morale Division had the same autonomy as the infantry or the artillery. Never before had such an arm existed as a separate Army command.

This new division showed first-run movies at all bases. "No soldier should be surprised to find Hedy Lamar, Ann Sheridan, or any of the popular young starlets billed as their evening's entertainers, not to mention Mickey Rooney," wrote the Washington, D.C., *Evening Star*, noting that among other things the Army promised were libraries for the intellectually curious, a vast array of athletic facilities, and "motherly" Army hostesses to prevent homesickness and to run service centers.

"Every soldier loves to sing," stated U.S. Army public relations material, quoting a World War I general who maintained that a singing army was a fighting army. "The soldiers of 1940–41 will help keep up the Army's age-old traditions of song and good fellowship. Mass singing and individual singing, whether on hikes or on work details, will be encouraged." An article in the *New York Times* asserted that Army song leaders would prove effective in creating and maintaining *esprit de corps*.[7]

Attempting to appeal to men of refined tastes and private education, the Army offered to institute college or prep school amateur dramatics programs at every location. The Washington, D.C., *Evening Star* wrote that the "long-underfunded notoriously drab military bases sound more like college campuses than what they were in reality." Indeed, "reality" was a lack of structures—specifically warm, dry, clean living spaces—which proved initially to be a major problem.

Because the passage of the legislation enabling the enlargement of the Army had taken so long—until August 27 for the National Guard and September 16 for the draft—the War Department had been deprived of adequate funds and time to build roads, utilities, barracks, and the rest of the needed infrastructure, to say nothing of the movie theaters and football fields. At the end of May 1940, Marshall had begun to ask for funds for new construction to house the National Guard units. The funds were not approved until September, and work did not begin until October.[8]

The result was that the drafted men were often sent to tent villages rather than wooden barracks, and their most common complaints had to do with being cold and living in the mud. Many—but not all—of the tents were pitched on wooden platforms, but all the tents were damp when it rained and cold even when the inefficient wood-burning stoves were well fueled. Added to this was the commonly noted shortage of coats, blankets, and modern stoves that would have made the situation a bit less miserable.

Roosevelt's initial order of August 16 had called up four divisions of the National Guard, along with artillery units and observation squadrons, to report to their armories on September 16, 1940, for ten days of "shakedown." This involved final physicals, inoculations, and equipment testing while the men awaited orders to report to a Regular Army base or a new base being constructed to house National Guard units.

However, the armories often lacked the capacity to feed large numbers and could not provide adequate places for them to sleep. In the District of Columbia, the so-called armory was a decaying 123-year-old hotel that had been condemned as unsafe and could not be used as lodgings—so the men were sent home to sleep each night and ordered to eat breakfast before reporting back to the armory at an early hour. The National Guard had no legal way of compensating the men for their transportation costs or the costs of their meals, thus the term *shakedown* took on a new meaning, as men anted up for carfare and hot meals.[9]

In all, close to 65,000 officers and men in the National Guard were initially inducted into service and sent off to become part of the Regular Army, which gave the numbers for a standing army an immediate spike. These were the first peacetime tours of service since 1916, when National Guard units had been positioned along the Mexican border while General John Pershing mounted a punitive raid across the Rio Grande in search of Pancho Villa.

As the Army struggled to house, clothe, and equip this first group of men, a second increment of National Guardsmen was federalized on October 15, adding another 38,588 men to a system already bursting at the seams. The third and fourth increments in November brought in yet another 33,000 Guardsmen. By the end of November 1940, 135,500 Guardsmen were in the Regular Army. As camp conditions stood at their worst, the first group of 13,806 draft selectees entered the Army in November, adding new stress to the system.[10]

Fort Dix,* New Jersey, the closest large Army installation to New York City, had enough barracks space for a few thousand new men but was sent more than 20,000 from New York's 27th Infantry Division as part of the initial conversion of National Guard to Regular Army. The 27th had served with great honor in World War I; on its return it marched in a parade five miles long up Fifth Avenue, greeted by the largest celebratory throng in the city's history to that point. Twenty years later the 27th had been sent first to Fort McClellan, Alabama, for training and then moved to Fort Dix, where most of the men ended up in temporary tents pitched over wooden platforms. Amid a labor shortage, as ground was broken for new construction, water was found close to the surface and flooding ensued, producing an enormous amount of mud.[11]

In the East, the particularly wet winter of 1940–41 yielded mud of such quantity and depth that roads leading to newly constructed barracks became impassable. The incidence of influenza in the Army rose to approximately four times the level of the previous winter, along with a coincident rise in other respiratory diseases.[12]

Major Hal L. Muldrow, of the 45th Division of the National Guard, later recalled the supply system during the cold days of late 1940 at the division's temporary base at Fort Sill, Oklahoma: "They issued overcoats in bales. They'd throw them out and a man didn't know if he was getting Size 14 or 44. And we had men who had to wear their civilian shoes for several months because the shoes provided by the Army initially were all the medium size." The men of the 45th were housed in tents, and during that winter, some 2,500 came down with influenza.[13]

Aspiring cartoonist Bill Mauldin was in the 45th. When he arrived at Fort Sill in late 1940, he was issued a 1903 Springfield rifle, cracked hobnail boots, and leg wrappings that when properly cinched cut off

---

* Fort Dix was named for General John Dix, sent by Abraham Lincoln to New York City to ensure that the military draft of 1863 was implemented and that the city remained at peace.

circulation to his skinny legs. The 45th Division underscored the challenges besetting the National Guard once it was federalized. It drew heavily on men from impoverished areas of the Southwest who had become Guardsmen simply to get a $12 quarterly payment in return for weekly drill sessions and an annual summer camp. The unit had been called into service in the previous decade for such tasks as quelling miners' strikes and battling locusts in the wheat fields of eastern Colorado. The unit was also unusual because it was racially integrated, counting in its ranks a small number of black men and members drawn from more than 50 native tribes, including the Apache, Cherokee, Choctaw, Pawnee, Seminole, Sioux, Kiowa, Hopi, Comanche, Osage, Creek, and Navajo tribes.[14]

Yet, despite the well-publicized and very real problems, there were also examples, albeit less noticed, of base construction moving like clockwork. On the morning of July 29, 1940, a massive construction program began at Fort Jackson, South Carolina, to provide housing for an additional 23,000 officers and men, a 1,000-bed hospital, and a variety of auxiliary buildings to support this influx, including mess halls, latrines, warehouses, firing ranges, water and sewage filtration plants, and a gigantic "movie theater" tent. To access all this, 23 miles of roads, six miles of railroad tracks, 30 miles of sewers, a water supply system, and electricity to light the area had to be built and put into operation.

By Christmas Eve, a workforce ranging from 6,000 to 7,000 at any given time had erected 1,000 permanent structures and 6,000 tent-frame structures (at the rate of one every 90 minutes), which were now ready for occupancy. A few finishing touches were still required, but what amounted to a new military city was, in the words of a local newspaper, "virtually complete."[15]

Marshall took all complaints from his growing force seriously and personally. When a recruit sent him a steak deemed inedible, Marshall fired off a message to Major General Frederic H. Smith, the man's commanding officer.

Dear Smith:

I am sending you directly the attached letter, which came to me with a tough steak. The latter had reached a point where it had to be disposed of. Do not trouble to answer this letter, but I pass it on to you as a possible hint toward a poorly run mess, for which I find few excuses.

As you will see, it is not anonymous, and I am putting this man Gardner rather out on a limb by passing it on to you. However, there may be something in it, so do not kill him until you have looked into it.[16]

Reading and responding to a letter about a bad steak was typical of Marshall, who turned reading—and often responding to—a sampling of letters from soldiers and their families into a daily ritual. To anyone paying attention during the winter of 1940–41, it was clear that Marshall was more finely attuned to the needs of a Recruit or Guardsman needing a dry pair of soft socks than he was to an officer whining about some minor annoyance or system malfunction. Whining—especially by a man in a leadership position—was a cardinal sin to Marshall.

On November 29, Marshall took a page from Roosevelt's playbook and staged his own version of a fireside chat, addressing the nation on NBC Radio on the issue of national defense. A significant portion of the broadcast was devoted to explaining the shortcomings of the Army. He apologized for the lack of housing, yet observed: "A contract to build something within a period of a year is not to be compared in difficulty with the contract which must be completed in three months' time, involving the construction of complete utilities, and roads, hospitals, offices, and barracks for twenty to fifty thousand men."

Marshall freely admitted to the failure to provide uniforms and the resulting social implications: "This has been a particularly pressing matter from the viewpoint of public opinion, because each mother looks to her son's uniform with a very critical eye, and the young soldier himself feels it is of great importance especially if his best girl happens to be in the neighborhood."

He expressed regret for the shortage of chaplains, and he apologized to the National Guard families that had relocated for a year to be near bases in rural areas, only to find virtually nothing to rent at an affordable price. One issue troubled him "more than any other": young men from remote bases "who flood into the small nearby communities over the weekends." Liquor was a problem as was an influx of prostitutes, whom Marshall referred to euphemistically as "persons of questionable reputation."[17]

On December 12, Secretary of War Stimson held his own press conference to announce that 25 of the 40 camps that were under construction to house National Guard troops were from one week to two and a half months behind schedule. As a result, the induction of the January draftees was to be delayed. Stimson noted unexpected construction hitches, including problems of excavation, lumber shortages, and extreme cold weather and suggested they were inevitable when carrying out a huge and intricate project of building what amounted to sizable cities in an extremely short period of time.

Marshall's chat and Stimson's explanations notwithstanding, the National Guardsmen faced endless problems. From Camp Murray in Washington State came a report in December that half of the 12,000 men encamped there had influenza. Compounding this infirmity, the Guardsmen were housed in tents pitched on platforms over wet grounds, while the draftees coming in were ushered into new, dry barracks with both heating and air-conditioning, because the draft legislation specifically stated that the conscriptees be adequately housed. The commanding officer of the National Guard was asked by a reporter from the *Seattle Times* how this situation affected his men. "They're patriotic," he replied, "but they have wet feet."[18]

"A gigantic mess ensued," General Omar Bradley, then a member of Marshall's staff, later said about these efforts to enlarge the Army.

> Despite all the years of planning—the files bulging with mobilization plans—the army was simply not prepared to assimilate such vast numbers of new manpower. There were no organized

basic training camps for draftees. Recruits were sent directly to existing or organizing Regular Army units for basic training, even though those units might be engaged in maneuvers. The Guard units . . . were ill-equipped and in some instances so ill-trained that the officers in charge had not the slightest idea of their jobs or how to train the men in their units.[19]

Bradley was not alone in his dire assessment. After inspecting one division, Lieutenant General Lesley J. McNair, the new chief of staff of the Army's General Headquarters and in charge of training the draftees, observed with foreboding that it was "often a case of the blind leading the blind."[20]

Marshall addressed these problems at many levels, the most basic of which was his willingness to listen to the complaints of new recruits and then to address them if they seemed legitimate. Biographer Forrest C. Pogue later wrote that this practice was "the essence of democracy."[21]

Marshall visited many bases, and at each of them he carefully determined what single thing Washington could do to improve conditions there. As he left each base, he would ask the local commander what was most needed from government, writing the answer down in a notebook that he transferred to a master list. "I reached my office this morning," he wrote to one division commander the day after visiting the camp in question, "and have immediately taken up the matter of getting some additional authorization for construction at your camp." Marshall showered his staff and division chiefs with long lists of specific needs, ranging from minor to major. He was working to build a bridge between reality and the ideal that had been stated as recently as October 1940, when the Army had publicly promised each base a pair of thousand-seat movie theaters, separate fields for baseball, football, and track, and service clubs with a 90-by-70-foot dance floor and a 5,000-volume library.[22]

For many of the early draftees and Guardsmen, the situation was exacerbated by local custom and regulation—especially in locales in the portion of the country H. L. Mencken had dubbed the Bible Belt. Almost all 53,000 Reservists from Ohio and Indiana sent to Camp

Shelby near Hattiesburg, Mississippi, beginning in late 1940 and into early 1941, were living in tent villages and forced to confront a culture many found puzzling and demoralizing. State law banned Sunday movies, and Hattiesburg forbade dancing within the city limits. One movie operator defied the ban, only to be so heavily fined by the state that he gave up after a few Sunday openings. The only amusement open on the Sabbath inside the city limits was an arcade housing pinball machines—colloquially known as "nickel-grabbers."[23]

Marshall realized that he had, in the words of his main biographer, Forrest Pogue, "an alarming situation" on his hands. The problems of drinking, prostitution, boredom, and disorder were getting worse. The houses of prostitution that opened near bases caused the spread of venereal diseases, which had sidelined tens of thousands of troops in World War I and remained a huge concern in an era before antibiotics.

The problems were no abstraction to Marshall, who had secretly appeared in civilian clothes in a small Georgia town located near two large and rapidly expanding military bases. He checked into a local hotel, without aides, and went out early in the evening to find a place to eat. Every seat in every restaurant and every stool at every counter was filled, while long lines of men waited to be seated. "The net result," Marshall recalled later, "was it was half past six when this started and I never got anything to eat until it was half past ten that night. Every place was crowded and I got up to a lunch counter where I just had some warmed over biscuits and things of that sort." To Marshall, the situation could not continue "without some outbreak of some sort or other" in towns overwhelmed by thousands of soldiers on leave. Marshall was particularly fearful about what might happen near large bases in the Deep South where there was no nearby town of any size.[24]

Members of Congress, home for the holidays, got an earful from constituents whose sons and husbands had been sent off to installations that lacked adequate shelter and who were clothed in garb from the Great War, much of which had been rendered threadbare by the Civilian Conservation Corpsmen who had worn it in the interim.

The challenge for Marshall was solving immense structural problems with one hand while building a citizen army full of *esprit de corps* with the other. Marshall never lost sight of the necessity for good morale if this unprecedented expansion was going to succeed. He also knew that this new army could not be disciplined by fear and intimidation but only through respect—a lesson he had learned from both the Army and his work with men of the Civilian Conservation Corps, who had needed to be convinced rather than coerced.

Brigadier General James Ulio, chief of the Morale Division, explained to a reporter that morale was not just athletics and club rooms but rather what made a soldier willing to get along without comfort when he had to. "Making his life as pleasant as possible helps build his morale. But so does good, hard training." Ulio, who had previously served as the Army's chief adviser to the Civilian Conservation Corps, felt that the opportunity for those men to learn a job like stonecutting or highway construction had been the basis for high morale. "If the government had just fed them and clothed them and made their lives easier, it may have spoiled them. Instead, they got something to give a meaning to life. That's morale."[25]

Marshall's speeches and the news accounts of his pronouncements in the days before Pearl Harbor reveal his near obsession with morale. He defined it again and again and revised old maxims and adages about its importance. Napoleon had estimated that "morale is to matériel as three is to one"; in February, Marshall made headlines when he claimed it was "six to one."[26]

In the wake of Marshall's visit to the small town in Georgia, he and Stimson—who occupied adjoining offices with a usually open door between them—began to work with the Morale Division on a broad program to create recreational halls on every major base in which men could buy light refreshments, listen to music, and meet and dance with female hostesses.

In early 1941, Marshall began creating special off-base camps where men could go on the weekends to relax and get away from the drab, disciplined life on base—a place where they could "shake the dust of the parade ground off their shoes" and sleep until noon if they so desired. Entertainment was provided by local civilian groups, and local concessionaires provided home-style meals at a cost of 15 to 30 cents.

To sustain this massive initiative, the United Service Organizations (USO) was legally established in New York City on February 4, 1941, when several national charities banded together to raise the morale of members of the armed forces providing them recreation, education, and entertainment.* The government was willing to build the first 350 USO centers, while the fledgling organization was responsible for operating them at an initial cost of $11 million, raised through an advertising campaign in national magazines such as *Life*. The ads told of towns with populations of 1,000 to 5,000 people, into which 3,000 men might arrive on a single evening. "Not half of them can find a place to eat; hardly any can find opportunities for wholesome entertainment."[27]

By the summer of 1941, seven USO camps were in operation, and dozens more were under construction, including one outside Washington, D.C., for African American soldiers. The camps were being built by the Civilian Conservation Corps, a force that Marshall knew he could rely on and was proud to enlist. But the camps, regardless of how quickly they were built, were able to handle only a small percentage of the men in uniform. By the end of the year, they could accommodate only 20,000 men per weekend.[28]

Starting in late 1941, the USO began to send star-studded shows to camps around the country. The catalyst for this idea was Albert Capstaff, the radio producer for British-born comedian Bob Hope, then a top radio and movie star. In late April, Capstaff urged Hope to do a live broadcast of *The Pepsodent Show*, the most popular weekly variety show on radio, at March Field in Riverside, California, on May 6. The base housed officers and men of the Army Air Corps and included many

---

* The United Service Organizations: the YMCA and YWCA, the Salvation Army, the National Catholic Community Service, the Jewish Welfare Board, and the National Travelers Aid Association.

aviators. At first, Hope did not quite see the point, arguing that it would be a lot easier to bring the airmen to the studio, but Capstaff told him that would be impractical because they numbered in the thousands. Hope thought that if nothing else, the excursion would bring publicity to his upcoming movie, *Caught in the Draft*. A troop that included Hope's comedic sidekick, Jerry Colonna, singer and comedienne Frances Langford, and bandleader Skinnay Ennis and his orchestra headed east from Hollywood to March Field.

Hope opened by telling his live audience and the millions at home listening on their radios that he was performing in the gymnasium of March Field in Riverside, California, adding: "And I tell you that I'm thrilled being here. And what a wonderful welcome they gave me! As soon as I got into camp, I received a 10-gun salute . . . They told me on the operating table." That line was one of many that brought down the house; Hope had a gift for poking fun at himself as he played the role of the timid civilian in front of an audience of brave warriors.[29]

The following week the show was back in the Hollywood studio but then, as the success of the March Field show sunk in, it began to show up regularly at military bases. By that time, *Caught in the Draft*, which was released on July 4, had become the most popular Paramount film of 1941. In the movie, Hope played a nervous actor who fainted at the sounds of gunshots while filming a war movie and then accidentally enlisted in the Army, there to be transformed from coward to hero. Hope's shows became a mainstay in the USO stable of traveling shows, which eventually featured singers, female movie stars, and other comedians. The entertainer observed that the men in uniform were so hungry for entertainment, getting them to laugh was easy—akin to "stealing money."[30]

Taking their master cue from Hope's lead, a succession of live radio broadcasts moved out of the studio and onto bases and camps. The next performance at March field was the *Edgar Bergen and Charlie McCarthy Show* starring ventriloquist Bergen and his wisecracking wooden dummy. During the live performance, McCarthy was made an honorary master sergeant in the Army Air Corps. According to the *Fresno Bee*, McCarthy caused a record number of young men to apply to become air cadets at March Field.[31]

Hope and the USO became an essential element of a new G.I. culture that had actually begun to take hold in January 1941 in Hollywood with the release of the Bud Abbott and Lou Costello musical comedy *Buck Privates*, the first movie based on the peacetime draft. The film featured four songs by the Andrews Sisters, including "Boogie Woogie Bugle Boy," an up-tempo tale of a jazz trumpeter who is drafted and becomes the bugler for his unit but insists he cannot play without sidemen to back him up. His commanding officer thereupon drafts a jazz band so he can perform at his best. The message of the movie and the song underscored that the Army could make room for misfits (Abbott and Costello) and demanding jazz musicians. As one critic noted, watching the Andrews Sisters belt out "Boogie Woogie Bugle Boy" made you want to enlist. *Newsweek* noted that the movie was important "chiefly because it launched the forthcoming cycle of films dedicated to the adventures of Uncle Sam's new rookie Army." The film went on to become the year's biggest box office hit,* and the song an instant and ever-so-danceable classic.[32]

This emerging G.I. culture was also revealed in the popular daily newspaper comic strips. The comic hero of the moment was the soft-hearted heavyweight boxing champion Joe Palooka of the comic strip of the same name, who joined the Army in late 1940 as a volunteer draftee against the advice of his manager, Knobby Walsh. In the weeks following his enlistment, Joe was depicted by his cartoonist creator, Ham Fisher, as the ideal soldier adjusting well to military life. This behavior by a cartoon character did not go without official notice, and in early June 1941, Fisher was summoned to Washington where he met with and was personally thanked by Roosevelt, Stimson, Marshall, and other top military leaders for his contribution to the morale of the emerging new army. Roosevelt was quoted as saying that Joe Palooka

* In some cities, the movie ran second as a moneymaker only to the 1939 smash hit *Gone with the Wind*.

had, among other things, "an uplifting effect on the minds of boys entering the service."

Fisher then wrote an account of the visit in the imperfect but sincere voice of Palooka, who described the personal meetings he and Fisher had attended at the War Department. The cartoon character's illuminating take on Marshall: "Well he is a hansome type of specimum an taller than me. And he treated us like we was old friends and I come to the seclusion that the bigger people is the more there liable to be understandin an human. Evry soljer knows what a great soljer Gen. Marshall is but I wish they all could have had the now opportoonity to know what a grand gent he to jist a plain private like I'm jist."[33]

Marshall also understood that one of his first missions was to educate his new army on the context of its mission in terms of American history and values. On all bases, American history texts were given to the troops, who listened to lectures on the United States, diplomacy, and the world situation, usually delivered by an officer with a knack for public speaking.

Beginning in early 1941, all new recruits and draftees were handed a slim paperback, entitled *FM 21-100 Basic Field Manual: Soldier's Handbook*. Marshall had supervised the preparation of the book and used "ghosts" on his staff to write individual sections, which he edited. The final result was pure Marshall. The first print run was two million copies, and the booklet was not only a giveaway to all new inductees but was also offered to civilians for 35 cents, postpaid.

The style of the book was so dramatically different from the usual publications of the War Department that the *Washington Post* reviewed it as a standard work of nonfiction. The reviewer noted the informal, direct form of address, couched in the second person.

The book described onerous circumstances in a softer, simpler tone. Military discipline was "not punishment or reprimand" but was invoked in "the spirit of team play." Saluting was not a distasteful nuisance but rather "a courteous recognition of privilege enjoyed only by members of the military service in good standing." It was at once a book of etiquette (three pages were devoted to how and when to salute), a manual of war (detailed instructions on what to do when attacked by tanks), and an explanation of rules (the dire consequences of desertion). At its harshest, it laid out the conditions under which deductions could be made from one's pay—if a soldier was determined to be responsible for "loss or damage to Government property and if you are absent without leave or absent sick, not in line of duty." A man making $21 a month could therefore be docked pay for a lost helmet or for days spent off duty recovering from a dose of the clap—otherwise known as gonorrhea.[34]

The book's tone was that of a scoutmaster talking to a group of young tenderfeet; it was not unlike that of the *Boy Scouts Handbook*, which had been published regularly since 1911 and with which many, if not most, of the men entering the service had grown up. As with the scout manual, the underlying premise was that discipline and regimentation were "based on respect rather than fear."

At the back of the book was a "Glossary of Common Military Expressions"—essentially a seed planted to enhance the culture of a new army. It was mostly common military slang, such as *chow* for food and *dog tags* for identification disks. Also included was the entry: "G.I.— government issue; galvanized iron." *G.I.** was gradually adopted into Army slang in numerous phrases, becoming synonymous with the Army, and later it was commonly used to describe an individual infantryman, just as *doughboy* had been used in the Great War.[35]

The Army itself distributed press releases noting new terms popping up in the camps, and the lesson of this emerging American jargon was not lost on outsiders. One valuable piece of evidence that the young men now engaged in serious military training were taking to their work

---

* The use of the term *G.I.* to describe an individual did not really take hold until the latter half of the war. As late as April 1943, an article on Army slang by Private Richard A. Herzberg in *Word Study* said the use of *G.I.* to mean a soldier himself was "a comparatively rare usage." Toward the end of the war, it carried great significance. General Dwight D. Eisenhower, alluding to the death of Ernie Pyle, war correspondent and confidant of many soldiers, said: "Every G.I. in Europe—and that means all of us—has lost one of his best and most understanding friends."

in good spirits lay in the glossary of slang terms they had invented, reported a correspondent for Britain's *Manchester Guardian* in February 1941. "Even an American expert on contemporary slang would be lost in the Army camps without a special dictionary. In keeping with tradition, the new jargon is cynical, contemptuous of authority and sentimentalism, and hard on symbols of patriotism or heroism. Yet its good humour, combined with lively inventiveness, indicates that Army spirits are high."[36]

Hardly a day passed during the winter and spring of 1940–41 that Marshall, his staff, or the Morale Division did not come up with a scheme to improve the lot of the men in the new army. Reserve officers who were too old for the general call-up were coaxed back into service as volunteers to run recreation programs on the bases. Local priests, ministers, and rabbis were persuaded to allow the men on nearby bases to become part of their congregations until a corps of U.S. Army chaplains could be recruited. Someone came up with a well-promoted plan for locals to invite a serviceman to Sunday dinner. And $12,816,880 was appropriated in March 1941 to build 604 non-denominational chapels on military bases across the country for the use of Catholic, Protestant, and Jewish soldiers.[37]

Despite the problems he faced on a daily basis, by mid-March 1941, Marshall was describing the Army as "magnificent." He had just returned from a tour of southern bases where, he reported, units of all types were crystallizing into a great army. Thanks to the draft, the draft volunteers, and men coming into the Regular Army from the National Guard, he now had his million-man army—1,058,500 to be exact—a fivefold increase in land forces in a year. In celebrating Army Day on April 5, Marshall declared: "In spirit, morale, intelligence and fortitude, we have never had a finer army."[38]

In a commencement address in June 1941 at Trinity College in Hartford, Connecticut, Marshall heaped special praise on the group he called the Selective Service Army for its spirit and intensity of purpose. "I do not believe a military force has ever been developed with so much attention to morale, the spiritual factor."

Morale, in his words, took on the aspect of a secret weapon that would turn the tide in battles to be fought in the future:

> Morale is a state of mind. It is steadfastness and courage and hope. It is confidence and zeal and loyalty. It is élan, *esprit de corps* and determination.
>
> It is staying power, the spirit which endures to the end—the will to win.
>
> With it all things are possible, without it everything else, planning, preparation, production, count for naught.

Marshall also used the Trinity address to make an appeal to the nation. "The time has come for the people to unify completely behind this Army and Navy; to unify as quickly as we can," Marshall said. "The day for bickering has passed . . . These are days for courageous men with unselfish purpose."[39]

The bickering had in fact intensified, and the divide between the forces of isolation and intervention was widening. One of the sparks that ignited a renewed isolationist spirit was the America First Committee (AFC), founded in September 1940 by a law student at Yale University named R. Douglas Stuart Jr., the son of a Quaker Oats Company vice president. The AFC opposed any American involvement in the European war and was harshly critical of the Roosevelt administration, which it accused of pressing the United States toward war. Launched with the help of speeches given by Charles Lindbergh and Earl Browder, head of the Communist Party USA, it grew into a powerful movement in a matter of weeks, attracting a number of powerful businessmen who financed it and gave it wide publicity. Soon, several of the nation's top advertising agencies were spreading its message. The AFC had the editorial backing of an assortment of newspapers, including the *Chicago Tribune*.

A key member of this operation was William Castle, who had been undersecretary of state under Herbert Hoover and remained a confidant of the former president. He openly expressed the belief that Germany would win the war and also advocated a conciliatory approach to Japan. Among the leading big names atop the AFC were automaker Henry Ford, meat packer Jay C. Hormel, and Senators Robert A. Taft and Burton K. Wheeler.

The leaders of the AFC directed a constant barrage of criticism and insult at Roosevelt and his administration. Wheeler portrayed Roosevelt as a tyrant who would take dictatorial control of the country once he had led it into war and was able to get under Roosevelt's normally thick skin. Early in 1941, the United States had enacted the Lend-Lease Act, which offered aid in the form of food, oil, and weapons to Great Britain and other anti-fascist powers. Wheeler described it as "a measure designed to plow under every fourth American boy." FDR's standard response to his harshest critics was skepticism and dismissive humor, but Wheeler's comment enraged him. Roosevelt responded by calling the statement "the most untruthful, the most dastardly, unpatriotic thing that has ever been said."[40]

While Marshall struggled with the problems of equipping and building a new citizen army, the forces of isolation had a new boldness and resolve aimed at ending the draft and sending home the thousands of draftees who had been brought into the Army for one year. Less discussed but of singular importance was extending the service of the National Guard, which had been drawn into federal military service starting in the autumn of 1940. By the summer 1941, Guardsmen made up one-quarter of Marshall's Army. Of the 18 National Guard infantry divisions the first four would complete their single year of service in September and then head home—unless Congress extended their tour of active duty.

Despite all of Marshall's good works, word was reaching Washington in the spring and early summer of 1941 that draftees and Reservists were becoming bored, restless, and resentful in increasing numbers. They had been taken from their families and jobs to be stationed at remote military bases where they did little more than train for hypothetical war and waste time because of a paucity of recreational facilities. At one hot, dry southern post, 8,000 men shared one small swimming pool.

But no matter how many movies a man got to see or how many hours he was free to lay about on his bunk and read comic books, nothing could take away from the reality that to this new recruit, Army basic training amounted to hours of drilling on parade grounds under all weather conditions. The drills were commonly followed by forced marches with a full field pack over rough and sometimes muddy terrain. Recruits were required to memorize the names of hundreds of parts of rifles and other weapons in a prescribed order and then recite them back in a certain cadence. They faced the endless task of keeping their rifle and uniform spotlessly clean and subject to demanding and sometimes capricious inspections, during which one might be punished for an infraction as simple as sporting a loose thread on one's uniform or wearing one's cap at the wrong angle. One's bunk had to be made with sheets so tight that a quarter could be bounced off it and shoes polished to a mirror-like state.[41]

Many of the new men believed that—barring the United States entering the war in Europe—they would head home after one year and go back to life as civilians, remaining in the Reserve for ten years, ready to be called up at a moment's notice if the nation went to war. The men in uniform as well as their families regarded this service as a contract of sorts between the individual and the government.

In fact, rather than a contract it was a compromise between those trying to build a new army and those who opposed the idea. Anyone with an eye on the calendar and an idea of what the original legislation actually said regarding the term of service realized that a showdown over extending the draft was inevitable. With this in mind, Marshall and Stimson emphasized the need to build a new army in the face of an ever-increasing world threat. Marshall avoided the word *peacetime*, preferring to refer to the present as a *time of peril*.

* * *

At the beginning of 1941, the situation for African Americans in the military seemed especially unfair. There was considerable foot-dragging in the calling up of black men, who in terms of stated policy were supposed to have been called up at the same 10 percent level they represented in the population, according to the 1940 census. In fact, they were being registered at a rate higher than 10 percent but called up at only half that rate, and a host of reasons were offered for the disparity, including the shortage of local doctors available for screening examinations and that black Americans tended to be migratory workers and were often harder to keep track of.[42]

The initial reaction, as expressed in interviews conducted by the black press, was positive, and many of the young black men in the first waves of draftees were pleased by their new status as Army privates. "Tell them back home we're doing fine and we have no complaints" was the consensus according to a reporter from the *Baltimore Afro-American* who visited black troops at Fort Bragg, North Carolina. The reporter commented: "This to me was an astonishing phenomenon as I looked about the floorless tents in which the lads are spending the winter, while their white contemporaries a few hundred yards away, languish in snug, freshly built barracks with steam heat." One man, reading the amazement on the face of the reporter, volunteered that living in tents had been fun: "It's healthy. I feel 100% better physically than I did when I came here. It's been great." No matter how substandard the facilities were for the black soldiers—inadequate medical care, a tumbledown barn as a recreation hall, staffed with no hostesses—the reporter could not get the men he interviewed to complain.[43]

Nonetheless, the black Americans who were drafted and ended up in southern camps were subjected to Jim Crow rules of segregated facilities—including seating on trains and buses—and to white law officers and civilians who might take offense at any breach of local laws or customs. Incidents were soon being reported in the black press, and not all the racial inequities took place on southern bases. A March 8, 1941, story in the *Baltimore Afro-American* about Fort Dix, New Jersey, observed: "While more than 20,000 well equipped white soldiers go through daily drill periods with armored tanks, rifles and other modern equipment, the 381 colored selectees of Company E are forced to drill on an acre plot without as much as a broomstick." The article also pointed out that a movie theater was being built on the base for black soldiers, in deference to white men from the South who objected to being seated with black men.[44]

Furthermore, as the defense industries grew, the only opportunities for black Americans appeared to be in janitorial positions. Some companies went as far as to declare that they would hire only Caucasians. One major aircraft company actually wrote back to a journalist who had inquired about black employment and told him that no black Americans would be hired. Three other leading aircraft manufacturers were asked the same question and refused to answer.[45]

In January 1941, civil rights and trade union leader A. Philip Randolph had called for a march on Washington to protest the exclusion of black Americans from "the defense industries and their humiliation in the armed forces." He called on 10,000 African Americans to make the trek to the capital on July 1. The slogan for the march was: "We loyal colored Americans demand the right to work and fight for our country."[46]

Randolph's early attempts at recruiting marchers went well as word spread that the campaign was a bold new initiative by the civil rights movement. The black press announced the march in banner headlines, quoting Randolph's assertion that the black community had "power, great power" to effect change. As this talk increased, industrial contractors went out of their way to underscore their unwillingness to hire black workers. "We have not had a Negro working in 25 years and do not plan to start now," Standard Steel told the Urban League, one of the groups supporting the march. At least one trade union stated that it would not allow black workers to join.[47]

In April, Randolph demanded that Roosevelt issue an executive order to integrate the armed forces and open jobs for black Americans in the war industries. As he wrote in a manifesto that appeared on the front page of the *Baltimore Afro-American*: "President Roosevelt can issue an executive order tomorrow to abolish discrimination in the Army, Navy,

[Army] Air Corps, Marines, and on all defense contracts awarded by the Federal Government, on account of race or color, and discriminations against colored people would promptly end." Clearly implied in Randolph's demand was that such an order—effectively enforced—would serve to end his mobilization of black Americans around the issue of racial discrimination.[48]

Absent a response from the White House, Randolph felt confident about leading 25,000 marchers into the District of Columbia in July. As men and women from across the country signed up for the march, Randolph enlisted the support of the NAACP, and quickly he and his allies began talking about doubling the number and bringing 50,000 marchers to Washington, a city where Jim Crow ruled to the extent that separate air-raid shelters were being built for whites and blacks.[49]

Through the late winter and early spring, Randolph made repeated attempts to meet with Roosevelt, but he was constantly rebuffed. Meanwhile pledge forms were mailed to potential marchers by the NAACP, the Urban League, and other organizations asking for the signatures of individuals willing to march on Washington on July first.[50]

As the day of the march drew closer, the president asked First Lady Eleanor Roosevelt to intervene, because she was much closer to the nascent civil rights movement than her husband. Respectfully rejecting the first lady's advice to cancel the march, Randolph refused to back down.[51]

On June 18, as the march organizers were chartering trains and buses, Randolph and Walter White of the NAACP finally met at the White House with Roosevelt, Undersecretary of War Robert Patterson, and other top military officials. Roosevelt tried to engage Randolph with small talk, sometimes awkwardly:

Roosevelt: "Phil, when did you graduate from Harvard?"
Randolph: "I never went to Harvard, Mr. President."
The small talk went nowhere and Randolph quickly got to the
    point:
Randolph: "Mr. President, we want you to issue an executive

order making it mandatory that Negroes be permitted to work in these plants."

Roosevelt: "Well Phil, you know I can't do that. If I issue an executive order for you, then there'll be no end to other groups coming in here and asking me to issue executive orders for them, too. In any event, I couldn't do anything unless you called off this march of yours. Questions like this can't be settled with a sledge hammer."

Randolph: "I'm sorry, Mr. President, the march cannot be called off."[52]

The president turned to White and asked: "Walter how many people will *really* march?"

As White later recalled: "I told him no less than one hundred thousand," adding: "The President looked me full in the eye for a long time in an obvious effort to find out if I were bluffing or exaggerating. Eventually he appeared to believe that I meant what I said."[53]

The ultimatum posed by the threat of the march forced Roosevelt to frame and sign Executive Order 8802 on June 25, which banned discrimination in defense industries that received contracts directly from the government and prohibited trade unions from keeping black people from membership. The exact wording of the order called for an end to discrimination based on "race, religion or national origin" and established the language of non-discrimination for the coming decades.

The march was called off.

A few days after the order was signed, an editorial in the *Chicago Defender* declared: "If the 'March on Washington' does nothing else, it will convince white America that the American black man has decided henceforth and forever to abandon the timid role of Uncle-Tomism in his struggle for social justice." One battle had been won, but African Americans would continue to wage both an aboveground and a subterranean campaign throughout the war: one for victory over the Axis, the other for victory over Jim Crow.[54]

Indeed, equality was a long way down the road. In April, at Fort Benning, Georgia, the body of a black soldier, Private Felix Hall, was found hanging from a tree in a wooded section of the base, with his hands tied behind him and his feet bound with wire. Although investigations by the Fort Benning military police and the Federal Bureau of Investigation produced no convincing evidence of murder, Lieutenant Colonel Herbert Laux, the camp's provost marshal, thought that Hall had been lynched. However, as no witnesses had come forward, the case was closed, despite demands from the Negro Youth Congress, the NAACP, and other groups that it be investigated as a lynching. The NAACP was unequivocal in terming Hall's hanging "the act of a mob."[55]

CHAPTER 7

THE BATTLE OF TENNESSEE
AND THE "YOO-HOO" INCIDENT

George Marshall thought the United States' burgeoning Armed Forces needed a new series of bold training exercises—exacting maneuvers in a setting that would attempt to approximate the realities of the battlefield, whether it be North America or Europe.

But he also had something else in mind that would clearly differentiate these maneuvers from those of 1939 and 1940: the creation of situations by which the Army could be tested and purged of deadwood. Marshall had previously concluded that before the nation could go to war it had to be ready to replace incompetent officers with rising young officers who had proved themselves worthy. In 1939, before becoming chief of staff, General Marshall had discussed this matter with Colonel Matthew Ridgway, who would later recall that Marshall knew from his own experiences and his substantial study of military history that political pressure and organizational inertia had put many mediocre and incompetent officers in command. A month after becoming chief of staff, Marshall let it be known that many of the Army's line officers were too old to command troops in battle. "Most of them," he told a reporter, "have their minds set in outmoded patterns, and can't change to meet the new conditions they may face if we become involved in the war that's started in Europe."[1]

The U.S. Army of 1940–41 had an old and poorly motivated offi-cer corps, in which advancement was almost always based on seniority. Many National Guard units were led by undertrained men with little leadership ability. Some Regular Army units were led by officers who, for reasons of age, ability, temperament, or dependence on alcohol, were unfit and ill prepared to lead the men under their command. Marshall had already begun to work on this onerous problem, but he felt that the real test for culling would come from observing officers in the field, where their shortcomings would be on full display. Marshall envisioned that the umpires who would judge these training exercises would be especially alert to failures of leadership.

The public failure of the 1939 maneuvers at Bull Run and the lackluster results of the various maneuvers of 1940 made the idea of new and even bigger mock battles a hard thing to sell to the general public, with whom such field exercises tended to be unpopular. The general per-ception was that these operations were "confused and expensive affairs in which troops and vehicles moved haphazardly along the highways, interfering with traffic and disturbing honest working people, or across fertile fields, knocking down fences, ruining cornfields and frightening cattle, as they played at war."[2]

Marshall was undaunted and moved forward with plans for a series of three large-scale maneuvers to be conducted in 1941: in the moun-tains of Tennessee in June, Louisiana in September, and the Carolinas in November. Smaller drills were scheduled for Arkansas in August and in various locations on both coasts for the practice of amphibious and airborne warfare. Marshall was determined that the 1941 maneuvers would be unlike any peacetime military exercise ever staged anywhere.

All of this had to be set up quickly. In early January 1941, the Army gained permission from the U.S. Departments of the Interior and Agri-culture to take over 500,000 acres of national forest and parkland across the country to use as testing grounds for air, gas, chemical, and mechani-cal training around the country. In the words of the *New York Herald Tribune*, these lands, previously set aside for "peace and conservation," were now part of the war effort. By the time the announcement of this transfer of land had been announced, sawmills on the appropriated lands had been shut down, and people with houses in national forests were forced to abandon them. Among the lands taken were five separate tracts in the Kisatchie National Forest in Louisiana.

Unlike conventional war games, the maneuvers would be unscripted, with the commander of each army free to find a way to defeat the other. Live ammunition would be banned; nonetheless, men would die in the maneuvers, drowning in river crossings or being killed in vehicle accidents and plane crashes. A large corps of umpires would roam the mock battlefields, determining who had been "killed" and who was now a prisoner. Regular Army and National Guard units would join forces in these opposing armies rather than being pitted against one another. Which officers were ready to lead them in real combat and which were not would be readily apparent to the umpires.

Calling these maneuvers the most strenuous exercise in American military history, the Army excluded all men who had not yet received at least 13 weeks of basic training, considering them not ready. Troops began to be moved into Tennessee weeks before the exercises were to begin. On March 10, the 12,000 men of the 33rd Division of the Illinois National Guard were sent for extra training before the actual maneuvers to Camp Forrest, 75 miles southwest of Nashville, where they encountered a vast sea of rich, red Tennessee mud.

The maneuver area was 350 square miles in the middle of Tennessee—an area similar to the mountainous regions of Europe where Americans might be asked to fight. The principal feature of the terrain was the Duck River, which was crossed by a number of light bridges and several modern concrete ones. Between these points were fords for vehicles. The banks were generally steep and the bottoms rocky. Between the vehicular crossings, individuals could cross the river at a number of shallow points. The main town in the maneuver area was Tullahoma (population 1,400), which was some 70 miles equidistant from Nashville and Chattanooga.[3]

The emerging popular focus of the exercises would be the Second Armored Division, which the *New York Times* called "a full strength 'Panzer' Division of American troops." Patton had been promoted to Commanding General of the Second Armored Division on April 4th after Major General Adna Chaffee Jr., known as the "Father of the Armored Force," stepped down due to illness (he would die from cancer on August 22). Patton quickly became the most prominent figure in U.S. armored warfare, as well as one of the most colorful of all Army officers.[4]

Lieutenant General Ben Lear was put in charge of the Tennessee exercises. He was a veteran cavalry officer who was born in Canada and had enlisted in the U.S. Army during the Spanish-American War. Lear became an accomplished horseman and a member of the U.S. equestrian team that won a bronze medal at the 1912 Olympics in Stockholm. The epitome of a strict, disciplined commander who did things by the book, he had risen to commander of the Second Army on October 1, 1940—an extraordinary achievement for a man who had entered the army as a private and had neither graduated from West Point nor been born in the United States.

In mid-May, Lear issued a five-page advisory memo outlining the scope and purpose of the Tennessee exercises. After pointing out that maneuver rules were substitutes for actual bullets and bombs, he advised the participants: "Maneuvers are not contests in any sense of the word and will fail of their purpose unless commanders exercise the necessary control of the competitive urge for both themselves and their units. Attempts to determine a winner at maneuvers—that is, looking upon them as contests—is more than pointless, it is detrimental." Lear was simply parroting Army policy, which saw maneuvers as exercises and not competitions.[5]

This directive was sent to Patton, who had a deep and abiding competitive urge. From the outset, Patton was headed to Tennessee to win big and, by extension, to become the spokesman for his brand of hard-nosed, obscenity-laced leadership. Even before leaving Fort Benning, Patton urged his men to do their utmost in the maneuvers. He told them it was time to form habits "stronger than the fear of death" in these exercises, which he said "may be the last time you have to practice." The tactics he would employ in Tennessee could be reduced to the simplest terms: "Hold the enemy by the nose while you kick him in the pants." But Patton also cautioned his men to do nothing that would anger the umpires and reminded them: "The umpires have the job of representing the bullets."[6]

The conditions were meant to simulate a real combat situation. Even the highest-ranking officers in the field would sleep on the ground in pup tents like the men under their command. Enlisted men were searched before they went into simulated combat to make sure they were not carrying any food, because in real combat, one had to rely only on food supplied in the field.

At their height, the maneuvers in Tennessee involved 75,000 troops and 10,000 motor vehicles. The mock fighting was intended to be swift and bold. Commanders were given the freedom to act as they would if fighting in Europe. Umpires were ordered to assess significant casualty counts for inferior officers who led their men into mock slaughter.

On the eve of the maneuvers, a crisis developed when those in charge realized they had no safety pins with which to affix the armbands needed to identify the two armies and the umpires. With time running out, a factory was found in Connecticut that could supply the Army with the 80,000 safety pins it needed. A unit was dispatched to bring the pins back to Tennessee.[7]

Unlike the 1939 and 1940 maneuvers, the ones in Tennessee attracted a lot of press attention and some newspapers sent two or more reporters—one to be embedded with the Blue forces and a second with the Red.*

The first half of June was dedicated to training and small exercises, while the maneuvers themselves aimed to address four stand-alone

---

* The circulation for the nation's 2,400 newspapers was 74 million at a time when the nation's total population was 132 million. *Newsweek*, January 6, 1941, 45.

challenges designed to test the Second Armored Division as it opposed and fought with infantry divisions and other elements. The armored unit was accompanied by the streamlined Fifth Division and the 153rd Infantry Regiment. The Blues, with 46,000 men, were made up of two National Guard divisions augmented with draftees—the 27th of New York and the 30th of Tennessee, Georgia, and the Carolinas. The tanks of Patton's newly nicknamed "Hell on Wheels" division were set to be the star attraction of these exercises and were not even brought in until halftime. In the early morning hours of June 14, a final inspection was done at Fort Benning of the personal effects carried by troops about to depart for Tennessee. The officers wanted to make sure that no live ammunition had been accidentally stowed with the blank cartridges issued for the maneuvers. All units of Patton's Red Army moved into position over the weekend of June 14–15 as the division moved into concealed areas, unloaded its half-tracks (vehicles with regular wheels at the front and tracks at the back) and tanks (which had been sent by railroad freight cars), and got ready to enter the exercise. Patton sent reconnaissance units to gather information, while the bulk of the division provided protection for the unloading operation. Patton himself flew a solo reconnaissance mission over the battleground, while his officers made use of the division's fleet of 500 motorcycles to scout the area. "Consequently," historian Woody McMillin noted, "many Tennesseans got their first close looks at airplanes and motorcycles that hot June weekend."[8]

Patton's arrival in Tennessee was met with press coverage treating him to the kind of breathless prose that he (with the aid of his public relations officers) was starting to achieve nationally. The Nashville *Tennessean* heralded his arrival:

The Second Armored Division is led by Maj. Gen. George S. Patton, Jr., a man who was flying his own airplane in reconnaissance this afternoon, played his first polo game at 11, who attended Virginia Military Academy and finished at West Point, who set a record on the 220 dash at the latter school, who sailed his own boat from Los Angeles to Hawaii, who placed fourth in the pentathlon in the 1920 Olympics, and who was the first officer assigned to the American Tank Corps in the First World War.[9]

The Red attacking force had moved into position in the early morning by the light of blue headlights that were all but impossible to spot from the air. Patton was working to develop new techniques for his tanks that he felt would be essential in actual combat. He pioneered the use of total blackout operations in which even a flashlight or lit cigarette was forbidden, and his division's tents had been dyed black at a Georgia cotton mill so that his men could bivouac without being observed. Patton had begun experimenting at Fort Benning with an early version of this operation that required men to walk in front of tanks using only a white handkerchief to guide the driver. Drivers of other vehicles followed the tanks, and when the dust was heavy and made goggles useless, they often had to navigate by ear, reckoning by the sound of tanks to the front and rear.*

On Monday June 16 at 5:00 a.m. under the cover of darkness, Patton quickly moved his troops and tanks into the area, so they could jump into the first maneuver without warning. As he told a reporter for the Associated Press, "Our greatest advantage is surprise and we plan to make the most of it."[10] The Red Army mounted an attack on the Blue defenders from the southwest. In that first encounter, the Blues were met with 350 tanks and hundreds of other armored vehicles of Patton's Second. Patton was in a lead tank, broadcasting his orders through a radiophone: "Push hell out of them—they're running."

As the two divisions clashed, the mock fighting turned frighteningly real. Rocks were thrown, and Associated Press reporter Rice Yahner reported that some soldiers charged the enemy with fixed bayonets when they were out of sight of the umpires; some soldiers picked up

---

* *Bivouac* is a term then officially defined by the Army as "a temporary encampment without shelter."

acid-filled bottles intended to release smoke when run over by a tank to simulate land mines and tossed them at their opponents. "Several men were reported burned," Yahner wrote, "but none seriously."*[11]

In spite of the Blue Army's tenacious anti-tank defense, the Second Armored Division drove Blue units to positions west of the town of Bell Buckle, Tennessee, surrounded them, and then cut them off from reinforcements and supply lines. During the offensive, one of Patton's tank drivers swerved to avoid hitting a civilian truck, rode up on the sidewalk, lost control of the tank, and tore through the front brick wall of Bell Buckle's two-story town hall bringing down all two stories of the structure. Bricks and much of the contents of the second floor were dumped onto and into the tank. The rescuers had to dig the tank commander out of the wreckage, but no one was injured save for the tank commander who had a small bruise on his head. Patton's response was that the accident was not the fault of the tank driver since "the damn city hall was not on the map."[12]

A reporter watching the event from an aircraft flying 500 feet above the action said the tightening of the circle around the trapped division appeared "cool and calculating, efficient and deadly." The reality on the ground was less dramatic; the Reds had indeed encircled the Blues but were unable to deliver a knockout punch because the umpires brought a halt to the exercise six hours after it had started.

By the end of the day, the Red Army reconnaissance and small armored vehicles were on the prowl, probing soft spots in the lines of the defending Blue Army. Patton also waged a verbal war that was meant to inspire fear in the defenders. He expected that he would be able to deliver "Caesar's message"—I came, I saw, I conquered (veni, vidi, vici)—less than 24 hours after the attack by his army, which he was now

---

* The mock land mines used in Tennessee could be dangerous. Another more dangerous type of mock land mine then being used by the Army was triggered by a trip wire; a common clothespin (with a wire hinge) snapped shut, setting off an electrical charge triggering a small block of TNT, which exploded, spewing nails with some force—enough to drive a nail through an inch-thick piece of oak. "Engineers Improvise 'Clothes Pin' Mine," Evening Star, June 18, 1941, 13.

terming "the strongest force ever devised by the mind of man." Hilton H. Railey, one of two reporters covering the events for the *New York Times*, wrote: "Mobility, shock and psychology are on the side of the daring ebullient Reds, man—and fire—power on the side of the Blues."[13]

Despite Patton's declarations and the good press he was getting, the outcome of this segment of the maneuvers fell far short of what Patton had hoped for, as the performance of his Second Armored Division was less than a ringing success. Some outside observers termed the exercises a failure, because Patton's "unstoppable" armored division was unable to move across the landscape with the speed and agility the commander and his officers had promised. A headline in the *Washington Post* declared: ARMORED UNIT TAKES BEATING IN TENNESSEE MANEUVERS.[14]

A United Press reporter invoked the officers of the Second Armored who claimed that the division was "woefully handicapped" by the rules of the maneuvers, which did not allow tanks to run across fields or through wooded areas. The tanks were confined to roads, most of which were too narrow to allow tanks to turn around. For understandable reasons of public relations, the War Department was doing all it could to limit crop damage.[15]

While both armies claimed victory, the umpires declared neither side a winner, pointing out that the Red Army had lost about 400 of its tanks as well as many of its men in the simulated fighting. Frustrating to both the men fighting and the press following the action, all a man had to do to "destroy" a tank was point a simulated anti-tank weapon at it—the Army equivalent of a kid cocking his index finger at another kid and saying: "Bang! Bang! You're dead." The Blue defenders attracted their share of praise in the umpire's report, which noted: "An armored division operating against a skilled and determined defense in a difficult terrain finds itself canalized, denied freedom of movement and opposed by effective anti-tank defense."*

Patton had captured the commander of the Blue force but had driven his tank through a simulated artillery barrage to do so and had,

---

* *Canalized* in this context means to be conveyed through a duct or channel.

it was ruled, become a casualty himself. Patton was incensed, arguing that the .37 mm gun that had theoretically brought down the command tank was not powerful enough to do so. Protests notwithstanding, the performance of Patton's division in that first major exercise was largely unimpressive to the judges, who stood by their ruling. But for the press at the event, it was very exciting, especially if they kept their eyes on Patton and their ears tuned to his steady stream of obscenity and hyperbole.[16]

Patton's mouth became an element of the mock war in Tennessee. He had learned to fly a small plane and now had a pilot's license that permitted him to oversee the maneuver area at low altitude to check on the units under his command. Captain Norris H. Perkins, who served under Patton, later noted that at one point the airborne general observed a group of his tanks bunched together in a swampy area, inviting disaster. Using a loudspeaker mounted to his plane, he let loose with a stream of profanity that, as Perkins put it, both "cowed" his men and "edified" the locals.[17]

On June 17, the third day of the maneuver, waving his pistol above his head, with powerful air horns blasting, Patton again led his armored division, with 2,300 vehicles and 11,000 officers and men back into action. The division had light tanks, each with a .37 mm cannon protruding from its turret, jeeps, 6x6 personnel carriers, ambulances, supply trucks, and engineer units carrying sections of pontoon bridges. A reporter for Nashville's *Tennessean* newspaper watched as the division raced across middle Tennessee and saw it as "a simulated duplication of the tours of terror that have swept across Europe and Africa."[18]

The tankers went on to a quick, decisive victory less than three days after the offensive began despite the fact that the umpires had for the second time declared Patton himself a casualty because of his exposure leading his tanks. Later, some reporters made the inflated claim that this attack was Patton's first victory of World War II. As one author framed it, "His victory marked the first time in the annals of American military history that a full armored division had engaged in maneuvers and had an opportunity to test itself in combat."[19]

Even though the umpires gave Patton demerits for becoming a casualty, the press seemed to love his tactics. Nationally syndicated columnist Henry McLemore, one of the reporters on the ground with the troops in Tennessee, noted the changes he was observing in modern warfare as evidenced by the Second Armored Division, whose officers put themselves in the thick of the action. "General Patton of the Second Armored has aroused in this reporter a suspicion that he exposes himself to danger as casually as a strip teaser does to the front row orchestra," he wrote. The columnist was convinced that in actual warfare, Patton would dress up in an Uncle Sam costume and stick his head out of the tank to be sure he was the first to draw fire, giving the impression that he was either incredibly courageous or incredibly foolish.[20]

On June 23, an exercise that was supposed to last for two days was over in seven hours as this next-to-last maneuver began as Patton's forces feinted to the right and left of a line held by the Fifth Division and then drove into the middle of the line and, as Jerry Baulch of the Associated Press described it: "struck with the full force of its thunderbolts to split the enemy lines." The attack was called off but not before the men manning anti-tank guns were declared dead by the umpire. One of these hapless defenders was baseball slugger Private Henry Greenberg, allowing the *Tennessean* newspaper to run the front-page headline: HANK GREENBERG 'KILLED!' TANKS COMPLETE 2-DAY JOB IN SEVEN HOURS.[21]

The final mock battle of the maneuvers began on June 26 just as Secretary of War Henry Stimson arrived in Tennessee. He chose to ride in a jeep—"the army's midget open car"—rather than in the larger command car reserved for his use. Photographs of Stimson distributed by the wire services all showed him with Patton, who had been Stimson's aide when he was secretary of state in the Hoover administration, underscoring the respect the two men had for each other.

Stimson witnessed the third and final maneuver, whose objective was to capture Tullahoma. Patton's tanks and half-tracks roared toward the town at top speed ignoring the ground rules of the exercise by ripping through fences, leveling fields of cotton and corn, and knocking down fences and stone walls. The defenders were quickly backed to the outskirts of Tullahoma and drew all of their light artillery in a circle, with the infantry packed behind it. One observer compared it to "driving jack rabbits into a corral and then beating them to death." Like the one before it, this exercise, which was meant to take place over a two-day period, was finished in a matter of hours. Patton was again the winner, but the victory was personally disappointing because he was ruled killed by a simulated land mine.[22]

One high-ranking defending officer told a reporter: "We had scouts out—on motorcycles, in cars, and on horses—but we could not do much about stopping the Reds. At times our scouts were so close to the enemy's mechanized forces that they could count the number of tanks and cars. However we could not move our antitank defenses fast enough to stop them. All we could do was to hold them off as long as possible and then watch them tear through."[23]

Patton bragged to Stimson that while his division had traveled significant distances, "in some cases over 110 miles, every fighting vehicle in the division, except two tanks and a scout car, got to the place it was supposed to be in time to deliver the attack."[24]

These long marches not only tested Patton's machines but also his men. Captain Perkins later recalled four marches of 100 or more miles under the cover of darkness staged so that the unit could reassemble at an appointed location and attack the enemy army at dawn. "In each case," he recalled of these night operations, "we were up all day, all night and all the next day." Movement on the ground was treacherous even when the roads were good because the tanks moved at high speed at night with only tiny, blue blackout lights that were invisible to aircraft but that only gave a few yards of illumination to the road ahead. As Perkins sadly noted in his 1988 memoir, "One tank missed a curve, hit a cliff and killed all four men in the crew."[25]

As the maneuvers ended and the Army moved into the area with a special squad whose job was to pay for the damages left in the wake of the battle for Tullahoma, the umpires had their final word, which was in large part disturbing to Patton. Despite the big win, Patton was upset by the criticism and penalty of the umpires who thought it improper for him to lead the charge when he should have been managing his forces from a command post some 15 to 25 miles from the battle in order to lead his forces into combat. To Patton, this critique was nonsense. He asserted that a commander could not see how his men are behaving in the field from a desk far removed from the combat zone. Patton's response, framed a few days later, was to demand that all generals of mechanized units lead from the frontlines, or as he told his officers in a general meeting: "You can't move a string of wet spaghetti by pushing it from the tail end."[26]

Nothing was less photogenic to a nation preparing for war than an image of a commander sitting at his desk and cradling a telephone headset. So when *Life* magazine put Patton on the cover of its July 7 special defense issue, he was posed standing in the turret of his command tank, resplendent in what *Life* referred to as his Green Hornet costume: football helmet, shoulder holster, pistol, and carefully tailored, non-standard uniform. The image was stunning.* For the nation—or at least the millions who subscribed to *Life*—the new army now had a face. It also had a narrative: *Life*'s Defense Issue lauded the performance of the Second Armored Division and declared it and the other emerging tank divisions a match for Hitler. The issue featured dozens of images of the Second Armored Division in operation, including a picture of men leading tanks with handkerchiefs in a total blackout, along with dozens of other images of the Second Cavalry Division in operation.[27]

   Life editor Henry R. Luce wrote to Patton to tell him how much he and the division had done for the magazine. Patton responded that the article had done at least as much for the Second Armored Division. "The important thing in any organization is the creation of a soul which is based on pride, and no member of the division reading your magazine could fail to be filled with pride," Patton wrote.[28]

---

* The image did bring its share of derision. One writer pointed out that Patton was taking liberties with regulations by wearing a shoulder holster with side plates of ivory or bone instead of cross-hatched walnut, and then asked, "What use has a major general for a pistol, anyway?"

Patton's respect for his troops, a majority of whom were draftees, seemed to reach a new high after the Tennessee Maneuvers. On July 8, Patton assembled his division in the immense auditorium he had ordered to be built at Fort Benning, so that he could address all of his men at once. He used four large maps to show what the division had done in Tennessee and went on to praise his men for their performance. He encouraged them to think and rely on their own imagination and judgment. He then began talking about the division shoulder patch that he had wanted his men to wear. "As it turned out," Patton remarked, "the shoulder patch was not necessary because your soldierly bearing, meticulous attention to military courtesy, and your neatness in dress told the world to what unit you belonged." He went on to say that if the men were able to keep up their good work, their patch "would cause as much dread to the nation's enemies as it caused pride among its friends."[29]

Patton continued to generate headlines well after the maneuvers were over. On July 8, he honored two privates and a sergeant for having captured a general and his staff during the Tennessee Maneuvers. The men split the cash reward, but the real winner was Patton, who was now mastering the art of publicity.[30]

If Patton was the star of the show, he had competition from baseball slugger Hank Greenberg, whose unit took part in the maneuvers. Autograph seekers swamped Greenberg in every small town his unit passed through. Finally he appealed through the Associated Press: "I'll appreciate it very much if the public will just let me get lost in the Army and forget about me. It's awfully nice and considerate of my friends, but all this publicity is doing me more harm than good. I just want to be another one of the boys." The appeal failed, and Greenberg had to fend off autograph seekers and well-wishers for the rest of the exercises.[31]

Part of what Greenberg experienced may have been attributed to native hospitality rather than celebrity worship. Hospitality seemed to have been the order of the day in Tennessee. "Soldiers who participated in maneuvers had thick rule books. Citizens had three rules: don't feed the soldiers, give them directions or give them a place to stay. We broke all three," said native Woody McMillin, author of the definitive work on the Tennessee exercises.[32]

Besides making Patton into a household name, the Tennessee Maneuvers—especially the finale—were a catalyst for creating a new type of anti-tank unit. Within a week of his return to Washington from Tennessee, Stimson announced the formation of 22 "tank destroyer battalions," calling them a radical new type of division. These battalions, Stimson said, would be unlike any units used by any army in the world and would feature self-propelled artillery, to be developed and ready for testing in the Carolinas later in the year. Stimson alluded to what he had seen in Tennessee as justification for these new battalions.[33]

Perhaps the best news reported from the maneuvers concerned the degree to which the men involved—Regulars, Guardsmen, and draftees—had adapted to the difficult life in the field and proved they could take its rigors. Various harsh external factors had come into play, but the dust was probably the worst, edging out the mud of the early days of the exercises. The *Boston Herald*'s Bill Cunningham reported from the maneuvers: "The country roads and trails back in those hills are unpaved, and the dust clouds have been so thick from the marching columns and rolling trucks that the cars were forced to use their headlights in the broad light of day and the soldiers all but choked for something to breathe."[34]

Americans were now hearing about soldiers who had previously griped about tough steaks and endless weeks of drills enduring a stiff dose of life in the field with little complaint. Lewis B. Sebring of the *New York Herald Tribune* reported that food was delayed in reaching the soldiers, sometimes because of actual difficulties in supply caused by impassable back-country roads and sometimes because of orders from headquarters, meant to test the men so they might learn to skip a meal or two as they would on a real battlefield. Sebring pointed out that on some nights the men were lucky if they got two hours of sleep, and when they did sleep were likely to wake up with painful chigger bites.[35]

And yet, despite the privations, the men were in better spirits in the field than in the relative comfort and boredom of an Army base—and better able to show their abilities. Morale seemed to improve in direct proportion to the distance the units got from the drill fields. Sebring told his readers that the nation should have no second thoughts as to the fighting ability of its men. "Mentally and physically they are ready for whatever the future may bring. They are personally a splendid group of men and now they need only the encouragement of the public to put them across in the job of defense for which they are being trained." Sebring was quick to add that this was not just his opinion but the consensus of the experienced military men he had spoken to during the maneuvers.[36]

What was missing from the official accounts of these war games was that their emotional component belied the thought that these games were meaningless to the men who played them. Captain Norris H. Perkins later recalled that "grievances caused by infractions of rules and disputed umpire decisions brought about fist fights, fixing of bayonets and firing of tinfoil pellets from blank cartridges." Perkins quickly added: "A fine time was had by all."[37]

The sick call rate for the 75,000 men in Tennessee was 1.7 percent, as compared to the normal rate of 3 percent on military bases. As the chief medical officer for the Second Army reported these figures, he noted: "Soldiers on maneuvers don't have time to get sick." But there seemed to be more to it than that. Rice Yahner, who had covered the maneuvers as thoroughly as any reporter, looked at the numbers and commented: "The withering heat and choking dust that covered everything wherever the Army went in the Cumberland Highlands would've laid low less hardily trained men."[38]

These soldiers "fought" 24 hours a day, ate from rolling kitchens, and drank chemically purified water from questionable sources. They slept on the run but never in the open, where they could be run over during the night by a tank or other vehicle. Soldiers slept in barns, corncribs, and front porches, to name a few of the safe places the tide of battle left them. Even with 10,000 vehicles operating in the maneuver area, there were only seven accidental deaths. The desertion rate was in the single digits, and there was a lone suicide.[39]

The War Department also learned some important lessons in Tennessee. One was the value of light, nimble civilian aircraft, a dozen of which, including several of the famous J-4 Piper Cub, flew during the maneuvers. They were paid for by their manufacturers and were used in a variety of ways, including surveillance, communications, transporting key officers, and directing artillery fire. These trim and tiny planes were easy to handle and could be hidden under a tree with just a touch of camouflage. During the maneuvers, pilots landed on 102 different fields, roads, and pastures to demonstrate the Piper Cub's singular capabilities. When one of the light planes signaled the end of a maneuver to the tank divisions, one armored group did not understand the signal, so the pilot landed in a field and caught up to the moving tanks by taxiing down a road to deliver the news.[40]

Before the exercises began, Lieutenant General Ben Lear, commander of the Second Army and the officer in charge of the maneuvers, had warned: "Elimination of unfit, inefficient, and incompetent leaders is of greater importance than the elimination of defective and inefficient weapons." During the maneuvers, he had reported a widespread lack of discipline throughout his command—with the single exception of the Second Armored Division. Among other things, Lear was upset with men who did not maintain a soldierly appearance.

Lear was a widely respected no-nonsense leader—who soon found himself in the headlines, serving for a good portion of the summer as an unwilling symbol for what was wrong with the Army.

Sportswriter Robert Creamer lived through this period and recalled it later in the context of baseball. "The country was still pretty lighthearted on the surface, as interested in batting streaks and pennant races as it was in war and the threat of war. The military action that got the most attention in mid-summer was the conflict between a general and some soldiers who yelled 'Yoo-hoo!' I still laugh, thinking back on the enormous fuss raised in the summer of 1941."[41]

After the maneuvers ended on Sunday, July 6, 1941, Lear was playing golf at a course in Memphis, Tennessee, when a convoy of 80 vehicles and 300 men of the 110th Quartermaster Regiment, a unit of the Missouri National Guard, passed through as it was returning from the exercises. The convoy slowed down, and members of the unit made catcalls to a group of young women playing on the course who had turned to watch the convoy pass by.

As Lear addressed the ball, he heard soldiers yell, "Fore!" and "Hey buddy, do you need a caddy?" Lear exited the tee and headed to the road, where he ordered the convoy to stop. When he began to speak, he was mocked by some of the men on the trucks, to whom he appeared to be nothing more than an old man in white golf shoes and seersucker knickers yelling at them. According to several sources, vile language and offensive hand gestures ensued.[42]

Officers present quickly realized Lear was in fact their commanding general and listened as he ordered them back to their base at Camp Robinson, 145 miles away, to await further orders. When they arrived at sundown, they found orders instructing them to drive back to the Memphis airport, where they camped for the night. The next morning, Lear assembled the men, delivered a severe dressing-down, and emphasized their lack of discipline and lack of respect for civilians. Lear ordered the men to get a good night's sleep, because the next morning, they would return to Camp Robinson. However, this time, 15 of the 145 miles of the trip would be made on foot, in three segments of five miles apiece.

The punitive march was conducted publicly and the temperature hit the 97 degrees Fahrenheit mark along the return route. The wire services were there with their cameras, and an Associated Press photograph showed Private George Morrow of St. Louis lying by the wayside, a victim of heat exhaustion. The photograph helped fuel a firestorm of criticism from Congress—not of the troops, but of what Representative Everett Dirksen of Illinois called "grouchy golfing old generals." Dirksen defended the soldiers as healthy, vigorous American boys acting naturally and was highly critical of General Ben "King" Lear. Some members of Congress also seemed particularly incensed that Lear had been playing golf at the time of the incident. Days later Representative William F. Norrell of Arkansas announced on the floor of the House that he had just received word that Lear was "still on the golf links" and then said, "He is not the kind of general we need, standing on the brink of war. He apparently is engaged all the time in playing golf."[43]

A member of the House sent a telegram to Lear demanding to know what right the general had to punish the men without a proper hearing. Lear's response was immediate and clear, emphasizing that it was his job to raise all the men under his command to "the highest attainable standards of combat and combat efficiency." He said he would not tolerate loose conduct and rowdyism. Lear also made the point: "I am responsible also that members of the Second Army treat the civilian population with respect and consideration." He added that the behavior of the men on the golf course was "in marked contrast to the gentlemanly and soldierly behavior of the vast majority of the men who had taken part in the maneuvers."[44]

Congress demanded an official investigation by the War Department, which remained detached. Reporters with access to high-ranking officials learned that nobody from Stimson and Marshall on down was concerned by Lear's disciplinary method. Insiders termed the 15-mile hike a busman's holiday after the rigors of the maneuvers. On July 17, the War Department officially ruled that Lear had acted within his authority and no reprimand would be issued.[45]

Despite what many regarded as a career setback, Lear's next big assignment was to lead his Second Army in the Louisiana Maneuvers. His opponent would be Lieutenant General Walter Krueger, who would lead the Third Army. Like Lear, Krueger was born outside the United States, in West Prussia, which was then part of the German Empire, and had joined the Army as a private and served in the Spanish-American War. Between them, they now commanded close to a half million privates, non-coms, and line officers. Both men would spend the summer of 1941 creating complex field armies, while facing, as one writer put it, "great problems of administration and supply to say nothing of moving in strange country—to demonstrate how they will function as a great machine of modern war."[46]

The first wave of arms and equipment for a large army was now available or on its way. At the beginning of May, Roosevelt called for a new expansion of the defense effort, specifically demanding that munitions, ships, and aircraft be produced "in even larger quantities and schedules assigned to them." He wanted every industrial machine capable of contributing to defense to be put to work on a 24-hour-a-day, seven-day-a-week basis, speeding up the arms effort.[47]

By mid-1941, the ranks of the Regular Army had risen to 1,460,998 men: "The ground forces in the continental United States form four armies of nine army corps and twenty-nine divisions, and an Armored Force of four divisions, soon to be increased to six," Marshall reported in his *Biennial Report on the US Army* released on July first, adding that: "The Air Force includes 54 combat groups, and the initial equipment requirements of these forces will be met with the stocks now on hand and under manufacture, plus those to be produced from funds set up in current estimates."[48]

The maneuvers in Louisiana would be an even bigger test of whether this collection of men and machines actually worked.

CHAPTER 8

"OVER THE HILL IN OCTOBER": TREASON, SABOTAGE, AND THE VOTE

As the Tennessee Maneuvers played out in June, and as the number of men drafted was quickly adding up, with an additional 105,200 slated to be inducted by the end of July, George Marshall gave his fullest endorsement of conscription to date. "I believe the Selective Service provides the only practical and economic method of maintaining the military force . . . I think, with all my heart, that Selective Service is necessary to the maintenance of a true democracy."

Among other things, Marshall was signaling that the Roosevelt administration was mounting a campaign to extend the term of service for those already drafted beyond the initial 12 months and to increase the term of service for the National Guard and Reserve troops who had already been called up. Some 957,000 men, all told, needed an extension of their terms of service; the first of them were to be sent home in September. Only two divisions had fewer than 30 percent draftees in their ranks; most had more than 50 percent, and some had as high as 85 percent.[1]

Without an extension for the men already in uniform, the Army, preparing for its maneuvers in Louisiana and the Carolinas, would face a large-scale disintegration. Marshall warned Congress in late July that such disintegration was all that was needed to encourage the Japanese to continue their armed aggression in the Pacific. The public and the press were becoming increasingly focused on the looming national battle to hang on to the Army's men—who had gone off saying or singing: "Goodbye, Dear, I'll Be Back in a Year!"[2]

Around the time the administration began the discussion of the need to extend terms of the draft, the world situation changed radically in a day. Germany launched a surprise invasion of Russia on June 22, 1941, after which the American Far Left dropped its support of Hitler as a former ally of Stalin's. Nevertheless, the isolationists seemed to gain strength every time the word *extension* was uttered by a member of the administration, and numbers of draftees wrote to Roosevelt or members of Congress opposing the action. *Newsweek* reported that on July 21, several men stationed at Fort Meade, Maryland, had been confined to quarters after writing letters to Senators Wheeler and Taft protesting moves to extend their one-year term. Reports included complaints by National Guardsmen; one guard unit passing through Fredericksburg, Virginia, tossed penciled notes from its trucks stating: "One year's enough! Send this to your newspaper." One note stated that while the general in charge had said that his men did not mind serving another year, nobody had asked the men themselves.[3]

Marshall's effort to boost morale with movies, reception centers, and better food in the mess halls was being muted by the undeniably unattractive reality of life on an Army base. "An Army post in peacetime is a dull place," novelist Carson McCullers wrote in her 1941 novel *Reflections in a Golden Eye*. "Things happen, but they happen over and over again. Perhaps the dullness of a post is caused most by all the insularity and by a surfeit of leisure and safety, but once a man enters the Army, he is expected only to follow the heels ahead of him."[4]

Despite the resistance, Roosevelt continued to warn congressional leaders that the failure to extend the service of draftees beyond a year would mean the disintegration of the Army at an exceedingly dangerous period in American history. Syndicated columnist David Lawrence, among others, felt the president had done a bad job of keeping the American "home front" on his side. "It has been assumed by the administration that those who disagreed on foreign policy either were sympathizers with the fascist idea or totally unaware of the dangers of a Hitler victory." Lawrence argued that a large group of Americans was not inclined to fascism and understood the evil of Hitler but simply wished to stay out of a European war and preferred not to send their sons, husbands, and sweethearts off to prepare for that war. He thought the Roosevelt administration was ignoring this group, which could have a major impact on the next election.[5]

The campaign to end conscription and keep the United States out of the war created unusual alliances. The isolationists did not shy away from using the "Negro issue" in their campaigns against the nation entering the war in Europe. On June 4, 1941, the *New York Daily News* carried an image of a Ku Klux Klan cross burning juxtaposed with a photo of black sharecroppers. "Should We Fight to Save the World . . . While These Things Continue at Home?" read one caption, while another declared: "Negroes Have No Freedom of Speech, No Freedom from Terror in the South." The tabloid advised its readers: "Tell your president, senators, and congressmen, that you want democracy to work properly at home before you fight." The images and copy for the piece, which appeared on the paper's opinion page, were supplied to the tabloid by the New York Chapter of the America First Committee.[6]

Roosevelt and to a lesser extent Marshall and Stimson were obliged to play a con game of sorts in which they portrayed the Army they were amassing as more like the Civilian Conservation Corps than a peacekeeping force to stop Nazi troops trampling Europe. "No civil leaders dared call them *soldiers* as if there were something shameful in the word," said Eric Sevareid, the young reporter for CBS News, just back from Europe. "An impression was given that they were herded together for some reasons that had to do with moral upbringing and physical training; few were so bold as to suggest that their job was to learn to kill."[7]

In July, the battle over extending the draft involved Stimson in a headline-grabbing clash with Democratic senator Burton Wheeler from Montana, who had become the most tenacious and loudest critic of Roosevelt's ongoing efforts to make the United States the "great arsenal of democracy" by supplying military aid to countries fighting Nazi Germany and Imperial Japan. In a March speech, Wheeler had declared that Roosevelt's policies were the soil that would produce a postwar "Hitlerized America—even though Hitler will be dead and buried."[8]

Under Wheeler's postal frank, a million antiwar postcards, usually costing a penny apiece to mail, were posted in July, containing material designed to illustrate the folly of Roosevelt's policies, including direct quotes from Charles Lindbergh, former ambassador Joseph P. Kennedy, former president Hoover, and Roosevelt himself, from his October 30, 1940, assurance to America's parents that their sons would not be sent into any wars overseas. The postcards asked that recipients write to the White House and demand that President Roosevelt keep the nation out of war. The messages echoed the party line of the America First Committee, and the printing and addressing of the postcards had been managed and paid for by the group.[9]

An undetermined number of these postcards were delivered to soldiers in training camps, and many more were sent to their families at home. A few of the men in uniform replied, including a first lieutenant in the infantry named Alford T. Hearne, who pointed out that it was against Army regulations for him to express a public opinion on staying out of war. "But regardless of the Army regulation, I do not feel myself qualified to advise the president of the United States on political affairs. Neither do I have the time to devote to studying political affairs, as my present job requires that I devote my entire energy to its accomplishment."[10]

Furious about the postcard campaign, Roosevelt decided that Stimson should go after Wheeler. At a press conference, Stimson said of the postcard: "This comes very near the line of subversive activities against the United States—if not treason." Roosevelt then backed up Stimson's assertion by saying that he agreed with the recent headlines of two newspaper editorials—ON DANGEROUS GROUND and MR. WHEELER GOES TOO FAR—that had appeared, respectively, in the *New York Times* and the *New York Herald Tribune*. Wheeler responded in kind, regretting that he had not gone far enough: "The only regret I have is that I wasn't able to send postcards to every mother in the United States."[11]

To the accusation that postcards had been sent intentionally to men in the military, Wheeler replied that this was totally unintentional—an honest response, because he did not control or have direct access to the mailing list. He then accused Stimson and Roosevelt of mounting a smear campaign against him, rising on the floor of the Senate to declare, "I accept these low and perfidious charges of 'near treason' as another badge of honor!"

Wheeler's rhetoric against the president intensified; he now called FDR one of the "wolves of war," terrifying the American people. Some of the rhetoric in the Senate was as defiant as Wheeler's: "Stick to it, Brother Wheeler! Standup! Never mind how many are with you. I'll be with you if you go to a concentration camp. I'll go with you and there will be two of us standing there together," exhorted the isolationist Republican senator Hiram Johnson, of California.[12]

Wheeler also said in a prepared statement that the secretary of war could probably be excused on the grounds of his age and incapacity, and that he was "ga-ga." He also repeated his mantra that the administration was actively "seeking to plow under every fourth American boy."[13]

Newspaper columnists were quick to engage with the issue of the postcards. Dorothy Thompson, who in 1933 had been the first American to see and report on Hitler's overall plan for conquest and his desire to exterminate Jews and other minorities, sent a dispatch from London entitled: "The Unexplainable B. K. Wheeler."* She not only supported the use of the term *treason* to characterize his actions but also sucked the wind out of Wheeler's sails. "War is now on our doorstep, but Mr. Wheeler thinks he can fill the vacuum by postcards sent to servicemen. If only we can get enough sabotage in our armed forces, he apparently thinks we shall certainly have peace. This is a highly gratifying thought to our enemies."[14]

---

* Thompson was also among the first to be banned from Germany. She had called Hitler an ordinary man. Her knowledge of and reporting on fascism no doubt influenced her husband, Sinclair Lewis, when he wrote his dystopian 1935 novel *It Can't Happen Here* about a fascist takeover of the United States.

Syndicated columnist Henry McLemore mocked Wheeler by envisioning an American army in which all actions had to be ratified by a postcard plebiscite. "We may well see the day when, under the Wheeler influence, the writing desk is just as important [a] piece of military equipment as an antiaircraft gun, and a soldier's side arms will include a blotter and a pen wiper."[15]

Wheeler threw fuel on the fire on July 20, when he told the *Washington Post* that large groups of privates had gone AWOL at two undisclosed camps—124 at one camp and 24 at a second—and that no action had been taken at either because the sentiments of the men who did not desert were with the deserters. Wheeler claimed the information had reached him by telegram but refused to either show the telegrams to the *Post* or to reveal the location of the two bases in question.[16]

On July 30, against the advice of members of his staff, Stimson apologized for using the term *treason*, and Wheeler accepted the apology. Stimson's prepared statement took some pressure off, but it was only a momentary reprieve. The apology was seen as a major win for the most determined isolationists, who claimed the smear against Wheeler had blown up in the face of the administration. "The smearers have gone too far; and the objects of their smearing—Father Coughlin, young Charles Lindbergh, and now Burton Wheeler—are bigger and more respected in the nation than ever before," intoned Father Coughlin's *Social Justice* magazine.[17]

Now Marshall invoked the kind of inflammatory term that had caused Stimson to apologize. He infuriated the isolationists by calling the opposition to extending the tours of National Guardsmen and selectees *sabotage*. Marshall testified to the Senate Committee on Military Affairs on July 24 that an organized movement was afoot to subvert the Army by urging draftees to protest to Congress to prohibit their extension. Marshall pointed out that Army regulations forbade soldiers from attempting to influence legislation and then asserted forcefully: "We have got to deal with it: we've got to treat them as soldiers. I regard these moves as sabotage. We cannot have a political club and call it an Army. I won't have these boys victimized. We cannot have that kind of an Army."[18]

Marshall had no plans to apologize for the use of the word *sabotage*. One source for his claim was General Hugh Drum, now heading the First Army, who had reported to him that some of the 1940 draftees were threatening to desert if the original 12 months was extended. A slogan popular in the camps was "Over the Hill in October," presented as an acronym (sometimes *O.H.I.O.* but more commonly *OHIO*), which suggested that conscriptees intended to desert at the end of their 12 months, beginning with those drafted in October 1940. The letters *OHIO* began appearing on the walls of latrines, on road signs, and painted on the backs of military vehicles.

Nobody has ever been able to pinpoint where this campaign started. Primary instigators were thought to be America Firsters and other isolationists, but just as likely it was a spontaneous idea among the men, and it spread, much to the glee of those opposing American involvement in the war in Europe, including those spreading Axis propaganda. The administration believed that if the Wheeler postcard had not actually started the movement, it had been a catalyst in moving it forward, and its very existence put an already nervous Washington on notice that mass desertions might occur should the draft be extended.[19]

On July 21, 1941, Roosevelt asked Congress to declare a "national emergency" allowing the Army to substantially extend the term of service of draftees, Reservists, and National Guardsmen for whatever period the legislators deemed appropriate. FDR warned that if two-thirds of this new Army went back to civilian life, almost a year would pass before its size could again reach one million. Referring to the 1940 draft legislation, he declared: "I do believe—I know—that the danger today is infinitely greater." The next day, Marshall threw another log on the fire. "An emergency exists," he warned, "whether or not the Congress declares it. I am asking you to recognize the fact that the national interest is imperiled."[20]

Working with Grenville Clark, who had again set up a "war room" in a local Washington hotel, Representative James Wadsworth of New York renewed his sponsorship of legislation to extend the terms of military service and was the lead Republican in gathering support in the House. Wadsworth then assembled a group of House Republicans to listen to Marshall explain what was at stake for the Army and the nation. One member responded to Marshall by saying, "You put the case very well, but I will be damned if I am going to go along with Mr. Roosevelt." Marshall's response was quick and to the point: "You are going to let plain hatred of the personality dictate to you to do something that you realize is very harmful to the interest of the country!"[21]

After seven days of heated debate and failed counter-proposals that would have shortened the extension, the Senate approved a joint resolution with the House of Representatives on August 7 authorizing Roosevelt to extend the term of service by 18 months. The vote was 45–30, as 21 abstained or chose to duck the vote, claiming they were ill, out of town, or "just-away." The Senate was not willing to declare a national emergency, which would have given the president a blank check. Rather, it decreed that the "national interest is imperiled"—and the isolationists saw the change in language as a minor win.

The Senate vote came hours after a Gallup Poll was released revealing that the nation was split on the issue: half wanted the extension, 45 percent wanted the men released, and the other 5 percent expressed no opinion.[22]

The lead story in the next issue of *Life* magazine addressed the problems now facing the military, including "the growing restlessness and boredom of the great civilian army" and the issue of whether it had the will to fight. Although the number of potential OHIO deserters was believed to be relatively small, the *Life* magazine report claimed that half the soldiers in a 400-man sampling of four separate units threatened to desert if their period of service was extended. One man said he considered the base nothing more than a "concentration camp" and said he was prepared to desert and head for the Mexican border if the extension was passed. Another told of having already gone AWOL when the base commander refused to give him a few days leave to attend the birth of his first child. Nearly 95 percent of the men in one unidentified unit believed the president's claim of a national emergency was nothing less than "a complete sham."

Besides cataloguing the deficiencies of military bases, including the paucity of recreational facilities, *Life* described the ineptness of young officers, who commonly got lost in the woods while leading their men. *Life* also reported increasing violence on the bases, including Fort Bragg, North Carolina, where a week before the article appeared a riot between black soldiers and the military police resulted in the deaths of a white sergeant and a black private as well as a number of injuries. The *Life* article implied that the draftees overall were neither willing nor able to defend their country.[23]

On August 18, 1941, the same day that the *Life* article appeared, its sister magazine, *Time*, published an article that reported low morale affected two-thirds of the 1.5 million men now in uniform, and troops in a Mississippi camp booed the newsreel footage of Marshall and Roosevelt. In a letter dated one day after the magazines' issue date, Marshall alluded to these articles, playing up the morale problems of the Army as one of the reasons he was "in for a hard winter."[24]

Although not publicly revealed at the time, the unidentified unit discussed in the *Life* article was the 27th Division of the New York National Guard, whose 408 privates in five regiments had been interviewed by the magazine. The 27th was a division made up predominantly of men from the New York City metropolitan area and the Hudson River valley and given especially close coverage by the New York newspapers. The *New York Times* sent young reporter Anthony H. Leviero south with the unit when it was moved to Fort McClellan, Alabama, in 1940. Leviero's many dispatches covered everything from the 27th's lack of equipment and weaponry (the men practiced throwing grenades by pitching rocks) to reporting that the men of the unit were of a "high order" of intelligence, based on Army testing, but in contrast to *Life*, he never once hinted at low morale.[25]

The 27th had distinguished itself in the Tennessee Maneuvers and was given an award for its efficiency. NEW YORK'S 27TH TERMED BEST IN ARMY EXERCISES was the headline in a *Chicago Tribune* article, which quoted General Lear saying: "Morale is very high. An extraordinary example of this is found in the 27th Division. The day after payday only 40 men out of 17,000 were absent without leave. To me this is an indication of the high type of soldier we are developing in the army today."[26]

With *Life* magazine's circulation of 13.5 million and *Time*'s close to that number, the articles had a significant impact, especially because they appeared in American mailboxes just after the draft extension bill hit the floor of the House on August 11. The collective power of Henry Luce's *Time*, *Life*, and *Fortune* led Robert Hutchins, educator and former chancellor of the University of Chicago, to observe that "Luce's periodicals had more of a collective impact on the American mind than the country's entire system of public education."[27]

In Washington, the House was much more divided than the Senate. Members of the House had a host of collective and individual reasons to oppose the draft extension. Different groups opposed the bill: the Republican leadership; Democrats who felt the extension violated the implied "contract" with those in uniform; a handful of pacifists who opposed all defense bills; a cohort of members of both parties who opposed anything that Roosevelt favored; and 17 Irish-American members opposed simply based on their anti-British sentiments.

The man given the task of moving the bill forward was Sam Rayburn of Texas, the Speaker of the House, who had been elected to that position the previous September to fill the vacancy created by the passing of Speaker William B. Bankhead. In early July 1941, Rayburn had told the president that a majority of the House did not approve of the draft extension and that he was among them because it violated the terms given to the men who had gone into service with the 1940 legislation. The following day, Marshall and Stimson met with Rayburn for more than an hour to discuss the matter. No public statements were made at the time, but Rayburn was clearly convinced to change his mind, based on his sudden support for the move to extend.[28]

With Marshall working as a point man, Rayburn now worked behind the scenes for days in tandem with Republican Wadsworth and his fellow Texas Democrat, Lyndon B. Johnson, to create the majority he had promised the president he would aim to achieve. On August 8, four days before the vote, Johnson made an emotional appeal on the House floor: "I am confident that, at this time, every American knows his country is an island in a world of danger . . . If we vote down this proposal we will send two-thirds of our present Army home ... [at a time when it is] reaching a point where we may begin to think of it as approaching adequacy." He then urged his colleagues not to sell out the welfare of the United States for the sake of gaining a few votes back home.[29]

Wadsworth was the key factor in changing votes. Representative Carter Manasco, a freshman Democrat from Alabama, was wavering because of the implied one-year contract, but he praised Wadsworth's efforts. Nearly 40 years later, he remembered how Wadsworth "sat on the table down in the Well dangling his legs ... telling how [General] Marshall had told them that the Germans had asked the Japs to come in in March." Until Wadsworth stepped forward, Manasco "thought it was going to lose by ten or fifteen votes ... [That was the] only speech I ever heard that swayed votes."[30]

By comparison, the House Democratic leadership performed erratically. Not only had Speaker Rayburn and Majority Leader John McCormack of Massachusetts come out against an extension when it was first proposed, but they had also failed to keep an accurate head count as the bill advanced. Not until August 6, after FDR, Marshall, and others had left for a top secret meeting with British Prime Minister Winston Churchill in Placentia Bay, Newfoundland, did McCormack inform the White House that 45 Democrats were against it, 35 were undecided, and the bill appeared headed for defeat.

The House debate and vote was set for Monday, August 11, but Rayburn postponed it for a day to honor Representative Albert G. Rutherford, who had passed away over the weekend. With Roosevelt out of town, Rayburn, Johnson, and Wadsworth used the additional day to roam the corridors of Capitol Hill pressing for votes.

At 10:00 a.m. on August 12, the final debate began on the resolution to extend the time of service by 18 months, already passed by the Senate. The capacity crowd on hand to witness the vote was opposed to the extension and included a number of men in uniform who wished to return to their civilian lives. The debate dragged on for ten hours without a break, continuing through both lunch and dinner, as amendments designed to soften the impact of the bill went down to defeat, aided by isolationists who demanded an "all or nothing" vote on the resolution.

Finally, at 8:05 p.m., the clerk began to call the roll. Then, as required, the clerk went back through the list, checking the names of members who had not answered in the first roll call. Finally, almost an hour later, the vote was completed and tallied: 204–201 in favor of extension, with 97 members abstaining.

But before the vote could be announced, which would have made it official, New York Democrat Andrew L. Somers rose to his feet demanding recognition. Rayburn obliged but quickly regretted the move, as Somers switched his vote from aye to nay, opening the door for additional defectors.

Then Rayburn recognized Missouri Republican Dewey Jackson Short, a leader of the anti-draft forces and a key member of the isolationist Committee to Keep America out of the War, who sensed a shift taking place and called for a recapitulation or confirmation of the vote to make sure that no counting errors had been made. If Rayburn had made an error calling on Short, Short made an offsetting error by calling for "recapitulation," instead of "reconsideration." Under a reconsideration, members would have been able to change their votes; a recapitulation, however, simply allowed for a recount of those votes already cast. Rayburn acted quickly to start the recapitulation and prevent members from changing their votes.

"Does the gentleman desire that before the vote is announced?" Rayburn asked.

Short agreed, apparently not understanding what Rayburn was doing. The confirmation of the vote then took place, and when it was done, the tally remained the same and Rayburn quickly announced the results: "On this roll call, 203 members have voted aye, 202 members nay, and the bill is passed." He then banged his gavel, and in his so doing, under the rules of the House, the vote was frozen and final.

A discordant chorus of cheers, rebel yells, boos, and catcalls erupted from both the floor and the House gallery.

"Mr. Speaker," Short cried out. "I was on my feet . . ."

Rayburn looked at Short and repeated the count.

Short again exclaimed, "Mr. Speaker, I wanted to move to reconsider the vote by which the bill was passed."

"The gentleman, in the first place, is not eligible to make that motion. Only a member from the winning side could do it," was Rayburn's curt reply.

Another opponent of the extension rose to question this, but Rayburn would have none of it and for the second time banged his gavel to end the protests and signal that the bill had passed—by a single vote.[31]

The next morning the *Baltimore Sun* reported on "scenes of high drama which are witnessed seldom in that historic chamber" and devoted more than 80 paragraphs in attempting to give a moment-by-moment explanation of what had actually transpired on the floor of the House during the eight hours of debate. Readers needed nothing more than the headline to understand the outcome: DRAFT PASSES HOUSE BY 203–202 VOTE: SCENE DRAMA PACKED.[32]

In the hours and days following the vote, Rayburn was accused of wielding a "quick gavel" and, depending on one's point of view, of either bending, exploiting, or skillfully observing the rules of the House to ensure the outcome he wanted. By the margin of a single vote, the draft extension would be made, and Rayburn had engineered one of the slimmest—and most important—wins in the history of the United States Congress.

The House vote was immediately dubbed the "gamble of the decade" by political columnist David Lawrence, who collated the vote by party and warned the 133 Republicans opposed to extension that they might pay the price, especially if the nation was at war in November 1942. Some editorialists at the time actually charged the Republicans with trying to make a "party issue" out of Army training and readiness. "This effort to inject party politics into the issue is no credit to Republicans. Far from it," said an editorial in the *St. Louis Post Dispatch* the day after the vote was taken. "The state of the army is no more a partisan issue than is the state of our national defense in general."[33]

Rayburn immediately announced he was headed for Texas and seclusion. His protégé, Lyndon Johnson, had learned that knowledge of the sometimes arcane rules of Congress was a valuable tool in amassing political power. The administration now knew it had men on Capitol Hill it could rely on in a pinch in the months ahead.

But the bill still had to go back to the Senate for confirmation before it could be sent to the president. If any changes were made, and the bill coming out of the Senate was not identical to the House bill, the House would have to vote on it again, with no guarantee that it would survive another vote. In order to ensure that the Senate vote was as strong as possible, those in favor of the bill sent airplanes out to pick up as many friendly senators who were now outside Washington as possible. Two pro-extension senators—Sherman Minton of Indiana and World War I veteran Harry S. Truman of Missouri—held the floor and delayed the vote until a minimum number of ayes was on hand to pass the bill. The final tally was 37–19,* and the bill was sent to the White House.[34]

The isolationists, now insisting they be called non-interventionists, cited the razor-thin margin of victory for extension as "proof" that Congress was opposed to entering a foreign war. The one-vote majority also helped fascist propagandists overseas, who claimed the American people were not behind the president and his anti-fascist agenda. "The House vote on the draft extension bill . . . pleases the Nazis enormously," was the lead to an editorial in the *Springfield (Mass.) Republican*, which added: "The authorized spokesman at Berlin has expressed his satisfaction."[35]

Citing both the homegrown and foreign propagandists, who saw the close call in the House as a defeat for Roosevelt and the Army, Gladstone Williams, a columnist for the *Atlanta Constitution*, spoke for many when he wrote: "No doubt the country is also confused over the House results."[36]

If morale among the troops was as low as it seemed to be at the time of the *Life* article, the enactment of the extension pushed it even lower. In late August, 25 soldiers from Army bases in and around Washington were

---

* The low total number of votes was ascribed to the number of members who "paired" with a member on the other side of the issue, with neither having to record his vote when the vote was taken and with neither vote counted in the vote totals.

interviewed by a team of reporters. The number-one reason stated for poor morale according to these men was the extension. A man identified as Soldier 15 boiled it down to nothing less than a "bad break"—one that would take time from their young lives that they would never regain. Others had harsher words. "I'm sick and tired," said Soldier 4, who had been in for four months. "This army does not seem to have any aim: we don't know what's expected of us."[37]

On August 18, FDR was back in Washington after his no-longer-secret meeting with Churchill in Newfoundland, which had led to the signing of the Atlantic Charter, a bold statement of principles about a post-war world of freedom and self-determination that had been announced to the world on August 14. Immediately on his return, he signed the extension into law, extending the draft for the men in uniform by months and setting the time of service of new draftees at 30 months. The legislation also increased the base pay for draftees after their first year of service by $10 a month. The battle proved to be, as Roosevelt speechwriter and biographer Robert E. Sherwood later put it, "one of the narrowest escapes of Roosevelt's wartime. He had almost let it go by default."[38]

As the nation and official Washington digested the *Life* magazine article, its veracity was challenged by many, including *New York Times* publisher Arthur Hays Sulzberger, a member of Grenville Clark's ad hoc committee that had originally framed the 1940 draft. Sulzberger felt the *Life* report was grossly overblown. At the urging of Marshall, who was alarmed by the article's findings, Sulzberger assigned Hilton Howell Railey, 49, to examine the story with an eye to debunking it. Railey's beat on the newspaper was America's preparedness for war, and he had covered the Tennessee Maneuvers, where he had concluded that "the morale of both the foot and the mechanized soldier is higher than ever, 'at fighting pitch.'"[39]

Railey had already established himself as a dynamic figure with a Zelig-like ability to work his way into history. A veteran of the Great War who had written for the *Times* as an officer in 1918, he had developed a flair for public relations and become the spokesman for Admiral Richard E. Byrd's Antarctic expeditions and later recruited Amelia Earhart to fly across the Atlantic, helping to launch her to international fame. When Earhart disappeared in the Pacific Ocean in 1937, Railey regretted his role in making her a household name. The list of his brushes with fame included an offer in the mid-1930s from a representative of the Third Reich to become Hitler's public relations man in the United States, an offer he turned down.[40]

As Railey was beginning his investigation, on August 14, Marshall wrote to Bernard Baruch, the New York banker, who was a key adviser to Roosevelt on military preparedness and war production, to discuss the effect of the two magazine articles and the debate over the extension. "It has been intensely interesting and quite tragic to watch the violent change in morale commencing with the recent debates on the prolongation of service. Up to June we really had a remarkable state of morale, but seemingly in a moment with these violent discussions, parents became stirred up and individual soldiers were taught to feel sorry for themselves." He then summed up the dilemma facing him: "There is no more delicate problem than troop morale, and with such a slender margin of public approval to back us, it is no easy matter to build up the highly-trained and seasoned fighting force that we must have available as quickly as possible. However, we are going to do it if too many of us do not lose our tempers."[41]

Marshall's ability to control his well-known temper and veil his anger in this moment was crucial. More than a decade would pass before he expressed publicly how he actually felt at the time. "People have forgotten entirely the hostility of that time," he said in a 1957 interview. "*Life* magazine played it up at great length—this OHIO movement . . . Certain phases of democracy make it quite a struggle to raise any army—probably should, I guess. But in the great tragedy the world was in at that time, it made it doubly hard."[42]

The question of morale now loomed more important than ever. The Army's first public response to the *Life* and *Time* articles came from General Ben Lear, then in Arkansas getting his Second Army ready for the upcoming maneuvers in Louisiana. He stated that the morale of America's fighting forces was in direct proportion to that of the citizenship; and if it was low, it was not the fault of the Army. "If the morale is poor it is only because the morale of the people is poor."[43]

In Denver the following day, Marshall made the same point when he stated that Army morale had been excellent until public debate on the question began, adding that Army morale was dependent on the morale of the country and its unity of purpose.[44]

The day before, August 19, 1941, the Associated Press in a totally unexpected story revealed that despite the provisions of the draft extension bill, the Army was planning to release a selected 200,000 draftees, Guardsmen, and Reservists before Christmas, meaning that these men would have served, on average, less than 18 months rather than the 30 months just authorized by Congress. Unnamed military sources said the announcement would give a pronounced "lift" to troop morale. These early releases were not automatic; men had to request them. Those with a proven hardship would be released first, followed by married men and those who would be 28 years of age or older by July 1, 1942. This was good news to a lot of older draftees who wanted to resume their civilian careers, including 30-year-old baseball slugger Hank Greenberg.[45]

Allowing the men over 28 to be discharged made sense. In his report, Hilton Railey suggested in the strongest words possible that the loudest malcontents he encountered were draftees over 28, and their removal from the service would in and of itself help boost morale.

The next day C. P. Trussell of the *Baltimore Sun* published a front-page story with the banner headline ARMY MORALE IS CAUSE OF WIDE CONCERN, which claimed the morale problem was so huge it went way beyond the Morale Division. Taking into account many reports from the field, which he had been allowed to see, Trussell determined that the foundation of the problem was that the men making up the great draft force were still "civilians," who had not yet been separated from the rest of the country's population. Trussell, who clearly had strong sources within the Army, added that congressional debates and votes figured heavily in the lowering of morale among the "civilians in uniform."[46]

Nor was there vindication for the Army in the confidential "Railey Report" delivered in early September. Railey and Sulzberger brought a copy of the report to Washington, where they met with Roosevelt and promised that it would not be released to the public. "I, for one" Sulzberger later wrote, "did not propose to make Hitler a present through the columns of the *New York Times*." The new report made the *Life* article, in Sulzberger's words, "look like a Sunday School version." Sulzberger indicated that FDR was deeply disturbed by the report, which was immediately classified SECRET by the Army and kept out of sight for years after the war. In 1987, Lee Kennett noted in his book *G.I.: The American Soldier in World War II*: "Even today its existence is not widely known among military historians."[47]

Railey had interviewed 1,000 men and found that more than 90 percent of them expressed hostility to their officers and to the government. The "Railey Report," like the *Life* magazine report before it, blamed the sorry state of affairs in the Army on poor leadership, lax discipline, inferior training, a lack of proper equipment and, of course, low morale. Railey said the extension and the closeness of the vote in the House had lowered morale even further. "Now it is obvious that the army is not truly fit to fight unless the men in it are inspired by some belief in the things for which they are fighting," Railey wrote. He concluded: "With extraordinary uniformity . . . the morale of the United States Army, as I've sampled and verified it from the Atlantic to the Pacific, is not reassuring."[48]

As a firsthand observer, Railey was appalled by the behavior of undisciplined draftees and officers, whom he witnessed becoming drunk and disorderly. When Railey asked one officer if he and his fellow officers were afraid of the men under them he replied, "We are scared to death of them." One general was so appalled by the level of disloyalty among the National Guardsmen that he told Railey he thought the National Guard needed to be disbanded immediately. At Fort Meade, Maryland, the enlisted men believed that they were "superior to their officers in everything except rank."[49]

This conclusion had also been reached by Secretary Stimson, who in a diary entry of September 15, 1941, was quick to admit that low morale had gotten lower with the extension. "The trouble has come from the fact that we have [been] trying to train an Army for war without any declaration of war by Congress and with the country not facing the danger before it." Marshall also agreed with Railey about amusing and entertaining the troops. In a report to the president, he wrote: "At the same time that we leave no stone unturned for the protection and welfare of our soldiers, we must not forget that it is not the American ideal to bribe young men into the patriotic service of their country by thoughts of comfort and amusement. Moving pictures and soda water fountains have their places, but endurance of hardship, sacrifice, competition, and the knowledge that he is strong and able to inflict blows and overcome obstacles are the factors that in the last analysis gave the soldiers morale."[50]

Contradicting the *Life* and Railey reports, Stimson claimed after traveling 14,000 miles inspecting the troops that Army morale was as sound as ever and that when the Army went into action, there would be no problem of morale. He predicted that a day would arrive soon when the nation would actually draw strength from the patriotic spirit of its armed forces.[51]

Stimson was not alone in his feelings about morale. CBS Radio reporter and columnist Eric Sevareid, who had just returned from London, read the *Life* article and immediately headed to the nearest Army base, where he ate with and listened to the men. To be sure, Sevareid said, they bickered and complained and cursed the Army, but they did it out loud. Reflecting back on his firsthand observations of the French army, he reported: "I have learned something about soldiers in Europe. These men [the American enlistees] will not desert . . . It is when men say nothing to one another, when they bend silently over their food, when they lie listlessly in their bunks in the evening, that spirits are breaking, that the danger point is reached."[52]

Two conflicting narratives thus gripped official Washington: one that low morale had a hold on the Army that would be difficult to deal with and the other that a high degree of morale existed that would come to the fore when an actual war began.

By his actions, Marshall appeared to have acted on the former while believing in the latter. He had already realized that one of the Army's key morale problems stemmed from the simple fact that commanders were not giving their men a proper sense of responsibility for what they were doing in the field. He learned that the men in many units were ignorant of what their tactical purpose was in the maneuvers in which they were engaged.

Marshall had already embraced Railey's key point that the Army had a "magnificent opportunity" to use basic training to teach largely uneducated young Americans what war was about and the threats at play in the world. He initiated a program of 15 lectures prepared by West Point educators that were to be made an integral part of basic training. The lectures began late in the year and each was followed by an open discussion of what was going on in the war.

And yet the OHIO impulse seemed to grow as the effect of the extension set in. A group of men calling themselves Disillusioned Soldiers wrote a letter from "Somewhere in Louisiana" to the *Hartford Courant* complaining of deteriorating morale after the extension. "This is not a feeling of just Connecticut boys but a national feeling throughout this maneuver area, and it's really immense. All you see is placards which say OHIO."[53]

Attention to the movement also spread to the African American press and persisted close to the October desertion date. Columnist Charley Cherokee of the *Chicago Defender* noted in his National Grapevine column of September 13 that black Americans everywhere were asking for a black member to sit on the Army's Morale Division and that the lack of one was causing low morale among black troops. "It must gladden Hitler's heart to know white and colored American soldiers are whispering the chant OHIO in increasing volume."[54]

*   *   *

Through all of the turmoil of the summer of 1941, Marshall quietly and with little public attention established and staffed a new institution that had first been outlined in a report created in 1938 but then shelved. The concept was to develop a new group of junior officers from the body of the men already in the service—the best of the enlisted men, Regulars, and draftees. In late 1940, Marshall had begun to express the belief that the next war would require a new breed of intelligent, motivated junior officers specifically trained to be platoon leaders able to successfully lead 50 to 60 men into battle. He argued that a group of Officer Candidate Schools could be created without great expenditure and housed on existing Army facilities. Marshall also firmly believed such a plan would not only strengthen his new army but also improve the morale of its ever-increasing mass of enlisted men if they appreciated that some of their officers had come up from the ranks.

The idea challenged military dogma of the time and met strong opposition from the highest level of Marshall's own staff and, most significantly, from Henry Stimson. Along with Grenville Clark and many of the individuals who had gotten the 1940 Selective Service Act passed, Stimson had been involved with the Plattsburg Plan during World War I, when tens of thousands of college graduates were trained to be officers in special camps, beginning with the prototypical camp in Plattsburg, New York.

The earlier program was known officially as the Citizen Military Training Camps, and its graduates were dubbed "90-day wonders" because of the swiftness with which they were moved into officer ranks at all levels, up to and including a few colonels. Stimson wanted to adapt the old Plattsburg system, in which businessmen, who were mostly college graduates, self-nominated themselves to the new army. Marshall, who had actually worked at one of the camps in 1916 and seen some of the Plattsburg graduates fail on the battlefield, felt the system was flawed and vastly inferior to the idea he now championed.[55]

Stimson and Marshall were so profoundly at odds on the issue that Marshall was forced to play his strongest hand, threatening to quit if Stimson's position was allowed to prevail. He told Stimson to get himself a "Plattsburg man" and let him run the Army. Stimson backed off. In early 1941, Marshall ordered then lieutenant colonel Omar Bradley to Fort Benning, with a promotion to brigadier general and instructions to design the Officer Candidate School (OCS) program. Bradley immediately began designing a system based on the rigor and routine of West Point, including a similar code of honor. As military historian Joseph R. Fischer later summarized: "'The Benning method,' as Bradley's teaching pedagogy came to be called, was simple: demonstrate the skill desired, explain it, then have the cadet do it."[56]

The first OCS opened in July 1941, and the hunt was on to identify men who had been in uniform for at least six months and were intelligent, ambitious, and able to lead. Roughly one in 100 would qualify for entrance into OCS.[57]

Military historian Geoffrey Perret later reflected on Marshall's decision, noting that giving natural talent a chance to rise in a people's army was only right and that, among other things, eventually it proved to be a tonic to enlisted morale. "OCS represented the Napoleonic approach, a modern way of telling soldiers that their general assumed each of them carried a marshal's baton in his pack."[58]

The first group of men to enroll in the Officer Candidate School "were a fine, selected group of noncommissioned officers," Bradley reported to Marshall on July 26. However, at the program's inception, he also warned that because of the added service time required with an OCS appointment and a commission: "Many of the best qualified selectees are not interested in attending the candidate school. Apparently they want to finish their year and get back to their jobs."[59]

Now that the nation was in the early days of creating a new junior officer corps at Fort Benning and several other locations, the focus of the Army turned to Louisiana, where men who were already officers—both newly minted and veteran—would be tested.

CHAPTER 9

STAGECRAFT:
THE EXTRAORDINARY
PREPARATIONS FOR THE WAR
IN LOUISIANA

The Louisiana Maneuvers were the largest of the 1941 mock battles and the centerpiece of Chief of Staff Marshall's plan to give the Army fresh vigor, a higher level of morale, and a new cohort of leaders. Marshall also saw Louisiana as a place to show the nation what it was like to go to war and what it would take to win that war.

The chief of staff also hoped this big event would focus the nation's attention on the Army's weaknesses, especially its shortages of equipment. It was one thing to say the Army was short of tanks, quite another to show the shortage in an actual battle simulation where, as had been the case in 1940, small trucks were deployed with cardboard signs reading TANK.

Even during the planning stages, the Louisiana Maneuvers were labeled the largest-ever military exercises in size and scope. More than 19 full divisions and some 400,000 men were to be made ready to engage in a mock war, which was approximately the same number of troops on active duty in the United States Army in 2019.

The main event in this battle would take place in September and would follow warm-up maneuvers beginning in May, staged in Louisiana as well as Texas and Arkansas. The two forces pitted against one another in the main event would be the Second and Third Armies. The maneuvers were ballyhooed by newspapers as the first clash between two complete armies in this country since the Civil War. Fittingly, the Second Army was drawn primarily from eastern and midwestern units, while the Third was from southern, southwestern, and western states.

The planning and logistics challenges of the Louisiana Maneuvers were huge and unprecedented. To support the exercises, Camps Polk, Livingston, Beauregard, and Claiborne were hastily constructed or embellished in Louisiana, along with Army Air Corps fields at DeRidder, Lake Charles, Alexandria, Pollock, and Pineville. By early August, Louisiana governor Sam H. Jones was able to boast that his state had received more new defense facilities over the previous year than any other state in the union.[1]

Starting in early May, the Army mounted a public relations campaign to alert the American public to the upcoming maneuvers. Major General Robert C. Richardson, an affable, talented, and highly decorated cavalryman, had been handpicked by Marshall to head the new Bureau of Army Public Relations, and he sold the maneuvers like a coming attraction, promoting the plan to use parachutists for the first time in any American war game. No fewer than 500 of them would drop from the skies over Louisiana and float to the ground ready and armed for mock battle. Actual tanks, including those under Patton's command, as well as mounted cavalry divisions would participate.[2]

The staging would borrow a page from Hollywood. Smoke canisters would be released to shroud battlefields, large bags of white flour would be fired from artillery or dropped from aircraft to simulate attacks and mark direct hits while loudspeakers would blast the recorded sounds of battle.

In mid-July, Major General Richardson went to Hollywood to confer with movie industry leaders to arrange to have the maneuvers filmed and the films shown in theaters. Richardson said that he wanted maximum coverage and would resort to censorship only when it was absolutely essential: "We want people to see how their money is being spent, and we want no secrets other than those which, if told, might endanger the lives of our soldiers."[3]

Although the Army had already obtained the rights to exercise on federal and state lands, including the massive Kisatchie National Forest in Louisiana, the plan called for a much larger combat zone. Beginning in May, more than 100,000 letters were typed, addressed, and mailed to landowners whose property would be part of the battlefield. Recipients were told to stay in their houses and on their farms when operations were nearby and that there would be trespassers on their lands, but the Army would do everything possible to protect their property. Landowners, many with properties of as little as an acre, were told that they would be fairly compensated for any damages, including livestock killed or stolen during the operation. Files were created to track every response to the letters. The Associated Press reported that the task at hand made the Louisiana Purchase of 1803 look like a simple real estate deal.[4]

May was also the month when the Army began its campaign to raise the money needed to fund the maneuvers, which would require the majority of its training budget. On June 30, Congress awarded nearly $13 million for training, almost all of it earmarked for the maneuvers. Some agreed to the expenditures with trepidation. During and after the 1940 maneuvers, all the errors had made the Army look bad. When one senator questioned support of new exercises in 1941, Marshall shot back: "My God, Senator, that's the reason I do it. I want the mistake down in Louisiana, not over in Europe, and the only way to do this thing is to try it out, and if it doesn't work, find out what we need to make it work."[5]

In the spring of 1941, George Marshall, Henry Stimson, and the chief of training, Lesley McNair, expanded their big-picture event. At the end of June, Marshall announced that he was now taking dramatic steps to weld American land, sea, and air forces together into a closely coordinated fighting team, which would be put to its first real test in September. As logical as this seems in retrospect, at the time it was headline-making news in a country where separate branches of the service saw themselves more as rivals than allies. Roosevelt, a former secretary of the Navy, was prone to favoring that branch and relished being known as a "Navy man." Now, in Louisiana, Navy dive-bombers would be paired with Army ground troops for the first time. At the same press conference, Marshall announced that a high-ranking Marine officer was being put in charge of an Army-Marine task force to prepare for future amphibious landing operations. Marshall stressed the fact that he was following Germany's lead in creating a powerful and united armed force.[6]

While Congress wrestled with whether or not to extend the service of the draftees and Reservists, troops from all over the country began their trek to Louisiana and staging areas in neighboring states. Many units would remain in the field for five months. Enlisted men could possess only what they could carry, which would mimic the conditions of a real war. Everything else, including woolen uniforms, would be left behind or sent home for the duration. None of the big pyramidal tents would be taken, only pup tents. The Army planned to set up mobile cobbler shops to fix damaged boots at the front.

Some units arrived in Louisiana with large numbers of men who had not yet gone through basic training, which usually included 63 days of marching, drilling, firing weapons, and going to school. In one case 18,500 men from the Upper Midwest underwent this 63-day program in just 25 days, during which no passes or furloughs were issued. Although the men were given new uniforms, there was no laundry service during their early days in Louisiana and when available, their clothing had to be sent to Shreveport to be cleaned, which they paid for themselves. Many of the men carried emergency first aid kits in the field that were marked "1917." John Thompson, the reporter following this story for the isolationist *Chicago Tribune*, concluded that these conditions prompted "a rash of desertions."[7]

The First Cavalry headed in from Fort Bliss, Texas, with 7,000 horses, 17,000 men, and hundreds of trucks but almost immediately got hopelessly bogged down near El Paso after a cloudburst stopped the unit's scout cars and reduced the speed of the men on horseback from five miles an hour to three. General Walter Krueger, who was watching, let the unit have it: "Conditions here are bad, but they are nothing to what you will get in Louisiana. There is no excuse for scout cars bogging down. Let a man get out on his two tootsies and find a suitable trail." If the horse cavalry was wary of bad omens, this was one.[8]

The Second Army would get the bulk of its food shipped from Camp Robinson in Arkansas, while the Third Army would get its supplies—100 train carloads a day—from New Orleans. Just the food being shipped through New Orleans was estimated to cost $325,000 a day at the peak of the maneuvers and required a crew of 2,500 to unload and load onto other trains, which would take it to one of three "regulating stations," where it would be rerouted to other trains and then onto trucks for delivery.

An anti-aircraft regiment from Missouri, which had been moved into Texas in early June, reported that due to a lack of motor vehicles and weapons, it was able to operate at only 20 percent efficiency. At the most basic level, the men were supposed to have been trained with the new Garand rifle, but the only arms they had obtained thus far were the old 1903 model Springfield rifles. They had yet to see even a single example of the Garand. The long list of shortages included blankets and was featured in a report published by John L. Mortimer, Army editor of the *Houston Press*. Mortimer asked: "You think the colonel ought to have a headache?" He then answered: "He did. But for three weeks recently the army didn't even have enough aspirin in the camp hospital." He then went on to call the unit, the 203rd Coast Artillery, a "splendid organization" with a high degree of morale; it had, who were from his viewpoint, the hardest-working group of officers and men he had seen anywhere in Texas.[9]

According to the colonel in charge of the operation in New Orleans, his goal was not to accumulate a large supply of food at one spot but to keep a smooth level of supplies flowing to the regiments at the "fighting front." Based on an early estimate, 14 million pounds of fresh oranges would pass through the depot in New Orleans.* In addition, a million pounds of ice a day were needed to keep the food fresh on its journey. The amount of ice needed over the 60-day period of the maneuvers, if frozen into a single block and dumped into the North Atlantic, would have been big enough to show on maps.[10]

Bread for the half million men in Louisiana became an item of highest priority. Some 1,100 soldier bakers were brought in to bake 250,000 pounds of bread every 24 hours in kerosene-fueled ovens in a 500-foot-long bakery erected at Jackson Barracks in New Orleans. The bread came out of the ovens in circular thick-crusted loaves about a foot in diameter with a two-week shelf life.[11]

Fresh potable water—a gallon a day for each person in the maneuvers—required a virtual pipeline of trucks for the two massive armies. Heavily chlorinated water created from ponds and groundwater could be used in emergencies, but even when flavored to taste like lemonade, it was soon discovered to be almost impossible to stomach. Besides the food and drink for humans, the many thousands of cavalry horses also had to be fed and watered.

Fueling the 25,000 military motor vehicles of all types that would pour into the combat zone, as well as the large number of aircraft, was one more huge challenge. According to one early estimate, the ground vehicles alone would devour some 600,000 gallons of gasoline a day, with a commensurate amount of motor oil. Fuel would be brought into the area by railroad tank cars, and the gas would be pumped into tank trucks using transfer pumps, known as "cows," with eight nozzles that could fill as many trucks parked in a circle at once. But when the railcars

---

* Attempting to vividly describe the amount of food to be consumed led to some strange images: " . . . the eggs to be consumed would require the services of a champion egg-a-day hen for 100,000 years; the coffee to be brewed would be enough to float a 20,000-ton Navy cruiser; the hot dogs to be consumed during the exercises, if laid end to end, would stretch from Norfolk to New Orleans, with enough left over to encircle both cities" *Atlanta Constitution*, August 4, 1941, 4.

were not available, gasoline would have to be trucked into the area from the rear in ten-gallon drums.[12]

By the end of July, 20 million acres of land had been acquired in East Texas and Louisiana. The Third Army, based in San Antonio, had worked with local officials to obtain permission for Texas properties. One letter granting permission read: "You can dig it up or blow it up. I don't care. You have to have the land to do your job." A press release claimed that the letter was typical of the average landowner. Clearing these land rights had been carried out by an ad hoc group of state employees, college students, and National Guardsmen recruited on the spot because of their working knowledge of property law.[13]

At the same time, the state of Louisiana was undergoing a transformation. Toward the end of the summer, the Army Corps of Engineers came into the combat zone to repair roads, reinforce bridges, establish train and truck unloading platforms, and set up telephone and telegraph networks. Particular attention was paid to evacuation routes for casualties, both real and simulated. Army planners anticipated 136 real deaths and some 40,000 hospitalizations for real injuries and serious illnesses during the event and planned to place ten Pullman railroad sleeping cars throughout the combat zone to speed the afflicted to hospitals or evacuation centers.[14]

Local officials working with the Army shut down the gambling dens and houses of prostitution in "open" jurisdictions, notably the "sin cities" of Lake Charles and Leesville. Harder to eliminate were "trailer girls," who were arriving in large numbers in the maneuver area. They had long bedeviled authorities. They used mobile house trailers that were usually populated by two women and pulled by car or truck, with a male chauffeur-lookout, who also served as a procurer. "There won't be any trailer girls at these maneuvers like there were in last year's games," pledged Captain B. O. Yeldell, commander of the group of state troopers charged with clearing them out.[15]

The push to purge prostitution from the Deep South and the Southwest was driven by Congress's insistence that areas near military bases be cleansed of their red-light districts—even those areas with local means of disease control. In Corpus Christi, Texas, for example, a large area of sanctioned prostitution had flourished since 1846, when the Army of General (later president) Zachary Taylor camped there for some months during the Mexican War. Over time, the district had been sanctioned by the city, which registered the women and required them to have periodic medical exams and be granted "health cards" before they could continue working. On August 1, 1941, at noon, after a night of bacchanalian excess, the 86 houses of prostitution were closed, a movement prompted by a request from the commander of the new Naval Air Station being established in the city.[16]

For all the money the maneuvers would bring to the Pelican State, they would also create hardships. Commercial flights into, out of, and over the area were banned for the month of September. Because of the danger to school buses from military vehicles, the state education department asked public schools in the vast maneuvers area—comprising half the state—to delay school openings from two to four weeks.[17]

On August 1, 1941, Stimson announced that more than 1,000 aircraft would participate in the maneuvers, including Navy aircraft and 13 Army autogiros,* which were initially dismissed by the Army Air Corps as without merit but embraced by artillery units as flying observation posts with an ability to hover over an area.[18]

Marshall expected as much realism as possible in the upcoming war games, especially in the treatment of prisoners of war. Captured troops would be questioned for military information, searched for documents, maps, and ammunition, and then marched to the rear to be housed and fed in camps at the captors' expense. The United Press noted that these were the first Army exercises that would deal with the treatment of prisoners.[19]

Well before the first mock battle, commanders warned their troops that they would not only be fighting an opposing army but also dealing

---

* Autogiros were a precursor to helicopters. With a fixed wing and rotor blade they were able to move like a conventional aircraft but also to stop in midair thanks to the rotor blade or, depending on the design, blades.

with the dreaded three M's of tropical warfare: mud, malaria, and mosquitoes. Units were warned that the exercises were calculated to produce exhaustion. A veteran of the 1940 exercise warned that in Louisiana, "in addition to the enemy there are two redoubtable antagonists lurking to . . . break up the best laid plans of a commander—Old Man Fog and his twin brother Bog."[20]

Organizers of the maneuvers feared putting so many men into an area where disease could spread. A battle would be waged against malaria, which occurred with high frequency in the mosquito-rich states of Alabama and Louisiana. The Third Army would be given quinine and the Second Army would receive the cheaper drug, quinacrine (also spelled chinacrin), as a test to determine which was more effective.[21] A separate army of state and federal workers was put in place to bring a high degree of sanitation to protect the troops on the ground as well as the local population. The safety of milk, water, and the food supply was a major concern as was the safe disposal of human excreta.[22]

Like the Tennessee Maneuvers, these in Louisiana were unscripted; nothing was prearranged about how they would be conducted or how they would end. The generals in charge of the two armies were given wide latitude. Below the command level, the maneuvers were to test the resourcefulness of the men on the ground. There would be no time-outs, rest periods, or days off, as there had been in the Tennessee Maneuvers, during which fighting ceased on Friday night and began again on Monday morning. The goal was to approximate real combat in a way never achieved before. Marshall and his staff also saw something even larger that could come out of the maneuvers: they wanted to stage Louisiana as a big show, an ongoing melodrama that would capture the nation's attention and imagination.

Elaborate plans were made for the care and comfort of reporters, broadcasters, and newsreel crews. The Army suggested that all news organizations send at least two correspondents, one for each army. Each correspondent would be issued an officer's uniform with a green press brassard, transportation, and a set of maps. Initially, plans were made for 200 members of the press, not including reporters from the dozen or so local daily newspapers and radio stations. There had been no broadcasting during World War I, so no blueprints existed for the radio correspondents, or the Army, to follow. The radio companies, especially the big networks, were eager to test their men and their own equipment needed for remote broadcasting. CBS announced it was sending its A team of 15 technicians and broadcasters, including Eric Sevareid, John Daly, William L. Shirer, George Fielding Eliot, Bill Slocum, and Gene Ryder. CBS also brought in stage-and-screen star Burgess Meredith as a special narrator to give the games a melodramatic spin. The reports from Louisiana would be broadcast under the title "The Spirit of '41"—a clear allusion to the "Spirit of '76."[23]

A who's who of newspaper reporters would participate, including those from leading isolationist newspapers—among them Tom Watson of the *New York Daily News* and C. C. Corpening of the *Chicago Tribune*. Three of the star wire service men assigned to the maneuvers—Leon Kay and Richard C. Hottelet of the United Press and Charles Nutter of the Associated Press—were just back from the European combat front. Edgar Snow, known for his work in Asia and author of the 1937 book *Red Star Over China*, was being sent by the *Saturday Evening Post*. Even small outlets with an interest in only one unit deployed to Louisiana were invited to send a representative. Thus Granger Weil of the Port Huron, Michigan, *Times Herald* reported on Company L, 125th Infantry, 32nd Division composed mostly of former National Guardsmen from Port Huron.[24]

To provide a work space for all of these writers, photographers, and broadcasters, the Army built a giant press center three-quarters of a city block long that featured long tables, scores of typewriters, and a sawdust floor. These reporters were housed in their own camp nearby, which featured row upon row of canvas tents. More than 100 taxicabs were chartered for the duration to take the "war" correspondents wherever they wanted to go in the maneuver zone. The Army supplied a pool of cab drivers, part of a special detachment of 306 officers and men in charge of public relations, including a special photographic unit providing images for newspapers and magazines.[25]

In addition to wearing Army uniforms, news personnel were required to camouflage their equipment and understood that they were subject to capture, just as any other soldiers fighting in this "war." In addition to the press, certain VIPs asked to be accommodated, ranging from top brass and members of Congress to members of the British military and four people from Harvard Business School planning to study logistics in the field.[26]

In many small towns that had never seen a military convoy, the troops were greeted with applause, home-baked goods, and oceans of cold soft drinks and iced tea. The admiration for the maneuvers seemed genuine and heartfelt, despite feelings lingering from the Civil War about troops invading from the North. When a group of 1,700 Connecticut infantrymen were driven into Quincy, Florida, they saw a large sign strung across Main Street that said: WELCOME 43RD DIVISION. NO GENERALS PLAY GOLF HERE, a clear reference to General Lear. A few days later as the same unit passed through Alabama and Mississippi, the reporter from the *Hartford Courant* traveling with the men reported a new "menace" plaguing officers trying to maintain discipline and keep the troops from injury. Every town the unit passed through had its quota of "girls from 12 on up" intent on delivering "mash notes" to the soldiers, though many of these notes were attached to a rock, making them dangerous projectiles.[27]

The local newspapers treated the men in the maneuvers as if they were in a real war with real enemies. "I have information which convinces me that elements will try hard to poison the morale of both troops and civilians during this great concentration of manpower," warned Louisiana's Governor Jones in the *Baton Rouge Advocate* at the end of July. He advised residents to avoid "hysteria, witch hunts and wild suspicion" but to be quick to report to the Army or the FBI evidence of attempts to secure military secrets or to spread disunity or "un-American doctrines." Nobody quite knew what Jones was talking about, but it gave the operation an early sense of melodrama.[28]

On August 12, General Walter Krueger, commander of the Third Army, paid a courtesy visit to his host, Governor Jones, in Baton Rouge.

Krueger was accompanied by his chief of staff, Colonel Dwight D. Eisenhower, who was deeply involved in getting the Third Army moved and into position. He later described the challenge of having to move 400,000 men into unsettled country where the road network was designed for a car or two at a time, not an entire army.[29]

From the outset the good-natured colonel whom everyone referred to as Ike seemed content at being there. As he later wrote after first being told he was going to Louisiana: "All the old-timers here say, that we are going to a god-awful spot, to live with mud, malaria, mosquitoes and misery, but I like to go to the field, so I'm not much concerned about it."[30]

The upcoming maneuvers had a mixed effect on the African American community. Locally, the Army construction boom meant that many black male servants quit their low-paying jobs for the $5 a day they could receive working on construction crews building barracks. Whites in Alexandria complained to reporters that they were now faced with an "impossible" servant problem.[31]

But the black men whose units were sent to the Deep South faced frustration and deprivation. Ollie Stewart, a reporter for the *Baltimore Afro-American*, ventured to Camp Shelby in Mississippi in late July and found black soldiers longing to be transferred to bases where their treatment would improve. Their major complaint was an absolute lack of recreational facilities. Stewart ticked off the list: "They have no band. They have no service club. They have no guest house for their relatives and girlfriends. They have no library. They have no movie house. They have no hostesses. They have no recreational halls for Ping-Pong, cards and other games. They had a baseball field, I am told, but white soldiers came and saw and took it over."[32]

The most serious incident in the run-up to the maneuvers took place during the trek of the 94th Engineers from Fort Custer, Michigan, to Louisiana. This was a group of 1,000 black soldiers led by white officers, which drew heavily on men from Detroit and Chicago. It had been created in May, and its ranks were dominated by draftees.

As it headed south, the unit was cheered by flag-waving crowds through the Midwest. However, when it crossed the Ohio River into Tennessee, everything changed, as racial slurs replaced the cheers and the white officers were called "nigger-loving Yankees." In Nashville, several of the men were beaten and jailed. According to one of the men in the unit, conditions improved in Little Rock, where they were treated "swell," but deteriorated when they continued into Arkansas to an area outside the small town of Gurdon, where they were to establish a camp to await further orders.

Trouble started when local authorities herded the soldiers into the black section of the small town and told them they could leave and return to camp only by avoiding walking on the state highway, which meant they had to come and go by way of a culvert along the side of the road. When one of the white officers objected, he was punched in the face by a state trooper.

In the next few nights, locals began hurling insults at the soldiers. Tensions escalated, and white military police and the Arkansas State Troopers became involved. The spark appeared to have been a black soldier who refused to remove his cap when he went into a store to buy cigarettes. Pistols and shotguns were brandished, and the black troops then returned to their camp. The *Chicago Defender* published a letter from an eyewitness, who claimed that the state troopers fired shots at the camp, although nobody was hit.[33]

The critical moment occurred when the sentries guarding the camp were denied ammunition for their weapons by those charged with supplying the unit, which effectively disarmed the black unit. Without the ability to defend themselves from an armed mob and hostile state troopers, the men of the battalion claimed they were now living under a "reign of terror"—a term shared by their white officers, who were helpless to defuse the situation and who had been told that their "insignia meant nothing down here."[34]

As a result, 43 of the black soldiers deserted, claiming they were afraid for their lives. Most of them headed back to their base in Michigan, and four of them made it to the Jefferson Barracks in Missouri, a Regular Army base, where they surrendered and told their story to authorities and to the black press, now widely covering the story. For weeks to come, it defended the men as patriots forced to escape from a hostile situation, all the more credible because their officers agreed the men were in peril.[35]

By the end of August 1941, the *Atlanta Daily World* reported that the racial hostility among the troops camping in Arkansas had cooled to "a mild simmer," and a redemptive moment came when the 94th Engineers moved into Pine Bluff, Arkansas, early in September, on the final leg of its trip to the maneuvers. The men were welcomed by the mayor, police chief, and by a biracial committee of local notables and invited to camp on the campus of the local black college. One of their officers told a reporter that the treatment of his men in Pine Bluff had made them forget the unpleasantness of other communities.[36]

But the black press had not forgotten the unpleasantness in Gurdon. Charley Cherokee, the popular columnist for the *Chicago Defender*, now talked of a ban on black soldiers on the streets of 45 southern cities. "These," he reminded his readers, "are the same Negroes who are being inducted to defend democracy, remember?" Protests by the NAACP and others reached President Roosevelt and the War Department but got no immediate response.[37]

Despite all this, pride was expressed in the African American press over the fact that black soldiers were now part of the mainstream, albeit in segregated units. Black infantry, engineer, cavalry, and other units would square off on either side in the big September battle. A black corporal, J. A. Brown, bylined a piece in the *Atlanta Daily World*, titled "Our Military Might," in which the word *our* clearly referred to men of his race. "These colored troops to a large degree represent the 'cream' of the Selective Service men. They will give definite proof that the Negro is quite capable of performing his part with intelligence and skill."[38]

On August 16, hundreds of thousands of men now in Arkansas, Texas, and Louisiana listened in large groups, on radios powered by portable generators, to a speech by Secretary of War Stimson, explaining why the nation had decided to keep the Army in service for another 18 months. The broadcast was specifically aired for the Army in the field and given the ponderous title: "You Will Not Falter—You Cannot Fail."

Stimson was now in a tight spot. As *Time* magazine put it: "No U.S. Secretary of War in 75 years has faced such a situation as Henry Lewis Stimson faced. He had 1,500,000 soldiers under arms and many of them wanted to go home at a time when he was sure that they were desperately needed." What they were needed for at that one moment was "defense," and in this respect, Stimson himself thought he had done a poor job making his case when he looked back at it after the war.[39]

The speech droned and preached rather than inspired and seemed to drown in its own platitudes. "We are not seeking to rival the size of these possible enemy forces which surround us," the secretary said. "But we wish an Army which in equipment, in training and in spirit, aided by an unsurpassed air force and the full efforts of our Navy, will be able to meet and conquer any attack which may be attempted against any part of our homeland."[40]

The reaction was mostly negative, especially from men now camped in remote locations where, if one were lucky, one might get a ride on a dusty gravel road to a place like Alexandria, Louisiana, to see a movie or spend an evening in a nickel-a-beer roadhouse. The men never had a chance to spend even a few hours in New Orleans; such trips were reserved for senior officers and umpires.

William J. Clew, the writer for the *Hartford Courant*, reported that the young men he talked with disliked the idea of an extension but would try to make the best of a bad situation. But talk of desertion was most certainly in the air, and he already knew of a hundred men from Connecticut who had gone AWOL. Many of the men from the Nutmeg State, who had never been farther south than Norwalk, were now living "the most primitive kind of life," in the moist, muddy hell of the Kisatchie Forest.

By the time of Stimson's radio address, the Army had announced that men over 28 could be discharged earlier, and Clew talked with one man who said, "Well it's all right for these young fellows. But for us guys over 30 this cowboys and Indian stuff is the bunk." Clew posed a question in his report: "Would the Louisiana Maneuvers show an American fighting machine or a mere unwieldy mass of men?"[41]

D-Day for the maneuvers was set for September 15. A warm-up event known as the Arkansas Maneuvers began on August 17, as an imaginary war between two nations: KOTMK (pronounced *koatmik*, an acronym for Kansas, Oklahoma, Texas, Missouri, Kentucky), which would soon be known as the Red Army, and ALMAT (Arkansas, Louisiana, Mississippi, Alabama, Tennessee), to be known as the Blue Army.

According to the setup for the event, announced by the Second Army press officer Major R. A. Griffin and published in *Life* magazine, ALMAT had conquered a large portion of what was now Alabama, as well as the state of Louisiana, yielding the lower Mississippi, which included the Port of New Orleans. The newly acquired lands gave ALMAT an unprecedented level of prosperity, as it contained many productive oil wells. At the beginning of the maneuvers, KOTMK planned to renew warfare to regain its lost territory by moving from its base in East Texas over the border into Arkansas. But before the battle could begin, KOTMK sent raiding parties in armored vehicles into ALMAT to seize civilian hostages and simulate wrecking public utilities.

The maneuver then went into high gear, as borders closed and hostilities intensified. KOTMK blitzed ALMAT, with the object of gaining control of the Mississippi River itself as well as the Port of New Orleans. The invaders "blew up" dams, "destroyed" bridges, "knocked out" factories, and "torched" crops. Two target cities were then "blitzed" by raiding parties—Texarkana, on the border of the two states, and Fort Smith, deep in the state of Arkansas.[42]

Despite this grand simulation, which was meant to prepare for Louisiana in September, the action on the ground largely revolved around learning to move large groups of men through the principal types of field operations: advancing to contact an enemy, attacking, establishing a defensive position, and finally withdrawing. These were mostly "green" units that had not taken part in the Tennessee Maneuvers.

*   *   *

The ability to move troops quickly under difficult conditions was essential. On the night of August 25, 75,000 men of the ALMAT force were moved from a position where they had been trapped by KOTMK divisions to a safe location under total blackout conditions.[43]

Patton's arrival in Louisiana in early August was the very model of military stagecraft with his two 70-mile columns of 2,300 vehicles rolling through towns and villages in a three-hour parade. As the parade passed through, 15 freight trains carried 700 tanks, 44 artillery pieces, and their two thousand plus crew members. The flat cars carrying the big guns featured men at parade rest holding machine guns and armed with .45-caliber revolvers protecting the weapons. Second Army Division photographers were on hand to take pictures and hand them to the local newspapers for publication.[44]

At its peak, 120,000 men of the Second Army in Arkansas were bivouacked in densely forested areas, where they first learned to deal with heat (as high as 99 degrees Fahrenheit), dust, and the other realities of the southern wilderness, including snakes, chiggers, and the occasional razorback hog.[45]

The last hours of the fighting in Arkansas provided good theater for local residents. On September 6, people living in the town of Junction City, which straddles the Arkansas-Louisiana line (with half of the municipality in either state) awoke to find themselves in the middle of what the *Arkansas Gazette* termed the "most violent" engagement of the war games so far. Beginning at dawn and into the morning, troops of the Blue and Red Armies engaged in hand-to-hand combat moving from house to house with machine gun emplacements on many front lawns. Prisoners of war were taken after being driven into private homes, stores, garages, and, in one case, beneath a front porch. As the day wore on, the Blue Army lost ground and was driven from town and chased down into Louisiana—southeast to Bastrop and southwest to Homer. Meanwhile the highway running through Junction City had been clogged all day with military convoys, marching soldiers and civilian cars as many area people flocked to town to witness the show.[46]

One family memoir told of kids riding their bikes to see tanks and occasionally getting to ride in one. The kids also visited the Army camps with their friends during the maneuvers. "We would get in the mess line and eat with soldiers," said Gary Hymel, who added that the sight of cooks dumping Jell-O onto scrambled eggs in the soldiers' mess horrified his sister. Gary's brother Gene remembered the soldiers complaining about the chiggers, red bugs, and ticks. "They were a big part of the soldiers' social life," he remarked.[47]

The first big payday for the soldiers amassed in Arkansas and Louisiana came on September 1. The soldiers were also given the day off. With more than $16 million in their collective pockets, they cleared the shelves of country stores. Some storekeepers claimed to have sold more on that day than they would in an average year.[48]

Payday was a morale booster, as were the efforts of the nascent USO to provide a modicum of recreation in Louisiana. It sent three mobile motion-picture trucks able to deploy a massive movie screen into the maneuver area. The screen and projection and sound equipment setup on the trucks would be able to entertain thousands of men at a single screening. By early September, the USO had set up recreation areas in no less than 50 communities in the maneuver zone.[49]

In addition to the maneuvers in Arkansas and those about to commence in Louisiana, Marshall was closely monitoring maneuvers that took place in other regions of the country during the summer of 1941. On the same day the Arkansas Maneuvers began in the South, a mythical enemy force in the West began shelling the coast from Monterey Bay in California north to the Canadian border with heavy simulated casualties reported at coastal military bases. Enemy troops landed at Grays Harbor in Washington. The invasion was only on paper and attacks, battle lines, and casualties were simulated, but before this maneuver was over, more than 100,000 real servicemen would be involved in defending the West Coast. Because of its hypothetical nature and a nameless enemy that existed entirely on paper, the maneuvers attracted minimal interest in terms of the press or the public. Real troops were used in these maneuvers, but for the most part, they tangled with imaginary forces. For instance, on August 18, a dozen large motorboats carrying 400 infantrymen sped across an arm of Puget Sound so they could intercept an imaginary tank battalion said to be on its way to attack the Navy Yard at Bremerton. The exercise yielded odd headlines in the newspapers of the Northwest, such as MYTHICAL FLEET INVADES WASHINGTON.[50]

An editorial in the *Los Angeles Times* captured the *faux* reality of the situation: "Following mythical feints that have had our defense units from the Mexican to the Canadian borders in a state of complete theoretical bewilderment and uncertainty, the make-believe aggressor from the imaginary somewhere struck hard in the Puget Sound area just as yesterday's sun was reddening in the eastern sky."[51]

On August 28, a New England maneuver was staged for control of the Nashua River valley involving some 40,000 troops. This exercise focused on an 18-mile front in the hill country along the Massachusetts–New Hampshire line and was set to test, among other things, the viability of Army communications under combat conditions with extra credit being awarded by the umpires to the army showing the best ability to talk to itself. These maneuvers were hampered by the fact that so much of this part of New England was under cultivation or occupied by thickly settled towns and villages that restricted troop movement primarily to public roads.[52]

Though these two exercises were devoid of actual combat, they served as important tests of the military to move troops and weapons rapidly from one point to another. In the western maneuver, troops moved in large numbers from points in California into Washington at a rate of more than 275 miles a day at an average speed of about 30 miles per hour, up from a normal expectancy of 175 miles per day at a speed of 25 miles an hour. This ability would now be put to a severe test in Louisiana.[53]

War Flouters. Leaders of the Veterans of Future Wars: Louis J. Gorin, Jr. founder of the movement is flanked by Kathleen Krieger (left) and Linda Barnes, commanders of the Home Fire Division of the group.

Nerve Center. War Department workers departing the Munitions Building located on Constitution Avenue in 1941. Both Army Chief of Staff Marshall and War Secretary Stimson worked here before and during the early phases of World War II.

Frontline VIPs. Sen. Henry Cabot Lodge of Massachusetts (left) and Rep. John Sparkman of Alabama observing the First Army during the 1939 Plattsburg Maneuvers. Both men were members of the Army Reserves. Lodge would act as a major liaison between the forces in the field during the Louisiana Maneuvers and Congress.

Horse Power. Men, horses, hay, and a howitzer of the First Cavalry, an element of the Third Army during the 1940 Louisiana Maneuvers. The image underscores the degree to which the 1940 Army still relied on the mounted cavalry to move its artillery.

Draft Drafters. Army Chief of Staff George C. Marshall confers with Rep. James Wadsworth (R., NY), left, and Senator Edward R. Burke (D., Neb.), on the compulsory military training of civilians. The draft bill passed in both houses of Congress and was signed into law by President Roosevelt on September 16, 1940.

Prime Mover. Grenville Clark, the man who began the successful drive to create the 1940 military draft, shown here in 1943 testifying before the Senate Armed Services Committee on an ill-fated bill that would have made both men and women eligible for the draft.

R(egistration)-Day Celebrity. Heavyweight boxing champion Joe Louis, center, registering for the draft in Chicago on October 16, 1940. His half-brother Alonzo Brooks is seated to his right and his co-manager Julian Black stands at the rear. The draft registrar sits to the champ's left.

First Call. On October 29, 1940, with President Roosevelt looking on, a blind-folded Secretary of War Henry Stimson reached into the fishbowl and pulled out the first capsule containing the number 158. Across the nation, 6,175 young men who had been the 158th man to register at their local draft boards held that number.

Numbers Game. Brig. General Lewis B. Hershey, assistant draft director, points to the first of the first fifteen numbers pulled from the fishbowl on October 29, 1940. A high percentage of the men holding these numbers would pass their physicals and be in uniform within a matter of weeks.

Isolationist Icon. Senator Rush Holt of West Virginia holding his Selective Service Card. Holt was one of the angriest and most outspoken members of Congress in opposition to the 1940 peacetime draft which he termed "silly and unnecessary."

On Deck. Baseball slugger Hank Greenberg waiting to take his Army physical in Detroit in April, 1941. He was declared 1-A and soon in uniform.

Spud Patrol. Volunteer Draftee Clyde Odell Brown of Heard County, Georgia, was the first Southern draftee taken in 1940. He is shown here serving time in the Kitchen Police (or K.P.) where peeling potatoes was the commonest assignment.

Army Bound. The first group of draftees and "volunteer draftees" depart from Detroit to Fort Sheridan, Illinois, on November 23, 1940. While the group here is racially integrated, they would soon be segregated in what the black press often referred to as the Jim Crow Army.

Equal Eligibility. Winthrop Rockefeller (left), son of John D. Rockefeller shakes hands with Charles McCarthy who had been unemployed for the previous six months. Both men had been drafted the same day and met at the headquarters of draft board #20 in midtown Manhattan on January 22, 1941.

Special Straphanger. William McChesney Martin, Head of the New York Stock Exchange, traveling by subway from his draft board office to his Army induction at the 71st Regiment Armory in April, 1941.

G.I Jack. The jeep made an early appearance in the Tennessee Maneuvers (when it was still commonly referred to as "the army's midget open car"). Here three men act as a human jack for the lightweight vehicle.

Dynamic Duo. Secretary of War Henry L. Stimson (center) with the Red Army during the Tennessee Maneuvers, late June, 1941. Peeking over Stimson's shoulder is Major General George S. Patton, who had been Stimson's aide when he was Secretary of State in the Hoover administration.

Tail Tow. During the Tennessee Maneuvers, men of the Sixth Cavalry demonstrate how to hold onto their horses in order to cross an unfordable stream with full field equipment.

Bayonet Charge. Three hundred men of the Seventh Army emerge from a smoke screen in maneuvers in the state of Washington. From their helmets to their leggings they were outfitted with surplus equipment left over from World War I.

Radio Star. CBS reporter and commentator Eric Sevareid who returned from Europe after the French capitulation to report on the 1941 maneuvers. After watching men in action in Louisiana and the Carolinas, he came to believe the men of the American army had the determination and courage to beat the Nazi army.

203-202. Isolationist Rep. Hamilton Fish, Republican of New York meets with mothers of draftees opposing legislation that would require extending the duration of active service and keep men in uniform beyond the original one year period. Later in the day the bill to extend passed in the House by the razor-thin margin of 203-202.

Brain Trust. Third Army commander General Walter Krueger and his Chief of Staff Colonel Dwight David Eisenhower on the eve of the second phase of the 1941 Louisiana Maneuvers.

Show Stopper. Brig. General George S. Patton starred in all three major 1941 maneuvers as a tank commander, generating headlines and controversy. He is shown here in March, 1943, when he was in charge of the United States II Corps, part of the American force fighting in North Africa.

Early Work. Cartoon drawn by Bill Mauldin of the 45th Infantry Division during the Louisiana Maneuvers, which carried the caption "I've heard of some very peculiar things happening on these blackout maneuvers."

Heavy Traffic. 30-ton medium tanks roll through the town of Castor, Louisiana, which had been defended by 75-mm field artillery guns deserted by ground troops during September, 1941.

Boot Hospital. Army private of the 5th Army Corps mobile shoe repair shop unit at work inside his truck in Louisiana. The logistical skill of the army on display in the 1941 maneuvers was seen as an important dress rehearsal for actual war.

Walkie-Talkie. Airborne Infantry officer using a new two-way radio field telephone, during Third Army maneuvers in Louisiana.

Armored Mascot. Men of the 69th Armored Regiment show off their pet armadillo with divisional insignia on its back. The armadillo had been "taken prisoner" at one point in the exercises underscoring the point that the maneuvers were a far cry from real combat.

Dry Crossing. A pontoon bridge strong enough to handle tanks being assembled during the Louisiana Maneuvers. These instant bridges were later put into play in the crossings of the Rhine and other rivers during the war in Europe.

Sitting Ducks. Planes of the 105th Squadron "strafe" troops of the 13th Infantry Division in an open field near Columbia S. C. during the Carolina Maneuvers. Throughout the 1941 maneuvers men on the ground displayed a "fatal" disregard for attacks from the air.

Instant Airfield. The first portable airfield being assembled from perforated steel plates in the field in Marston, NC, during the Carolina Maneuvers. The finished runway, 150 feet wide and 3,000 feet long, could handle every type of aircraft up to a large, 5,000-horsepower bomber. Known as the Marston Mat, it proved invaluable to the American war effort in both theatres of World War II.

Iron Horses. Tanks from Camp Polk, Louisiana, being unloaded from flatcars for action in the Carolina Maneuvers. During the course of the 1941 war games the importance of armored cavalry increased as the importance of the horse decreased.

Dummy Aircraft. Burlap, string, and twigs are used to create the tail structure for a dummy plane used as a decoy at the Marston airport during the Carolina Maneuvers. The use of decoy aircraft and armored vehicles was common during the war.

Chow Depot. One day's ration of fresh food for various units of the First Army piled on a field in Chester, SC, awaiting pickup by individual units. Learning to efficiently supply troops in the field with food, fuel, and ammunition was seen as one of the most valuable lessons of the 1941 maneuvers.

Cutting Loose. A member of Company C of the 502 Parachute Division uses a knife to cut himself loose from a pine tree during an attack by his Provisional Airborne Task Force during the Carolina Maneuvers. Making one of the great debut performances of the 1941 maneuvers were the combat paratroop units.

Action Team. A machine gun unit of the 60th Infantry Division of the First Army springs into action during the Carolina Maneuvers during which the ability to rapidly set up weapons was stressed.

Infamous Night. The White House as it appeared on the evening of Sunday December 7, 1941, after the attack on Pearl Harbor. War Secretary Henry Stimson saw the attack as the country's great awakening.

War Planner. Brig. General Dwight D. Eisenhower (left) becomes head of the Army's War Plans Division on February 19, 1942. He replaces Major General Leonard T. Gerow (right) who then commanded the 29th Infantry Division.

Combat Ready. During the 1943 Louisiana Maneuvers women were part of the action as members of the Army Nurse Corps. As the war progressed Army nurses were called to serve closer and closer to the front lines.

Morale Booster. Comedian Bob Hope entertaining troops in the Solomon Islands in 1944. Hope was a leading force in morale building for the military before, during and after World War II.

CHAPTER 10

THE BATTLE OF THE BAYOUS

As the two massive armies positioned themselves for the big games in Louisiana, events in the news had an impact on the morale of men who were far from home. For all the many deprivations of the Louisiana camps and bivouacs, the men on the ground had access to news via radios and daily newspapers locally produced in Baton Rouge, New Orleans, and Shreveport often sold to the soldiers by local kids on bicycles.

On September 4, Undersecretary of War Robert Patterson announced that approximately 5,000 Regular Army, National Guard, and Reserve officers were to be removed from active duty in the next few months because of newly established age limits, ranging from 62 years for major generals down to 30 years for second lieutenants. The move was part of an effort to "revitalize the field forces." A few of these overage men might be promoted and others reassigned to administrative or staff positions, Patterson said, but the bulk would be given honorable discharges. The Army Air Corps was immune from most of these cuts because it was so desperately in need of officers.

This news, unexpected and dramatic, signaled in concrete terms the wide-ranging changes to the officer corps that had been promised by Lesley McNair, George Marshall, and Henry Stimson. Many of the men reassigned to non-critical jobs or sent out to pasture at the end of the maneuvers would express their anger and bitterness. Stimson, Marshall, and others behind this move insisted it should not be called a purge because of the negative impact of such a word on the morale of both the officers and the men they commanded, but that was exactly what the men losing their commands insisted on calling it.[1]

The action to remove officers was given a jump start on September 12, when Stimson announced that 170 mostly senior officers had been deemed unfit for active duty by a secret panel composed of five generals, with the final decision left up to Stimson. The names were never made public, and the selected men had the right to request voluntary retirement in lieu of forced retirement, an option many of them took. The next day's front-page headline in the *Baltimore Sun* screamed: 170 OFFICERS AFFECTED BY ARMY PURGE.[2]

Coming three days before the start of phase one of the Louisiana Maneuvers, Stimson's announcement alerted all officers that if they did not perform well they could be out of a job. "Through the maneuver area ran the rumor that when next week's battle was over the cleanout of substandard officers would be terrific—perhaps as high as 30%," reported *Time* magazine. General McNair did nothing to dispel the rumors when, with characteristic frankness, he said: "A lot of these Generals who want to fire their Chiefs of Staff ought to fire themselves. We're going to start at the top and work down. We've got some bum Generals, and maybe I'm one of them, but we're going to weed them out. Have we the bright young Majors and Captains to replace them? Yes."[3]

Marshall, in advance, carefully set up a system by which he could do his pruning of Regular Army officers with a minimal amount of outside (that is, congressional) interference. Legislation was proposed and passed by Congress in late July, giving him the authority to establish a special Removal Board (which became known informally as the Plucking Board) headed by General Malin Craig, the former Army chief of staff, who had come back to active duty to perform this important job.[4]

On September 4, the same day the initial purge had been announced, a German submarine operating off the coast of Iceland fired two torpedoes at an American destroyer, the USS *Greer* (DD-145). The ship was carrying mail to servicemen based in Iceland and flying a clearly visible American flag. The torpedoes missed their mark, and the destroyer made it safely to its destination. The Germans may have fired on the American ship in error, thinking it was actually a British ship that had attacked them. But the incident was enough for Roosevelt to frame a new policy, which he explained in a fireside chat delivered a week after the attack. Because of its importance, the speech was carried live by all three major radio networks. An address by Charles Lindbergh, scheduled to be broadcast live at the same time by the Mutual network, was moved back by more than an hour.

Lindbergh's speech was to be given in Des Moines, Iowa, at an America First rally, which had an expected attendance of 10,000. When the live broadcast time of Lindbergh's address was moved back, the rally organizers decided to add Roosevelt's speech to the program, giving the America Firsters ample reason to boo and heckle their warmongering president.

At 8:00 p.m. Eastern Time, on Thursday, September 11, Roosevelt delivered what would later be described as his "shoot-on-sight" speech, declaring war on any nation that attacked American ships in the North Atlantic: "If German or Italian vessels of war enter these waters, they do so at their own peril." As commander in chief, Roosevelt had now declared war at sea. Roosevelt chose his closing metaphor carefully: "When you see a rattlesnake poised to strike, you do not wait until he has struck before you crush him. These Nazi submarines and raiders are the rattlesnakes of the Atlantic."

Roosevelt's declaration was broadcast over the BBC (British Broadcasting Corporation) and other outlets throughout the world and had a listening audience estimated in the millions, including the America Firsters in Des Moines and the armies now in place in Louisiana. The Associated Press reported that Roosevelt's speech was cheered in Des Moines on 11 different occasions and never booed. Whether the cheers came from outsiders who had come to the event to heckle Lindbergh or from isolationists somehow moved by Roosevelt's combative stance, or a combination of the two, the effect was dramatic.[5]

Lindbergh came on the radio moments after Roosevelt finished and delivered a speech he had been working on for months, one that his wife had begged him not to deliver—not because of its content but because of the headlines she knew it would generate. The speech blamed three entities for leading America into war—the British, Roosevelt, and American Jews. He labeled these three "the war agitators." He warned the American Jewish community that entry into the war would be contrary to their interests, because a war could bring devastation and could lead in turn to reprisals against Jews in America. "Tolerance" he pointed out, "cannot survive war and destruction."

Lindbergh's words about Jews suggested that they were "other" people, whose interests were not America's interests.* "Their greatest dangers to this country," he added, "lie in their large ownership and influence in our motion pictures, our press, our radio and our Government."[6]

The response to Lindbergh was immediate, stunning, and widespread, as even chapters of America First turned on the former American hero. Merle H. Miller, chairman of the Indianapolis America First Committee, announced: "It is deplorable that Mr. Lindbergh has singled out groups who are supposed to comprise the interventionists. Of those named, the Jews will, of course, bear the brunt of public resentment, for they have been the historic scapegoat in all lands, and history teaches us that people looking for a scapegoat do not solve the real problem— witness Czarist Russia and Nazi Germany." Miller added that several members of his local committee were Jewish. The denunciation of the

---

* On a factual level, at least one commentator with an eye on demographics pointed out that the South and Southwest, where interventionist feeling was strongest, was where the Jewish percentage of the population was smallest. On the other hand, because of the large number of military units from the large metropolitan areas of the Northeast and Midwest, the percentage of Jewish troops on the ground in Louisiana was relatively high and attested to by the members of the National Jewish Welfare Board at work in and around the maneuver area, including some who went to the most remote regions as part of the USO's effort to minister to the religious needs of all soldiers. The active Jewish press of 1941 covered the maneuvers as if the men were another far-flung but vibrant congregation.

speech among leaders of the America First movement in New York City was so loud that some wanted Lindbergh to come to the city to make a public apology. A special irony of the speech in New York was that it was carried on WOR, the Mutual Broadcasting outlet in the city, owned by Bamberger's Department Stores, which were in turn owned by the proudly Jewish Louis Bamberger.[7]

The consensus at the time, and ever since, was that Lindbergh's speech torpedoed the isolationist movement at the exact moment America's involvement in the war was escalating. Virtually every major and most of the minor newspapers and magazines denounced Lindbergh, including the isolationist press. The *New York Herald Tribune* called the speech an appeal to the "dark forces of prejudice and intolerance," and the *Kansas City Times*, in an editorial entitled "Lindbergh Hits Below the Belt," said: "Such an attack upon the Jews from any source would be cheap, unfair and un-American. It comes with singularly poor grace from a man who requires tolerance himself."[8]

As finally configured, the first exercise of the Louisiana Maneuvers, on September 15, pitted the Red Second Army under General Lear against the Blue Third Army of General Krueger. Lear's army was to the north and Krueger's to the south. For those still following the scenario described in the preliminary encounter, Lear headed the forces of KOTMK and Krueger those of ALMAT. A few newspapers would keep the imaginary country names alive in the days to come, but to most observers, the battle was now between Red and Blue, Lear and Krueger, Second and Third Army. The Blue Army was outfitted with blue armbands and floppy cloth fatigue caps. The Red Army wore red armbands and flat-brimmed steel helmets.*

---

* The steel helmets were almost all flat-brimmed models used in the Great War and known to the troops as "tin hats." The wide-brimmed sage green herringbone-tweed fatigue hats were known as "Daisy Mae hats," a reference to the voluptuous woman who was hopelessly in love with Li'l Abner of comic fame.

General McNair's assistant, Brigadier General Mark W. Clark, 45, had roughed out the maneuver area in Louisiana in pencil on a filling-station road map. He used the Red River and the Sabine River as the eastern and western boundaries, respectively, and Shreveport and Lake Charles as the northern and southern limits. To many of those involved, the battle zone resembled a gigantic football field on an eleven o'clock to four o'clock axis, with the Red River serving as the line of scrimmage. The river, often described as a "muddy channel," had in many places more exposed areas of marshy riverbed than flowing water. Beginning in East Texas, it runs southeast, crossing the Sabine River at the state line.

Wounded in combat in the First World War, Clark was a rising star in this new army. Promoted to brigadier general on August 4, he thus had authority over officers with much greater seniority and he was now positioned to become the voice, guiding light, and main critic of the maneuvers.

The opening act called for Lear's small (130,000 men) armor-heavy Red Army, which included Patton and his tanks, to attack and attempt to destroy the larger (270,000 men) but armor-light Blue Army. This combination would put more than a quarter of the U.S. Army in the field in the same area at one time.

The two armies faced a stark reality: that due to the military's limited production capability, its manpower now far outstripped its weapons inventory, resulting in the widespread use of dummy weapons and obsolete equipment in the mock battle. Supply officers quipped that the Army was about to put its best foot forward but it was, at this point, a bare foot. The situation in the air was marked with equal austerity. Owing to the shipments of aircraft overseas under the Lend-Lease agreements and the need to use existing aircraft to train pilot cadets, both the Army and Navy air forces were short on aircraft during the maneuvers—down to fewer than 800 from an earlier estimate of more than 1,000.

Dozens of small Piper Cub, Taylorcraft, and Aeronca aircraft, nicknamed "grasshopper planes," were added to each army at the last minute. These small, light planes, which had previously been shunned

by military planners, had decisively proved their worth in Tennessee*
and had acquired a number of nicknames, including "flying jeeps," which
was meant as a compliment.[9]

Speaking to the reality on the ground, Joseph C. Harsch, a former
Berlin correspondent for the *Christian Science Monitor* and now with the
Second Army in Louisiana, observed his surroundings and deemed them
the worst terrain in the entire United States, writing: "Nothing could try
the spirits of men more than the swamps and dense jungle undergrowth
of this country. Nowhere is there worse terrain for tanks and modern
motorized equipment." He then predicted that if the morale of the men
in Louisiana could survive this, the Army could laugh at the stories of
bad morale that had been so widely circulated—precisely the outcome
the War Department leadership in Washington was hoping for.[10]

Lest there be any question, the conditions in Louisiana were intended
to be tougher and more demanding than they had been in Tennessee. As
Captain Norris H. Perkins of the Second Armored Division, who had
served with Patton in Tennessee, later testified: "Unlike frequent long road
marches and encirclement in Tennessee, in Louisiana we were forced to
operate in narrow quarters between great boggy areas, sometimes covering only a few miles of front with a whole tank regiment."[11]

Perkins, like all of Patton's men, went into Louisiana with a special
sense of being above and apart from other units. "The Blitzkrieg tactics
developed in Tennessee were to be polished in Louisiana. We were now
THE HELL ON WHEELS division. We saw Patton as the great star among
the 400,000 soldiers in Louisiana and all of us down to lowliest private
prayed with Patton at the altar of violent force and audacity."[12]

The rules for the maneuvers were set out in advance; they included
a scoring system that baffled reporters and most of the men on the

---

* The Army had become so aware of the importance of these "grasshoppers" that in early
August it placed a large order for them. One feature that appealed to the Army was that
they could depart from and land in almost any cow pasture and perform a number of
tasks, including rapid secure communications. A person of average intelligence could
also be taught to pilot one in ten hours.

ground, especially regarding the declaration of winners and losers. After the maneuvers, Vincent Hooper, one of Patton's men, remarked, "Without umpires, you might expect every battle to end up in a fistfight; because there was nearly always an argument as to whether or not one side had made a legitimate conquest." As in Tennessee, the umpires were—as George Patton had explained to his men—the "bullets and bombs" of these exercises. The umpiring crew for these maneuvers, however, was 2,000 strong.[13]

The melodrama afforded by network radio was immediate. At 5:30 p.m. Eastern Time, on Tuesdays, Thursdays, and Saturdays, the Mutual Broadcasting System broadcast recordings of the real battles, and on Mondays, Wednesdays, and Fridays, it provided analyses of the maneuvers. The all-star CBS crew had arrived well in advance, and at least two broadcasts a day were sent out live over the network. NBC aired coverage as well, and Americans could spend a good portion of every evening listening to reports from the "front" in Louisiana. These maneuvers seemed to have been made for radio. Sound trucks were now in the field prepared to pump out the noises of bomb blasts, cannon fire, machine guns, and rifle fire—all at high volume.[14]

On the eve of the first phase of the exercises, the combat zone came within an eyelash of a direct hit by a hurricane, which changed course and made landfall in the area near Galveston, Texas. The heavy rain and wind only added to the power of the enemy both armies faced: "General Mud."[15]

The maneuvers were testing whether a superior force without tanks (Blue) could defeat a smaller force with two mature armored divisions (Red). Not stated as such by the men in charge, but understood by a few of the reporters, this setup was akin to the situation the allied nations faced in Europe. As Leon Kay of the United Press noted, when Krueger gave the order to "advance and engage the enemy," it was essentially the same order given to the vastly smaller armies in the Netherlands, Belgium, and Yugoslavia when Germany's columns of tanks and armored vehicles thundered over their borders. Kay, who had witnessed firsthand the war in Europe and had watched the German invasion of the Balkans, would view the maneuvers through a prism that saw Lear, as the Nazi, sending his two Red Army Panzer divisions into a nation holding on for its life.

The maneuvers officially began at 12:01 a.m. on September 15, 1941, as rain fell over most of the area. Close to a half million men were now at war. The day got off to an inauspicious beginning, as the 400 aircraft of the Blue Third Army were grounded before dawn after two planes collided and one pilot was killed. Three other soldiers were killed in predawn traffic accidents—fatalities that immediately underscored the exercises were more akin to real war than simple war games.

Print and radio journalists described the opening both in terms of historic precedent and real combat. "The largest Army maneuvers in the history of the United States, exceeding in number the soldiers engaged in any single battle of the Civil War or the Revolution, were in full swing in the northern half of Louisiana today," wrote Lewis Sebring in the *New York Herald Tribune*.[16]

Life magazine reported on the opening hours:

> With two fast-moving, hard-hitting armored divisions leading the way, Lieutenant General Ben Lear, commander of the Second (Red) Army which for this exercise included Patton and his men, had pushed his troops across the muddy Red River, and was already sending long tentacles down the highways to the south, where Lieutenant General Walter Krueger's Third (Blue) Army lay in wait. Overhead, armadas of pursuit planes fought great dogfights, while sleek A-20 attack bombers and Navy dive bombers strafed the columns of tanks and trucks moving up to the front.[17]

During that first exercise—officially referred to as Phase I but quickly dubbed the "Battle of the Red River" by the press—the Second Army quickly found that getting across the river was tougher than expected. A lack of bridges strong enough to carry tanks forced Lear to deploy three temporary pontoon bridges. These, along with three strong highway bridges, allowed him to send his First and Second Armored

Divisions on a wide pivot northwest, to cross the river at Shreveport and Coushatta, with Patton's tanks in the lead. Patton's men crossed before dawn in blackout conditions under the added protection of a heavy smoke screen. Horse cavalry, assigned to clear out snipers and small patrols on the other side of the river, followed the tanks and armored cars.

As they began, it was clear that the maneuvers were well staged and above all augmented by top-notch sound effects. "This added realism was so loud that we had to shout to be heard," commented Captain Norris H. Perkins. Added to this were the other sensory cues suggesting real warfare including the smell of burned powder and diesel exhaust and the distinct odor of cavalry horses as well as the presence of billowing clouds of smoke and dust. "The news writers and photographers were having a field day," Perkins observed.[18]

By nightfall, the greater part of Lear's Red Army had met little opposition as it occupied several hundred square miles of Blue territory. If there was a great success on opening day, it was the placement of those massive pontoon bridges across the Red River.[19] As September 15 came to a close, the expectation was that there would be conflict the next morning.

Inside the maneuvers, a contest within a contest was going on. Before the opening, Major General John A. Greeley, commanding the Second Infantry Division of the Blue Army, had offered his men a $50 reward for the capture of "Georgie" Patton, "dead or alive." Upon hearing this, Patton offered $100 for the capture of Greeley. After crossing the river, a group of Patton's men went looking for Greeley and found him in his command post near Lake Charles. The bounty was collected.[20]

Lear's infantry ran into problems on its move south. In one case, a Red Army unit was marching in formation down an open, paved highway when an umpire suddenly stepped from behind the bushes on the side of the road and informed the men that many of them had been killed by the fire of two machine guns, and that two 37 mm anti-tank guns of the Blue Army had killed most of the rest of them. What was left of the unit, ordered to take cover in the brush, would not be allowed to advance until its reinforcements arrived on the scene. The unit had been given a lesson in the need for concealment, as it had walked into a mock ambush.[21]

One of the day's few true successes for Lear came when early in the morning of September 16, the Second Army's public relations radio staff took over station KALB in Alexandria for seven hours and interrupted normal programming with false announcements of traffic conditions,* which fooled the opposing forces and enabled Lear's forces to drive a small bulge—or salient—into the Blue line.[22]

Later that night, a small band of Blue Army men made a bold attempt to kidnap General Lear, detouring several hundred miles around Red lines in a captured truck. The plan failed because Lear was not at his headquarters, in Winnfield, Louisiana, north of the Red River, but rather in the field. The attackers were captured, but because of the close call, Lear was forced to move his headquarters.[23]

Earlier that day, on his way to Louisiana, George Marshall appeared in front of the American Legion convention in Milwaukee, where he made headlines decrying the "pressure groups and individuals" hampering the effort to build a strong Army. At one point he asked, "But must we declare war in order to facilitate training and morale? Must you burn down the building in order to justify the fire department?"

He then moved to the maneuvers, whose importance he said was difficult to overemphasize.

> The present maneuvers are the closest peacetime approximation to actual fighting conditions that has ever been undertaken in this country. But what is of the greatest importance, the mistakes and failures will not imperil the nation or cost the lives of men. In the past we have jeopardized our future, penalized our leaders and sacrificed our men by training untrained troops on the

* The Associated Press deemed this the first use of radio waves to spread military disinformation.

battlefield . . . Tremendous sums of money have been spent on our national defense effort, but I know of no single investment which will give this country a greater return in security and in the saving of lives than the present maneuvers.[24]

Marshall's speech was broadcast nationally, as were the remarks of comedian Bob Hope, who acted as master of ceremonies at the convention. Hope was fast becoming an important voice supporting Roosevelt, Stimson, Marshall, and the Armed Forces. At a VIP reception later in the day of the Marshall speech, Hope told the assembled group that he was happy to be out of Hollywood, because he was ducking a subpoena from Senator Gerald P. Nye, who was spearheading a congressional investigation of the movie industry, which he and his fellow isolationists had accused of stirring up pro-war propaganda. "Bing Crosby recently gave five horses to the cavalry and he's suspected of being a fifth columnist," Hope quipped.[25]

Early the next morning Marshall left for Louisiana to see his new forces in operation. Marshall regarded the fact that his Second and Third Armies were now where they were supposed to be and on the move as the first success of the Louisiana Maneuvers.

At nine thirty on the morning of September 17, General Krueger employed a new tactic that brought sudden drama to the mock combat. He ordered the first tactical use of paratroopers, dropping men 30 miles inside the Red Army's frontline, behind Lear's new headquarters, which he had moved to Natchitoches after the attack on the first headquarters. In a zone east of Clarence, Louisiana, Krueger's planes first dropped supplies and weapons, which floated down under blue, green, and yellow parachutes, followed by 127 men, whose mission was to capture a bridge. There was a minor complication when the maneuver panicked farmers on the ground, who thought it looked like an invasion from outer space. As the men landed, 55 pursuit planes circled overhead to give them cover. The paratroopers then proceeded to destroy the bridge,

thereby cutting off traffic on a vital highway, and then surprised a communications unit stringing wire, which they cut. The surprise attack was
described by one of the pilots involved in the operation as "the slickest
thing you ever saw." Watching the historic jump was a group of high-
ranking military leaders, including Marshall.[26]

Two of the paratroopers later made their way to Lear's headquarters, where they convinced the sentries they had been sent to deliver
typewriters. They got in the building and wandered around for ten
minutes looking for Lear before they were captured. By the rules of
the maneuvers, all the parachutists were to surrender to the opposition,
if not captured, 20 hours after landing. When the 20 hours expired on
September 18, more than half of them were still on the loose, cutting
wire lines and playing havoc with Red communications.[27]

The parachute landing had relatively little impact on the course of
the maneuvers, but it made the headlines and yielded some spectacular
photographs in the next day's newspapers. The larger mock war moved
slowly on the 17th as mud continued to inhibit the movement of men
and machines. In the words of Harrison Salisbury of the *New York Times*,
the tanks were "strangely quiescent," leading him to label it the day of
the "blitzless blitz."

On September 18, after three days of preparation, the Red Army
thrust more than half of its 130,000 men at the Blue Army along a
75-mile front in central Louisiana, while sending its armored divisions,
based on airborne reconnaissance, east rather than west, where the Blue
Army had positioned its anti-tank units. The armored divisions had
virtually disappeared for two days, setting up the surprise attack.

However, Krueger's forces discovered Lear's armored divisions,
and the Third Army's B-26 aircraft attacked them before dawn, dropping flares on the columns. All morning and afternoon, the Red tanks
advanced slowly and broke through the Blue Army lines only in small
numbers; many were either captured or destroyed by anti-tank units and
infantry or hit with tons of hypothetical bombs from a steady stream
of dive-bombers. By the day's end, the attack had failed; the tank columns had advanced only a few miles and had sustained severe losses—a

setback for Patton as well as Lear. Reporter John O'Reilly concluded, after watching this day of fierce fighting, that the moment had arrived when the Louisiana war games resembled the vast battles in Europe.[28]

By nightfall, observers felt that each side still had a chance at defeating the other, but the tide turned quickly the following morning, September 19, when the Blue Army captured most of two regiments of the New York 27th Infantry, which led Hanson W. Baldwin to declare, "Had today's finale been real war, General Lear's Second Army would probably have been annihilated." In a final masterstroke, the Blue First Cavalry rode out of East Texas, smashed through the western flank of Lear's Red Army, and captured its gas supplies. Baldwin said the raid was reminiscent of those bold cavalry raids staged by J. E. B. Stuart or Nathan Bedford Forrest in the Civil War.

Within hours, the Blue bombers, which earlier had dropped flares and small flour bags on the Red Army, now dropped propaganda leaflets, which read:

> Your commanders are withholding from you the terrible fact of your defeat. Your gasoline stores have been captured. From now on, if you move, you do it on the soles of your shoes. Your food stores have been captured. Your dinner today is going to be what was left over from yesterday. No one is going to bring up any of the steaks that the men of the Third Army will have tonight. Rout, disaster, hunger, sleepless nights in the forest and swamps are ahead of you—unless you surrender, surrender while there is still time.[29]

The Red Army was fast losing ground, as Krueger's forces now held Lear's headquarters, and at 3:30 p.m. Central Time, McNair declared the battle over, as the momentum of Lear's smaller army was stalled and unable to penetrate any deeper into Blue territory. The invading Second Army, Leon Kay reported, was "tired, hungry and confused as it lay down its arms Friday as the first phase of the mass maneuvers in Louisiana ended."[30]

The *New York Herald Tribune* termed what had happened an "armistice victory" by the defending Blue Army, and the Associated Press termed it a "rout." Many years after the fact, a scholar stated in his thesis on the subject: "Lear had started out hard and fast, but ended up cold."[31]

Richard Hottelet, who reported from the Red Second Army for United Press, had just recently returned from Berlin and the European battlefields where he reported on the blitzkrieg from the German side. He noted that no official notification had been made by the umpires as to who "won," but the Blue Army thought it was the clear victor over the tank-rich but smaller Red Army. Hottelet noted that a combination of terrain and tactics had stopped the tanks. The swamps and heavy rains that had fallen as the maneuvers began forced the tanks to keep to the main paved roads, which exposed them to dive-bomb attacks from the air and to nests of Blue Army snipers positioned along the main roads. "There was no opportunity for swift and dramatic dashes like the encircling movements of the German Panzer divisions I saw over the firm dry ground of Northern France," Hottelet wrote, adding that when the Nazi tanks encountered flooded areas in the Netherlands, they simply drove around them.[32]

After the exercise ended, the Blue Army issued a communique claiming "an unquestioned victory," to which the Red Army responded by saying: "Quick moves used to confuse an enemy do not constitute flight." The Red Army blamed its showing on "Krueger's 5 to 1 numerical advantage," though the actual ratio (still consequential) was 1.7–1.

A few lessons appeared to have been learned—or at least underscored—during this exercise. Major General Charles L. Scott, commander of the First Armored Division, concluded that air superiority and a motorized infantry were needed for the success of tank attacks. "The day of trying to operate without aircraft is past," he asserted. "And putting foot troops with tanks is like sending a race horse and a plow mule out together and expect them to go at the same speed." Scott believed that Lear's forces lost because the tanks had to wait for troops on foot to catch up, when they could have cut Krueger's forces to shreds if they had just gone in.[33]

George Patton's Second Armored Division had met with overpowering infantry and anti-tank opposition and was essentially destroyed. There was general agreement that the combination of inhospitable terrain, weather, unfavorable umpire rulings, and the anti-tank battalions had combined to defeat Patton's men. Patton was not only frustrated to be on the losing team but also unhappy that he was unable to pay the $50 reward he had promised to his officers and men for the capture of "a certain s.o.b. named Eisenhower."[34]

Patton and Eisenhower were old friends, united in part because they both saw a future in tanks. Despite their vast differences in temperament and personal wealth, they enjoyed the highest personal respect for one another. Having been placed on the opposite side in a mock war, Patton thought the best way to humiliate Eisenhower would be to capture him, but his attempt did not avail. On the other hand, reporters in Louisiana had no trouble finding Eisenhower.

Patton had stood out from the crowd since his debut in Tennessee, but the most prominent of the new faces noticed by the cadre of reporters in Louisiana was 49-year-old Lieutenant Colonel Dwight D. "Ike" Eisenhower, who became the face and voice not only of Krueger's Blue Army but also of the leaders of Marshall's emerging new U.S. Army. As Ike's son John Eisenhower explained, Krueger was a reticent man who still retained a trace of a German accent, and he was glad to hand over the role of keeping the press happy and well informed. Eisenhower turned the headquarters tent into a veritable open house, where reporters were welcome to drop in and discuss what was going on without an appointment. There was hot coffee and hard liquor for those who wanted it. Eisenhower was welcoming, quick to laugh, and eager to explain what was going on in Louisiana in plain English. Because of his good nature, genuine humility, and love of telling stories, he became the counter-stereotype to the no-nonsense, tight-lipped Army field officer.[35]

Robert Sherrod of *Time* magazine relied heavily on Eisenhower's interpretation of the war games and found him to be much more articulate than any other officer he encountered during the maneuvers: "He was a deeply impressive man. He looked like a soldier. He talked like an educated man." Sherrod told Eric Sevareid about the man called Ike: "He makes more sense than any of the rest of them." Sevareid observed about reporting: "War in Louisiana is rougher than war in Europe. Over there you sit around waiting for communiqués. Over here you go to the front or you don't find much to report."[36]

Robert S. Allen, who co-wrote the syndicated Merry-Go-Round newspaper column with Drew Pearson, had attempted to meet with Krueger at the end of the first phase of the maneuvers. He was told that the general was not available, but his chief of staff, Dwight Eisenhower, could meet with Allen and Joseph C. Harsch of the *Christian Science Monitor*, who was traveling with him. The name Eisenhower meant nothing to either Allen or Harsch, but at one point in the conversation, Allen mentioned that Harsch had just returned from Germany, and Eisenhower immediately began asking him about the German army. "He interviewed me as much as we interviewed him," Harsch later recalled.[37]

For his part, Krueger seemed to want to do everything he could to advance Eisenhower's career and reputation. During the first day of the scheduled intermission in the maneuvers, Krueger and his whole staff flew to Baton Rouge to have lunch with Governor Sam Jones. During the meal, Krueger turned to Jones and said: "Governor, I want you to know my Chief of Staff. He's the colonel at the end of the table. He's one of the brightest minds in the American Army. In my opinion, he is going places." Jones asked for the man's name, and Krueger said, "Eisenhower."[38]

The good press generated by Krueger and his chief of staff was remarkable. In his last Merry-Go-Round column from Louisiana, Robert Allen's highest praise was reserved for Eisenhower and his deputy, Lieutenant Colonel Alfred M. Gruenther. Describing Eisenhower as the man who had both "conceived and directed the strategy that defeated the Second Army," Allen wrote, "Eisenhower has a steel trap mind plus unusual physical vigor. To him the military profession is a science, and he began watching and studying the German Army five years ago." Both men, he reported, were of that rare military species: "Regular Army officers who can think in terms of the civilian and the citizen soldier."[39]

Krueger, however, was clear that he, not Eisenhower, had been responsible for the plans and orders for the Third Army in Louisiana, and he later bridled at the assertion by Mark Clark, in his post-war autobiography, and others that Eisenhower had been awarded his generalship "because of the planning he had done in Louisiana."[40]

Many secondhand reports have assigned Eisenhower a much greater role in the maneuvers than he actually played, including at least one that put him in charge of the Louisiana Maneuvers as a whole. However, neither Eisenhower himself nor his son and biographer, John Eisenhower, nor others who served under him, including then colonel J. Lawton Collins, commander of the VII Corps, ever made such a claim. Collins would later single Eisenhower out for his "public relations savvy" during the maneuvers. Eisenhower himself later recalled that the maneuvers served to introduce him to the press,* which in turn introduced him to the American people.[41]

Eisenhower's ability to get along with the press may have led to his getting credit for running the maneuvers. "Shortly afterward, I was given unsought publicity in a newspaper column whose author attributed credit to me that should have gone to General Krueger," Eisenhower noted. "I still have no idea why I became the target for his praise."[42]

During the maneuvers, Eisenhower met Marty Snyder, a chef who had been conscripted into the Army in April 1941 and sent to Louisiana shortly thereafter to take part. Eisenhower inspected Snyder's mobile kitchen and found that he was bending mess hall tradition by trying to make the Army chow tasty by adding spices and flavorings that he had paid for out of his own pocket. Eisenhower was also impressed by the way Snyder kept his heavy stoves on the trucks rather than having to unload them at each stop like other mess cooks. Snyder was able to do this with the asbestos pads on the trucks. Eisenhower, who liked to cook, sampled Snyder's food. As Snyder later recalled in his own memoir: "He

---

* Eisenhower noted later that he was also introduced to the press camera in Louisiana, where he was an unknown face to the men who used them. An early photo of Ike, Krueger, and a British military observer identified him as "Lt. Col. D. D. Ersenbeing."

was the first inspecting officer I had met who was interested in the food. And obviously he knew food. The way he tested the gravy, examined the spices and sauces, tested the bread and could tell the quality of the coffee by its color were all tricks of the good cooks with whom I had worked in restaurants." Eisenhower made a mental note to keep track of this likable and talented cook.[43]

George Marshall, who was in Louisiana for Phase I, saw political value in the maneuvers, which he gladly exploited. He invited and transported members of the House Appropriations subcommittee in charge of War Department expenditures to Louisiana during the first phase of the exercises, where they were given a 600-mile automobile tour of the war in progress and then a day watching the action from the air. The goal of this effort was to let the men holding the purse strings see how the equipment worked and what equipment was still needed. Clearly, the sight of a large tree branch perched on the back of a two-and-a-half-ton truck as a stand-in for an antiaircraft gun made an impression.[44]

At this point, Marshall knew that great progress was being made in national defense—1,854 military aircraft had come off American assembly lines that very month, light tanks were rolling off the production lines at a record speed, and more than one Garand rifle was being created per minute—but it was not enough, and there were still shortages. More money, attention, and determination had to be put into rearming the nation while also keeping England well enough supplied with weapons to allow its forces eventually to turn the tide of battle against Germany.

The British had been spending large amounts of money on aircraft and other arms since before the war, and as the country began running out of money in early 1941, the Lend-Lease program was created to serve America's desire to see Nazi Germany defeated without actually having to enter the war. The United States would hand over the arms and other military supplies needed by the British but would not insist on immediate payment, instead deferring payment and "lending" the ships, aircraft, and other weapons. The goal, as expressed by Senator

Claude Pepper of Florida, one of the strongest supporters of aid to the British, was "to keep America out of the war by defeating Hitler with a flood of American production."[45]

On August 24, 1941, the *New York Times* ran a feature story on the progress of rearming the nation, in which it declared the "tooling up" period for war production was just about over, noting that tens of thousands of aircraft were in production and that all the aircraft plants needed to fight the war were either built or being built. Roosevelt's stated goal of producing 50,000 new warplanes annually was still a year away. The article concluded: "One year of defense preparations is over. Peak production is forecast by July 1942."[46]

Just as the congressional delegation headed back to the District of Columbia, the *Washington Post* pointed out, in the first of a series of editorials on the state of arming the nation, that despite the higher production levels, if production could not be speeded up the United States would not be ready to engage in major air combat until the spring or early summer of 1942. Roosevelt himself made the point on September 1, 1941, in his Labor Day address to the nation that despite enormous gains in arms production, the United States' enemies knew "that our American effort was still not enough."[47]

After Phase I in Louisiana, four days were needed to separate the armies, reorganize them, and get them to their new starting points. Released prisoners had to find their way back to their units. Thousands of men did nothing more than catch up on their sleep. One reporter noted that these soldiers didn't look at all like the same men who had been drafted into the Army in the spring. "They were dirty, sunburned, and they had a tough appearance," John O'Reilly wrote in the *New York Herald Tribune*. "Some of the infantry units had marched 70 to 100 miles." The intermission fell over a weekend, and many used whatever means of transportation they could find to get to the larger cities, in a few cases to New Orleans. Saturday night saw the "granddaddy of all Saturday nights," as hundreds of thousands of men headed for town.[48]

That Saturday, the Army hauled 100 overage tanks to an area outside Shreveport and let aircraft participating in the maneuvers bomb and strafe them with live ammunition. It was more than a sideshow; it gave the crews of the 81 aircraft involved in the exercise a feel for real munitions. The UP's Richard Hottelet commented that the Germans had conducted practice bombings with real bombs for years before the war. He recalled being told by an officer of the Luftwaffe that this was the only way a bombardier could get a feel for his mission.[49]

Beginning on Sunday of the intermission, which lasted through Wednesday, September 24, large numbers of men and their arms and equipment were moved considerable distances, with all the logistical problems that such a move entailed. For Phase II, the center of action shifted to the northwest, where the Red Army would be positioned to defend Shreveport from the Blue Army, located to the south. This massive movement of troops and equipment kept supply lines open and flowing to both armies, a condition that had been insisted on by Marshall, who regarded it as one of the most important elements of the maneuvers. When he had initially ordered the two armies to move in the middle of the exercises, he met with resistance. "Well, I said, they would have to do it anyway," he later recalled.[50]

The most significant change in the armies came when Patton's Second Armored Division was reassigned to the Blue Army. One of Patton's men likened the situation to a football game in which your team changed sides at halftime. The photogenic paratroopers were also transferred from Blue to Red for the second phase.

Action on the first two days, starting on September 25, was light and limited to reconnaissance missions. The ground remained soaked. "General Mud stepped into the Army maneuvers in Louisiana today and took command of virtually every road but the main concrete highways," Lewis Sebring wrote on opening day. In addition, rivers and creeks were rising, which slowed the Blue attackers and aided the Red defenders, who were blowing up as many bridges as they could to slow the advances of the Blue Army.[51]

On September 26, the same group of paratroopers that had earlier landed behind Red Army lines did the reverse, splashing down behind the Blue lines in a marshy area inhabited by a herd of cattle, which scattered in all directions. The landings were witnessed by a small army of reporters, photographers, and newsreel crews that had been hastily assembled and secretly brought in to see the drop. The paratroopers' goal was to inflict as much damage to the Blue Army as possible.

The exercise was not without problems—the support aircraft sent in to destroy antiaircraft guns and other impediments did not arrive in time—but the drop itself created a wave of excitement among the observers. This and the previous drop had been "two magnificent shows . . . and perhaps the most memorable sight of the whole maneuver."[52]

For Stimson and Marshall, the key function of the maneuvers was to answer a set of questions, among the most important being whether the Army's newly created paratrooper units could be dropped in large groups, which had been proved beyond a doubt. Remarkably, the only injury reported in the two 127-man drops in Louisiana had been a sprained instep one man suffered when he hit the ground in the second drop.[53]

Gradually, the Blue Army moved north toward Shreveport. Lear's defensive task was thankless and perhaps hopeless, as the superior Blue Army crossed rain-swollen rivers via pontoon bridges and dealt with other obstacles both natural and man-made. Eisenhower was impressed by the ingenuity of some of the men under his command. One story he loved to repeat: "An umpire decided that a bridge had been destroyed by an enemy attack and flagged it accordingly.* From then on, it was

---

* Often overlooked among the accounts of the maneuvers by reporters looking for the big story were dispatches that told of umpires behaving capriciously or, in some cases, vindictively. A report that appeared in one Louisiana newspaper told of an umpire who refused to deem a bridge destroyed when a satchel filled with simulated TNT was swung into the side of the bridge. The umpire ruled that simply hitting the bridge with a package of TNT would not have destroyed it. The colonel in charge of the "bombing"

not to be used by men or vehicles. Shortly, a corporal brought his squad up to the bridge, looked at the flag, and hesitated for a moment; then resolutely marched his men across it. The umpire yelled at him, 'Hey, don't you see that that bridge is destroyed?' The corporal answered, 'Of course I can see it's destroyed. Can't you see we're swimming?'"[54]

As Patton advanced toward Leesville, the Red Army believed he would attack from due north. But he suddenly wheeled his tanks west into East Texas, beginning a bold end run that involved a wide hooking movement that took him hundreds of miles from his supply lines. He kept his mobile forces up and running by using cash from his own wallet to purchase gasoline from commercial filling stations. The swing through Texas and back into Louisiana was a 380-mile journey that ended with a mass attack on General Lear's flank in a nighttime raid under blackout conditions. After surrounding much of Shreveport, Patton took the waterworks and the airport and was heading into the city. Controlling the water supply meant the battle was effectively over as a city without potable water was a city that would be forced to surrender. At this point, the Red Army claimed that its bombers had inflicted severe damage on Patton's tank columns and pointed out that Krueger's main force was still 25 miles south of Shreveport, albeit moving steadily toward the city.[55]

Captain Norris Perkins was on this end run through western Louisiana and East Texas with Patton and later put it into historic perspective as "the longest and most completely self-sustaining maneuver ever made by a large force in a short time." Perkins recalled troops and vehicles moving through river bottoms, swamps, and poorly maintained side

---

operation was furious and called the umpire a liar. The umpire retaliated by making the colonel a casualty. The colonel apologized, and the umpire accepted the apology but refused to retract his decision. At this point, the umpire searched through his supply of casualty tags and pinned one on the colonel reading G.S.W. (gunshot wound), which meant he had to relinquish his command and sit by the side of the road waiting for an ambulance to take him to a dressing station for treatment of the imaginary wound. Arthur Halliburton, "Umpire Rulings Also Get Hoots in War Games," New Orleans *Times-Picayune*, September 21, 1941, 10.

roads to accomplish what he called "a feat never before attempted or thought possible by a large armored unit."[56]

The maneuver ended on an explosive note: two massive smoke bombs were set off in front of Lear's headquarters by a Blue Army captain, who jumped out of a jeep to detonate them. Smoke billowed over the downtown business district, which some officers claimed was a simulation of artillery fire. The umpires declared the attack illegal pointing out that artillery fire could be shown only by a display of flags. Nonetheless, it was an effective way of underscoring the Blue Army's belief that it was about to take Shreveport.[57]

The games ended suddenly at 4:15 p.m. on September 28, when General McNair declared an armistice while the Red Army still held Shreveport. Church bells and factory whistles sounded loudly in the besieged city, presumably in thanks that the city's streets had not been torn up by Patton's tanks. McNair made it clear that the armistice was declared not because of the tactical situation but because of the calendar. Lear was to have been relieved by a fresh theoretical force on October 6; whether he could have hung on until then was a much-debated question. Minutes later, Marshall sent a message to McNair declaring the maneuvers "a great success" and proclaiming that "this new citizen army is on its way to becoming a powerful machine with all its parts in close cooperation."

To the great disappointment of the press and others who wanted to see a clear winner and loser, McNair refused to make such a declaration. Lear had prevented Shreveport from falling, and Krueger's main force was still 25 miles from Shreveport when the game was called. Even reporters disagreed. Lewis Sebring, who reported from the Second Army, stated that all the observers he talked with gave the Red Army the victory because it had held off an army three times its size. However, Jerry Baulch of the Associated Press asserted that even though the main force of the Blue Army was still miles to the south, one of Patton's columns of tanks had reached the gates of the city from the north, only to be stymied by the obstacle of a bayou five blocks from Ben Lear's headquarters. Baulch and others thought that if the games had been allowed to play out, the Blue Army would have won, especially when it came to street-by-street, hand-to-hand combat inside the city. Hanson Baldwin of the *New York Times* reported on a city under siege, almost ringed by enemy forces, with the city center within range of Blue artillery.[58]

Even after the maneuvers had ended, the question on the ground was how Patton's men had been able to fuel their tanks for their end run through Texas, which took them from Jonesboro to Leesville in one night. Don M. Ewing, associate editor of the *Shreveport Times*, had traveled with Patton on the trip through Texas and later reported that protests had been lodged against Patton based on the fact that he refused to say how he had fueled his tanks. According to Ewing, Patton's response was "the tanks are there what are you going to do about it."[59]

Life in the areas affected by the maneuvers began to return to normal after the soldiers left. On September 29, Eastern Air Lines resumed flights into Atlanta, New Orleans, Houston, San Antonio, Corpus Christi, and Brownsville. A few days later, three state colleges and 1,200 public schools in 31 Louisiana parishes opened.

Digesting and interpreting the results of the Louisiana Maneuvers began immediately after the September cease-fire. On October 3, the Army revealed its final death count of 94, the last two fatalities being a man killed in a taxicab accident in Vicksburg, Mississippi, and a private killed when the stove in a mobile kitchen exploded in Arkadelphia, Arkansas. This was below the estimate of 119 deaths made by the Army Surgeon General before the main exercises began, and the lower death count was regarded as an achievement. The Army maintained that the death rate among young men serving in Louisiana was lower than it would have been among men of the same age at home in the civilian population.[60]

As good as the average soldier proved to be, the exercises confirmed that he needed more training. "The Germans were training for seven years," General McNair said at the end of the games. "We are on our first lap. We expect more time than one year to fix us for the battle."[61]

Communications had been poor and relied to a large extent on commercial telecommunications, causing McNair to ask rhetorically whether the Germans had Bell Telephone in Europe. Two-way radios were in short supply in Louisiana, and most of those on hand had been used by the umpires rather than the troops. Human and pigeon couriers* were responsible for a large percentage of communications during the maneuvers. More than 1,000 pigeons had been sent into action, including many that rode inside tanks, whose radio equipment was often jarred out of adjustment and required avian assistance.[62]

Based on the effectiveness of Choctaw tribesmen as code talkers in the waning days of World War I, members of 17 Wisconsin and Michigan tribes effectively transmitted and received coded messages for the Third Army during the maneuvers. There were limitations on this form of communication because the men who could communicate this way were few and far between and the ancient tribal vocabularies did not contain modern military terminology. According to one report, a tank became a turtle and different types of aircraft became certain insects.[63]

To outsiders, one of the biggest surprises of the maneuvers was the success in moving large numbers of men and equipment. Visiting British officers were impressed by the American skill at handling convoys. Eric Sevareid told his CBS Radio listeners that the art of handling a modern army in combat is the purely mathematical business of controlling traffic. Marshall regarded this as one of the main accomplishments of the games.

Late in September, Sevareid found himself in the imaginary line of fire and was declared dead by an umpire. The same day that Sevareid was theoretically killed, John Charles Daly, also reporting for CBS, was gassed, and this was anything but theoretical. What stopped and stunned Daly was not same poison gas that rolled across the trenches in World War I but rather the noxious, blinding, irritating chemical smoke used as a stand-in

---

* The pigeons had received much press coverage in Louisiana since the day in July when the 280th Signal Pigeon Company traveled to Louisiana from Fort Monmouth, New Jersey, and set up a two-way communications system between Camp Claiborne and Camp Beauregard, 23 miles apart. Most of the nine officers and 134 men in the unit were pigeon fanciers in civilian life, and they created a system of pigeon mail during the maneuvers. Because the pigeons flew at altitudes above 5,000 feet, they were generally out of actual shell-fire range.

for the real thing in the maneuvers. Daly was choking and was saved from serious injury when he somehow found a gas mask that allowed him to escape the area in which he seemed trapped. He complained of a sore throat for the next three days. All of this made for melodramatic radio and underscored the fact that there were dangers inherent in reporting from a war zone—even one where there was no live ammunition.[64]

Systems designed to feed the troops in the field worked remarkably well. Paydays were conducted on time, even in remote areas, and laundry no longer had to be sent to Shreveport but was now done and delivered in an expedient manner. Louisiana saw the introduction of armed laundry units that performed a full cycle of washing and drying in 68 minutes. These units, such as the "Fighting Laundrymen" from Camp Lee, Virginia, were also full-fledged combat units. Tied to the 16 laundry companies in Louisiana were as many sterilization units, which deloused uniforms in the field before sending them to the laundry. The laundrymen were accorded the honorific moniker "button-choppers." The Quartermaster Corps, which supplied the Army, was learning the ratios it needed to keep the troops moving and content—one humble example: a roll of toilet paper served 45 enlisted men per day.[65]

The exercises also led to some disturbing discoveries. Perhaps the most dramatic was that men on the ground had a potentially fatal disregard for air attacks. Another shortcoming was their lack of discipline during blackouts, with the notable exception of Patton and his men. One general reported, "Troop discipline under attack by air forces was exceptionally bad." These battle faults he warned would result in "extremely heavy losses in time of war."[66]

Efforts to clean up the sin cities of the Delta had been only marginally effective. The worst example was Leesville, Louisiana, which had become the temporary capital of vice and corruption during the maneuvers. The governor of Louisiana had rejected all entreaties to clean up Leesville and dismissed criticism of its filth as "Yankee propaganda." The Army was coming to the realization that the key to controlling venereal disease was not in shutting down red-light districts but in equipping the troops with prophylactic care. Starting in 1940, all new soldiers received a 16-page pamphlet entitled "Sex and Venereal Diseases," which suggested abstinence but then cautioned: "If you do not have self-control, then do not fail to take safety measures."[67]

Two questions prior to the maneuvers had been whether mobile units could adequately replace horse cavalry and whether the horse cavalry was obsolete in modern warfare. Horse cavalry units took part in the maneuvers and acquitted themselves well, especially in their ability to safely move large distances over difficult, often muddy terrain. The First Cavalry Division covered 600 miles by hoof in 60 days in Louisiana, which included multiple river crossings. In one part of the exercises, thousands of cavalry mounts and cavalry troopers swam across a river at night, and neither a man nor a horse was lost in the crossing. For the 5,000 horses and 10,000 men of the cavalry who took part in the maneuvers, there seemed to have been earned one more chance to prove their usefulness in a modern army, as a large group of cavalry units were scheduled to take part in the upcoming maneuvers in the Carolinas.[68]

While Marshall and the war planners in Washington looked at such matters as the strength of supply lines and the comparative usefulness of the square vs. the triangular division, most of the men and women who had been brought in to report on the maneuvers were more interested in the morale and skill of the soldiers. The question they asked was not only would they fight but did they have the ability to fight.

The night the maneuvers ended, General McNair issued a statement that started and ended with a nod to the outstanding stamina of the men on the ground.[69] To McNair, stamina seemed to be an outward expression of the morale of the troops. As the maneuvers moved along, press coverage of morale drifted from bad to at least, as one observer termed it, satisfactory. The journalist-historian Mark Skinner Watson said, "The published whinings about the soldiers' sorrows and about the mud or dust perceptibly dwindled."[70]

Syndicated columnist Robert S. Allen, while embedded with the Second Army, stated without equivocation that there was nothing wrong with the morale of the Army. "It is as patriotic, as courageous as any army in U.S. history." Allen also said that when the men were confronted with Burton Wheeler and Charles Lindbergh's claim that the nation need not worry about an Axis attack, they dismissed it with a "short-blunt word." The men of the Second Army, he asserted, were aware that neither the Atlantic nor the Pacific Ocean made the United States immune to attack.

One of the units being most carefully monitored for its morale and leadership was the 27th Infantry of the New York National Guard, which had been featured in *Life* magazine weeks before, with a potential 50 percent desertion rate threatening. The 27th had been assigned to Lear's Red Army for the time in Louisiana. Mark Skinner Watson, writing for the *Baltimore Sun*,* revealed that as soon as the *Life* article appeared, the Army did a counter-inquiry and found that the division had a low percentage of men absent without leave or under extra discipline, an excellent health record, and an above-average efficiency rating. Watson watched troops of the 27th during one of the longest marches of the maneuvers, conducted in extremely uncomfortable weather, and saw no stragglers. Watson theorized that morale lagged in camps where soldiers rose at a fixed hour and were free after their exercises until it was time to sleep on orderly cots, but that morale picked up under the constant duress of the maneuvers.[71]

To ascertain the incidence of the kind of deep disaffection some military leaders feared, John H. Cline, a seasoned reporter for the Washington, D.C., *Evening Star*, was embedded with the Third Army for several days and spoke to dozens of men. Afterward he observed: "If there is anything wrong with the morale of the men of the Third Army, somebody down here is doing a swell job of camouflaging the

* Like many other writers at the maneuvers, Watson used the U.S. mail to get his dispatches from Louisiana to his newspaper, where each was published as soon as it was received. It is a testament to the system and the efficiency of air mail that the dispatch cited was written and mailed from Lake Charles on September 28 and appeared in the newspaper on September 30.

disaffection." One soldier he interviewed declared that if all men in his unit were discharged after their term was up, 75 percent would reenlist if there were any real danger of war.[72]

Morale also may have been buoyed by the tone of the exercises, which was serious but at certain moments downright amusing. Donald V. Bennett, a young officer who took part, described the maneuvers as an "equal measure of vision and farce." The term *farce* fit, as comic events and misunderstandings were common. Patton, who would later brag that he had never lost a battle, was stymied on September 26 during the second phase of the maneuvers when he heard the sound of cannon fire and assumed that light artillery had focused on his unit. He did not move for several hours until his scouts returned with three young boys and their harmless but noisy toy carbide cannon. The incident was awarded the mock-heroic title: "The Battle of Bermuda Bridge."[73]

Almost every day during the maneuvers, a story appeared about a humorous incident that would have been anything but humorous in actual warfare. For example, on September 18, a Red Army motorized column rushing to the front came upon a soldier at a fork in the road vigorously jerking his thumb. Without stopping, the column sped up the road indicated by the thumb jerker. As reported in *Newsweek*, after going three miles, the officers discovered their mistake: the soldier had been merely thumbing a ride, not directing traffic.[74]

As he had done in the 1939 maneuvers in Plattsburg and the 1940 maneuvers in Louisiana, Senator Henry Cabot Lodge Jr. was back on the ground in Louisiana, this time for two months of active duty with Patton's Second Armored Division, serving in both Louisiana and the Carolinas. Again he was the only member of the Senate to see active duty thus far in 1941. This time he came back to Washington with a new take on the status needs of the Army. He advocated an even stronger, larger army that should be relieved of "housekeeping duties," by which he meant, for example, that troops should not have to carry out such menial tasks as planting trees around barracks but instead stick to training in the field for war. He also believed that the Army needed to put a new emphasis on training specialists.

Lodge also reported that morale was "streaky," as it varied with different units and that the difference between those with good morale and those lacking it was "due to its officers." Lodge seemed to be giving Marshall encouragement to move ahead with the officer purge he had promised.[75]

Many of the troops came back from Louisiana spouting a new and irreverent slang. "Newly coined words flip from the agile tongues of sweating, marching 'gravel agitators' (foot soldiers in the infantry). Out of the 'hell buggies' (army tanks) come other, indelicate phrases," wrote journalist Ralph Martin. He reported many new terms, including "glamor boys" (draftees), who referred to their squad tents as "boudoirs" and their sleeping bags as a "snore sacks." Aviators told Martin that heavy bombers were called "flying box cars" and a "Chinese landing" was a landing with one wing low. Bess Stephenson, one of the female reporters brought to the maneuvers, noted that among the first things Army public relations people did when they welcomed new correspondents was to hand them a mammoth envelope. In addition to maps, it contained a dictionary of maneuver terms and a glossary of Army slang, strongly suggesting that the Army saw slang as a morale builder no matter how cynical it became. SNAFU, an acronym for "Situation Normal All Fucked Up," seems to have either debuted or been given a big push in Louisiana."[76]*

The maneuvers signaled a change in attitude about race, as black infantry, cavalry, and anti-tank units were widely praised for acquitting themselves well in mock combat, even in the press of the Deep South: "Negro

---

* SNAFU/snafu (pronounced *snaffoo*): A completely confused situation, short for "situation normal all fucked (fouled) up." It is defined in a 1944 slang dictionary as "temporary turmoil resulting from an abrupt change in orders . . ." The slang guides of the day insisted that the f-word was either "fouled" or "fuddled." The first report of the use of this term outside of the military came during the Louisiana Maneuvers when Henry Allen reported in his October 1, 1941, "Washington Merry-Go-Round" in the *Washington Post*: "Popular expression in the new citizen army, 'Situation normal, everything snafoo.'"

soldiers drew high praise from white officers and white soldiers in the ranks, all agreeing the Negro troops were superbly disciplined, ready to serve, and proud of their job."[77]

Praise also came from Marshall and other leaders who did not agree with General Douglas MacArthur and others who saw no place in the Army for African Americans outside of menial work and dangerous jobs such as handling live munitions. Still, despite the good showing of black troops, no talk of integration ensued. The African American press viewed the experience through a different prism, insisting that the black units—including three black regiments—saw little action in the games and received little combat training.[78]

Young cartoonist Bill Mauldin, whose 45th Division went to Louisiana, honed his skills during the maneuvers and found a growing audience for his work among his fellow soldiers as well as readers of the *Shreveport Times*. One morning, two civilians drove up to the camp asking for the "renowned" soldier-cartoonist. The men were from the Universal Press, a printer and publisher located in San Antonio, and they wanted to commission Mauldin to create a souvenir book of cartoons and sketches of the maneuvers. Mauldin created the book in a marathon 48-hour session. It was published as a small paperback, titled *Star Spangled Banter*, and sold for 25 cents. "I was nineteen years old and suddenly I was watching people with their noses buried in a book I had published," Mauldin later wrote. "The fact that I didn't hear another word from Universal Press and never learned where they mailed my royalties hardly hurt at all."[79]

Mauldin was quickly learning to see the world through the eyes of the guy on the ground. One of his Louisiana cartoons depicted an unshaven soldier crawling in mud during a rainstorm. A fellow soldier gestures at a reporter standing behind them, holding an umbrella, and says: "It's the press, he wants to know how's our morale?" Mauldin was still far from becoming a household name, but Louisiana showed that the men who populated the new Army needed and would support humor that was geared to their wry and somewhat cynical view of the world and the Army.[80]

CHAPTER 11

PROMOTION AND PURGE

A humorous finale to the Louisiana Maneuvers occurred the morning after the cease-fire, at the end of General Mark Clark's remarks to an assembly of senior officers of both armies. Clark was handed a list of officers whose promotions had been approved by Marshall, Stimson, and Roosevelt—ten to be major generals and ten to be brigadiers. While Clark had an inkling of what it contained, he had no idea who was on the list.

Aware of the fact that Eisenhower was sitting in the front row, Clark took a quick look and saw that his friend and West Point classmate was number three on the list for brigadiers, but when he read the list aloud, he deliberately omitted Eisenhower's name. "I tell you, you could hear a pin drop, and I didn't dare look at his face," he recalled later. "I knew what must be going through his mind and I knew that his face had to be red, and that vein had to be throbbing, but I left out his name and I said, 'That's all gentlemen. Congratulations.'" As the assembled group stood and prepared to leave, Clark banged the gavel and said, "Please be seated. I have an apology to make. I have made a grievous error. I neglected to mention the name of another officer to be brigadier general; he is number three on the list."

Clark heard Eisenhower say, as he rushed to the podium, "You sonofabitch, I'll get you. I could kill you."

"Ike," Clark pleaded. "I couldn't resist the temptation."[1]

Eisenhower accepted the promotion with what his granddaughter Susan later termed "characteristic modesty." He wrote in a note to a friend: "When they get clear down to my place on the list, they are passing out stars with considerable abandon."[2]

In the wake of Eisenhower's promotion, a myth arose that he had been virtually unknown and plucked from obscurity by George Marshall just before he appeared in Louisiana. "In reality," wrote Colonel Ty Seidule, an Army historian, "the last three Chiefs of Staffs [MacArthur, Malin, and Marshall] leading up to World War II considered him one of the top two or three officers in uniform."[3]

Little noticed in the final hours of the Louisiana Maneuvers, the first class of second lieutenants graduated from Omar Bradley's new officer candidate program at Fort Benning on September 27. Marshall had staked the Army's future, not to mention his own career, on these new officers who had come up from the ranks and wrote a speech for their graduation that was read by Brigadier General Omar Bradley, as Marshall was still in Louisiana. Marshall had a vision for these men and did not mince his words when he wrote: "Mental alertness, initiative, vision are qualities which you must cultivate. Passive inactivity because you have not been given specific instructions to do this or to do that is a serious deficiency. Always encourage initiative on the part of your men, but initiative must of course be accompanied by intelligence."[4]

Marshall believed this new junior officer corps being created under Bradley's leadership was absolutely essential for the United States to win a war. His biggest challenge now was to eliminate that element in the existing senior officer corps that hung over the Army like the Spanish moss hanging down from the trees of the Louisiana bayous.

While the morale of the men during the maneuvers was praised, officers received bad marks. Shortly after the maneuvers, General McNair held a meeting, open to the press, during which he demanded the immediate replacement of "weak officers." His major complaint was that officers had been unable to maintain discipline during the maneuvers, which he blamed on "the comparatively low training ceiling of officers"—a clear reference to Reserve officers and officers of the National Guard. The cardinal sin these men committed was sending masses of troops onto a road or path before making sure it was safe from enemy fire. The list of shortcomings included a disregard of orders for complete blackouts at night, inadequate scouting, and a failure of troops to be impressed by danger from the air. In certain National Guard units, men drank with their officers, called them by their first names, and were not punished when they went absent without leave.[5]

The fact that the Army was saddled with a large number of officers unable to lead could not be hidden from the experienced military writers who witnessed the maneuvers. In his last dispatch from Louisiana, Hanson W. Baldwin wrote of "officers who not only knew little but displayed no initiative and little common sense." He recounted how one officer allowed two soldiers under his command to drown while crossing a treacherous stream that in places was 20 feet deep. This officer, yielding to his men's enthusiastic desire to cross, permitted them to enter the water in full uniform, carrying heavy packs on their backs, and watched as they were swept away to their deaths. Baldwin's conclusion from the Louisiana exercises was that all problems exposed there, aside from lack of equipment, stemmed from poor or ineffective leadership.[6]

Baldwin also complained that the so-called purge was too slow in coming and needed to be pursued vigorously. The same day the new cohort of Army generals was named, Marshall wrote to the commanding generals of each field army urging them to reexamine officer fitness in their commands. The month of October, which had been long feared as the month in which draftees and Reservists would go over the hill, turned out to be the month in which many of their officers were forced over the hill.

The first major dismissal came on October 3, when Krueger fired Major General Morris B. Payne, 56, commander of the 43rd Division and the senior division commander in the U.S. Army, who had 10,000 men under his command. The War Department did not publicly state the cause for his removal, but the *Hartford Courant* reported about his active life outside the Army. He headed a New London, Connecticut, architectural firm, was an actively engaged Freemason, and was a Republican member of the Connecticut state senate—ample evidence of his part-time role as a soldier.[7]

In the purge now underway, rank and longevity could not guarantee immunity. In October, of the 42 corps and division commanders who had participated in the maneuvers, 31 were either relieved outright and reassigned to dead-end duties or allowed to retire. Hardest hit were the National Guard and Reserve officers. Marshall's restaffing of the National Guard had the full support of Stimson, who had himself been a Guardsman and by his own admission had an appreciation for how little the Guard had prepared many of its officers for the field of battle.[8]

Marshall had served in France during the First World War and learned firsthand the problems of having to relieve officers overseas after their worst defects were displayed at the front. This time Marshall wanted to avoid the enormous leadership disruption. At one point in the fall of 1941, Marshall confided to a friend that he might become as unpopular as Pershing had been when he had 32 generals scheduled for return to the United States during World War I.[9]

Both Stimson and Marshall did all they could to conceal the names of the officers who were being replaced, as it would have been harmful to the morale of the units involved and was deemed unfair to the men to be relieved of duty. Although most attention was focused on National Guard and Reserve officers, a greater number of Regular Army officers also were being either let go or reassigned to positions well removed from potential combat. Marshall, upon whom the heaviest responsibilities for the shake-up fell, said it was "the hardest thing we have to do."[10]

Marshall was personally affected when officers close to retirement had to be relieved of duty. In some cases, he faced the unpleasant task of telling an old friend that a long-sought promotion would now go to a younger man better suited to the demands of combat. As much as possible, he attempted to find new positions for these officers. But Marshall biographer Forrest C. Pogue noted that while many of these men understood and expressed gratitude, others became "convinced that Marshall was paying off old wrongs" and created "a small, bitter band within the ranks of the Army, eager to listen to personal attacks on Marshall and to offer their views later as ammunition for campaigns against him."[11]

The Regular Army men left or transferred to new posts, no matter how angry they were, but the National Guard senior officers were a different problem. Marshall feared that some of the National Guard generals would apply as much pressure as they could to stay in place for as long as possible. Marshall wrote to General Hugh Drum at the end of October that he feared these men would "hold on like grim death to their divisions, but we cannot make exceptions on this age business."[12]

The removal of the National Guard officers was often brutal and humiliating for those on the firing line. Even as units arrived in the Carolinas in October for the final set of maneuvers, Marshall's purge continued, and officers were relieved of their duties while hundreds of miles from their home base. Unlike the earlier dismissals, which had been done quietly, those in the field resulted in men being named publicly. On October 5, for example, 195 officers of the Massachusetts-based Yankee Division, a large National Guard unit, were relieved of their commands while bivouacked in a rural area of North Carolina and told to relinquish command to younger men on the spot. The order included three full colonels. (The official reason given for the overhaul was that the 195 officers removed were too old for their jobs.) The officers who were removed were told they had to serve immediately in non-active roles such as umpires, and most were told they would be removed from the service entirely on the division's return to Camp Edwards in Massachusetts. The division was told it had to move out at dawn the next morning with a new group of men in command.[13]

Age was only one reason for removal. One major general, whose National Guard unit was based at Fort Dix, New Jersey, was removed because of "dissatisfaction" with the poor morale and discipline of his unit, which had an unusually high desertion rate that had peaked when the draft legislation was extended.[14] As one historian of the National Guard wrote: "It was found necessary to make almost 100% replacement of the commissioned officers with troops from the grade of Major General down through the grade Col. and to replace an extremely high percentage of officers of lower rank."[15]

One of the forced replacements became a national story. Major General Ralph Emerson Truman, commander of the 35th Infantry Division of the Missouri National Guard in the Louisiana Maneuvers, part of Lear's Second Army, was relieved of his command in early October and given the choice of retiring or accepting a marginal position in an administrative role on the Second Army's reclassification board. He chose to retire. On the evening before he officially surrendered his command, Truman gave an insightful speech in Jefferson City, Missouri, in which he talked about the high level of morale and good spirits among his men and then addressed the impact of civilian morale. "Army morale will remain high unless it is torn down by civilian morale, and this would mean catastrophe."[16]

Truman had fought in both the Spanish-American and the First World War, during which he had been given a battlefield promotion to captain. He was a popular leader of the National Guard, and his first cousin was fellow World War I vet and former National Guard captain Senator Harry S. Truman. The senator said nothing in public, but two other senators—one a Republican, the other a Democrat—weighed in on what they regarded as outrageous and unfair treatment of Ralph Truman by Marshall and the War Department.

Senator John Chandler Gurney (Republican of South Dakota) demanded a congressional investigation of Ralph Truman's treatment, which went nowhere. But Democrat Bennett Champ Clark, the senior senator from Missouri, grabbed headlines after he asked Lear why he had taken Truman's command away. Lear replied to Clark in a telegram, saying that Truman had done outstanding service and that his departure would be regretted by Second Army headquarters. Clark fired back at Lear, telling him that he was the one who should retire rather than making Truman the "goat" for a tactical defeat Lear had made in the maneuvers. The reality was that for some months, General McNair had been highly critical of Truman's leadership of the division, and Lear, as head of the Second Army, had been attempting to remedy its shortcomings.[17]

General Pershing, now hospitalized, wrote to Marshall about Clark's charges, noting that such reactions were unavoidable and to be expected. Marshall responded by pointing out that the Clark attack was emblematic of the larger matter of the "unnecessary or rather the avoidable rumpuses" resulting from the unfortunate or tactless methods for removing and replacing those who had proved themselves to be unfit.[18]

Marshall told his old boss that the replacing of the unfit had led to a new problem, the controlling of senior officers who were so fearful of their own possible loss of authority that they were now "inclined to terrorize everybody below them." He explained: "It doesn't matter much how great the deficiencies are in leadership, I find myself very impatient with the man in the field who orates too much, and tactlessly, to his subordinates. The job is hard enough at best and it is awfully hard for these higher commanders in the field, but under present conditions in the development of the Army, some finesse is required."[19]

Finesse seemed to be in short supply as the purge continued. In fact, just as the Clark story broke, Stimson held a press conference to announce that 2,000 National Guard pilots and flight crew members who had been adjudged overage for combat duties would be reassigned to jobs on the ground.

Clark's charges were off base and ill considered, but one line in Clark's message to Lear seemed to resonate with members of the National Guard: "It is, of course, the old Army game which does not intend to leave a National Guard officer, no matter how efficient, in command of a National Guard division." This became a rallying cry for National Guard officers still in place who believed this to be the case.[20]

Veterans of the 35th Infantry Division, meeting in convention in Salinas, Kansas, condemned the purge of its leader and demanded that the governors of Missouri, Kansas, and Nebraska open an investigation of the Truman firing and other removals in the 35th Infantry.[21]

Less newsworthy were the protests over firings of other National Guard officers, many with strong political ties. It was announced by the Army in October that General Edward Martin, commanding officer of the 26th Division and head of the Pennsylvania National Guard, would be replaced because of his age (he would turn 62 on September 18) but would be kept on until the end of the Carolina Maneuvers. In the wake of Martin's dismissal, the entire Pennsylvania congressional delegation demanded and got a meeting with Marshall. He explained that he needed the best men in position for field leadership and with full military backgrounds, not part-time officers. When it became clear to Marshall that these arguments were failing to convince the delegation, he declared: "I'll put it this way, gentlemen. I don't understand your position because I should think that your constituents should be your principal interest—and here it seems to me that you are only considering one constituent and ignoring all [your] other constituents who are members of the division. I am concerned with them." Then he threw a stick of dynamite into the proceedings: "I am not going to leave him in command of that division. So I will put it to you this way—if he stays, I go, and if I stay, he goes." Marshall then recalled, "That broke up the meeting."

The following morning, one of the senators returned to the War Department, met with Marshall, and told him that he had told his wife about their meeting the previous day. She reacted by reminding him that one of the constituents Marshall alluded to was their son and that she was very happy he was in a United States Army headed by General Marshall.[22]

By the end of October, only 8 of the 18 National Guard divisions involved in the maneuvers were still under Guard commanders. The others had been replaced by Regular Army officers. In all, 269 National Guard and Army Reserve officers were either forced to retire or discharged from active duty during the late summer and early fall of 1941; among them were 31 colonels, 117 lieutenant colonels, 31 majors, and 16 captains of the Regular Army. Adding in the officers moved to positions without combat responsibilities, the total came to nearly 600.[23]

No matter how strongly Washington insisted that no purge was underway, rumors circulated that it would continue and reach into the highest echelons. On October 22, columnists Drew Pearson and Robert S. Allen announced that Hugh Drum, 62, commanding officer of the First Army; Ben Lear, also 62, commanding officer of the Second Army; and Lieutenant General John L. DeWitt, 61, commanding officer of the Fourth Army on the West Coast, were the next to go in the purge, and that Walter Krueger, 60, would be the only commanding general left standing. Word of the column leaked to Marshall the day before it appeared, so he sent telegrams to these generals letting them know that their removal was news to him. The report proved to be pure rumor but was indicative of the climate created by the purge.[24]

The transformation in Army leadership in Washington was not lost on others. British writer turned military gadfly H. G. Wells had become intensely critical of the older British generals, who he felt were incompetent and making blunder after blunder. He called for a British purge, which he noted Germany and Russia had already done. He added, "They are even having a purge in America." Wells believed that Britain was now paying dearly for not having had its own.[25]

The new American officers owed their promotions less to their "paper" record and time in service and more to their performance in the 1941 maneuvers. The officers who survived the October purge became, in the words of historian Carlo D'Este, the "nucleus of the new army," which in turn was improving the way it trained its newest members. Of the 18 former colonels on the list of new brigadier generals, seven were immediately assigned to one of the new Replacement Training Centers, where they were in charge of giving new recruits rigorous basic training. The Army now saw separate basic training as the essential means of turning rookies into well-disciplined soldiers, a departure from the old way of just placing them in divisions where they would be trained in place. So important were these new centers that officers put in charge of them who did well were promised important combat commands when war came.[26]

Meanwhile, the new army continued to build. In October, it stood at 1.6 million men, with an 11,000-member cadre of uniformed physicians, surgeons, and dentists to care for them. This would be the first time many of the soldiers had access to competent medical care.

On October 10, the president held a press conference in which he reported that of the first two million men called up, 900,000 were found to be physically or mentally unfit—enough to populate 13 full Army divisions. Some 200,000 of these men could be made available for full active duty, to which end the government was setting up a health rehabilitation program in which the potential draftees would be treated by local civilian physicians and dentists, who would in turn be reimbursed for their services. More than half of the remaining group could be restored to sufficient health to enable them to perform limited military service. The remainder included men with mental, nervous, heart, and lung conditions, and 100,000 who lacked the equivalent of a fourth-grade education.

The officer purges and health issues played against an international backdrop that underscored the new urgency to prepare for war. The Nazis were driving toward Moscow, slowed only by the rains and mud of the Russian autumn. The militant regime in Tokyo was increasingly belligerent. German U-boats torpedoed the U.S. Navy destroyer USS *Kearny* on October 10 and then sank the destroyer USS *Reuben James* on October 31 near Iceland. Suddenly, voluntary enlistments in the Navy started to go down, as young men and their parents realized that ships were not safe havens but targets, even before war was declared. For the first time in its history, the Navy warned that unless enlistments picked up, it might have to draft men from the general population instead of being all volunteer.[27]

CHAPTER 12

THE CAROLINAS:
THE FINAL SCRIMMAGE

As the Louisiana Maneuvers ended, plans were in place to stage the final set of 1941 Army maneuvers in a 10,000-square-mile historic military ground between Fort Jackson and Fort Bragg in North Carolina. This area had been occupied in part by British troops under Lord Cornwallis, who defeated the Americans during the Battle of Camden in 1780, and was also terrain over which Union general William Sherman had marched and burned stores of cotton and tobacco in 1865 during the Civil War. Some writers could not resist commenting on the irony of Northern soldiers in action in the Carolinas. "We judge from the history of Sherman's marches," wrote newspaperman and short story writer Damon Runyon, "that it will be a novelty to North and South Carolina to have a lot of soldiers running around down there without arson on their minds."[1]

These games would employ a mostly new cast of approximately 300,000 troops of the First Army, two armored divisions, and tank, engineering, and aviation units, as well as the horse cavalry, given another chance to show its value. The Army announced that it was adding 3,119 new mounts to its stable of 37,000 horses. It was also buying 140 new mules. The fiercely loyal horse cavalry contingent could point to its shining moments in the previous maneuvers, especially when horse and rider got to swim rivers when bridges had been destroyed and pontoon bridges had yet to be erected. In November, during the Carolina Maneuvers, the horse cavalry unit would get a new test against a motorized unit, meant to see which had the upper hand in reconnaissance.[2]

A series of preliminary exercises involving basic operational issues such as transportation, feeding, and supply were scheduled during the month of October and the first two weeks of November. The maneuvers themselves were scheduled to begin in earnest on November 16, 1941, as a battle between an infantry-superior Blue force, numbering 195,000, and a smaller but highly mechanized Red force, numbering 100,000. These maneuvers would end on November 30 and leave plenty of time to get the participating troops back to their home bases and furloughed in time for the 1941 Christmas season.

The commander of the Blue Army was General Hugh Drum,* while the smaller Red Army was led by Major General Oscar W. Griswold of the IV Corps, an example of an important new breed of officer, having jumped from colonel to major general in a little more than a year. At 55, he was now the youngest corps commander in the Army. Griswold's temperament appealed to reporters. "General Griswold is not the swashbuckling type of Army man," said Eric Sevareid on his CBS Radio show. "He never roars his commands, nor is he the grim, silent, incisive type . . . He is as amiable as the proprietor of a country store . . . The liking and respect in which his men hold him is obvious even to a layman's eye."[3]

Assigned to the smaller army, General George Patton's Second Armored Division would attempt to repeat his bold showings of the previous war games. In the weeks between the end of the Louisiana Maneuvers and the start of the Carolina exercises, the division had received more tanks and, more important, had been given new two-way radios to replace a primitive communications system dependent on the use of Morse Code. With a reliable, high-quality communications system in place, Patton felt his unit was "fit and capable of immediate

---

* Damon Runyon commented that Drum had the most appropriate surname for an Army officer he had ever heard.

and decisive combat in the event of a national emergency."[4] Another unit reassigned to this exercise was the once-infamous 27th Infantry of the New York National Guard.

The Blue Army was composed primarily of units from the Northeast, one of them the 26th Infantry Division, a Boston-based National Guard unit that attracted special attention because of the men in it. Colonel Theodore Roosevelt Jr., son of former president Teddy Roosevelt and a World War I veteran, headed the unit. His son, Lieutenant Quentin Roosevelt, and Sergeant Winthrop Rockefeller, 28, a grandson of the late John D. Rockefeller, were in the division. Colonel Roosevelt had a special bond with the 26th, as he had commanded the unit during World War I. Though young Rockefeller would be sent off to Officer Candidate School as the unit was en route to North Carolina, his presence nevertheless stood out as evidence to Americans that the rich and powerful were not exempt from service in the new army.[5]

The rolling terrain and numerous streams in the Carolinas were considered ideal for testing the mobility of armored units. At one point in the staging of the event, a line of more than 2,500 military vehicles stretched 425 miles, from Fort Benning to Rock Hill. The November weather in North Carolina was valuable in teaching the men how to survive in a colder climate like that of much of Europe.

Before the major exercises began, training battles in late October and early November got the troops ready for the main event. Reporters observing the men in the Carolinas marveled at the ability of the Army to feed itself in the field. The food, one of them said, was more varied and better prepared than the soldiers could find in the cafés and restaurants in the small towns scattered through the maneuver area. While complaints were shared about such things as the drudgery of kitchen duty, the discomfort of sleeping on the ground, and the monotony of daily life, one private said morale was "better now than it was when all that stew was going on in Congress about the length of service."[6]

What had first become evident in Louisiana and was underscored in the Carolinas was that the Army made no obvious attempt to censor the gripes of the troops on the ground, even when they became public. The Army being fashioned by Marshall and Stimson seemed to view public griping as a blessing—a way to blow off steam—rather than a curse. What had been deemed intolerable in earlier wars was now seen as a display of high spirits. The *Dallas Morning News*, quoting from a division newsletter, cited an example of the new freedom:

> Troops of the 45th were marching in the heat of the day. Sweat rolled down their faces and pasted their shirts to their backs. Presently the column passed a small house.
>
> Out in the garden a man was puttering leisurely. He looked cool and comfortable.
>
> "Say Buddy," sang out one of the soldiers. "If you ever get a letter from the government—don't open it!"[7]

A November report from the War Department noted that desertions in October were no higher than at any other time in recent history and that AWOL figures were low overall. On November 6, the *Washington Post* observed that October had come and gone and the OHIO movement had failed to materialize, because soldiers were "too busy making themselves cogs in what promises to be the greatest Army in American history."[8]

On November 11, General Marshall addressed the nation over the NBC Radio Network to announce the formation of a civilian defense force, by which the nation at large would participate in its own self-defense by the appointment of air-raid wardens, police auxiliary, firefighters, first aid workers, and hospital service staff across the country. The force would be alert to Nazi sabotage, which, Marshall said, included Nazi propaganda. Marshall then read from the instructions issued by Germany's ministry of propaganda the previous April: "'It is more effective,' these instructions state, 'when the American press provides propaganda for our mill than if we do it ourselves.'"

"Now what happened last summer?" Marshall asked in his radio address. "The [draft extension] debate was on, the criticisms of our good faith and judgment were naturally frequent, and the more unfavorable reactions of individual soldiers were broadcast. Mass desertions were reported to threaten the Army in October." Marshall noted that "the cleverest move to capitalize on this golden opportunity for sabotage" was for the Nazis and their agents to plant the false report rumors among the troops in certain National Guard units that more than 1,000 men of the Regular Army had already deserted as a group from an unidentified division. "The men had been fed this particular rumor because such an occurrence in the Regular Army was indicative of a general breakdown in discipline. The actual fact in this matter was that the division in question had one lone desertion in the period referred to." Marshall, who had done his best to neutralize the America Firsters, now alleged that they and their allies in the press were actively—even if unknowingly—working with the Nazi propaganda machine.[9]

The United Service Organizations (USO), now calling itself the "army behind the Army," had quickly learned from the lessons of Louisiana how it could provide maximum aid and comfort to the troops and became an even more powerful and efficient force in the Carolinas. For example, in the September maneuvers, many service stations had locked their men's restrooms when they saw troops approaching. The station owners argued that the many troops were too messy to deal with. The USO took them at their word and organized a traveling cleaning service that would tend to the messy restrooms if the owners of the service stations agreed to keep them open.

In hundreds of small towns, the USO set up a system by which locals would place barrels of ice water under shade trees along country roads. Patriotic citizens wanting to organize tea parties and other social events for the troops were told by the USO that they would do more for morale if they instead allowed their garages and other outbuildings to be rigged with the pipework needed to convert them into showers and to distribute benches for tired troops to sit on. For those willing to have showers built, the USO would install the necessary hardware.[10]

The USO was learning to respect religion and actively helped to provide for the religious needs of all, as attested to by the widespread observation of Yom Kippur, which fell on October 1.* But the USO was not to go over the line into proselytizing or evangelizing the troops. Under Marshall, the Army regarded religion as an important element in the lives of its men, but the commander made sure that it was not in the business of saving souls. "If you rush the soldier he'll run away and you never will see him again," was the message delivered to a USO convention on October 9 by a high-ranking Army morale officer, who added: "And besides he doesn't have horns and probably doesn't need saving anyway because he has never been lost."[11]

For the first exercise of the Carolina Maneuvers, the "international boundary" was the Pee Dee River. The orders for the two sides were simple: Drum's Blue Army was to cross the Pee Dee and sprint westward into Red territory and try to prohibit the Red Army from crossing the Catawba River, which was 60 miles to the west; at the same time Griswold was to move across the Catawba and head east to the Pee Dee to stem the Blue Army invasion. Drum planned to get across the Pee Dee along a 75-mile line while Griswold's plan was to speed three motorized divisions to the Pee Dee to defend the position it held there, while his infantry divisions occupied Monroe, North Carolina, a town halfway between the two rivers.

As the exercise began at 6:30 a.m. on November 16, Griswold's Red Army began crossing the Catawba, while reconnaissance troops sped toward the Pee Dee. Some of Patton's troops crossed the Pee Dee and immediately captured General Drum, who was returning to his Blue headquarters after watching his own men cross the river. He was stopped and greeted by a young officer who took him into custody.

---

* Captain Bernard Segal, a Jewish chaplain, reported to the Boston-based *Jewish Advocate* that he had brought the Jewish families of Jennings, Louisiana, who for years had been isolated from Jewish affairs, together with Jewish soldiers for Yom Kippur services.

General McNair was then notified that the Blue Army commander had been taken prisoner. Shortly following his capture the umpires ordered Drum's release, ruling that the capture was unrealistic and would not have occurred during the conditions of a real war. Unfortunately for Drum, the incident was reported in the newspapers, often under the most unflattering headlines.*

The Drum story hung on as reporters who had not actually witnessed the capture wanted the Army to officially confirm it. On November 25, after avoiding the issue for more than a week, McNair reluctantly confirmed it at a press conference and ineptly attempted to defend Drum: "I think considerable credit should attach to General Drum for being up there where he could be captured."[12]

The significance of Drum's early capture underscored Patton's strategy, which was likened to a raid by the Confederate cavalry in the American Civil War. His armored units continued to mount raids behind enemy lines, although Patton had to be routinely reminded of the delicate balance between raw strength on the battlefield and the mundane business of keeping his tanks fueled and functioning. Drum had an intense dislike for Patton, based on several past incidents, the most public occurring in 1936 during a polo match in Hawaii, when Drum—then Patton's commanding officer—rebuked him for his strong and offensive language. Then colonel Patton's teammates, who were largely from Honolulu's moneyed class, stood up for the well-heeled colonel and Mrs. Patton, thereby humiliating Drum, who used the occasion to give an official reprimand to Patton.[13]

Aside from the capture of Drum, the first phase of the maneuvers tested the ability of the anti-tank divisions to hold the armored divisions in check. Although it appeared to those observing the action that the armored divisions held the upper hand through the next few days and nights, the final critique announced that the tank-fighting

---

* One of the South Carolina newspapers later reported that after Drum's capture his troops nicknamed him "Snare Drum." Orangeburg *Times and Democrat*, December 26, 1941, 4.

methods, which included the use of 4,000 guns of all types, had proved themselves against the tanks. The two armored divisions had begun the exercise with 800 tanks and were judged to have lost 983 tanks during the action. (Under the rules, a destroyed tank came back to life after a certain number of hours, thus allowing a given tank to experience more than one destruction.) In his critique, General McNair said that the First Armored Division had been "substantially destroyed," and Patton's Second Armored Division had been bottled up and split into feeble elements. The "tank killer" units were praised for their bold and aggressive abilities.

Drum and his First Army had won the most decisive battle of the 1941 maneuvers thus far but had done so with a certain amount of cheating, which was pointed out in a confidential report on the operation by McNair. Among other infractions, Drum had used trucks carrying rations, which were immune from capture under the rules, to practice espionage deep behind Red lines. One such truck confiscated by the umpires contained "a single can of coffee, one box of sandwiches and a half dozen men of the Blue Army.[14]

McNair put it all into the context of events in Europe: "Lack of massed guns in France was a major cause of the disaster there. In Russia, the Russian inferiority in tanks was increased when tanks had to be used to fight tanks instead of guns being used to stop tanks and the Russian tanks saved for the counterattack. That is the situation we were trying to avoid." The harshest criticism was leveled at the pilots, who lost aircraft at a tremendous rate—far more than could be afforded in actual combat—because pilots constantly flew too low over antiaircraft defenses.[15]

After five days of mock combat, the two armies got the weekend off. Unexpectedly, the nighttime temperatures in the Carolinas in late November dropped dramatically. Campfires were banned as blackout conditions were ordered, and each man was issued three blankets. One participant in the exercise later recalled that the only thing he actually learned in the Carolina maneuvers was how to deal with the cold: "We found out what it felt like to sleep on the ground in pup tents and with no pup tents, in rain, sleet, and snow. It taught every soldier to remember where he last left his overcoat, raincoat, dry socks, long underwear, gloves, scarf, and anything else that he could put on to stay warm. The loss of one glove could make a soldier no use on the open field."[16]

Captain Norris Perkins was also in the Carolinas with Patton and later described how the tank men dealt with having to sleep on the cold ground between trees where you were less likely to get run over in the middle of the night. He noted that reporters covering the maneuvers commented on how quickly soldiers of the Second Armored were able to fall asleep. "This," he explained later, "is based not only on mental and physical fatigue but on the security and equanimity of being part of a well-trained unit."[17]

In 1941, Thanksgiving was celebrated nationally on November 20, when the two armies were still in the field "fighting," so their observation of the holiday was moved to Sunday, November 23, between the two phases of the maneuvers. It was a testament to the ability of the Quartermaster Corps that every man was promised—and got—a pound of turkey, celery dressing, mashed potatoes, giblet gravy, lettuce and tomato salad, fresh celery hearts, and sliced pickles.[18]

After the weekend, in response to Marshall's insistence that the armies be able to move quickly and adroitly, as they would have to in a real war, the armies were transported to new areas in South Carolina for the beginning of the second phase of the maneuvers. Thousands of tanks and other vehicles rolled over both hard roads and rutted dirt roads. One journalist traveling with the troops reported that crossroads were jammed over hundreds of square miles of countryside as "military police labored valiantly to untangle the snarls."[19]

Although the Army proved its ability to get fresh food into bivouacs deep in the Carolina woods, the ability to deliver gasoline was an even more dramatic one. Approximately 6.5 million gallons were needed. "Think of enough gasoline to take your automobile to the sun—93,000,000 miles—and that will give you an idea of the amount of fuel needed to keep Uncle Sam's motor vehicles moving during the First

Army maneuver," is how one newspaper expressed the thirst for gasoline that had to be quenched in the Carolinas. Oil companies brought fuel into the 16 counties in which the maneuvers were conducted by railroad tank cars and tank trucks.[20]

Even before the main event, a truck loaded with gasoline containers crashed into a truck carrying soldiers, who were showered with burning gasoline. Four soldiers were burned to death and another 11 were seriously wounded, one of whom, an early report stated, was not expected to live. The accident focused attention on the difficulty the Quartermaster Corps had in fueling armored vehicles and tanks. Prior to the games, since not enough trucks existed to keep the armored divisions moving, locally leased railroad tank cars were employed for tank refueling.[21]

Almost all the men who died in the Carolinas were killed in road accidents. The nation slowly realized that these deaths in mock combat were heroic. As an editorial in the *Miami Herald*, titled "Died for Country," put it: "Even playing war is dangerous. These young Americans are as dead as if felled by an enemy bullet."[22]

Many of the reporters covering the mock war in the Carolinas were less interested in the actual battles than in the officers and men fighting them. Eric Sevareid of CBS became infatuated with the mettle and spirit of the men in the Carolinas. Each night for the better part of two weeks, he reported on live radio from an embedded position with the troops of Griswold's army—the David in this mock war against Drum's Goliath. This was a faster contest than the one waged in Louisiana. Sevareid told his listeners on the night of November 17: "The new American armored force, the pride and hope of the army, is getting its first real chance to show what it can do . . . The forests aren't so thick, there are more side roads [than in Louisiana] . . . There are wide stretches of flat land where the tanks can cut across in a swirling cloud of dust presenting a much more difficult target to the enemy planes and guns."

One soldier Sevareid interviewed in his first report from the Carolinas was Massachusetts senator Henry Cabot Lodge Jr. He was now Captain Lodge and was helping to run a tank exercise: "Lodge is the most impeccable man in the Senate," Sevareid reported. "Today the grime was so thick on his unshaven face the most eager lobbyist couldn't have placed him, but you never saw a happier man." As in earlier exercises, Lodge was not without expressing his opinion on what the Army needed to make it more efficient. Speaking from the "front," he advocated the widespread use of half-tracks to move infantry units into combat. "This would speed the movement of infantry and give the men more protection against artillery."[23]

The syndicated newspaper columnist Walter Lippmann flew to the Carolinas to form his own opinion. In 1941, Lippmann was the most influential political columnist in America. His column in the *New York Herald Tribune*, entitled Today and Tomorrow, was syndicated to more than 100 other newspapers, connecting him to millions of readers. Lippmann had served in France as a captain in the intelligence service in 1918. In the Carolinas, he saw a new army as different from the old army, "as New York City is different from the New York where as a small boy I kept a goat in the stable around the corner."

Lippmann viewed the Army of 1917–18 as "alien" to American traditions and aptitudes: "The mass armies of the First World War were the culminating phase of a European tradition in which highly drilled masses of men were used, without regard for human life or respect for individual capacity, as living weapons." Lippmann now saw a U.S. Army that was a complex organization of spirited small teams built around a tank, an armored car, or an airplane—a far cry from the desolate band of recruits he had seen the previous spring and summer, who had reminded him of garage attendants out of a job. As he watched the soldiers in the Carolinas, he saw an army, no longer a collection of uniformed civilians. His highest praise was saved for General Marshall and the War Department, which he thought had done brilliant work in transforming the state of the institution in just 12 months. The nation, he felt, had prepared itself for any emergency.[24]

On November 24, seasoned military writer Frederick Palmer filed a report from Washington on his return from the Carolinas. Palmer, whom Theodore Roosevelt once called "our best war correspondent," had been the first reporter to be given the Army's Distinguished Service Medal for his coverage of the First World War. He, too, took great satisfaction in watching this new army, which he felt was on its way to becoming a cohesive force for mass action. The Army he saw in the Carolinas, he judged, was now out of the bush leagues and into the minor leagues in terms of efficiency. "But it cannot qualify for a major league status with wheel spokes for bats," he added, alluding to the need for better and more equipment.[25]

Palmer and other observers could see the usefulness of the para-troopers who put on a compelling show in the Carolinas. On November 25, the Blue Army parachutists performed a double twilight drop that was stunning in its simplicity and effectiveness. The first drop was a feint, in which 50 men landed and drew defensive forces away from the second landing area, where an hour later 100 men floated to earth and charged a company of black infantrymen before dispersing and hiding in the dark woods. Almost the entire first group of paratroopers was captured, but few members of the second group were. More than 1,000 Red Army soldiers looked for the second group, which within two hours had cut telephone and telegraph lines and "destroyed" one highway bridge and two pontoon bridges.[26]

As had been true in earlier maneuvers, the troops were forced to use makeshift stand-in objects for real weapons. "Jokes and wisecracks about our make-believe weapons circulated among the troops," a participant later recalled. "A supply sergeant, tending a wooden-barreled tank gun, would say with a straight face that he was waiting for the anti-termite stuff he had requisitioned; others would complain that they had not received the paint and varnish for their stick rifles."[27]

Two days after the special Thanksgiving celebration, the second and final phase of the maneuvers got underway, with the action switching from roughly north–south to east–west. Griswold's orders were to station his Red Army to defend a bridge crossing the Wateree River, as the Catawba is called in South Carolina, at Camden. Drum and his Blue Army were not told that Griswold's mission was to defend Camden. Drum was only informed that a strong Red force was advancing from the southeast and fording the Wateree River near Camden.

Drum now advanced cautiously against the Red Army as his warplanes bombed the bridges that crossed the Wateree. Griswold then created defensive lines protecting Camden, while columns from his three mobile divisions launched successful attacks. Patton located and then attacked the Blue line west of Monroe, North Carolina, as Monroe itself was attacked by the Red Fourth Motorized Division.

Believing that the Red Army intended to make the Monroe front its main line of defense, Drum ordered that Monroe be held while his other forces struck from Cheraw, South Carolina, to attack the Red force from the rear, driving the Red Army from both Monroe and Cheraw on November 26. Drum made several bold offensive moves and by the end of the day on November 27 announced to his troops that the Red Army east of the Catawba was now surrounded and would soon surrender. According to the account given by Rice Yahner of the Associated Press, who was traveling with the Red Army, it had been forced into a "great funnel with the little end at a vital river crossing."[28]

But with victory within his grasp, Drum made a series of moves that allowed Griswold to counter-attack, and so early on November 28, Drum found himself defending against well-executed armored counterattacks, though with a heavy loss of Red Army tanks. At the end of the day, as Griswold regrouped for a second attack, McNair ended the final phase of the 1941 maneuvers. The Red Army was still hemmed in and Drum was quick to claim victory while Red Army officers claimed a moral victory based on what they saw as bad calls and restrictions made by the umpires.[29]

The following day, the Army announced that 93 soldiers had died during the exercises—81 accidental and a dozen from natural causes.*

---

* This total was remarkably close to a War Department estimate made on September 10 that 70 participants would be killed and 30 would die of disease in the Carolina Maneuvers. As had been pointed out at the end of the Louisiana Maneuvers, this toll would be considerably lower than that among a corresponding number of male civilians of the same age during the same period of time.

* * *

The three maneuvers gave the Army an appreciation of how much work still needed to be done on the quality of its weaponry. Captain C. Lincoln Christensen, who had been given a commission in the Army's Ordnance Department in August, was sent to the maneuvers to evaluate various weapons in the field. His primary assignment was to look at the suitability of the M3A1 tank for combat operations. He later recalled, "There was some concern, based on what had been learned from armored operations being conducted in Europe, that the M3A1, which was our standard medium tank, would be unable to compete against the tanks of some of our possible opponents." This concern focused on the tank's engine, a Wright Aeronautical nine-cylinder, air-cooled radial model, which Christensen noted was a more powerful version of the type of engine that powered the *Spirit of St. Louis*, the plane Charles Lindbergh had flown across the Atlantic.

Christensen quickly discovered that the tank was flawed. Its lack of power caused sluggish performance, and its engine overheated, generating a host of mechanical problems. Certain design weaknesses affected its combat performance, particularly its high silhouette and the limited traverse velocity and the low muzzle velocity of its 75 mm gun. His report was presented to top brass from the War Department in a large tent near Camden, South Carolina, right after the maneuvers ended. The officer responsible for the performance of the M3A1 fleet gave a detailed and spirited defense, declaring that it was better than the British heavy tank. "At that," Christensen reported, "a high-ranking general at a command level in the maneuvers exploded, saying, '[Expletive]! We're not going to fight the British!'" Although not named by Christensen, it can be easily surmised that the comment came from Patton. Almost immediately, work began on a modification package for the tank that greatly improved its engine and turret design and thereby its performance and reliability.[30,*]

* As Christensen noted: "The later M3A5 tank with lower silhouette, fully rotating turret, and higher muzzle-velocity cannon—called the General Grant by the British—was used

If the tanks themselves fell short, tank leadership was another matter. On November 27, the next to last day of the maneuvers, George Marshall and members of his staff flew to North Carolina for a final look at the troops before they began their return home. Since Marshall's first visit earlier in the month, the threat from the Japanese had become more severe, and it was becoming clearer that war with Japan was potentially imminent. Negotiations with Japan for a non-aggression pact had ended abruptly that same day. Later, Senator Homer Ferguson (Republican of Michigan) questioned Marshall's decision to leave Washington at the height of the Japanese crisis. Marshall biographer Forrest Pogue reported the general's reaction: "Forgoing the obvious rejoinder that the President and other top government officials were still in the city, the Chief of Staff rested his defense on one episode of the trip. He recalled with relish the splendid performance of one of the armored force commanders, a certain George S. Patton. As a result he had set that fiery soldier on the road to high command." What had impressed Marshall most about Patton had been the way he handled his division.[31]

Patton's behavior at all three of the 1941 maneuvers was controversial in that he followed his own freewheeling instincts, such as the prankish capture of Drum that disrupted the first exercise in the Carolinas and infuriated McNair, especially when Patton disappeared with his high-ranking captive. Additionally, Patton gave scant respect to the umpires. When they determined that he and his men had violated the rules by going outside the designated area, Patton retorted that he was unaware of any such rules in actual warfare. He was accused of grandstanding and worse.[32]

But Patton's hell-raising approach to mock warfare demonstrated the very spirit and determination that Marshall and McNair found lacking in so many officers. Patton was censured by both the umpires and McNair for his audacity, but his reputation in the eyes of Marshall and

---

very effectively by Bernard Montgomery in the desert fighting against Erwin Rommel and his somewhat better armed tanks, beginning at the Battle of Gazala in June 1942 prior to U.S. troops entering the war in North Africa."

Stimson had risen by employing the very audacity the new army so badly needed.

At the end of the maneuvers, public perception of the Army, helped by on-the-spot radio reports and front-page coverage in most newspapers, had shifted from negative to positive. People began to understand that the American soldier was tough, resilient, and ready to defend the country. One defense expert, writing for the International News Service, noted that the final cost of bringing a soldier into the 1941 maneuvers, over and above the cost of keeping that same man in camp for the same amount of time, was approximately $22. He added: "That's probably the cheapest cost there has ever been for turning camp soldiers into field soldiers. And it's field soldiers that you fight wars with."[33]

The new recruits were children of the automotive age, and Patton and others discovered that a man able to tinker under the hood of a Ford or Chevy could do the same with the engine of a tank or an aircraft. For many of these men, their first encounter with jeeps and half-tracks was love at first sight. The draftees were also, for the most part, adroit map readers, thanks to the millions of maps given away by gasoline and oil companies. As one Second Army intelligence officer put it: "Give an American soldier a map and a compass and you'll have a hard time losing him."[34]

One chaplain told a reporter at the end of the maneuvers: "Morale isn't a problem anymore now that the men are busy." Mary Hornaday, one of six female reporters brought to the Carolinas to get the "woman's angle" on the exercises,* reported in the *Christian Science Monitor* that the morale shoe was on the other foot: the soldiers now worried about civilian morale. "The people back home don't take this business seriously

---

* The women reporters wore special green armbands and, unlike their male counterparts, could not be captured. Ruth Cowen of the Associated Press wrote that the effort to bring women into the mock conflict was an effort to mix "face powder with gun powder." In her dispatch of November 17, Cowen mentioned that she had brought a complete wardrobe to the war zone, including an evening dress. AP, "Powders—Face and Gun—to Mix in Army Games," *Seattle Times*, November 17, 1941, 5.

enough," a grimy Army Air Corps pilot complained. "They think we're down here playing."[35]

Eric Sevareid, who had seen the power of the Germans and watched the collapse of the French army in 1940, now lavished praise on the paratroopers, whose drive, fight, and *esprit de corps* were, in his words, "enough to take your breath away."[36] At one point he watched paratroopers drop and then destroy a bridge, only to be told by an umpire that the bridge had not been properly rigged before it was blown up and was ruled to still be standing. The young paratroopers were furious with the ruling and demanded that the umpire change his mind.

> One young boy, the one who had supervised the dynamiting, was trembling with rage and disappointment, like a high school football player pulled from the game for fouling, and almost on point of tears. His voice shaking with anger, he informed the umpire that his men still controlled the area and they could blow the bridge a dozen times if need be, until it went down. In the end, the umpire was an engineer himself and hated to see the engineers defeated, and gave in. The bridge was officially out.

The next morning, traffic again moved over the bridge, which had been restored under the rules of the game. But the paratroopers had done a thorough job on the phone lines, which still did not function. "But by grace of chance, this broadcast line was overlooked," Sevareid said, live on the radio, as he switched the broadcast over to his partner, Bill Slocum Jr., embedded with the Blue Army.[37]

The parachute drop that Sevareid witnessed was one of several staged in the Carolinas, which saw greater involvement of the Army Air Corps than the previous 1941 exercises. Some new equipment and techniques were tested for the first time, and one innovation stood out above all others. Although little noticed at the time, in early November in the small town of Marston, North Carolina, the Army aviation engineers had spent 11 days constructing an all-weather airport

runway composed of 1,000 tons of perforated steel plates that were
each ten feet long, 15 inches wide, and a mere eighth-inch thick. The
finished runway, 150 feet wide and 3,000 feet long, was used to land and
launch every conceivable type of aircraft, from a Piper Cub to a large,
5,000-horsepower bomber. It was judged by the pilots who landed on it
to be less slippery in wet weather than conventional airstrips. Because
it was perforated, grass would quickly grow through the mat giving
it natural camouflage The engineers in charge said that with a little
practice they could learn to lay a runway in two days. General Henry
H. "Hap" Arnold, the head of the Air Corps, saw the strip in action
and immediately labeled it the year's greatest advance in aviation. At
the conclusion of the maneuvers, it was taken apart, loaded on flatbeds,
and removed to Langley Field in Virginia, where it was immediately
named the "Marston Mat."[38]

Choking clouds of dust had long plagued the Army, but they
became a major problem with the rise of motorized warfare—especially
in a period in U.S. history when parts of the country had been plagued
by fierce dust storms. Standard gas masks were effective against poison
gas but could not filter out dust particles. The Army experimented, in
all three maneuvers, with commercially available dust respirators used
by coal miners, which proved to be highly effective, and then began to
create its own version.[39]

On November 30, General McNair issued a statement to those
who had fought in the Carolinas, which he shared with the Associated
Press. He opened with the oft-asked question of whether these men
now returning home were ready for war and then answered it: "It is
my judgment that, given complete equipment, they certainly can fight
effectively. But it is to be added with emphasis that the losses would be
unduly high, and the results of action against an adversary such as the
Germans might not be all that could be desired."

He spoke of the "remarkable progress" that had been made in
one year but pointed out that further training was clearly necessary. He
called the American soldier "an inspiration and a challenge to leaders

who he would follow anywhere, [and who] asks only that they bring him success and victory."[40]

On December 3, Secretary Stimson brought key members of the military to his office to determine the collective lessons learned in all the 1941 maneuvers. General McNair led the discussion, repeating much of what he had said several days earlier and pointing out that training had progressed satisfactorily and leadership in the larger units had improved noticeably over the course of the maneuvers. The anti-tank experiment had worked favorably and one lesson coming out of the maneuvers was that tanks could be stopped with properly positioned heavy artillery. However, McNair noted disturbing deficiencies in the training of individuals and in small-unit leadership, which, with some notable exceptions, had been called to task in Louisiana.

McNair admired the horse cavalry, which he admired for its "magnificent" performance and high degree of morale in both Louisiana and the Carolinas—but in the end, the maneuvers cast it in an unfavorable light as the mechanized cavalry had shown a distinct advantage over the horse cavalry in the exercises, despite determined attempts to make it relevant to modern combat. In some exercises in both Louisiana and the Carolinas, horses had been loaded onto truck trailers, hauled for considerable distances, unloaded, mounted, and ridden into battle, but the results were uniformly poor when compared to the performance of motorized units. Henceforth and to the dismay of many, the era of the soldier on horseback had ended, and only a few horses would be kept for ceremonial purposes. Those at the meeting also reached the conclusion that ground-to-air radio communications were simply terrible and that communications in general were way too slow.[41]

Very few first-person accounts of draftees who served in the 1941 maneuvers exist, but one that has is a memoir from Private Jack Womer of Dundalk, Maryland, who took part in the Carolina Maneuvers as an infantryman in the 29th Infantry Division, which had been first created in February 1941 and mostly comprised of men from the National Guard and draftees.

Womer, who had been drafted in April 1941, actually saw the maneuvers as a joke in the sense that it was so easy to trick the system by disguising yourself as the enemy you were fighting. "All you had to do was find out when and where the colored identification material (usually armbands) of the opposing army was being handed out, and go there and act just like the other guys that were supposed to be there. In essence, you were getting false identification, which you would carry in your pocket. During a war game, if you saw enemy troops and felt that you were going to be spotted or captured, all you had to do was remove your own identification, hide it, and put on the fake colored identification."

But Womer was actually loath to use his false identification because, as he later explained, he was "delighted" to be captured for the simple reason that a prisoner in the Carolina games was well fed and allowed to sleep as much as he wanted.[42]

At this point in his military service, Womer hated both the Army and the maneuvers but was quick to admit that life in the field with all of its privations—including going for days with little to eat or drink and no change of clothing—had made him tough. "I had learned how to survive off the land, and I was determined to withstand anything the army could dish out at me." He added: "A lot of us felt the same way."[43]

The Veterans of Future Wars had been all but forgotten for four years, until November 30, 1941, when the *Washington Post* carried a feature entitled "'Veterans of Future Wars' Are Becoming Just That," by Edward T. Folliard. It opened with: "Where are they now, those droll college boys who, back in 1936 organized the Veterans of Future Wars and demanded a $1,000 bonus in advance? Answer: Some are in the Army and some are preparing to go into the Army—for the usual $21 a month without bonus." Folliard talked about Future Wars alumnus Tommy Riggs Jr., who was registered and ready to go overseas with the Army.

*   *   *

As had been true of the two earlier 1941 maneuvers, the troops return-ing to their home camps from the Carolinas often left with something more than they came with. The 1941 maneuvers created their own culture and generated their own memorabilia, including felt pennants, *faux* campaign ribbons and medals, commemorative pillowcases, and both pictorial and comic postcards dedicated to the event. Snapshots abounded. One of the most common items the men took to the maneu-vers were box cameras (most commonly the Kodak Brownie), which were used to photograph everything in sight. "They are not official items of equipment and are frowned on by the high command, but everywhere you go the inevitable camera appears," a reporter from the *Kansas City Star* observed. He described watching a group of soldiers gather around a jeep and take snapshots of one another, posing in the vehicle and in front of it. Umpires reported that at their worst, some troops responded to air attacks by running into the open to enjoy the show and often take photos.[44]

One enterprising private drew, published, and sold a souvenir map of the route of the First Armored Division through the main Louisiana Maneuvers areas, which included such non-tactical sites as swimming holes. *Army Laughs* magazine, which debuted in early 1941, was one of several new monthly humor magazines catering to the citizen army. Humor often revolved around plays on the word *maneuvers*, as a term for both military exercises and moves made during the ritual of seduc-tion. The December 1941 cover showed a corporal leading a scantily clad woman into the woods with the caption: ARE THESE MANEUVERS OR JUST MANEUVERS?[45]

This culture was wry and whimsical, with more than a whiff of insubordination. Soldiers would later claim that in some cases the OHIO declaration (Over the Hill in October) had been an easy way to blow off steam more than an actual declaration of intent to desert. *OHIO* was just one of hundreds of freshly coined slang terms and expressions coming out of the mouths of the men, who seemed to like to attach the initialism *G.I.* (government issue) to many terms. A *G.I. haircut* was hair cut to one inch; the 1941 maneuvers became known as the *G.I. War*; and a *G.I. struggle* was a dance held at the post.

Before the attack on Pearl Harbor, commercial publishers and printers were offering dictionaries of military slang, and several books about the draft contained extensive glossaries. The most popular of these was Park Kendall's *Gone with the Draft: Love Letters of a Trainee*, published in 1941.* Kendall's dictionary of Army slang is particularly rich in food slang, which ranges alphabetically from *armored cow* (canned milk) to *zeppelins in a fog* (sausages and mashed potatoes).[46]

By late 1941, almost every Army camp and large unit had its own daily or weekly newspaper, ranging from mimeographed four-sheeters to printed dailies with paid advertising. These periodicals were often similar in tone and content to the college humor magazines of the time and thrived on topical jokes and cartoons drawn by talented selectees. Nationally syndicated newspaper columnist Jack Stinnett plowed through scores of these papers and concluded that the cartoonists were surprisingly good. He cited a number of examples, including one depicting a befuddled draftee dashing about in the dark and moaning to a lieutenant: "I know it's after taps, sir, but I camouflaged my tent and now I can't find it."[47]

Some of these cartoonists had extraordinary talent. Bill Mauldin and Dave Breger had participated in the Louisiana Maneuvers and both captured in their cartoons the life of the "dog face" foot soldier. Mauldin had already published his first book of cartoons about Army life. Breger, who was drafted in 1941 and assigned to duty as a truck mechanic, sold the first cartoon in his self-satirizing series *Private Breger* to the *Saturday Evening Post* on August 30 that year. George Baker, a Walt Disney cartoonist who worked on such classic films as *Pinocchio*, *Fantasia*, *Dumbo*, and *Bambi*, was drafted in June 1941. During his early days in uniform, he created the hapless private of the comic *Sad Sack*.

---

* Given the sensibilities of the time, these published works shied away from scatology and obscenity. *SOL* in Kendall's dictionary stands for "sure out of luck."

This new G.I. culture was bolstered in the larger popular culture, in Hollywood movies, radio, and Tin Pan Alley songs. "Boogie Woogie Bugle Boy," "'V' Stands for Victory," and "I'll Be Back in a Year, Little Darling," the country music smash by the Prairie Ramblers, were popular even before the Louisiana Maneuvers. Several of the songs catered to a wartime nostalgia for European cities that had fallen or were under attack. "A Nightingale Sang in Berkeley Square" evoked an England before Dunkirk and the Blitz, and "The Last Time I Saw Paris" became a sensation after the 1940 conquest of France by the Nazis.

The first movie to be inspired by the 1940 draft was the Abbott and Costello musical comedy *Buck Privates*, which turned the barracks and the drill field into venues for slapstick. *Caught in the Draft* starred Bob Hope playing a famous movie star who does his best to avoid the prewar draft but ends up in uniform. The theme of the hapless civilian thrown into the alien universe of the Army spawned a new genre, "camp movies." A prime example was an October 1941 film entitled *Great Guns*, in which the slapstick stars Stan Laurel and Oliver Hardy played a gardener and a valet who enlist in the Army to follow their millionaire employer, who has been drafted, to make sure he is happy and well cared for. The men participate in the Louisiana Maneuvers, where they take a wild ride in a jeep and miraculously cross a field of exploding mines, are bombed from the air with bags of flour, and become captives of the opposing army. Actual footage from the maneuvers was spliced into the film, giving many Americans their first look at jeeps in the field. The *Chicago Tribune* labeled *Great Guns* the year's funniest movie: "Not since Charlie Chaplin's *Shoulder Arms* have I seen an audience cotton to a war-minded comedy as they do to *Great Guns*," wrote the newspaper's movie critic, May Tinée.[48]

A host of films released before the United States entered the war were built around America's ability and willingness to fight, including: *A Yank in the R.A.F*, *Flight Command*, *Dive Bomber*, *I Wanted Wings*, and *Parachute Battalion*. Many of these films used real aircraft and military personnel. In the first paratrooper epic, *Parachute Battalion*, released within weeks of the public debut of parachute operations in the maneuvers, real paratroopers at Fort Benning were used for action shots.

None of this was lost on the Army. The strongest booster and facilitator in the use of film as a motivator and morale builder was Marshall, who had first realized when he was a leader of the Civilian Conservation Corps in the Pacific Northwest that movies served as an inexpensive and effective way to inspire working men and started showing them in the camps by projecting them on the sides of trucks.[49]

"More than any other senior official in the Roosevelt administration, Marshall had a vivid vision of the critical role filmmaking could play in the war," wrote Mark Harris in *Five Came Back*, his book about Hollywood and the Second World War. "He saw it as a medium that could help the army with the ardent confidence not just of civilians but of its own recruits." Even before Pearl Harbor, Marshall had been instrumental in getting the great film director Frank Capra (who had already directed such American classics as *Lost Horizon, It Happened One Night*, and *Mr. Smith Goes to Washington*) to leave Hollywood for a new career in the Army. Within days of the Pearl Harbor attack, Capra, a World War I veteran, left Hollywood to become a major in the Signal Corps.[50]

The collective impact of film and radio on the war was such that in the fall of 1941, Senate isolationists began to demand an official investigation into whether motion pictures were being used as pro-interventionist war propaganda. Their September 1 resolution called for an investigation of radio and movies, "the most potent instruments of communication of ideas." The resolution demanded that the Senate Committee on Interstate Commerce "or any duly authorized subcommittee" make a thorough investigation of propaganda in movies and radio shows designed "to influence public sentiment in the direction of participation by the United States in the present European war." Those behind the resolution directed their greatest anger at pro-British and anti-Nazi films, which included *That Hamilton Woman*, a period film with Anglophilic overtones, and Charlie Chaplin's Hitler satire *The Great Dictator*, which was especially odious to the America Firsters.

The same day the resolution was introduced, Senator Gerald Nye delivered a radio address, in which he contended that "American motion-picture companies have become the most gigantic engines of propaganda in existence to rouse the war fever in America and plunge this Nation to her destruction." He named the men—he called them refugees—who he believed dominated the industry. It was an anti-Semitic laundry list, totally dominated by what Nye termed "non-Nordic names," among them Harry and Jack Cohn of Columbia Pictures, Louis B. Mayer of Metro-Goldwyn Mayer, Adolph Zukor of Paramount, Murray Silverstone of United Artists, and Sam Goldwyn, of Samuel Goldwyn, Inc.[51]

Hearings began on September 10, and the Motion Picture Producers and Distributors of America hired the recent Republican presidential candidate Wendell Willkie to represent them for a reported fee of $100,000. A man who had the reputation of loving a good fight, Willkie attacked the legislators with the same venom the isolationists were tossing at the movie producers and radio broadcasters, charging them with using their senatorial powers "to disseminate unsubstantiated gossip" and in the process "destroying reputations by whim and fancy." When the senators brought up a specific film, Willkie asked whether the questioner had actually seen it; if not, he would be glad to show it in the hearing room.[52]

The Senate group that sought to uncover the pernicious influence of radio and the movies kept up its investigation through the fall of 1941 and scheduled a new series of hearings for early January 1942.

On November 25, word came from Washington that between 700,000 and 800,000 soldiers would be granted holiday furloughs, with one group leaving on December 12 and a second leaving on December 20. Some men would get two weeks off, while others would be granted a full month away from duty. This was predicted to be the largest strain on bus and train lines since the 1918 armistice, when two million began their journeys home.[53]

The discharging of draftees over the age of 28 picked up pace in late November and early December, so that the men could be with their families for the holidays. On December 5, 1941, 30-year-old sergeant Hank Greenberg was handed his discharge papers. He immediately set out for Detroit to begin preparing for spring training and the 1942 season.

On November 29, 1941, the *Saturday Evening Post*, circulation four million, published a cover illustration by Norman Rockwell depicting an Army soldier in bed, next to a valise with a tag that said, "Property of Pvt. Willie Gillis, Fort Dix, N.J." The caption, HOME SWEET HOME, announced that Gillis had just returned from one of the southern maneuvers. Gillis was Rockwell's "everyman" draftee, and the young private immediately gave a name and face to the new army.

Most of the units that had fought in the Carolinas had gotten home by Saturday, December 6, and looked forward to Sunday as a day of rest and relaxation. Technical Sergeant Max Bloom of the First Infantry Division, known as "the Big Red One," had been drafted from his home in Brooklyn in 1940. "A lot of men got drunk on the night of August 12—when the House of Representatives extended the draft for another 18 months by a margin of one vote," he recalled, adding that talk of OHIO and "OHIO clubs" was not uncommon then. "But by December 6," he explained, "nobody in the First had gone over the hill, and the Carolina Maneuvers were over." As the division arrived at its home base, then Fort Devens, Massachusetts, early that afternoon, Brigadier General Theodore Roosevelt Jr. had the post band play "Old Soldiers Never Die." Most of the men had been given a pass to go into Boston that Sunday night—but they never made it. Word of the attack on Pearl Harbor came first.[54]

At Fort Benning, on December 6, Patton issued a directive that praised his men for their six months of active training in the field under difficult conditions, where they had acquitted themselves well, individually and in units. "You were commended by the highest and most experienced officers in the Army for your appearance, your discipline, your soldierly comportment, and your combat efficiency. By every test short of war you are veterans.* Protect your record."[55]

Despite rulings from the umpires that went against him in both Louisiana and the Carolinas, Patton's reputation had risen considerably. "In both maneuvers, Patton broke all the old-fashioned rules, smashing his mechanized forces ever onward with speed and surprise." Omar Bradley later recalled, "But it was clear to anybody in the U.S. Army with the eyes to see that we had on our hands one of the most extraordinary fighting generals the Army had ever produced."[56]

Before the Carolina Maneuvers, the 366th Infantry, an African American division of the First Army stationed at Fort Devens, Massachusetts, was disinvited, the only First Army unit left behind. Colonel William A. Smith, camp commander, was taken aback by the order. Smith had spent part of the previous Sunday with the men of the regiment, as well as its officers and chaplains. "I wore civilian clothing and I don't believe that one of those enlisted men knew me as post commander," he told a reporter from the *Boston Globe*. "I found them without exception, extremely enthusiastic about Army life. I expected high morale, but theirs really surprised me. They are as fine a group of soldiers as there is in the Army."[57]

The reason the 366th was left behind, all but certainly, is that unlike other black units, which had white officers in command, this unit was commanded by a black man. Colonel West A. Harrison led 133 other black officers in supervising the 3,000 black men in the division. Had this unit been taken to the Carolinas, white officers below a certain rank as well as all enlisted grades would have been compelled to salute and defer to the officers of the 366th. In September, Ollie Stewart of the

---

* It has been pointed out by Second Armored Division historian Donald E. Houston that Patton used the terms "*soldier* and *veteran* sparingly and only in the most complimentary fashion," which makes it all the more remarkable that the vast majority of the men under his command had been put in uniform through the 1940 draft.

Baltimore Afro-American, who had written earlier about the problems at Camp Shelby, visited the unit as part of a tour he took of military bases while investigating the treatment of black troops. He wrote:

> If anybody wants to see the morale of enlisted men at a very high point: if anybody wants to see colored soldiers hold their heads up, and go about their jobs minus the resentment that results from abuse, insults, and open discrimination on account of color, my sincere advice is this:
> Go to Fort Devens and take a look.

The strongest reaction to the 366th's exclusion from the maneuvers came from the *Chicago Defender*, which saw the action as a manifestation of an official War Department Jim Crow policy intended to keep elite northern black units out of the South.[58]

Racial issues, which had remained unresolved through the maneuvers, intensified. The treatment of the 94th Engineers in Gurdon, Arkansas, during the Louisiana Maneuvers animated protests by the NAACP and others that reached the president and the War Department. A final and dispiriting decision came down from the War Department on Friday, December 5, judging that the civilians and troopers involved in the Gurdon incident were not "amenable to trial by court-martial for violations of the articles of war."

Criticism of the military's inability to deal with segregation and unequal treatment of black Americans in uniform was growing. Marshall scheduled a meeting with 22 editors and columnists from African American newspapers on Monday, December 8, 1941.

CHAPTER 13

DECEMBER 7, 1941

If Americans were still divided on Sunday morning, December 7, 1941, a clear consensus existed among interventionists and isolationists, believers, and non-believers that the Sabbath should be off-limits as a time to discuss the war and that clergy should refrain from using the pulpit to discuss possible American participation. In the custom of the time, sermons were regarded as news and reported in newspapers. With few exceptions, the sermons delivered on December 7 shied away from any mention of the war or the world crisis and instead focused on abstractions such as serenity, inner peace, and spiritual renewal. One notable exception was Congregation Rodeph Sholom, a Reform synagogue on the Upper West Side of Manhattan, where the theme of the address on Sunday was whether the United States could win the war without sending the Army overseas.[1]

At 12:55 p.m. Eastern Time, after most of the sermons had been delivered and many Washingtonians were getting ready to watch the Redskins football team play its final game of the season against the Philadelphia Eagles, the attack on the U.S. Navy base at Pearl Harbor had already begun. In the stands, no one knew this at the opening kickoff. But shortly after Philadelphia took a 7–0 lead on its first drive, a steady flow of announcements began coming out of the public-address system asking military officials by name to report to their offices. "We didn't know what the hell was going on," Redskins quarterback Sammy Baugh later recalled. "I had never heard that many announcements one right after another. We felt something was up, but we just kept playing."[2]

Team owner George Preston Marshall knew what was happening but refused to make an announcement about the attack. He later confessed, "I didn't want to divert the fans' attention from the game." When the fans finally exited the stadium, they were shocked by newsboys hawking newspapers with giant headlines screaming: U.S. AT WAR! JAPAN BOMBS HAWAII, MANILA.[3]

Prominently displayed in those special editions of Washington's five daily newspapers—and papers countrywide—was the name Pearl Harbor. Many, if not most, Americans had no idea where Pearl Harbor was located or what it represented. In Camp Blanding, Florida, one of the men who had just returned from the Carolina Maneuvers had gone to bed dead tired on the night of December 7 before word of the attack had reached his unit, when, as he later recalled, "some GI came into our tent and shouted that the Japs bombed Pearl Harbor. In unison, practically everyone shouted, 'Where the hell is that place?'"[4]

Those who knew about Pearl Harbor and the fleet based there on the Hawaiian island of Oahu had seen it as one of the reasons Japan would *not* attempt an attack on the United States. On December 4, syndicated columnist Jay G. Hayden proclaimed that Japan would be held in check by the overwhelming naval and air supremacy of her potential enemies, including "an American fleet, bigger than her own . . . poised at Pearl Harbor." He added, "American, Russian and British bombers based at Manila, Hong Kong and Vladivostok are in easy flying reach of Japan's papier-mâché cities."[5]

General Marshall was home having lunch when he received the call that Pearl Harbor was under attack. Before December 7, Marshall had been adamant that Pearl Harbor was "impregnable" and that Oahu stood as "the strongest fortress in the world"—a view seconded by Navy Secretary Frank Knox and Secretary of War Stimson.* After December

---

* In his annual report, issued on the morning of December 7, 1941, Secretary Frank Knox declared: "I am proud to report that the American people may feel fully confident in their navy." Donald W. Mitchell, *History of the Modern American Navy: From 1883 through Pearl Harbor* (New York: Alfred A. Knopf, 1946), 389.

7, Marshall began to ship troops west, making preparations should an attack, or worse still, a West Coast landing, be in the offing.[6]

According to Marshall's wife, Katherine, when her husband came home late that evening, his face was grim and gray. "Since June, 1938—three and a half years—he had labored relentlessly against impossible odds to arouse and prepare America; yet America was still unprepared. Panama, Alaska, the Hawaiian Islands, Wake, Guam, the Philippines—our outposts were woefully unprepared. Now the blow had been struck."[7]

At 2:31 p.m., those whose radios were tuned to CBS heard John Daly say: "The Japanese have attacked Pearl Harbor, Hawaii, by air, President Roosevelt has just announced. The attack was also made on naval and military activities on the principal island of Oahu." The radio waves were soon consumed by commentators and newsmen condemning the bombings, some commenting on how foolish the Japanese had been to launch an attack on such a powerful nation. None of them were aware of the actual devastation wrought on the Navy in Hawaii.[8]

Within minutes of the attack being made public, sanctions were issued against Japanese citizens living in the United States, under the assumption that they might be spies and/or saboteurs. Mayor Fiorello La Guardia of New York City ordered all Japanese residents to lock themselves in their homes or apartments and not show themselves on the streets of New York until their status had been determined by the State Department.

On the morning of December 7, the White House was an unguarded mansion in the middle of Washington, D.C.; during daylight hours, one could enter the grounds through the gates without challenge. By sundown, armed guards had been placed around the building's perimeter, and crowds had gathered three or four deep in front of the mansion. The gates were now locked. The nation was at war.[9]

When the attack was announced, cartoonist Bill Mauldin was in a camp with the 45th Division. The men around him had been convinced that they faced combat soon somewhere, so the news came almost with a sense of relief. "We didn't even have the sense to get scared," he remembered. Hollywood leading man and Army Air Corps corporal Jimmy

Stewart stood guard duty at Moffett Field, south of San Francisco, the day after the bombings. Stewart was horrified by Japan's attack in Hawaii, but he also believed that it meant he would finally get his commission as a second lieutenant and his aviator's wings.[10]

Andy Rooney, who had been drafted on July 7, 1941, was stationed at Camp Blanding attached to an artillery regiment. He was reading in a recreation room when he heard the news on the radio. "I had that awful feeling in the pit of my stomach," he later recalled. "I don't know why fear strikes there." John F. Kennedy, by then in Washington, D.C., with the Office of Naval Intelligence, had just finished playing a pickup game of touch football and was driving back to his apartment when the news came over the radio. In the car with him was LeMoyne "Lem" Billings, his close friend, and the two men witnessed the billowing smoke rising from the Japanese embassy on Massachusetts Avenue as Japanese diplomats burned documents.[11]

Some of those who had been discharged from the Army because of age decided to reenlist, but on their own terms. Late on the night of December 7, Hank Greenberg, who had spent 180 days in the Army as a draftee, decided his country still needed him. He announced to friends the next morning that he was going back in. "We are in trouble and there is only one thing to do—return to service. I have not been called back. I am going back of my own accord. Baseball is out the window as far as I'm concerned. I don't know if I'll ever return to baseball."[12]

Harrison Salisbury, who had covered the maneuvers for the *New York Times*, had been at a New York Giants football game and left early to go to a friend's house for a drink when the news came over the radio. He immediately told himself that the Japanese attack would prove to be suicidal and that "those poor little bastards" were finished and did not have a chance.[13]

Brigadier General Dwight D. Eisenhower, who had worked during the morning and still felt tired from the long and exhausting staff work of the maneuvers and their aftermath, was taking a nap—after giving an order that under no circumstances was he to be disturbed—when he was awakened and told of the attack. Within an hour of being notified,

Eisenhower was ordering antiaircraft units of the Third Army to head for the West Coast. Fearing the possibility of a Japanese assault on the mainland, he put anti-sabotage measures in place. "Immediacy of movement was the keynote," he wrote later. "The normal channels of administration were abandoned . . . A single telephone call would start an infantry unit across the country."[14]

George Patton received word while at home with his family. According to his wife, Beatrice: "It was an incredible thing, but not as shocking to us as to the rest of the country. George had tried and tried, while we were in Honolulu, to get it across to General Drum, the War Department, and anyone who would listen that the Japanese were enemies. He had had his wrist slapped repeatedly for rocking the boat and making waves."[15]

Henry Stimson was finishing lunch at about 2:00 p.m. when he got a call from President Roosevelt, who told him in an agitated voice about the attack. Stimson confirmed that he had been following Japanese movements in the Gulf of Siam.

"Oh, no," Roosevelt responded. "I don't mean that. They are attacking Hawaii. They are now bombing Hawaii."

Stimson then called Grenville Clark, asking him to come to his office immediately to draft a declaration of war for the president's approval. Clark drew it up, basing the language largely on that of Woodrow Wilson's 1917 declaration of war.[16]

Secretary of War Stimson saw the attack as a great awakening, as his memoirs reveal: "The Japanese attack on Pearl Harbor restored to America the freedom of action she had lost by many cunning bonds of her own citizens' contriving. The self-imprisoned giant was set free." To Stimson, the reality of the attack was "easier to bear than the fearful former sight of America half-asleep." Stimson's diary entry for December 7 dwelt on a crisis that would now unite the people, of which a united America had nothing to fear.[17]

Brigadier General Omar Bradley, commander of the infantry school at Fort Benning, was tending his garden with his wife, Mary, when a colleague stopped by and told them the horrific news. Bradley put on his uniform and immediately began to direct the troops under his command to protect key installations around the state of Georgia. When he finally got to bed late that night, he would recall, he thought about how "lucky" the nation was to have George Marshall as its Army chief of staff: "In his two and a half years in command, he had laid the necessary groundwork for us to go to war."[18]

Eric Sevareid, who had returned to Washington from the Carolinas a few days before, heard the news and quickly began reporting about what the nation needed to do. Roger Burlingame wrote in his biography of Elmer Davis, director of the nation's Office of War Information: "For the first time, [Sevareid] told the grim truth about Pearl Harbor: that the damage to the American fleet had been disastrous, that it would be impossible to exaggerate it—that indeed the very core of naval defense in the Pacific had been wiped out." Davis believed that Sevareid's broadcast became a rallying cry for Americans and that the broadcast journalist was the one who set the wheels turning in American factories to create a full-fledged, three-shifts-a-day wartime economy.[19]

Sevareid later recalled that although he knew the stunned and anxious nation would sleep badly, he had seen the draftee army first-hand, and he knew its men had something he had not seen in Europe in terms of their spirit and desire to win. "For me, there was a feeling of enormous relief; the feeling that we had won, even before the fight began, and survived, even before the onslaught. I slept like a baby."[20]

At the highest level, Marshall knew who would command his new army in the event of war. He had already screened his roster of senior generals and eliminated most, with the notable exception of Walter Krueger. Generals Lear and Drum were not on the list of those to be retained. He then made a list of senior officers in whose judgment he was confident. The names he had collected over a long period, a list refined during the 1941 maneuvers, included Bradley, Clark, Courtney H. Hodges, Jacob L. Devers, Patton, J. Lawton Collins, Alexander M. Patch, William Hood Simpson, Lucian K. Truscott, Robert L. Eichelberger, and Eisenhower.

Some of these men Marshall knew personally; others he knew only by reputation and recommendation.[21]

The new officers at lower levels had come from Omar Bradley's Officer Candidate School at Fort Benning and a dozen other sister institutions spread throughout the country that had been nicknamed "shave-tail colleges"—an allusion to Army slang for a second lieutenant, derived from the practice of shaving the tails of young, newly broken mules.

On the morning of the attack on Pearl Harbor, Hanson Baldwin's article "The Making of the American Officer" appeared in the *New York Times Sunday Magazine*. It underscored the nation's progress toward a new and "vibrant officer corps." For the first time in the nation's history, he noted the Army had begun turning its most talented and motivated enlisted men into officers. Even in these early days, this seemed to be working exactly the way Marshall predicted it would. To Baldwin, this group "more emphatically than any other" would provide the answer to the need for leadership of the Army's "platoons and other small tactical units." Baldwin thought the lack of leadership at this level had been "one of the greatest deficiencies of the American Army." He noted that this was similar to the radical innovation the Germans had made and the British had somewhat adopted. In Baldwin's view, the OCS system would upgrade the Army in the wake of the October purge of the untrained and poorly motivated.[22]

Supporting the preparation of enlisted men, an important Army institution was up and running by December 7: 21 Replacement Training Centers had been built in the winter and spring of 1940–41 and become an integral part of the nation's preparedness. At these centers, men now coming into the Army as draftees and volunteers were given 13 weeks of basic training before being placed in tactical units.[23]

Another reason Eric Sevareid may have slept well the night after the attack was the Selective Service System, which was ready to expand based on the 1940 legislation that had established it. Perhaps the most important aspect of the original implementation was the willingness of unpaid citizens to staff local draft boards. The system already had at least one draft board in every county and parish in the United States—6,442 local boards and 274 boards of appeal above them. Before Pearl Harbor, the system had operated for 14 months and was ready for immediate wartime expansion. The beauty of the system and a prime reason that it had not caused any serious disruption during those peacetime months was that it was decentralized and local, keeping the process, in the words of its director, Lewis B. Hershey, "close to the people." The system attracted thousands of uncompensated medical professionals*— including the physicians who provided physical examinations and the dentists who repaired and replaced rotting teeth with dentures that allowed men who had been registered to become draft eligible.[24]

As the Army itself improved, so did its materiel, and as the maneuvers of 1941 concluded, arms and munitions that were needed to successfully fight a war were either in production, available in prototype, or on the drawing boards. Counting from Roosevelt's initial call for the United States to rearm on May 16, 1940, the nation had had an 18-month head start on the war. Seeds had been planted for gargantuan projects that were now coming online. A prime example: on March 28, 1941, the Ford Motor Company began to clear land for the massive Willow Run Bomber Plant, which would produce B-24 Liberator bombers, each one held together with 360,000 rivets and weighing more than 36,000 pounds. The plant had a 17-acre footprint and boasted an assembly line more than a mile long. The first bomber to come off the assembly line was still months away,** but the project was moving rapidly forward.[25]

"Monday was almost worse than Sunday, a merciful kind of shock had prevailed under the first impact and now as that wore off, the truth was inescapable," observed journalist Marquis Childs. The Navy was now

---

* Late in 1942, when it was reaching its peak operating level, the Selective Service System had 32,372 unpaid examining physicians and 8,535 dentists.

** The first B-24 was produced at Willow Run on September 10, 1942; 8,685 of the bombers would be produced by the end of the war. By November 1942, all the airplane factories required to build the aircraft needed to win the war had been built.

severely damaged. It was clear that the nation was unprepared for war in the Pacific and that the Japanese had been able to mount a major attack 4,000 miles from home. Tokyo, in fact, was farther from Hawaii than Berlin was from New York City.[26]

As President Roosevelt worked on the final draft of the speech he would give at 9:00 a.m. on December 8, in which he would declare war on Japan, a group of 20 newspaper editors and columnists from the National Negro Publishers Association arrived at the Munitions Building for their scheduled appointment with General Marshall to discuss racial discrimination and segregation in the U.S. Army. Invited by the War Department, the group had been buoyed on Sunday morning—before news of the attack—by a letter published on the editorial page of the *Washington Post* stating that "the most stupid thing is the failure of the Army to provide for the training of Negro fliers in the Aviation Corps." Some 200 African American men had passed all the required tests for flight training but were being held back at a time when the Army was begging for new aviation recruits. Black aviators were being trained as pursuit pilots in Tuskegee, Alabama, but only in small numbers.[27]

The Army's policy, set in 1940, was that black aviators could not be deployed in racially integrated situations, "since this would result in having Negro officers serving over white enlisted men," Major General "Hap" Arnold, chief of the Air Corps, declared flatly. "This would create an impossible social problem."[28]

Marshall began his remarks to the journalists by saying that on a personal level he was not yet satisfied with the progress made toward ending discrimination in the Army. He praised black enlisted men and offered the group something newsworthy: the hope that one, and perhaps two, African American divisions would soon be activated.[29]

Marshall then excused himself, because of the urgency to mobilize in the wake of the Pearl Harbor attack, and turned the meeting over to others. About an hour after Marshall's cordial welcome, Colonel Eugene Householder, of the Army's Adjutant General's Department, read a statement that essentially overrode Marshall's overture: "The Army is not a sociological laboratory. To be effective it must be organized and trained according to principles which will ensure success. Experiments to meet the wishes of the champions of every race and creed for the solution to their problems are a danger to efficiency, discipline and morale and would result in ultimate defeat."[30]

Householder then criticized the black press for "frequently" writing about alleged mistreatment of African Americans in the service, only to have those charges proved false by Army investigations. Householder strongly suggested that going forward any stories about the treatment or disposition of African American servicemen should be checked out with the Army before they were published.[31]

The adversarial relationship between black newspapers and the military only deepened after Householder's declaration. Clearly the status quo would be maintained; as historian Neil A. Wynn later explained, "This fear of jeopardizing white morale and of creating a white backlash during the war was, often, a greater force against change than the fear of black protest was for it."[32]

The Army entertained the press delegation through the end of the following day. Columnist Charley Cherokee of the *Chicago Defender* wrote in his next column: "The War Department last week fed 20 Negro editors wine, chicken and propaganda." Cherokee reminded his readers that the black men killed by the Japanese at Pearl Harbor did not die manning guns and fighting back but were "shining officers' boots in the pantry."[33] The *Chicago Defender* pointed out that the delegates to the meeting had been invited to Washington and had come there at their own expense, only to be told that the Army was planning to continue its "undemocratic" policy of racial segregation.[34]

As scheduled, on the morning of December 8, before a joint session of Congress, President Roosevelt delivered his address, in which he asked for a formal declaration of war against Japan. Many did not realize, until Roosevelt spelled it out, that the attack on Pearl Harbor was only one element of a larger invasion still underway as he spoke. American ships had been torpedoed in the open ocean between San Francisco and

Honolulu, and Japanese forces had also attacked Hong Kong, Malaya, the Philippines, Guam, and Wake Island. On the morning of December 8, they attacked Midway Island. "Japan has, therefore, undertaken a surprise offensive extending throughout the Pacific area," said Roosevelt.

The Senate unanimously approved the resolution by a vote of 82–0, while the House of Representatives' tally was 388–1, the dissenting vote coming from Montana Republican Jeannette Rankin, an avowed pacifist. Representative Everett Dirksen (Republican of Illinois), seated next to Rankin, pleaded with her to vote "present" rather than "no," but she refused explaining: "As a woman, I can't go to war and I refuse to send anyone else." Angry spectators and reporters looking for a quote from Rankin followed her as she left the Capitol. Feeling threatened by her pursuers she took refuge in a telephone booth until the Capitol Police came to her rescue.[35]

Although the isolationists voted to go to war, some did so while blaming Roosevelt. Late on December 7, Senator Nye declared that the United States had done its utmost to provoke a quarrel with Japan and that the attack was the result of that provocation. On his way to hear Roosevelt's declaration, columnist Marquis Childs rode in a Senate elevator with one of the "recalcitrant isolationists," who complained bitterly about the plight the president had created for the country. "With this," Childs later wrote, "went dark hints that he would never vote for declaration of war." The man voted aye, but Childs suspected then that the conversion of the isolationists might be temporary.[36]

In contrast, Texas congressman Lyndon Johnson, who was a lieutenant commander in the Naval Reserve, wrote to Roosevelt on December 7 to urgently request that the commander in chief assign him to active duty with the fleet. Johnson obtained indefinite leave from the House and reported to the Navy on December 10 as a Reservist, hoping for activation. He then went to the White House and told Roosevelt that he was leaving Congress for the Navy. "He said he understood, and told me goodbye," Johnson reported. Roosevelt refused to ask the Navy to assign him to a warship, because he knew Johnson was not prepared for combat. Instead, Johnson and his aide John Connolly were assigned work in the Office of the Secretary of the Navy. Around the same time, Senator Harry S. Truman asked a similar favor of Marshall, to make him a colonel of artillery. "Senator," Marshall shot back, "you're too damn old."[37]

On Tuesday, December 9, telegrams went out to all Selective Service offices in the country, alerting them to prepare for the earliest possible induction of another million men. Recruiting offices were ordered to stay open 24 hours a day for the duration of the war. The day after the attack, thousands of men formed long lines in front of the massive Federal Building on Church Street in Manhattan, where they could volunteer for service in the Army, Navy, or Marine Corps. The *New York Times* reported on December 14 that the Armed Forces were "receiving applicants in numbers unprecedented in the history of the nation" and that "many of the men had been in line [at recruiting stations] the whole night."[38]

In Lower Manhattan, more than 2,000 stood in a discrete line to sign up for the Navy. When officials told 1,000 of the men to go home and come back later, the men refused to leave, and the Navy was forced to rescind the order to disperse. In Manhattan, as well as other localities, veterans' groups showed up to serve hot food and coffee to the men standing in long lines, shivering in the December winds.

The phenomenal young pitcher Bob Feller, 23, was driving from his home in Iowa to the annual winter meetings of baseball executives in Chicago when he heard the news about Pearl Harbor, just after he had crossed the Mississippi River. He decided to enlist at once and "throw a few strikes for Uncle Sam."* In Chicago, Feller contacted

---

* The Feller news shocked the baseball executives assembled in Chicago, where, among other things, the owner of the lackluster, attendance-poor St. Louis Browns was trying to get permission to move his American League franchise to Los Angeles. The war eclipsed any thought of moving a team to the West Coast, where troops were now taking defensive positions against potential Japanese attacks. The more important question raised at the winter meetings was whether baseball would be allowed to continue while the nation was at war. Although a friend of the sport, Franklin D. Roosevelt bore no goodwill toward baseball commissioner Kenesaw Mountain Landis, a severe conservative who openly loathed Roosevelt's liberal politics. Nonetheless, the president and

former heavyweight boxing champion Gene Tunney, who supervised the Navy's physical fitness program, and signed up to become a Navy petty officer. He took the oath of office the next morning, with orders to head to Norfolk, Virginia, for training.[39]

On December 11, Germany and Italy officially declared war on the United States, and the United States countered by declaring war on them. The nation was now in a two-ocean war, with a growing fear that Japan could mount an invasion of the West Coast. Antiaircraft units were already on their way west. Within a few days of the declaration of war, large groups of soldiers were on the move, employing a railroad system that was still trying to return to normal after the large-scale movement of men and materiel to and from the Louisiana and Carolina Maneuvers.

New York's 27th Infantry Division was back in Alabama at the time of the attack and had already shed the 3,000 or so conscripted men over the age of 28. All furloughs were immediately canceled, and troops were sent to guard key installations throughout the state, including power plants and reservoirs. On December 11, the division was notified that it had 48 hours to be ready to move from Fort McClellan to an undisclosed new location. The division rode west by rail to Southern California to defend against a potential seaborne invasion of the United States' suddenly vulnerable West Coast. Not only had the Japanese destroyed a large part of the Pacific fleet, but their attack on the Philippines had also taken out a large part of the American B-17 bomber fleet at Clark Field, 40 miles north of Manila.

---

the commissioner exchanged letters in January 1942, Landis asking about baseball's role in wartime, and Roosevelt replying with his famous "Green Light Letter," which argued that the nation needed more—not less—baseball: "I honestly feel that it would be best for the country to keep baseball going. There will be fewer people unemployed and everybody will work longer hours and harder than ever before. Baseball provides a recreation which does not last over two hours or two hours and a half, and which can be got for very little cost."

The first landing of Japanese troops in the Philippines came on December 10, the same day Japanese aircraft sank two British warships operating in the Pacific: the cruiser HMS *Repulse* and the battleship HMS *Prince of Wales*. As Henry Stimson noted in his diary at day's end, "The Japanese were for the time being the masters of the southwestern Pacific."[40]

CHAPTER 14

"LITTLE LIBYA,"
IRISH MANEUVERS,
AND OPERATION TORCH

On December 12, 1941, the day after the United States declared war on Italy and Germany, Brigadier General Dwight Eisenhower was ordered to report to Washington, D.C., to assume a job as a member of the War Plans Division of the War Department.

Eisenhower approached the position with apprehension, fearing that this promotion would condemn him to a desk job for the remainder of the war. Because he believed that missing combat experience in World War I had hindered his career, he thought he was being dealt "a hard blow" with this assignment.[1]

Arriving in Washington by train on December 14, Eisenhower headed directly to Marshall's office. The two men had only talked briefly on three prior occasions, so this all-important face-to-face meeting was clearly a moment for Marshall to get a better sense of the man he had just brought to Washington to help him run the war. Marshall began by outlining the American military position in the Pacific, which was dire and bound to get worse, as was the situation in Europe and North Africa. Although Germany held much of Europe, it was deeply embroiled in fighting the Russians on the Eastern Front. On December 5, Russia's Red Army began its counter-attack against the Nazis outside Moscow.[2]

Marshall looked at Eisenhower and said: "We have got to do our best in the Pacific, and we've got to win this whole war. Now, how are you and how are we going to do it?"

"Give me a few hours," replied Eisenhower.

Using a pen and a stack of yellow paper, Eisenhower wrote out his plan for victory in the Pacific. A few hours later, he delivered to Marshall his written report, "Assistance to the Far East," and followed up with a verbal briefing. The most important step, Eisenhower felt, was securing the sea and air routes to Australia, because the island nation would become the point from which the Allies could fight the Japanese and send reinforcements to the Philippines. He also concluded that the Philippines would fall to the Japanese, but the United States could not abandon its people. Marshall agreed. As Eisenhower started to leave, Marshall pulled him back to say: "Eisenhower,* the department is filled with able men who analyze their problems well but feel compelled always to bring them to me for final solution. I must have assistants who will solve their own problems and tell me later what they have done." As journalist/historian Mark Perry concluded in his book on Eisenhower and Marshall, "Eisenhower got the message—he was there to make decisions." The memo and Eisenhower's grip on the situation had amounted to a test that he'd passed with flying colors, and he had put himself on the path to an even higher level of leadership. Marshall biographer David L. Roll wrote of this moment: "Thus began a partnership that led to the greatest victory in American history since the Revolutionary War."[3]

On December 22, British Prime Minister Winston Churchill arrived in the United States after a storm-tossed ten-day trip across the Atlantic to meet with Roosevelt. Churchill had invited himself to the White House in a wire he sent to Roosevelt on December 8. The trip was shrouded in so much secrecy that First Lady Eleanor Roosevelt did not know about it until Churchill had landed in Norfolk, Virginia, and

---

* Even though Eisenhower had been known as "Ike" from the time he arrived at West Point, Marshall seldom called him that but rather chose to address him as "Eisenhower."

was flying to Washington in the hope of arriving at the White House in time for dinner.

Churchill's arrival was the stuff of upbeat headlines at a time when positive news was in high demand. "With Churchill at the White House, Washington became literally the wartime capital of the world," wrote Raymond Z. Henle in the *Pittsburgh Post-Gazette*. "It is the first time in history that the heads of two mighty nations at war have met in the White House to discuss methods of crushing a common enemy."[4]

White House press secretary Stephen Early announced shortly after Churchill's arrival that the purpose of the meeting was "the defeat of Hitlerism around the world." One of the main reasons Churchill had come to Washington was to make sure the United States adhered to a policy of "Europe first." A memorandum Marshall presented to Churchill made it clear that that policy was in place: "Notwithstanding the entry of Japan into the war, our view is that Germany is still the prime enemy and her defeat is the key to victory." The two leaders put on an inspirational show of solidarity.[5]

Even as Christmas approached, Americans kept a wary eye on the West Coast. Early in the morning of December 23, near Redondo Beach, California, an element of the New York 27th Infantry sighted a Japanese submarine and fired nine artillery rounds before it disappeared. One hit was recorded, and the Army Air Corps later confirmed that the sub had been sunk.[6]

On Christmas Eve, Roosevelt ordered the White House gates opened, so that the public could come in and witness the lighting of the national Christmas tree by these two powerful men, who both spoke to the crowd packed in tightly on the lawn. Their speeches, delivered from the South Portico, were broadcast over the major radio networks. Churchill said that although he was far from family and country, he could not say he felt far from home because of his deep friendship with Roosevelt and the United States.

On Christmas morning, the two leaders attended church together, where they sang hymns and carols. Churchill was taken with "O Little

Town of Bethlehem," a Christmas hymn he had never heard before, written by an American Episcopal priest after the Civil War.[7] But all their spirited singing could not drown out the bad news: on December 25, Hong Kong, then a British colony, fell to the Japanese after 18 days of desperate fighting, with some 4,000 dead on both sides.*

The next day, Churchill spoke to a joint session of Congress in which he expressed the opinion that the Allies needed no less than 18 months to turn the tide of war in their favor. While stating that "we are able to beat the life out of the savage Nazi," he also made the dire prediction that "many disappointments and unpleasant surprises await us."

The two statesmen and their military leaders spent many hours together discussing how to win the war. Marshall and Stimson were of the mind that a joint American-British force should attack Germany directly, as soon as possible, going across the English Channel and through France. Churchill felt the best approach would be to attack in North Africa later in 1942, and once territory there was taken back, to move to Sicily and up through Italy, which he saw as the "soft underbelly" of German-controlled Europe.

The reality of the Marshall-Stimson approach was that the United States would not have the necessary manpower and weaponry ready for such an offensive through France and into Germany until at least mid-1943. Churchill pushed hard for American intervention before the end of 1942, which pointed directly to North Africa. Roosevelt initially rejected the plan to invade North Africa, because Stimson and Marshall were strongly in favor of attacking Germany through France from bases in England.

Churchill left Washington on January 14, 1942, flying home to England via Bermuda, with the issue of how Germany would be attacked by an Allied force still very much up in the air.

---

* This was also the day popular crooner Bing Crosby first sang "White Christmas" live on the radio. The song, which had been written by Irving Berlin, became the greatest hit song of the war years and today is still listed among the greatest hits of all time. Carl Zebrowski, "I Heard the Bands on Christmas Day," *America in WWII*, December 2017, 61.

At the War Plans Division, Eisenhower had replaced his close friend Major General Leonard J. Gerow, who was taking a field assignment as commanding officer of the 29th Infantry Division, which had most recently taken part in the Carolina Maneuvers. Despite the importance of his new position, Eisenhower wanted to do what Gerow was doing, and his desire seemed to only get stronger. On January 19, just a few weeks into his new assignment, he wrote in his diary: "There are lots of amateur strategists on the job, and prima donnas everywhere. I'd give anything to be back in the field."[8]

Like his friend Eisenhower, General George Patton was given a new assignment after Pearl Harbor. On January 15, he was made commanding general of the I Armored Corps, an important, large unit comprising two armored divisions and a mechanized division. The promotion inspired him to write to his old boss General Pershing: "It will be a very interesting job, and, of course, I hope to get to a place where I can do a little fighting as soon as possible."[9]

In late January 1942, the Germans recaptured the port of Benghazi, Libya, from the British and a week later pushed more than 100 miles east through the desert toward Egypt, which underscored the urgency of blunting their momentum in the desert. Some feared that if the Germans could not be stopped by the British, the British Indian Army, and other troops drawn from the British Empire, they could push east and eventually join forces with the Japanese, if the Japanese cut through India. This potential was alarming on many fronts, not least the possibility that the Axis could attack Russia from several directions. Realizing the Army needed to be trained to fight in the desert, thoughts on how this could be accomplished pointed directly to Patton.

During the late winter, more and more Army units found themselves on the West Coast, both as defenders and potential troops for the war against Japan. While in California, as the 27th Infantry awaited orders to move into a war zone, it focused on bringing its numbers up to the authorized level of 1,012 officers and 21,314 enlisted men. While in

California, every man in the division received new equipment including an M1 rifle. The first companies of the division boarded ships bound for Hawaii on February 27, 1942, becoming the first infantry division to depart the continental United States after the Pearl Harbor attack. Whatever residual bad reputation had attached itself to the 27th from the 1941 *Life* article had now vanished as it became clear that this division was working its way inexorably into combat. Elements of the 27th would go on to fight in nearly every island campaign against the Japanese during the war, including Makin (or Butaritari) Atoll in the Gilbert Islands, Enewetak Atoll in the Marshall Islands, Saipan in the Mariana Islands, and Okinawa. It eventually became the last Army division to leave the Pacific.[10]

In March 1942, General Lesley McNair was assigned to lead the Army Ground Forces. Within weeks of his promotion, McNair asked Patton to establish training grounds in the desert for a new set of maneuvers. The 1941 maneuvers in Tennessee, Louisiana, and the Carolinas had been designed to mimic the terrain and climate of Europe, not the conditions now facing the British fighting the Germans in North Africa.[11]

Uncharacteristically, Patton all but disappeared from public view in early 1942, as he sought a unique area for desert maneuvers. In the late winter, he set out from Fort Benning in his private aircraft, a Stinson Voyager, to map out the site for his Desert Training Center. Near Indio, California, he found a patch of parched land 180 miles long and 90 miles wide, covering 16,200 square miles of the desert lands that straddled parts of California, Nevada, and Arizona. It was larger than Massachusetts, Connecticut, and Rhode Island put together. Patton enthused about it: "The area possesses tremendous advantages for all forms of training, because, in addition to its climatic and geographic similitude to Libya it is also the only place I know of where artificial restrictions are almost wholly non-existing and where there is room to burn."[12]

In late March, Stimson formally announced the creation of a new corps of 8,000 men who would train under Patton in the desert. The troops—units of the First Armored Corps and the Second and Third Armies—were to serve as the backbone of an American expeditionary force that would fight in North Africa and the Middle East. In his appointment, Stimson took into account Patton's growing reputation as one of the Army's most colorful and vigorous commanders: "Knowing him as I do, I believe he will approximate actual desert warfare as well as he is able, with consideration for actual citizens in the neighborhood."[13]

"Out here there is no civilization—nothing but barren mountains, sagebrush and bare parched desert which the beating sun reduces to a uniform white glare," wrote Gladwin Hill of the Associated Press, one of the few reporters allowed into the Desert Training Center area but with strict limits as to what he could report.[14]

When he arrived in Indio, Patton discovered that his advance party of officers was setting up headquarters for the training center in a hotel. Patton would have none of it and moved the headquarters into the desert, near the men. The original camp, spartan in the extreme, was ready to receive large numbers of troops and tanks at the beginning of April.

While Patton was setting up his operation in the desert in early April, George Marshall arrived in London to discuss strategy with the British. This led to speculation in both the British and American press that a joint attack would be mounted on Germany, either along the French coast of the English Channel or through Norway. Thousands of American troops were already in the British Isles preparing for a new series of joint U.S.-British-Canadian maneuvers in Northern Ireland, which would start small and become larger and more ambitious in the coming months.

On April 18, while still in London, Marshall was presented a copy of *Stars and Stripes*, the weekly tabloid newspaper serving the American forces overseas, as it had during World War I. In his memoir, General Pershing wrote: "I do not believe that any one factor could have done more to sustain the morale of the A.E.F. [American Expeditionary Force] than the *Stars and Stripes*." Written for and by the soldiers, without official control, it was staffed primarily by draftees with stateside newspaper experience. Marshall was thrilled by the appearance of the newspaper. It contained a statement of his support, in which he said that the morale and military efficiency of the American soldiers in the British Isles would be directly affected by the *Stars and Stripes* of 1942. The newspaper quickly doubled in size and began to be published daily.[15]

On May 18, some 14,000 Army men and the tanks, artillery, and other equipment needed to support them in combat landed in Northern Ireland. The troops crossed the Atlantic in a massive convoy that moved through thick fog, while salvos of depth charges from American warships kept German U-boats at bay. An Associated Press reporter embedded on one of the ships compared the men he met on the crossing to those he had known in World War I and noted: "They are sturdier, healthier and as cheerful as kids at a circus." He also noted that the men had nicknamed the freighter carrying them the "Berlin Express."[16]

Many of the men in this convoy were transported in the luxury ocean liners *Queen Mary* and *Queen Elizabeth*, which had been converted to troop carriers. A lieutenant colonel who had served in the previous war noted: "The last time I came over on an old cattle boat. This time it was a liner. The war is getting better." By the end of 1942, some 227,000 Americans had been transferred to British ports on the *Queens*.[17]

With this delivery of men and machines, the British Isles now had some of the most capable troops in the U.S. Army, including the First Armored Division, which secretly had been moved to Fort Dix to prepare for the trip to Ireland and now carried the nickname "Old Ironsides." Officially, American soldiers were prepared to defend Britain against a cross-channel invasion, but instead were quietly being prepared for combat in North Africa.

The maneuvers in Ireland were demanding, emphasizing long marches and physically challenging exercises and, like the 1941 American maneuvers, took their cue from imaginary states (Down, Antrim, and Tyrone), each with its own political intrigues and racial problems. In addition, an overseas state (Lancashire) landed at night, attacked, and turned the tide of battle. Many stories appeared in the press, such as one describing how a Canadian parachute unit almost kidnapped the major general commanding the Down forces, but he escaped through the back window of his headquarters.

Emphasis was placed on small units in which every soldier was expected to be an instrument of combat capable of functioning alone or as part of the team. Exercises were scripted and doubled as physical fitness tests: on the first day, one American unit was force-marched 32 miles and then ordered to sleep in the open without tents.* Another U.S. Army unit, which had been on the move for eight days with no more than two hours of sleep a night and no change of clothing, met with Scripps Howard novice war reporter Ernie Pyle and told him that they had gone through more in one day here than they had in the whole of the Louisiana Maneuvers. An officer who had been in the First World War added that he had not spent two more difficult days in France than he had during the last two days of the Irish exercises. Pyle especially focused on the men doing the fighting rather than the men commanding them.[18]

The Irish Maneuvers involved not only Americans, Canadians, and the Irish Home Guard but also many British troops who had already fought the Nazis in operations such as the Belgian offensive of 1940. It was clear that the Americans and British could work well together. As to preparedness, a key moment came in July, when Winston Churchill was again in the United States and witnessed recruits conducting drills using live ammunition in North Carolina. His military aide, General Hastings Ismay, commented, "To put these troops against Continental troops would be murder." Churchill shot back: "You're wrong. They are wonderful material and will learn very quickly."[19]

*　　*　　*

* One of the Americans' complaints about Northern Ireland was the cold. A *Washington Post* reporter in camp with an American unit wrote: "Men who never balked at subzero temperatures back home on snowed-in Minnesota farms swear that the raw damp, 40 degrees in Northern Ireland is the coldest they ever encountered." "U.S. Soldiers in Northern Ireland, Happy but Anxious for Action," *Washington Post*, May 31, 1942.

Half a world away, soldiers arriving at George Patton's Desert Training Center were immediately exposed to extreme high heat. To Patton, the desert became a laboratory in which his men were expected to adapt quickly to a new and altogether hostile environment. As the first units were sent out on maneuvers, Patton wanted his men to innovate, especially with such basics as "desert cookery." The men were sent into the field with water and canned combat rations that needed to be cooked to be palatable. The area was devoid of natural fuel, including twigs. The men quickly named their method of cooking "Patton's desert stove"; a tin can was filled with gravel, gasoline poured in, set alight, and a can of food was placed on top.[20]

Some 60,000 men—tankers, infantry, and artillerymen—were brought to the desert to prepare to invade North Africa. The pace of operations was relentless, with one major tactical exercise every two days, including overnight maneuvers. Without roads, let alone road maps, Patton's tank men had to navigate using the stars just as if they were sailors at sea. Unlike the 1941 maneuvers, which involved major phases with elaborately scripted opening scenarios, these were high-speed events in which tanks and infantry units battled one another.

Patton admitted to the rigor of the training, saying, "I want my men to take just as rough a beating as I can give them in as near the situation they will have in North Africa." In heat that reached 120 degrees Fahrenheit, he allowed his men only a single canteen of water a day. Temperatures inside the tanks measured as high as 156 degrees. One veteran of the Desert Training Center later called the area "one of those places God has forgotten but the Army remembers."[21]

Patton's water plan proved to be folly and led to numerous instances of heat exhaustion requiring hospitalization, some cases of heatstroke, and even several reported deaths. Fortunately, the Quartermaster Corps had stationed a team in the desert, including Australian polar explorer Sir George Hubert Wilkins, an expert on the effects of climate on human behavior, who was soon able to show the commander that the water ration had to increase dramatically, or men would soon begin to die in larger numbers. One member of that quartermaster team, Weldon F.

Heald, later reported that men in the maneuvers sweated as much as two and a half gallons in 24 hours—all of which had to be replaced.* Heald took part in the maneuvers as part of his research and reported losing two to four pounds an hour when the heat got well over 100 degrees.[22]

Patton trained his troops for every eventuality, including ambulatory escape. After a month in the desert, he expected all of his men, himself included, to be able to run a ten-minute mile in full battle gear every 24 hours. Patton also demanded that they learn to go without sleep for a minimum of 36 hours straight.[23]

Because the nation was at war, public access to the desert maneuver area was prohibited and press access was limited. Tactics and equipment were deemed secret. The American public knew little about the operation.** Almost all information made public was vague and melodramatic, such as a report from *Yank* magazine: "Somewhere in the California Desert, under a molten sun and in a country where the very earth feels like fire, American armored vehicles are training . . . It is this force that will someday leave death in its wake in the sandy places of Libya, or wherever it may be sent."[24]

As the first desert camp was being established, Patton purchased a commercial radio transmitter with his own money and created a radio station that broadcast with enough power to be heard within the whole maneuver area. It was programmed to play recorded music save for when he wanted to address his troops. He kept transmitting microphones by his bed and at his desk, allowing him to break into the music whenever he wanted.[25]

The first group of men spent a month in the desert. They ended their training with a three-day final maneuver, featuring a 76-mile tank attack that swept across the desert, with Patton in the lead during the

* One of the unit's discoveries was that a man needed a quart of water to walk five miles in the desert and that 20 to 25 miles was the limit for men walking in the desert.

** The story of this massive undertaking has rarely been told, and there are few references to it in the literature of the Second World War. Many of the details of life in the Desert Training Center in 1942 were not made public until a half century later, when information about it was declassified and a museum was created to celebrate the maneuvers.

final push against anti-tank and artillery units. A United Press reporter was allowed to watch but was barred from reporting details of the operation. He was permitted to write about the spectacular performance of jeeps (often referred to as "peeps" at the time) as vehicles with many roles to play: "Crewmen literally hung on with both hands and feet as the peeps ranged far ahead of the main body on reconnaissance missions, carrying small combat crews, handling messages and speeding key personnel from one battle section to another."[26]

The 81st Infantry Division provided a vivid example of how tough it was. The unit, which had suffered more than 1,000 casualties in 1917 in the Meuse-Argonne campaign during World War I, had been reconstituted and participated in the Tennessee Maneuvers. The 81st had been assigned its own 1,200-square-mile piece of the desert in which to exercise, an area inhabited by only two civilians, both keeping guard over inactive gold mines and living there as hermits. The division moved west in stages, and the whole unit was in a new camp in the Arizona desert by July 25, in the middle of a heat wave during which the temperature reached 126 degrees Fahrenheit. By July 28, two soldiers had died from the heat, and many had suffered severe cases of sunstroke. The heat wave, in which the daily temperature exceeded 110 degrees for 45 days in a row, broke with a monsoon rain that almost washed the camp away. To make matters worse, shortly after the 81st arrived, Patton decided to no longer provide ice or fresh fruit to the men in the desert; everything—meat, crackers, fruits, and vegetables—came from cans, which Patton termed an *experiment*. [27]

Finally, late in the summer, the men in the desert tested a new ration kit, dubbed K-2, on which they would survive for six consecutive days. One of the more attractive elements of the K rations was that each meal carried with it a small tin of fruit juice.[28]

William F. Boni of the Associated Press, who had covered the Carolina Maneuvers in 1941 and had been given a limited look at the California exercises, reported that there was no comparison between the two events. "On rest days in the Carolinas, the men could take showers whenever they please. Here showers are impossible after 8 AM because the water quite literally boils in the pipes."[29]

African American troops participated at the Desert Training Center as part of engineering battalions. In one United Press report from the desert, a white soldier praised the black troops training with him for their apparent disregard of the heat: "They get through working," he said, "and they organize a football game."[30]

Desegregation was still a distant dream, and barriers were coming down slowly. Black men still had difficulty enlisting, let alone being drafted, due to the shortage of segregated facilities. At the same time, black Americans demonstrated a keen desire to serve. While more than three million black men registered for the draft through 1942, fewer than 100 were indicted for draft evasion.[31]

The movement for equality had been given a slogan in early 1942 that became a rallying cry for black leaders and the black press. The expression *Double V* was coined officially in a 1942 letter to the *Pittsburgh Courier* from a black man working in a defense plant:

> The "V for Victory" sign is being displayed prominently in all so-called democratic countries which are fighting for victory over aggression, slavery and tyranny. If this V sign means that to those now engaged in this great conflict then let colored Americans adopt the double VV for a double victory: The first V for victory over our enemies from without, the second V for victory over our enemies within. For surely those who perpetrate these ugly prejudices here are seeking to destroy our democratic form of government just as surely as the Axis forces.[32]

Now the movement for racial integration had a name. "By mid-1942," one historian on the black experience in the American Armed Forces wrote, "the tide was turning on black morale and the black press began to relent. There were now blacks in the Marines, the Coast Guard and the Women's Army Auxiliary Corps and some of the harsh rhetoric of the black press began to soften." In May the first five pilots graduated from the Army's "first Negro flying school" at the Tuskegee Institute in Tuskegee, Alabama.[33]

But Jim Crow was still in force, and the Army and Navy did not give an inch on the matter of race. Meanwhile, individual actions seemed to have had greater impact on public opinion than all the editorials, in both the black and the white press, in favor of African American inclusion in the Armed Forces. Two examples burned brightest. In January 1942, heavyweight boxing champion Joe Louis defeated Buddy Baer in the first round at Madison Square Garden in New York. Louis announced that he was donating his $47,000 winner's purse to the Navy Relief Society. At the time, black Americans could join the Navy only as stewards and menial workers in the food service. Two months later, when Louis knocked out Abe Simon in the sixth round of a heavyweight championship match, he donated that purse of more than $36,000 to the Army Relief Society. Louis then entered the Army as a private.[34]

In April 1942, a 22-year-old black man, Doris "Dorie" Miller, son of a Texas sharecropper, belatedly emerged as one of the heroes of Pearl Harbor. Miller was a mess attendant stationed aboard the USS *West Virginia*. He was collecting dirty laundry from shipmates when the Japanese attack began. One of Miller's duties was to carry ammunition during an attack. The battery he was assigned to had already been destroyed, so he began to carry injured crew members to safety amid the chaos and destruction, wading through waist-deep water and moving across oil-slicked decks. Miller then took over a .50-caliber machine gun, a weapon he had not ever used before, and fired hundreds of rounds at marauding Japanese planes until he was ordered to abandon ship. Miller believed that he brought down at least one Japanese aircraft.[35]

Miller's name did not at first come to the nation's attention; he was described in early press reports only as an "unidentified Negro mess man." But after his identity was revealed by the *Pittsburgh Courier*, pressure from civil rights organizations and the black press eventually resulted in his being awarded the Navy Cross. In the aftermath of Miller's actions, all Navy men, including mess workers and stewards, were given antiaircraft training. In December 1942, Miller was brought back to the United States from the Pacific and heralded as a hero to boost morale and help sell war bonds.[36]

The debate over where and when American troops would first engage the Germans lasted throughout the spring and into the summer of 1942. Eisenhower was assigned to London in June and ordered to begin preparing for a cross-channel attack against the German army occupying France, a plan that had been agreed on by the American, British, and Canadian governments in April, as the Allies' principal effort to defeat Germany. It was clear to Eisenhower that the beaches of the Normandy region offered the greatest chance of success in an invasion of France.[37]

Unlike the war in the Pacific, where the United States could call the shots and determine strategy, the war in the Atlantic required close collaboration with the British, Canadians, and other allies—but especially the British. The Soviets pushed hard for a cross-channel invasion, wanting a second front that would pressure Germany from the west and alleviate the burden carried by Red Army troops. In the United States, homegrown members of the Communist Party USA and their allies on the Far Left, who had once lobbied for neutrality, now could talk only of this second front that would take the pressure off the Soviet Union.

Where the United States would enter the war was finally resolved by Roosevelt over protests by some of his highest-ranking advisers. In late July, Roosevelt decided to fight the Nazis in North Africa. His aide Robert E. Sherwood later pointed out that this was one of the very few major military decisions of the war that Roosevelt made entirely on his own.[38] Roosevelt's decisiveness at this point was based not only on Churchill's arguments but also on his own determination to get the American Army into combat with the Germans as soon as possible in 1942 rather than wait until later in 1943, which looked like the first time the United States would be strong enough to lead an Allied cross-channel invasion.

The Navy and the Marine Corps had been fighting the Japanese in the Pacific since December 1941, while Army units had not yet engaged in a single exchange of shots with Hitler's armies. Despite pressure from Stalin, the invasion across the English Channel was delayed until 1944.[39]

On July 26, 1942, Eisenhower received orders in London to take command of the Allied attack in North Africa, a suggestion made by the British, who saw it as an incentive to the Americans. They also knew that "because Vichy French antipathy to the British," in the words of historian James Holland, "knew no bounds," any French resistance would likely be stiffer against their own forces than those of the Americans.[40]

Patton himself got orders on July 30, 1942, to leave the California desert and prepare for a landing in North Africa. He arrived in Washington on August 3 and was given a loft in the Munitions Building on Constitution Avenue, where he was to plan his role in Operation Torch, the Allied invasion of North Africa. There would be two invading task forces. The Northern Task Force, consisting of British and American troops, would set sail from England and land on the northern coast of Africa by way of the Mediterranean. The Western Task Force, wholly American and under Patton's command, would cross the Atlantic and stage an invasion on the western coast of North Africa in French Morocco.

On August 5, Patton was summoned to London to meet with Eisenhower to coordinate the Africa campaign. He began to keep a diary, which he had done in the past when combat seemed imminent. Patton's diary entries for August 8 reflect a disdain for the operation: "No one likes the plan but we will do it." He also feared that it would not work: "The major difficulty in the planning was the paucity of the available troops. If the Vichy French which controlled the area resisted, the likelihood of getting ashore was slim."

On August 9, Patton had dinner with Eisenhower, and the two men talked until the early morning. Patton noted that both felt the operation was bad and was being staged mostly for political reasons. He wrote in his diary: "However, we are told to do it and succeed in the attempt or die." At worst, Patton saw the North African mission as impossible, but he added: "With a little luck it could be done at a high price; and it might be a cinch."[41]

While Eisenhower and Patton met in London, a new series of maneuvers was in progress in Louisiana. They had begun in late May 1942, and Walter Krueger's Third Army and others were back in the bayous. The new maneuvers would last into the winter of 1942–43, and similar exercises were staged in the Carolinas, Kentucky, and California. A large percentage of the men participating were described by the Army as "green," meaning they were either volunteers or had been drafted since the 1941 maneuvers. In the new Louisiana Maneuvers, the Army announced that every unit involved would have to prove its ability to make a continuous foot march of 25 miles with full field equipment.[42]

Despite a comparative lack of news coverage of these exercises, one newsworthy dispatch did come out of Louisiana on September 10, reporting that top Allied Army chiefs were at the games to watch the Third Army work out a problem of tank vs. tank destroyer, with "their eyes cocked towards the opening of a second front and driving [German general Erwin] Rommel out of Libya." Louisiana was no longer a place for just war games; it was now the stage for a full dress rehearsal.[43] Hanson Baldwin wrote in the *New York Times* that the Third Army was a training school for new divisions and had come a long way in a year under the "restless, driving energy and aggressive leadership of General Krueger."[44]

Patton returned from London to the United States on August 21 and was soon off to Hampton Roads, Virginia, from where on October 24 he sailed to lead the American invasion of North Africa with 24,000 troops and a convoy of 102 ships. Many in the convoy had just been built and were manned by crews on their first cruise. The second group sailed from Northern Ireland and Scotland, with 18,500 Allied troops, including 9,000 Americans.[45]

On November 8, 1942, Patton and his men invaded North Africa, launching Operation Torch. American soldiers waded through the surf at three separate North African landing areas, launching the largest amphibious assault to date in the history of warfare.

Patton's landing in the rough waters off French Morocco was bumpy and displayed American weaknesses in many areas, including communications. The U.S. forces still had much to learn about amphibious operations. When Patton first went ashore he found a chaotic scene of landing craft adrift, untended piles of supplies, and confused soldiers. "As a whole the men were poor, the officers worse," he noted in his diary. He spent much of the day on the beach restoring order, but thanks in part to the lack of resistance by the Vichy French, the objectives had been met. The key target for Patton was the capture of Casablanca. This he achieved on November 10, when he took the city unopposed, just two days after hitting the beach.[46]

In the coverage of the invasion, Patton explained where he had been during the previous year. *Time* magazine reported:

> In Morocco, tough, muscular Major General George S. Patton Jr. ran into just the kind of opposition for which he had prepared. Months ago, on the deserts of southeastern California, he had drilled his men to fight in blazing heat over terrain such as they would meet in North Africa. Patton had insisted that they keep their sleeves rolled down, that they get along on a minimum of water. He had forbidden that vehicles, moving or standing, be within 50 yards of one another, lest they provide a bunched target. Not long after his men reached Africa, their grumbles turned to praise for what the Old Man had taught them.[47]

The first anniversary of Pearl Harbor brought many assessments of how far the Army had progressed in a year. Patton's forces, along with the British, now held an "arc of steel" around the Germans, holding Bizerte and Tunis in Tunisia and positioning forces in the British Isles for the eventual crossing into occupied France. Although stalled for the moment, they seemed close to a position where they could push back Rommel's Afrika Korps and move the war out of North Africa and into Sicily.

Don Whitehead of the Associated Press was embedded with the British Eighth Army. He reported: "The first anniversary of America's entry into the war finds the eagle's wings spreading fast over this theatre of war." In the air, American pilots in American-made planes had shot down 44 enemy planes and damaged 20, while losing eight. Whitehead noted that jeeps that had just come off assembly lines in Detroit were everywhere and were proving to be ideal desert vehicles. "Everybody wants a Jeep," he wrote.[48]

In the Pacific, the United States had already posted victories in the Coral Sea, at Midway, and in the Solomons, and the United States had sunk 394 Japanese ships, 101 of which were warships of the destroyer class and larger, including two battleships, six aircraft carriers, and 37 cruisers. The United States had lost 86 ships, including those destroyed at Pearl Harbor. The most stunning comparison on the one-year anniversary date was that the Japanese had sunk 11 American merchant ships while 115 Japanese merchantmen had been sunk by the Americans. Meanwhile, practically all of the ships damaged but not sunk in the Pearl Harbor attack had been repaired and were now back in the fleet and ready for battle.[49]

By December 7, 1942, the U.S. Army had more than doubled in size, to 4.5 million men. There were now 14 armored divisions instead of four. Specialized centers for training the various parts of the military had been established around the country, including one for mountain troops in Colorado and another for tank destroyers in Texas. The nine Regular and 18 National Guard units in existence on December 7, 1941, had grown to 59 divisions, with the activation of 32 new divisions the following year.

The Selective Service System was working, with successively larger call-ups during the year, from 99,929 in January to more than 450,000 in November. On November 20, 1942, a Gallup Poll asked a sampling of Americans: "Do you think the draft is being held fairly in your community?" Eighty-two percent answered yes. George Gallup noted: "At no time has there been more than a small minority of dissatisfaction (to be expected as larger and larger numbers of draftees were called into the Army). It is interesting to note that for the first time, the steady growth of dissatisfaction has been arrested."[50]

Only now did some observers marvel at what George Marshall had accomplished in the days before Pearl Harbor in order to make the nation ready for global war. "The Army's most crying need, that for trained junior officers, was met by a solution so far superior to the 90 day training camps of the first world war that there is no room for comparison," wrote Marshall Andrews in the *Washington Post* on December 6. He added that the Army's Officer Candidate Schools were turning out more than 150,000 new junior officers a year. The *Post's* military editor, who had covered all the 1941 maneuvers as well as the 1942 maneuvers in Northern Ireland and Louisiana, gave Marshall high praise for pruning the army of deadwood officers. He also praised the citizen-soldier, whom he saw as "Mentally unequipped for this cruel business, disliking it thoroughly, fed on the unfairness of his plight, he has turned out to be one hell of a fighter."[51]

The Allied advance in North Africa experienced a major setback in February 1943, at the Battle of Kasserine Pass, during which the Germans outflanked the Allies and controlled the battlefield from high ground. The battle was over quickly, and more than 1,000 American soldiers were killed. But after that defeat the Americans regrouped and initiated battlefield reforms such as the use of greater air support and a tighter system of command, which later occasioned the comment of World War II historian Keith Huxen that "American reaction to Kasserine Pass showed the American Army's determination that next time the Germans would experience very different results." Henceforth the Army acquitted itself well, as the Allies then pushed Rommel's Afrika Korps all the way to Sicily, moving the war out of North Africa and into Italy. All remaining Axis troops in Tunisia surrendered in May 1943, thereby ending the North Africa campaign.[52]

The victory in North Africa would later be celebrated as the beginning of the long march that ultimately won the war in Europe—what Eisenhower later termed, in the title of his memoir, *The Crusade in Europe*.

Before it was dismantled by Italian prisoners of war in the spring of 1944 and abandoned, the Desert Training Center retained the harsh conditions initially created by Patton in 1942. Not every training mishap got reported to the outside world. One that did involved a company of 39 men lost in the desert for several days; when located, three men had died and another was missing. The temperatures during the period the men were lost were among the highest in several years, topping out at 124 degrees Fahrenheit.[53]

There were four more Tennessee maneuvers with the last being staged in March 1944. Collectively, more than 800,000 Army troops were trained here before fighting in such battles as El Alamein, Sicily, the Bulge, and Normandy. These maneuvers were not without risk and more than their share of fatal accidents, the worst of which took place on the last night of the last maneuver in the state when an assault boat overturned in floodwaters from the Cumberland River and 21 soldiers lost their lives.[54]

Before the war ended, Louisiana was host to three more maneuvers. The 1943 event again featured the Third Army under the direction of Lieutenant General Walter Krueger and featured a new diversity of troops. For the first time, a full "all-colored" division, the 93rd, took part in the maneuvers. The Army took great care in getting maximum coverage for the 93rd by flying in more than a score of newspaper editors and columnists, including Roy Wilkins of the *Crisis*, the magazine of the National Association for the Advancement of Colored People, and Dan Burley, editor of the *New York Amsterdam News*. As the black press covering the maneuvers was quick to note, very few officers were black and no combat officers were. But the unit was the largest and most important of its kind and before the year was out was on its way west for deployment in the Pacific.[55]

The other special unit participating, attached to the 34th Infantry Division, was a Japanese-American combat unit, the 442nd Infantry Regiment, composed entirely of volunteers from the United States and the territory of Hawaii. The 442nd combat team was later attached to the Fifth Army in Italy, where it was given high marks for discipline and morale. Daniel Inouye, later to become a U.S. senator from Hawaii, lost his arm in the assault on Colle Musatello in the Italian campaign.[56]

For some, however, the 1943 maneuvers were a less-than-fresh experience. Paratrooper Bob Bearden of the 507th Parachute Infantry Regiment recalled in his war memoir that he and his unit had been dropped into the middle of the maneuvering troops: "I can't recall what our mission was to be, and probably wasn't the least bit interested then. All I knew was that I was back for another—my third—miserable Louisiana maneuver. I had spent some of the worst days and nights of my existence chasing all around the boondocks of that state." Bearden was later dropped behind German lines in Normandy, captured by the Germans on June 8, 1944, two days after D-Day, and survived a series of Nazi prison camps.[57]

Late in 1943, *San Francisco Chronicle* columnist and Army Air Force lieutenant Herb Caen went to Louisiana and reported that the area had seemingly become a perpetual Blue and Red war zone. In this column, Caen may have been the first to report what would become a legendary comment underscoring the very real discomforts of Louisiana and the maneuvers held there. As he reported: An American on his way back from the front lines in Italy met a friend in a unit about to move up. The friend asked: "What's it like up there?"

"Well," came the thoughtful answer. "Well, it's like the maneuvers in Louisiana—only not as bad."[58]

The comment—and the sentiment behind it—would be uttered often before the war's end. A soldier who fought with the 27th Infantry in the middle of the battle for Saipan said succinctly in a later interview with unit historian Edmund Love, "If it wasn't for the shootin' I'd say the Louisiana-Arkansas Maneuvers were as tough as this." Edmund Love concluded, in his history of the 27th, "No man who came through them belittled them later, even after going through combat."[59]

A version of the comment was repeated in the 1945 film *A Walk in the Sun*, regarded by some as one the most realistic depictions of World War II combat to come out of Hollywood. The film features a scene in which a platoon of American G.I.s comes under heavy fire as they attempt to occupy an Italian farmhouse. Members of the platoon agree that the task ahead is going to be tough, but that "it can't be worse than the Louisiana Maneuvers."[60]*

Occasionally, however, a pleasant reminder surfaces of September 1941, when America got to meet the men who would be instrumental in winning the war. In 2001, a fundraiser was staged at Antoine's Restaurant in the French Quarter of New Orleans to benefit the National D-Day Museum (now the National World War II Museum), the Eisenhower Center for American Studies, and *At Ease*, a military radio talk show. The occasion for the event was a celebration of the trip George Patton had taken to New Orleans 60 years earlier, during the break between the two phases of the 1941 Louisiana Maneuvers, when he dined at the famous restaurant. His meal consisted of oysters Rockefeller, dinde Rochambeau, pommes de terre soufflés, and omelette Alaska Antoine.** Patton's dinner was replicated and served to those attending the event.[61]

---

* The Louisiana Maneuvers then became all but forgotten by the Army until 1992, when it created a large-scale set of exercises that it called the modern Louisiana Maneuvers—or as it was quickly abbreviated, the LAM. The exercise did not take place in Louisiana but rather in the circular corridors of the Pentagon and did not involve troops on the ground but rather was a digital war game that looked at combat on the battlefield of the future, through the year 2040. The one thing it had in common with the original was that competing forces in these games were known as the Red and Blue Armies.

** Dinde Rochambeau: turkey in wine sauce; pommes de terre soufflés: souffléed potatoes; omelette Alaska Antoine: Antoine's dessert specialty, pound cake layered with vanilla ice cream and topped with meringue, then flambéed.

Personal memories of the 1941 maneuvers have faded with the
passing of the men who participated in them and the people in the
locales where they were conducted. One of the last recorded recollec-
tions came in 2012 from a Louisiana woman who was 12 at the time
and whose home was in in the middle of the action in 1941. She wrote:
"My most vivid memory is walking out on our porch after supper and
seeing our large yard completely covered with soldiers resting, turning
flips, enjoying a break. I've wondered many times how many of those
precious boys made it back."[62]

The ultimate accolade accorded to the men of the G.I. Army that rose
in the 1941 maneuvers came from the man who rose with them and to
command them in North Africa and Europe. On Tuesday, May 8, 1945,
the war in Europe ended. Germany had agreed to the unconditional
surrender of its armed forces. That day General Dwight D. Eisenhower
addressed the world by radio broadcast from his headquarters in Reims,
France. During his short victory speech, he named the generals who
had led to the victory and then added:

> But all these agree with me in the selection of a truly heroic
> man of this war. He is G.I. Joe and his counterpart in the Air,
> the Navy and the Merchant Marine of every one of the United
> Nations. He has surmounted the dangers of U-boat infested seas,
> of bitter battles in the air, of desperate charges into defended
> beaches, of tedious, dangerous fighting against the ultimate in
> fortified zones. He has uncomplainingly endured cold, mud,
> fatigue. His companion has been danger, and death has trailed
> his footsteps. He and his platoon and company leaders have
> given to us a record of gallantry, loyalty, devotion to duty and
> patient endurance that will warm our hearts for as long as those
> qualities excite our admiration.[63]

CHAPTER 15

VICTORY LAPS: V-E, V-J, AND—LATER—THE DOUBLE V

By war's end in 1945, 50 million men between 18 and 45 had registered for the draft, and of them 11.5 million had been inducted into the military. The draft, as first envisioned and pushed by the visionary Grenville Clark and implemented by Roosevelt, Stimson, and Marshall, was a great success and, with some modifications, was still fully operational in the first years after the war, when the postwar Army was being created. The mechanism that was created to serve the Army also served the Navy and the Marine Corps, as the manpower needs for those services developed beyond volunteers.*

Looking back, clearly a series of prewar decisions spelled victory for the United States and its allies, beginning with Roosevelt's decision to choose Marshall as the U.S. Army's chief of staff over those with higher levels of seniority. The impact of Grenville Clark and other civilian allies was unprecedented. In 1950, historian Mark Watson, an artillery officer in World War I and military correspondent for the *Baltimore Sun*, noted: "One of the most surprising aspects of the case is that this measure, a vital impulse to the upbuilding of American defenses more than a year before Pearl Harbor, was designed and given its initial push, not by

---

* According to the National World War II Museum, 38.8 percent (6,332,000) of the members of the U.S. Armed Forces were volunteers, and 61.2 percent (11,535,000) were draftees.

Army or Navy or White House, but by a mere handful of farsighted and energetic civilians."[1]

The importance of Marshall's pre–Pearl Harbor leadership is impossible to ignore. To cite one dynamic example, fully three-quarters (more than 45,000) of the Army's lieutenants and captains who fought in all theaters of World War II were graduates of the Officer Candidate Schools he fought so hard to establish before the United States entered the war, in the face of strong opposition from both Roosevelt and Stimson. Omar Bradley later stated that he felt the OCS was Marshall's greatest contribution to the mobilization effort. After the war, some OCS graduates became career soldiers, but a greater number completed their terms of service and returned to civilian life. The Army's Officer Candidate School system still exists today, with its headquarters at Fort Benning, and operates with the same basic format, discipline, and code of honor Marshall and Bradley established in 1941.[2]

The same impulse that led Marshall to demand the OCS be set up led him to create a path for battlefield commissions, which allowed an enlisted man to become an officer in a combat zone on the decision of his commanding officer. Some 25,000 of these commissions were awarded before the end of the war. John W. Vessey Jr. was a prime example. He joined the National Guard when he was only 16. According to an obituary: "General Vessey rose to the rank of first sergeant in World War II and received a battlefield commission as a second lieutenant in 1944 during the Battle of Anzio [in Italy] while serving as an artillery forward observer . . . Vessey eventually became the 10th Chairman of the Joint Chiefs of Staff, the Nation's most senior military officer, from 1982 until his retirement in 1985."[3]

The officer purge of October 1941 had been essential to the Army's rapid development, as had the creation of new leadership, with men such as Eisenhower, Patton, Clark, Bradley, Gruenther, and many others whose wartime accomplishments are well recorded. What can never be known is how many disasters were averted by the dismissal of the officers who had displayed their leadership deficiencies during the prewar maneuvers.

Marshall, Stimson, and other key members of the group working to successfully build a citizen army showed the important ability to effectively fend off the forces of isolationism and Nazi sympathy—no small feat given the temper of the times.

By war's end, Marshall had built a multimillion-man army and had formulated much of the Allied strategy. His wartime leadership was such that Winston Churchill deemed him to have been "the true organizer of victory." Churchill marveled that Marshall could have revitalized the tiny U.S. Army of 1939, empowering it to produce a wealth of command talent "capable of handling enormous masses [of men and materiel] and of moving them faster and farther than masses have ever been moved before." After the war, as Harry Truman's secretary of state, the general revitalized Europe with a plan of economic recovery that was soon known as the Marshall Plan. He then remobilized the nation for the Korean War as secretary of defense. In 1952, for his role as statesman and father of the Marshall Plan, he was awarded the Nobel Peace Prize.[4]

A largely forgotten force in the outcome of the war was the Civilian Conservation Corps, whose graduates represented a new class of disciplined non-commissioned officers, more than a few of whom had originally been plucked from vagrancy and the brink of outright criminality. Estimates indicate that as many as one-half to two-thirds of the Civilian Conservation Corpsmen served during the war, and many of those who did not serve in uniform strengthened the domestic labor force.

General Mark Clark put it boldly: "To my way of thinking the CCC, unrealized by any of us at that time, became a potent factor in enabling us to win World War II. Because, though military training and drill were not authorized as such in the CCC Camps, nonetheless these young men learned the vital factor of being able to live together in the mass and were taught urgent and essential specialties . . . and so though we did not realize it at the time, we were training Non-Commissioned Officers."[5]

The CCC also affected the young Army officers who managed its many camps. "Marshall had looked into the hearts and minds of the Depression generation," World War II historian Geoffrey Perret wrote about Marshall's belief that the morale of his men was key to actually winning the war. "The CCC experience had given him a window on its soul. He didn't doubt that all the moral qualities of high morale were there, if only he could find ways to arouse it, and then sustain it."[6]

Many things influenced morale, but none more visual to the outside world than the films that director Frank Capra made for Marshall. These were not training films but rather documentaries explaining the nature of war to the troops. Capra later recalled the moment he got his orders from Marshall.

> "General Marshall, I've got to tell you I have never before made a single documentary."
>
> "Capra," Marshall replied, "I have never been Chief of Staff before. Thousands of young Americans have never had their legs shot off before. Boys are commanding ships today who a year ago had never seen the ocean before."
>
> "I'm sorry, sir. I'll make you the best damn documentary films ever made."[7]

After seeing the Nazi propaganda film *Triumph of the Will*, Capra was inspired to create a body of work that rebutted it. His first film in the Why We Fight series, titled *Prelude to War*, won the Academy Award for best documentary of 1942. In this film and those that followed,* Capra relied on footage made by the Germans, Italians, and Japanese. Goose-stepping Nazis, the guttural ranting of Hitler, the tragicomic

---

* *Prelude to War* was followed by six other films in the series: *The Nazis Strike* (1943), *Divide and Conquer* (1943), *The Battle of Britain* (1943), *The Battle of Russia* (1943), *The Battle of China* (1944), and *War Comes to America* (1945). Capra also directed other movies for the Army, including *The Negro Soldier* (1944) and *Two Down, One to Go* (1945), which starred Marshall himself. For his contribution to the war effort, Capra was awarded the Distinguished Service Medal in 1945. All of these films can be viewed today via YouTube.

posing of Mussolini, and the swagger of Japanese "liberators" were, in the words of historian Geoffrey Perret, "all that anyone needed to realize that this was what tyranny and terrorism looked like, sounded like, were like." Marshall ordered the films to be shown to every soldier in his army, and the British, Canadians, and Australians followed suit.[8]

The peace-loving American youth turned out to be as brave and determined as the enemy. Before the war began, Robert T. Oliver spoke for many when he wrote in the *Washington Post*: "While Hitler, Mussolini and the warlords of Japan were loudly teaching the glories and virtues of war, our youth were organizing peace demonstrations and mockingly joining the 'Veterans of Future Wars.'" Ironically, a great number of the young men and women of the Veterans of Future Wars and its affiliates would soon be in line for a more generous bonus than the one they asked for in jest in 1936. This one would be paid out as part of the G.I. Bill—properly known as the Servicemen's Readjustment Act of 1944—in mortgage subsidies, small business loans, and tuition payments. But first they would pay the price. As one Princeton alumnus wrote many years later in a letter to the *Princeton Alumni Weekly*: "The request of the Veterans of Future Wars for bonuses now was humor of a high style, and like all great jokes it had a bitter end. Those young men who foresaw a war and knew they would be fodder were, in fact, bundled off to war, and many did not survive." By March 1944, six of the eight Princetonians who had created the *faux* veterans group were in uniform, and one was working in a key war industry. John C. Turner, the only one not in the war effort, had lost the use of both legs in an auto accident during his senior year and was working for CBS News. Lewis Gorin, who started the group, was an artillery officer. All six of the men in uniform survived the war.[9]

In his wartime memoir, *Crusade in Europe*, Eisenhower concluded that the beneficial effects of the Louisiana Maneuvers, which he dubbed "that great maneuver," were "incalculable." He felt that the prewar exercises "accustomed the troops to mass teamwork" and "speeded up the process of eliminating the unfit." Eisenhower then saw a number of lessons from the Louisiana Maneuvers transferred to Europe: "The efficiency of American trucks and the movement of troops and supply, demonstrated so magnificently three years later in the race across France, was forecast on the roads in Louisiana in September 1941."

Eisenhower may have been speaking about himself when he wrote that the maneuvers "brought to the specific attention of seniors certain younger men who were prepared to carry out the most difficult assignments in staff and command." He also pointed out the lessons learned in Louisiana regarding the large-scale supply of troops on a constantly shifting frontline, which came into play in Europe.[10]

Many of those who had served with Eisenhower in Louisiana followed him to Europe, where he became their commander in chief—a jump from colonel to four-star general. In the spring of 1944, a sergeant who had served under Eisenhower in 1941 was now serving with him in southern England as his division was preparing for the invasion of France. A reporter asked the sergeant if he could see any difference in the general and he replied: "No difference, same old Ike except there is more brass on his shoulders."[11]

Marshall concluded that the maneuvers were "invaluable" and that the U.S. Army could never have made its way through Europe without them. For the first time, in Louisiana, Marshall would later explain:

> It was possible to train the high command. Eisenhower, for example, was chief of staff of General Krueger's [Third] Army in the South. All of them learned a great deal. I remember in the 500,000-man maneuver down in Louisiana, I directed that they change their bases on each side. They told me it would take a month for something like that and be very, very expensive. Well, I said, they would have to do it anyway. They would have to do it in Europe and they would have to do it here. *So* they changed the bases. I remember in one case it took ten days and cost 40,000 dollars. That seems a large sum for a maneuver like that. But it was a very economical sum when it came to the efficiency

it developed in the troops. That is the reason that Patton and Hodges and Bradley were able to move as rapidly as they did across the face of Europe.[12]

After the war, others who had participated in the 1941 maneuvers cited those exercises as key to their ability to lead in actual war. Prominent among them was General J. Lawton Collins, who had been chief of staff of the VII Corps under General Lear. Collins in Louisiana went on to fight in the Pacific and then to lead the VII Corps in the Normandy invasion and in other Western European campaigns leading up to the Nazi surrender in 1945. Looking back on the maneuvers, he observed that they were the first time many, including himself, had participated in large-scale operations in which infantry, armor, and air forces learned to coordinate on both offense and defense. Lawton's biographer, H. Paul Jeffers, writes: "Experience was gained in two of the most difficult military operations, withdrawals and river crossings, requiring coordination between engineer and ground troops in building and demolition of bridges, erection of tank obstacles, and the laying and clearing of minefields."[13]

George Patton died following a car accident in December 1945, shortly after the war in Europe came to a close, and thus had little time to draw conclusions on how he and his men had learned from participating in the 1941 maneuvers and the 1942 desert training exercises he led. Undeniably, the bold actions of Patton and his tankers in Europe had been developed and rehearsed in the United States. Dubbing his desert training center "Little Libya" allowed him to turn metaphor into reality, when he drove his troops 1,200 miles across Libya to Tripoli, which he entered in January 1943.

Nearly 23 months later, December 1944, after the German army attack that set off what became known as the Battle of the Bulge, the 101st Airborne Division had become surrounded at Bastogne, Belgium. Eisenhower asked Patton, who then commanded the Third Army, if he could relieve the besieged unit, and Patton said he would. Employing the same nighttime end run he had used when he took Shreveport in the mock battle in Louisiana in 1941, Patton attacked the Nazis' southern front and relieved the battered garrison at Bastogne. He made this point a few days after the triumphant move, in a letter to Don M. Ewing, associate editor of the *Shreveport Times*, whom Patton had befriended in Louisiana during the maneuvers. Ewing and Patton had corresponded with one another in the days following Pearl Harbor and this time Ewing had written to Patton first to extend Christmas good wishes and then to specifically ask about what he had practiced in Louisiana that was put into play in the Battle of the Bulge. Patton's letter to Ewing, dated January 7, 1945, less than three weeks after the breakthrough, contained this reference to 1941 when the two had traveled through Texas: "I recall very well our trip through the night; and I can assure you that our success, particularly in this present operation, has been due to the ability of our people to move rapidly at night." Patton asserted that the only way to know how to move rapidly at night in a blackout was to drive in one, which he had done in Louisiana.[14]

Somehow, Ewing was able to confirm what had been rumor when the maneuvers ended in late September 1941. Patton had indeed bought gasoline with his own money, and both General Walter Krueger and Colonel Dwight Eisenhower had called a foul on him, which was upheld by the referees. His victory in the battle of Shreveport was negated. Ewing noted that for a "long time" it was not fully revealed that Patton had left cash at filling stations along the route, with orders to attendants to "give any of my vehicles all the gas they want and keep the change." Ewing's article was syndicated nationally by the Associated Press and appeared under various headlines, including: PATTON TRICK OF 1941 AIDS HIM IN BELGIUM; PATTON'S NOCTURNAL DASHES IN MANEUVERS ARE PAYING OFF NOW; and A WAR GAME PAYOFF.[15]

Ewing wrote a tribute to Patton on his death in which he recalled a moment in 1941 when the two men reflected on the accidental deaths of several men early in the maneuvers. Ewing wrote: "At dawn, Gen. Patton and I crouched on a bank of the Red River at the bridge near Natchitoches watching his armored vehicles roar across. Airplanes simulated dive bombing from above, chemical warfare units sent up smoke screens, star shells broke in the skies. We talked of the sudden death of war and of the slow and agonizing death of the fatally wounded.

"'For my part,'" Patton said to Ewing 'when my time comes, I want to catch a 155 mm shell square in the belly—blooey, and that's all!'"

Ewing then bemoaned the fact that the great general died of a broken neck after the war in Europe had ended. In Ewing's words, Patton "died of the same affliction . . . that is administered deliberately to some of the war criminals.

"'What a hell of a way to die!

"Especially for George S. Patton Jr."[16]

The maneuvers provided the data and instructions for the American tank battles that lay ahead. British tank officers were amazed that the officers of the U.S. Army's First Armored Division quoted the results of the Louisiana Maneuvers "rather as others quoted from the Bible."[17]

The maneuvers showed that mobile anti-tank battalions backed by coordinated combat aircraft could successfully fight against tank divisions. Krueger called this matchup blitz on blitz. These "tank killer" units were still experimental and had no counterpart in Europe, and the military, led by McNair, quickly believed that more and better anti-tank units should be organized at once. On the other hand, the Louisiana Maneuvers had also shown that columns of tanks and other armored vehicles displayed tremendous punching power and could smash holes in elements many times their size, but they still needed infantry behind them to hold the ground gained.[18]

The deadly power of aircraft demonstrated that the Army would be at a tremendous disadvantage without adequate air support. Army and Navy aviation units working together had been a powerful force in Louisiana. Among the other lessons learned in the Louisiana Maneuvers and proven in Europe and especially during the Normandy invasion was that paratroopers could be very useful when dropped behind enemy lines for sabotage. Some described the two shows the paratroopers had put on in 1941 as "spectacular."[19]

In 1972, George Edwin Patrick Murray completed a master's degree in history at Kansas State University; he wrote his thesis on the Louisiana Maneuvers of September 1941. Murray argued that a key element of Marshall's genius was staging the maneuvers as a big show for the country, not only to display the progress of the Army in terms of modernization, mechanization, and motorization but also to let the nation know it was woefully short of trucks, tanks, and ammunition. "Without the Louisiana maneuvers, and the jolt they gave the army in the country, the United States would've been even worse off than it was on December 8, 1941."[20]

The most important scholarly examination of the maneuvers was Army historian Christopher Gabel's *The U.S. Army GHQ Maneuvers of 1941*, published by the Army's Center for Military History 50 years after the fact. After careful reexamination, Gabel recognized their importance as a "triumph of logistics," especially noting the military's newfound ability to quickly and efficiently move large numbers of troops, which came into play following a declaration of war three months later. He also felt the 1941 maneuvers bridged "a critical gap between theoretical training and the practical application of military skills." Even more important, Gabel concluded, the maneuvers showed that "a newly mobilized Army, fabricated from scratch after two decades of skeletonization" could function capably and that it "provided the medium in which an embryonic Army completed an important formative process, setting the stage for its metamorphosis into an Army that could fight and win."[21]

Like the jeep, the Piper Cub aircraft—known to G.I.s as the flying jeep—which had debuted in the Tennessee Maneuvers and shown its versatility in Louisiana and the Carolinas, was an immense success. By the end of the war, Piper had delivered 5,673 Cubs to the military. They were used for pilot training and artillery spotting, as well as aerial photography, reconnaissance, and medical evacuation. More than three-quarters of all pilots trained for World War II service received basic instruction in the Cub. Many years after the fact, William Piper revealed that he had given the Army a dozen Cubs to use as artillery spotters during the 1941 maneuvers, after the Army had advised him to move beyond the Cub and convert his manufacturing operation to accept subcontracts from larger warplane manufacturers. Without this bequest the military may have never seen the value of the light aircraft for use in combat.[22]

Lots of other equipment got a first real test in the 1941 maneuvers, including the first medium tank (the M3 Grant,) the walkie-talkie for station-to-station communications, the half-track truck, the two-and-a-half-ton truck, and field rations, to name some of the most important. The ability to lay down pontoon bridges was hardly new—it dated back in the United States to the Civil War—but the speed and skill required to lay them was sharpened and refined. Bridges fabricated for crossing unfordable rivers in Tennessee, Louisiana, and the Carolinas were put into play in crossings of the Rhine and other rivers in European combat.

Without question, however, the single most important hardware innovation to make its debut in the 1941 maneuvers was the portable runway dubbed the Marston Mat. Two million tons of Marston Mat panels were produced in World War II, enabling U.S. troops to bring almost instant airfields to each island captured from the Japanese and airfields to Normandy in the wake of D-Day. By the end of the war, a whole airfield could be carried across the Atlantic or Pacific in the cargo hold of a single Liberty ship and be ready for aircraft to operate from 72 hours after unloading.*

As G. Patrick Murray pointed out in his thesis, perhaps no other branch of the U.S. Army learned as much from the maneuvers as those involved with supply. They had to work the maneuvers as if they were a real war—unloading trains only at night, moving without lights to forward depots, and so forth. When Marshall moved his armies during the break in the maneuvers, Roy Lutes, the man in charge of supply, moved his center of operation in one night.[23]

---

* Surplus mats left over from the Vietnam War have been recycled as elements in sections of the wall between the United States and Mexico. Cindy Carcamo, "Border Wall Built in 1990s Cut Illegal Immigration, But It Also Brought Problems for Small Town," *Los Angeles Times*, March 9, 2018.

Beyond the 1941 maneuvers themselves was the impact of the Desert Training Center on the conduct and outcome of the war. Between 1942 and 1944, 1.8 million men were trained here under the same hell-on-earth conditions originally established by Patton. At its peak, the 18,000-square-mile facility was home to 190,000 troops who lived there in 100,000 tents and trained in 27,000 tanks and half-tracks. Twenty of the 87 Army divisions that fought in World War II trained here, including the 4th Armored Division, which trained here for two years before becoming the leading unit in Patton's Third Army sprint across France in the summer of 1944. According to military historian Jerry Morelock: "Essentially the 4th Armored made Patton's reputation as a blitzkrieg-type armored commander."[24]

Eleven of the 42 generals who had commanded troops in the bayous went on to command in combat in the war. They enjoyed various fates. Leslie McNair, at 61, was killed while observing the Saint-Lô breakout by Allied troops in France in July 1944, when U.S. planes dropped their bombs off target. He was immediately recognized as the highest-ranking officer to die in the war. Commenting on McNair's role in transforming millions of green inductees into hardened troops, Marshall called him the "brains of the Army." McNair was posthumously promoted to four-star general by a special act of Congress in 1954, making him the most senior U.S. military officer ever to die in combat.[25]

Ben Lear was jumped two ranks to brigadier general two months after the maneuvers and retired in 1943, but he was brought back to the Army in 1944 to become a deputy to General Eisenhower in Europe. His most important role in the war took place when he succeeded McNair as commander of the European ground forces. When he returned from Europe in July 1945, he was welcomed ashore from a transport ship in Boston by a large chorus of G.I.s chanting "Yoo-hoo," an allusion to the incident in which he had disciplined troops who had catcalled women on a golf course. It was a tag Lear could never shake, even in the obituaries written about him when he died in 1966 at age 87.[26]

General Hugh Drum, thinking he was going to rise to become the "Pershing of the Second World War," instead saw his military career falter at the beginning of U.S. involvement in the war. In the words of historian Barbara Tuchman, Drum was "a pompous man of large pretensions and self-importance," who quickly walked himself into trouble with Stimson, Roosevelt, and Marshall. In January 1942, Drum refused a position Secretary of War Stimson assigned to him in China, because he thought China was of marginal relevance to the whole war, and he did not want to get stuck there. Thus, his Army career came to an end, and he was forced to retire a few months later. Marshall could not get over the fact that Drum had turned down an assignment from the secretary of war in wartime.* The man who got the job Drum rejected was General Joseph "Vinegar Joe" Stilwell, one of a few standout officers in the 1940 Louisiana Maneuvers, who gained great acclaim for leadership in the Pacific theater.[27]

General Walter Krueger remained in charge of the U.S. Third Army until he was given command of the U.S. Sixth Army in January 1943, which was based in Australia; he led his troops on many combat assignments until the end of the war in Asia and was credited with playing a critical role in the defeat of Japan. Perhaps Krueger was most remembered for organizing a task force of specially trained Army Rangers to rescue the several hundred American survivors of the Bataan Death March who were imprisoned near the town of Cabanatuan in central Luzon, Philippines. In September 1945, his Sixth Army was assigned to occupation duty in Japan. Krueger was promoted to temporary four-star general in March 1945; but in January 1946 the rank reverted to lieutenant general. However, when he retired in July 1946, it was at the four-star level.

When Krueger wrote his own memoir in 1953, he reflected on the 1941 maneuvers as an "invaluable" experience, and he even had

* In reflecting on the fact that George Marshall has no weapon or Army installation named after him, Thomas E. Ricks noted in his book *American Military Command from World War II to Today*: "In the snowy reaches of remote upstate New York there is even a Fort Drum honoring Gen. Hugh Drum . . . There is no Fort Marshall."

a good word for the wooden rifles and stovepipe cannons when he wrote: "The woeful shortage of weapons and equipment of all kinds taught my staff and me how to do much with little and get along with what we had."[28]

Alfred M. Gruenther, who had served as Eisenhower's deputy chief of staff in Louisiana, eventually replaced Eisenhower as chief of staff of the Third Army and served as chief of staff for various groups during the war. At 53, he became the youngest general serving during the war. He was the primary American architect for the Allied invasions of North Africa in 1942 and Italy in 1943.

In contrast, the purge or forced marginalization of officers by Marshall in the fall of 1941 was, in the opinion of Eisenhower, essential to victory in World War II. "By God, he just took them and threw them out of the room," Eisenhower recalled some years later. But ultimately, Ike concluded, Marshall was vindicated. "He got them out of the way, and I think as a whole he was right."[29]

Senator Henry Cabot Lodge Jr. went on to serve as an active duty Army officer during the war beginning in 1942, when he took a leave of absence from Congress. When he asked for a second leave in 1944, he was forced to resign from the Senate based on an order from Secretary of War Stimson that barred members of Congress from active duty military service. In resigning from the Senate he said, "Given my age and training, I must henceforth serve my country as a combat soldier in the Army."[30]

Reelected to the Senate in 1946, Lodge became closely associated with Eisenhower, who he had first met in the 1941 Louisiana Maneuvers and whose command he had served under as an Army officer in Europe. In 1952, he helped persuade Eisenhower to seek the Republican nomination for president and then took charge of the campaign during which he won the nomination from Ohio conservative and former isolationist Senator Robert A. Taft. In that same election, Lodge lost his seat in the Senate to John F. Kennedy. At year's end, when President-elect Eisenhower appointed Lodge as his ambassador to the United Nations, Lodge recalled his time in Louisiana with Eisenhower and mentioned

Patton's offer of $50 for Eisenhower's capture and then quipped: "As far as I'm concerned nobody's caught Ike yet."[31]

In 1960, Lodge ran for vice president on the Republican ticket headed by Richard M. Nixon and lost to the Democratic slate of Kennedy and Lyndon B. Johnson. In 1963, President Kennedy appointed Lodge to serve as his ambassador to Vietnam, and he went on to fill diplomatic positions for Presidents Johnson, Nixon, and Gerald Ford.

The men and women who covered the maneuvers achieved various degrees of fame in the years to come. Richard C. Hottelet joined the crack CBS reporting team under Edward R. Murrow. He covered the war under the honorific banner "Murrow's boys," as did William L. Shirer, who went on to write the best-selling and still unequaled *The Rise and Fall of the Third Reich*, and Eric Sevareid, who had a long and distinguished career as a CBS commentator. John Daly, the affable CBS reporter who had covered the maneuvers, became the host of several early television shows, the best known of which was the CBS panel show *What's My Line?* The show made him one of the outstanding personalities of television's black-and-white era, along with Dave Garroway of NBC Radio, whose trail after the Louisiana Maneuvers led him to be the first host of the *Today* show—one of the longest-running shows in American television history. Two of the top print reporters covering the maneuvers went on to win Pulitzer Prizes for their work covering the war: Hanson W. Baldwin of the *New York Times* won his for dispatches from the western Pacific in 1943, and Mark S. Watson of the *Baltimore Sun* won his the following year for wartime reporting in Europe.

Hilton H. Railey, the *New York Times* reporter and author of the report that had confirmed the low morale in the Army in 1941, helped create and lead the 23rd Headquarters Special Troops, also known as the Ghost Army, which employed dummy tanks and aircraft, bogus radio broadcasts, battlefield sound effects, and phony war-planning material—left poorly camouflaged so it could be discovered by the Germans. Between the Normandy landing and V-E Day, the Ghost Army staged 20 separate operations. Among them, in March 1945 when the U.S. Ninth Army was poised to cross the Rhine, Railey's men distracted the Germans by simulating two full divisions. These extraordinary feats were kept top secret until 1996, when some of the operations were made public. In his 2002 book on the unit, Philip Gerard concluded that the efforts of the Ghost Army saved thousands of more conventional soldiers from facing massed German defenders.[32]

John Edward Lawton, the first man drafted in November 1940, was honorably discharged from the Army a year later, in accordance with peacetime conscription plans. He then spent a year working as a civilian at the Boston Navy Yard, was drafted a second time, and, without seeing any combat action, at the end of the war was stationed at Fort Lewis, Washington.[33] Dorie Miller, the African American hero at Pearl Harbor, died on Thanksgiving Day 1943, after a Japanese submarine torpedo struck his ship, the aircraft carrier USS *Liscome Bay*, in the South Pacific. In 1973, the Navy named a frigate after him.[34]

Captain Norris Perkins, who served with Patton through all three of the 1941 maneuvers, was still under Patton's command when he led a tank company in North Africa and into Sicily. On July 12, 1943, he was wounded in Sicily and was awarded the Distinguished Service Cross and Purple Heart. At the end of the war he was promoted to major and then studied medicine and practiced as a physician from 1957 to 1986. By his own admission, he could never get his time with the Second Armored out of his system and published several articles about his time with the unit. His memoir *Roll Again Second Armored: Prelude to Fame 1940–1943* was published in 1988. Perkins died on April 16, 2008, at age 95.[35]

Marty Snyder, the cook who had impressed Eisenhower in Louisiana, was over 30 and shortly after the end of the maneuvers was offered early release from the Army. This would have taken place on Monday, December 8, but because of Pearl Harbor, Snyder chose to remain in the Army. During the ensuing war, Snyder became Eisenhower's cook at Supreme Headquarters in London and prepared meals for such notables as Charles de Gaulle, Princess (later queen) Elizabeth, and Winston Churchill. After the war, Snyder and a colleague who had cooked with him in Europe opened the Headquarters Restaurant at 108 West 49th Street in New York City.[36]

Jack Womer of Dundalk, Maryland, who explained during the Louisiana Maneuvers how he could trick the system (by obtaining the armbands of both armies), was part of the 29th Infantry Division but later transferred to the 101st Airborne Division as a ranger and paratrooper. He became part of an elite squad of malcontents and troublemakers who were assembled to do the dirty work of demolition and sabotage. The unit was without a name until a reporter for *Stars and Stripes* counted them up, observed their habit of not changing their clothing, and dubbed them the "Filthy Thirteen." Beginning with the D-Day invasion, during which they destroyed a bridge spanning the Douve River, thereby preventing Nazi troops from reinforcing the front, the Filthy Thirteen fought fiercely for a year, spearheading Allied advances in Europe. Before the Battle of the Bulge, for example, they were dropped deep behind enemy lines to conduct reconnaissance missions. The 1967 film *The Dirty Dozen* was reportedly inspired by and loosely based on the real-life Filthy Thirteen.[37]

Three well-known men who had been drafted and initially rejected in the prewar call-up were able to enter military service and had celebrated war records. After finally being accepted by the Army and joining the Army Air Corps, actor Jimmy Stewart rose quickly and received his commission on January 18, 1942. Stewart, who had won the Oscar for Best Actor the previous year for *The Philadelphia Story*, appeared in uniform at the Academy Awards in February, where he presented the same award to Gary Cooper for his title role in *Sergeant York*, the saga of one of the most decorated infantrymen in the First World War. During the next eight months, Stewart became a flight instructor and then in the fall of 1943 was sent to England as commanding officer of the 703rd Bombardment Squadron, which flew B-24 heavy bombers. Stewart soon began flying combat missions and on March 31, 1944, was made operations officer of the 453rd Bombardment Group. He was later appointed chief of staff of the Second Bombardment Wing of the Eighth Air Force.

Stewart participated in 20 combat missions, including some during the period of saturation bombing known as the "Big Week," which established air superiority for the Allies and paved the way for D-Day invasion. By April 1944, the skies of Western Europe were largely clear of Nazi fighter planes and bombers, thanks to Stewart and his fellow bomber pilots, and on the eve of the D-Day landings, Eisenhower could assure his ground forces: "If you see fighting aircraft over you, they will be ours." By the end of the war, Stewart had won a number of decorations, including three Air Medals, two Distinguished Flying Crosses, and the French Croix de Guerre. Stewart remained in the Air Force Reserve and was promoted to brigadier general on July 23, 1959, by then president Eisenhower. Two years after flying his final combat mission, in 1966, as a backseat observer in a B-52 Stratofortress over North Vietnam, Stewart retired from the Air Force.[38]

After finally becoming an officer in the U.S. Navy, John F. Kennedy volunteered for duty in the South Pacific where, as a lieutenant, junior grade, he commanded a patrol torpedo craft, or PT boat, USS *PT-109*. This small, fast, highly maneuverable attack craft, armed with torpedoes, attacked the Japanese shipping that supplied troops occupying the island chains of the Pacific. On August 1, 1943, *PT-109* was sliced in half by a Japanese destroyer, leaving Kennedy and his ten surviving crewmen floundering in the water. Kennedy led his men ashore, then to eventual rescue. Kennedy actually pulled one of his crewmen through the water by his belt, which was clenched in his teeth. He was ultimately awarded the Navy and Marine Corps Medal for heroism and a Purple Heart for his wounds. The *PT-109* saga was turned into prose by the well-known writer John Hersey, who published it in the *New Yorker* and saw it reprinted in the *Reader's Digest*. The story followed Kennedy as he went into politics. As Stephen Plotkin, an archivist at the John F. Kennedy Presidential Library and Museum wrote, "The incident was a strong foundation for his political appeal: For here was a war hero who had not won battles but who had shown courage and dogged will, responsibility for those he led and the ability to inspire them—and it would be hard to better this as a short list of qualifications for a political leader."[39]

After spending time as a sergeant, baseball great Hank Greenberg entered Officer Candidate School and was commissioned a first lieutenant on graduation. Greenberg had singular value to the military, a prime example of someone who had willingly given up a tremendous salary to reenlist in the Army. A photo, supplied by the Army Air Corps, appeared in the April 1942 edition of *Our Army* magazine, showing New York Yankee slugger Joe DiMaggio in civilian clothes and Greenberg in his Army uniform, signing autographs at Florida's MacDill Field, where Greenberg was stationed. The caption read, in part: "Joe DiMaggio, at current writing . . . is reportedly holding out for something like a $45,000 salary for playing ball with the Yankees in 1942. This is the sort of folding money Sgt. Greenberg used to draw—but they don't pay such dough in Uncle Sam's Army, or do we have to tell you?"[40] Greenberg later served in the China-Burma-India theater and received his second honorable discharge on June 14, 1945. He returned to the Detroit Tigers on July 1 that year and hit a home run. A headline in the *Sporting News* read: HANK BREAKS IN AGAIN WITH A BANG![41]

On February 4, 1945, the USO celebrated its fourth birthday with open houses at its more than 3,000 clubs and centers in the United States. Initially, the organization had planned on celebrating at 341 centers but quickly expanded the celebration's scope when the numbers who wanted to attend became apparent. By the time of the anniversary, some three million servicemen and women were visiting the centers each month and another two million more were being entertained in camp shows, which featured top talent from Hollywood and Broadway. During the war years, the USO put on more than 400,000 performances, featuring entertainers from the comedy team of Abbott and Costello to Norwegian actress Vera Zorina.

The most important entertainer on the USO circuit was Bob Hope, who took personal responsibility for keeping morale high among service members. Hope's unparalleled war travel—some 300,000 miles—on his "Foxhole Circuit" took him to all fronts of the war. Of Hope's 144 wartime radio shows, only nine were broadcast from his NBC studio in Hollywood. The rest all took place at military sites at home or overseas, sometimes actually originating live from combat zones. For his radio listeners, Hope would mention the base or camp at the start, opening his monologue using the name of the location as his middle name, for example: "This is Bob 'Clark Field' Hope."[42]

John Steinbeck—who had published his most famous work, *The Grapes of Wrath*, in 1939—became a war correspondent for the *New York Herald Tribune* in 1943.* An early summer dispatch that year told of his experience witnessing a USO show from the mess hall of a military transport ship carrying men into combat. Steinbeck's dispatch not only described the show but also what it meant to the troops. Steinbeck was particularly taken with Hope: "When the time for recognition of service to the nation in wartime comes to be considered, Bob Hope should be high on the list. This man drives himself and is driven. It is impossible to see how he can do so much, can cover so much ground, can work so hard, and can be so effective. He works month after month at a pace that would kill most people." Steinbeck noted that he did not know Hope personally but could only guess at the effect it had on the comedian. "He has seen horrible things and has survived them with good humor and made them more bearable, but that doesn't happen without putting a wound on a man."

Steinbeck ended his piece by describing a group of entertainers working in the ward of a temporary overseas hospital treating severely wounded Americans. The group included singer Frances Langford, who spotted a man with a head wound and began to cry as she sang "As Time Goes By." Langford had to finish the song in a whisper; she walked away and then, when the men could not see her, she began to cry. The ward

---

* In September 1943, correspondent Steinbeck took part in the invasion of the Italian mainland at Salerno and was trapped with an Army unit in a German mortar and cannon barrage, during which his eardrums burst. He went home suffering blinding headaches and blackouts.

remained quiet with no applause. "And then," Steinbeck wrote, "Hope walked into the aisle between the beds and he said seriously, 'Fellows, the folks at home are having a terrible time about eggs. They can't get any powdered eggs at all. They have to use the old-fashioned kind that you break open.'" Steinbeck then added: "There's a man for you—there is really a man."[43]

The USO was part of a larger G.I. culture that had taken root before the war and flourished during the war years. It was displayed at many levels and in many arenas, including language, music, movies, books, and even the graffiti of the time. Men who had truculently chalked "OHIO" on the backs of trucks later marked walls all over the world with the cryptic morale-building slogan KILROY WAS HERE, which served as notification that the Armed Forces of the United States had passed through.*

No better example exists of that culture than the cartoons and comics of the era, which were ubiquitous. Dave Breger, the young cartoonist who participated in the Louisiana Maneuvers, turned his Army experience into comics that were soon published in the Army magazine *Yank*. Breger popularized (some claim created) the honorific nickname "G.I. Joe" for his comic strip. He soon became one of the most popular of the World War II cartoonists, and his term *G.I. Joe* or *G.I.* was widely applied as the nickname for the American foot soldier. The term achieved an added degree of immortality with the passage of the Servicemen's Readjustment Act of 1944, immediately given the popular title of the "G.I. Bill of Rights."**

---

* Who started this and who was Kilroy has been long debated, but before the war was over "Kilroy" had appeared at airfields, shipyards, and military bases all over the world. In his book *I Hear America Talking*, Stuart Berg Flexner called it the most popular piece of graffiti of all time.

** The legislation called for: (1) Speedy settlement of all disability claims; (2) aid from a veteran's placement bureau for job hunters and unemployment insurance for a maximum of one year; (3) government guarantee of 50 percent of any loan up to $4,000 to apply to a home, farm, or business property purchase or repair; and (4) a free year of college, and more for longer service, if the veteran was under 25 when he entered the service. The bill was signed into law by President Roosevelt on June 6, 1944—D-Day, the day on which the invasion of Europe got underway.

The cartoonist Bill Mauldin had entered the Army through the Arizona National Guard in 1940 and was moved into the 45th Infantry Division in time to take part in the Louisiana Maneuvers. There he began capturing the life of the "dog face" soldier, the Army foot soldier serving in the infantry. By early 1944, Mauldin had been reassigned from the 45th Division Infantry to the G.I. newspaper *Stars and Stripes*, and what had been the occasional cartoon in the newsletter of the 45th now began to appear six days a week in *Stars and Stripes* as well as some stateside daily newspapers.*

Although Mauldin's fans were legion, he attracted the ire of Patton, who felt that Willie and Joe, Mauldin's unshaven, unkempt, and war-weary cartoon heroes, were a threat to what was referred to as the "good order and discipline" of the Army. On several occasions Patton tried to get his work banned, to no avail. Eisenhower eventually overruled Patton on the issue, and Mauldin continued to draw. "There was one cartoon that just infuriated Patton," Andy Rooney, who worked with Mauldin at *Stars and Stripes*, later recalled. "There was a Patton-type general with one of his aides, and he was looking over this beautiful vista, and he says to the aide, 'Is there one of these for the enlisted men?'"

Mauldin would became an astute political cartoonist, penning such classics as one showing a sobbing Abraham Lincoln at the Lincoln Memorial on November 23, 1963, the day following the death of John F. Kennedy. As a civilian cartoonist, he won two Pulitzer Prizes.[44]

Throughout the war, Norman Rockwell's draftee private, Willie Gillis, adorned eight more *Saturday Evening Post* covers after his first appearance in the days before Pearl Harbor. After following Willie through the war, his final 1946 cover appearance shows him as a college student, taking full benefit of the G.I. Bill.

The print versions of this G.I. culture were the daily newspaper *Stars and Stripes*, which was published in many European and Asian versions, and the magazine *Yank*. During World War II, the paper published

---

* *Dog face* was a term of endearment rather than derision for infantrymen, who wore dog tags, slept in pup tents, and marched even when dog tired.

more than 30 different regional European editions, covering and serving various fronts, from Casablanca to London, from Nancy to Berlin. Army Chief of Staff Marshall supported and sustained the G.I. culture and had the eager backing of Secretary of War Stimson. Marshall was one of the strongest supporters of *Stars and Stripes*, of which he said: "A soldier's newspaper, in these grave times, is more than a morale venture. It is a symbol of the things we are fighting to preserve and spread in this threatened world. It represents the free thought and free expression of a free people."[45]

Stars and Stripes was the most visible, but almost every camp and outpost of the military boasted its own wartime newspaper or newsletter. By war's end more than 3,000 of these local post papers were published worldwide. They were supported by the Camp Newspaper Service (CNS), a syndicate operated by the War Department that offered cartoons and columns by civilian and military cartoonists and columnists as a supplement to the local news. Cartoonist Milt Caniff, of *Terry and the Pirates* fame, voluntarily drew his *Male Call* comic strip for distribution through CNS. It featured Miss Lace, a sophisticated heroine who looked a lot like Rita Hayworth and expressed no romantic interest in officers, only in enlisted men. Another popular CNS weekly cartoon was *The Wolf*, drawn by Sergeant Leonard Sansone, whose title character was a G.I. with a wolf's head and a voracious sexual appetite, often thwarted by canny females.[46]

Marshall personally intervened to make sure that frontline soldiers received all possible creature comforts, as well as access to entertainment. Movies were sent to combat zones even before they were released in the United States. At one point, the Mariana Islands had more than 200 outdoor movie screens, and many of the movies shown had wartime themes. Beer was sold at all domestic bases and was part of the ration for men serving overseas.[47]

Leading isolationists in the Senate and House were defeated just before or just after the end of the war. Senator Gerald P. Nye and Representative

Hamilton Fish Jr. lost in November 1944 re-election bids, and Senator Burton K. Wheeler was defeated in the 1946 primary election.

After Pearl Harbor, Charles Lindbergh, the hero of the isolationists, was denied reinstatement in the Army Air Corps by President Roosevelt, who simply did not trust the man. The president's denial extended to company after company in the aviation industry, for which he hoped to work. Lindbergh was finally hired by Henry Ford, who used him as a troubleshooter in the production of the B-24 bomber. Lindbergh later went to work for United Aircraft on the Corsair Navy fighter, and in that role got to the Pacific, where he copiloted more than 30 combat missions as a civilian.

After the defeat of Nazi Germany, Lindbergh pleaded for better treatment of Nazi leaders and condemned the war crime trials held at Nuremberg, claiming to be shocked that trials were even taking place. He insisted that if the United States were really a Christian nation, there would be no tribunal. Lindbergh's expression of shock about the trials—and not for the crimes—led Office of War Information Director Elmer Davis to wonder whether he had been reading the newspapers.[48]

The postwar world quickly forgot many of the details and realities of the 1940–41 period but not the 1941 vote in the House that came within one vote and barely extended the 1940 Selective Service Act. The incident seemed to loom larger as the war played out, and Sam Rayburn's "quick gavel" was seen as an instrument of destiny and redemption rather than a political shenanigan. As *Time* magazine correspondent Frank McNaughton commented in 1943, "Sam Rayburn for a moment literally played the role of dictator within the framework of representative government for the safety and good of the government itself."[49]

Sam Rosenman, Roosevelt's top speechwriter, later wrote: "One vote the other way and the Army would have been thoroughly disorganized and crippled. Marshall was reliably reported to have remarked a few days after Pearl Harbor to Representative James Wadsworth, who was instrumental in getting the necessary votes: "Jim, you have saved two million American lives and shortened the war we are about to enter by two years."[50]

In retrospect, some historians and others have wrongly determined that the vote for the Draft Extension Bill was for the existence of the draft itself rather than simply to ensure that the trained men already in uniform remained in service for another 18 months and could be sent beyond the confines of the continental United States. In fact, the draft would have remained in effect conscripting new draftees regardless of the vote.[51]

Even so, if the House had defeated the bill, the results would have been devastating. The process of sending home tens of thousands of men would have begun almost immediately. General Marshall testified before the Senate Committee on Military Affairs that without a draft extension, the recently expanded U.S. Army faced "disintegration." "If the term of service of the National Guard and the selectees is not extended," Marshall warned, "under existing limitations of the law, almost two-thirds of our enlisted men and three-fourths of our officer personnel will have to be released after completing 12 months of service." He added prophetically that "such a contraction would expose one vital U.S. bastion in particular to terrible vulnerabilities . . . the great naval base of Pearl Harbor." The Louisiana Maneuvers, which were underway at the time of Marshall's warning, and the Carolina Maneuvers to come, would have become exercises in futility.

The day after the vote, the *New York Times* editorialized that the extension meant that "draftees will give their time in order that an unprepared American Army may not be butchered by its own weakness."

Victory in Europe Day, or V-E Day, was celebrated on May 8, 1945, to mark the Allies' formal acceptance of Nazi Germany's unconditional surrender of its armed forces. It was followed on August 14, 1945, by Victory over Japan Day, or V-J Day, which effectively ended World War II. Collectively, some referred to these two days of victory as the double V, but this was a far cry from the Double V campaign—one *V* for victory over America's enemies and the other *V* for victory over segregation and discrimination—that had been waged by the black press and the NAACP, with its campaign of public and private protest during the war. This victory was yet to be won, and A. Philip Randolph, the African American labor leader who withdrew his threat of a march on Washington in 1941 to achieve the second victory, still had his eye on this particular prize.

The 1940 Selective Training and Service Act expired in March 1947, but in 1948, President Harry S. Truman and Congress responded to the United States' deteriorating relations with the Soviet Union by moving to restore the system for a new emergency. With legislation to renew the draft under consideration, the individuals and organizations that had demanded integration of the Armed Forces before and during the war sprang into action with a new determination and a new threat, which Randolph took directly to Truman on March 31, 1948. He hinted at a program of civil disobedience along "Gandhian lines"—referring to the policy of non-violent resistance Mahatma Gandhi had pioneered in India—unless the Jim Crow element of the draft ended. Truman, by all accounts, was sympathetic to Randolph's demand but disturbed by the threat of mass organized non-violent resistance.

Randolph spelled out this threat in a bold statement before the Senate Committee on Armed Services in hearings on the Selective Service. He pledged:

> . . . to openly counsel, aid, and abet youth, both white and Negro, to quarantine any Jim Crow conscription system, whether it bear the label of universal military training or selective service. From coast to coast in my travels I shall call upon all Negro veterans to join this civil disobedience movement and to recruit their younger brothers in an organized refusal to register and be drafted . . . I shall appeal to the thousands of white youths . . . to demonstrate their solidarity with Negro youth by ignoring the entire registration and induction machinery . . . I shall appeal to the Negro parents to lend their moral support to their sons,

to stand behind them as they march with heads held high to
Federal Prisons as a telling demonstration to the world that
Negroes have reached the limit of human endurance, that, in
the words of the spiritual, we will be buried in our graves before
we will be slaves.[52]

Support for Randolph's campaign appeared to be growing, especially among young African Americans. The NAACP conducted a poll
among black male college students and found 71 percent to be sympathetic to the idea of civil disobedience against the draft. A *Newsweek*
survey reported that among black college youth, "there were indications
of strong sympathy and support for Randolph." Little progress had been
made in the area of desegregation, and although black service members
were now allowed to train with white troops, they still rode segregated
trains, lived in all-black barracks, shopped at the black post exchange,
and watched movies in segregated post theaters.[53]

Black leaders, pushing for civil rights advances in all areas of American life, issued the warning that the black vote might swing to the
Republicans in 1948 if the president did not act to desegregate the Armed
Forces. On June 21, as if to underscore this possibility, the Republican
Party, meeting in Philadelphia to nominate its candidate for president,
Thomas Dewey, issued its platform, which included the statement: "We
are opposed to the idea of racial segregation in the armed services of
the United States," along with calls for an end to other Jim Crow laws,
including the abolition of the poll tax imposed on black Americans to
discourage them from voting.[54,55]

Three days later, on June 24, a new draft law was passed by Congress and signed into law by Truman later that day. Under the act, all
men between the ages of 19 and 26 were eligible to be drafted for a
service requirement of 21 months. No provision in the revised act dealt
with segregation or the practice of setting separate quotas for black
draftees. The well-entrenched status quo was maintained. Under the
new law, all men between the ages of 18 and 25 had to register for
the draft beginning on August 30. On July 12, the Democratic Party,

which also met in Philadelphia, nominating Harry Truman as its 1948 standard-bearer, called for equal treatment in the military as a plank in its platform.[56]

Truman, who had developed great sympathy for the rights of all Americans and who had expressed horror over the poor and sometimes violent treatment of returning black G.I.s that had occurred during his time in office, issued Executive Order 9981 on July 26. It abolished discrimination "on the basis of race, color, religion or national origin" in the United States Armed Forces as soon as possible.

The intent of the order was clear, but the means by which to achieve its goal was not. As an editorial in the *Cleveland Plain Dealer* termed it, the "joker in the pack" was that the new policy of military non-discrimination would be put into effect "as soon as possible . . . having due regard for the time required to effectuate any necessary changes without impairing efficiency or morale." This meant that movement forward on the issue would be extremely slow, as the many senior officers who opposed desegregation would be the ones who would rule on efficiency and morale.[57]

Truman did establish an advisory committee, the President's Committee on Equality of Treatment and Opportunity in the Armed Services, made up of seven members designated by the president, but it did not have any real powers of enforcement. It would serve only to examine the problem, cajole the leaders of the various branches of the service, and report on the progress of military desegregation.

Truman's executive order was not enough for some in the nascent civil rights movement, including Randolph. The morning after Truman signed the order, Randolph declared it did not go far enough and was "deliberately calculated to obscure" the whole question. He said that black Americans should ignore it, and he refused to call off his plan for civil disobedience when the registration began in August.[58]

Members of Congress were quick to criticize the order and offer legislation to nullify Truman's intention, including a bill that would require a volunteer at the time of enlistment to be able to state whether he wanted to serve in an all-white, all-black, or mixed unit. The military would be required to carry out his preference.[59]

Randolph later withdrew his order for a boycott of the draft before registration day, inducing an editorial in the *Baltimore Afro-American* to declare the turnabout a victory for the Truman for president campaign. In November, Truman carried the 1948 presidential election with 77 percent of the black vote. For the first time since Emancipation, a majority of African Americans reported that they now saw themselves as Democrats rather than as members of the party of Abraham Lincoln. The black vote provided his margin of victory in three key states: Illinois, which Truman carried by 33,000 votes out of a total of 3.9 million cast; California, which he took by 18,000 out of 3.8 million; and Ohio, which he won by merely 7,000 out of 2.9 million.[60]

Truman was hampered by southern segregationist Democrats in Congress, and a schism within the party almost cost him the election. Senator Strom Thurmond's breakaway Dixiecrat party cost the president four southern states. The nation was witnessing a split that would afflict the Democratic Party for years to come.

Truman's action on the desegregation of the Armed Forces was seen as an important milestone in the struggle for civil rights in America, even though he had seemingly little ability to implement it or even to grant others the power to do so. From the outset, Truman had faced stiff opposition from the Army. Within 24 hours of the executive order's issuance, Army Chief of Staff Omar Bradley said that the Army was "not out to make social reforms" and would only change its policy when the nation as a whole changed. Truman was more hurt than angry at the chief of staff's response and told friends that he might have expected trouble from many others but not from Bradley.[61]

Bradley had much support, including that of Hanson W. Baldwin of the *New York Times*, who defended his position. Baldwin argued that morale and efficiency had to be placed above compulsory change. Walter F. White, head of the NAACP, was quick to respond to Bradley and Baldwin in a letter to the newspaper, in which he accused both men of defending segregation "based on the Negroes alleged lack of intelligence."[62]

The findings of the President's Committee on Equality of Treatment and Opportunity in the Armed Services were published on May 22, 1950. After its final report, *Freedom to Serve: Equality of Treatment and Opportunity in the Armed Services*, the committee disbanded. The report argued that "segregation was detrimental to the military's efficiency," which stood in direct contrast to the assertions of pro-segregation officials, including the secretaries of the Army, Air Force, and Navy. In its conclusion, the committee declared:

> Military officials did not deny the claim of these ideals; they asserted, however, that in discharging their duty they must maintain military efficiency. The Committee on its part did not deny the claim of military efficiency; but it believed the assumption that equality of treatment and opportunity would impair efficiency was of doubtful validity. The Committee found, in fact, that inequality had contributed to inefficiency.

However, though the commission had a voice, it lacked any ability to enforce Truman's edict.[63]

By the end of Truman's administration, the limited desegregation that had taken place resulted more from the exigencies of the Korean War than from direct presidential action. "Armed forces integration occurred when the services saw it was to their advantage to integrate, not when Harry Truman gave a vague order to practice equal opportunity," said Alan Gropman, chairman of the Department of Grand Strategy and Mobilization at the Industrial College of the Armed Forces on the 50th anniversary of the Truman order. "The services integrated to get the most out of the blacks that they could, not do something for blacks." Gropman added that in Korea, "integrated units were more effective than segregated ones."[64]

Douglas MacArthur, commanding general of the Army, was one of the few voices in the military calling for the immediate end to Jim Crow.

On his return from overseas in 1951, after being relieved of his command in Korea by President Truman, he gave his first interview to Stanley Roberts of the *Pittsburgh Courier* and attacked those in Washington who supported military segregation. He claimed that when segregated troops were sent his way, he integrated them on the spot. "Now let's talk about my troops," he said to Roberts. "I have one criticism of Negro troops; they didn't send enough of them."[65]

Republican president Dwight Eisenhower, elected in 1952, was left to complete the job that Truman had begun. He was relentless in following up on Truman's edict and reached into corners the Truman order had not touched. Before he had finished his first year as president, he had received praise from the NAACP for ending segregation in schools, on military bases (including those in the Deep South), in the hospitals and nursing facilities of the Veterans Administration, and in civilian facilities in the shore establishments of the Navy.

The most visible element in all of this was Eisenhower's abolition of segregated washrooms and cafeterias in the Navy yards at Norfolk, Virginia, and Charleston, South Carolina, where the resistance was strongest and loudest. The press coverage of this action, especially in the South, was intense, as newsreel footage observed black workers using the formerly all-white cafeteria in Charleston.[66]

By the summer of 1955, Val Washington, Eisenhower's director of minority affairs, was able to report to the president and the press that when the administration took over, "nearly half [of the] Negro units in the military were still intact and now there were none."* He added that when Eisenhower took office, nearly three-fourths of the black men in the Navy were mess hall servants, but that system had been abolished, and black men were now serving in all branches of the Navy on an integrated basis.[67]

Even with these advances, some people still countered integration. The most noteworthy holdout was General Mark Clark, who had left the

---

* Segregation within the United States Armed Forces did not officially come to an end until Secretary of Defense Charles Wilson announced on September 30, 1954, that the last "all-Negro" unit had been dissolved.

Army in 1954 to become president of the Citadel, the private military academy in Charleston.* He quickly declared himself an opponent of the Supreme Court's 1954 *Brown v. Board of Education* decision, which ended segregation in public schools, and he denounced the court's effort to "force indiscriminate racial integration upon the South." In early 1956, Clark stated his opposition to mixing of the races in the Army. In an unwarranted charge, he asserted that in Europe, black troops had bolted and run under fire and did not have the discipline for soldiering. The *Chicago Defender* charged Clark with "inflammatory race-baiting."[68]

The July 1, 1941, march on Washington, which A. Philip Randolph had agreed to postpone because of the threat of war, was finally staged in the summer of 1963. Martin Luther King Jr. led the March on Washington for Jobs and Freedom, where he delivered his famous "I Have a Dream" speech. Walter White, who died in 1955, did not live to see the 1963 march, but Randolph was front and center in its planning and execution. His address that day included these lines about the multitude assembled before him: "We are not a pressure group, we are not an organization or a group of organizations, we are not a mob. We are the advanced guard of a massive, moral revolution for jobs and freedom."[69]

One of the hidden proponents of racial integration in the United States was Grenville Clark, whose impact on American life was long, persistent, and quiet. After the war, he spent much of the rest of his life supporting the United Nations, world peace, international law, and human rights. He became keenly interested in civil rights, and in the early 1960s, wrote checks totaling $80,000 to help meet the demands for bail that threatened to force many of the original Freedom Riders to give up their fight for acquittal of charges against them—a fight they won in the Supreme Court years later. During the early 1960s, he set up a multiyear system, which became known as the Clark Plan, to fund the NAACP Legal and Educational Defense Fund, enabling that group

---

* The Citadel accepted its first black cadet in 1967, the year after Clark's presidency ended.

to wage some of its more difficult and costly battles. In 1964, he and his wife gave the fund a gift of $500,000, to be matched by other donors.

The integration of the United States Armed Forces was eventually accomplished 50 years after the fact. On that anniversary of Truman's order of 1948, Secretary of Defense William Cohen was able to claim, with considerable pride, that over that half century, the U.S. military had become the model for the ideal, as the best-integrated section of the American economy.

ACKNOWLEDGMENTS

I was born a few minutes before midnight on July 30, 1939, which makes me a prewar baby by just a matter of a month, as the war began when the Nazis invaded Poland early in the morning of the first of September. I entered consciousness as the war proceeded and was soon fully aware that my two uncles were both in uniform serving in Asian combat zones. War was no abstraction to our family.

I mention this because my world was framed by the war and its aftermath, and I had long aspired to write about some aspect of it, but this was easier said than done. My chance came in 2005, while I was working on another project at the Eisenhower Presidential Library in Abilene, Kansas, where I first encountered material that suggested the importance of the 1941 Louisiana Maneuvers, not only to Eisenhower's career but also to the outcome of the war.

So, from the beginning, I would like to thank Eisenhower Library archivists Jim Leyerzapf and Herb L. Pankratz for their help as I began work on the subject. I would also like to thank Brigadier General Carl W. Reddel (retired), executive director of the Dwight D. Eisenhower Memorial Commission, who has been a great friend and supporter of this project from the very beginning and graciously read an early version of this book and made valuable suggestions.

Special thanks to military historian Ed Bearss, United States Marine Corps veteran of World War II, for his invaluable time in helping me shape this narrative, and to Chris Bradley for setting up that meeting. Bearss first alerted me to the importance of the Civilian Conservation Corps to the story told here.

At the Pritzker Military Museum and Library in Chicago, I would like to thank Paul Grasmehr, reference coordinator, and Theresa (Teri) A. R. Embrey, chief librarian, for their invaluable help on my visits there. At the Library of Congress I would like to thank Jeffrey M. Flannery, head, Reference and Reader Services Manuscript Division, Kathy Woodrall, Abby Yockelson, and Tom Mann. I also thank Jim Gandy, librarian/archivist at the New York State Military Museum, and Jeffrey Kozak, director of the library and archives at the George C. Marshall Research Library, for their professional help.

I would like to acknowledge many old friends, beginning with Bill Young, who graciously and skillfully performed the first edit of this manuscript, and Bob Skole, who made valuable additions and corrections based on real world experience. Bob is a World War II veteran who, among other things, rode Imperial Guard horses he helped liberate with the Eighth Cavalry in occupied Japan. I would once again like to thank Joseph C. Goulden, constant helpmate dating back to 1969 and my first book contract, which he helped me snag. Besides Tom Allen and Jim Srodes, to whom the book is dedicated, I would like to thank three other friends who encouraged and advised me on the book while it was a work in progress but did not live to see it published; they are Bill Mead, Fran Voigt, and Rick Bates. Other friends and acquaintances who helped include Florenz Baron, Donald Tirotta, Donald Cornell, Tom Dalzell, Frank Dorsey, Ernest B. "Pat" Furgurson, Frank Obrimski, and the Hamlet Group and the League of Extraordinary Gentlemen.

Many thanks to my agent, Deborah Clarke Grosvenor, for her devotion to this project. (It is noteworthy that Deborah's grandfather William P. O. Clarke was the naval officer who trained thousands of Navy personnel to land troops and equipment for the 1942 amphibious attack on North Africa as part of Operation Torch. In his definitive history of the U.S. Navy in World War II, Samuel Eliot Morison commented on Clarke's key role in the success of that operation: "Captain Clarke had less than two months, about one-third of what had been considered the minimum, to train these men to conduct night ship-to-shore landings. Considering the time limitations, his performance was remarkable.")[1]

Extraordinary thanks to editor and old friend George Gibson, who saw the immediate potential in this book and guided it through three rigorous line edits armed with only a no. 2 pencil. High praise is also extended to copyeditors Amy Hughes and Paula Cooper Hughes for their work on this project. Thanks also to Emily Burns and Julia Berner-Tobin at Grove Atlantic.

And finally, thanks to Nancy, who made it all possible.

PICTURE CREDITS

The author has been collecting original images since he began work on this project in 2005. Most of those used here come from the Army Signal Corps, and wire photos originally distributed by Acme, International News Service, Wide World, United Press, and the Associated Press. In addition, the photos of Stimson drawing numbers from the fishbowl for the 1940 draft, the image of George S. Patton, the soldiers lifting a Jeep in Tennessee, the officer using the walkie-talkie, and the White House on the evening of the Pearl Harbor Attack were obtained from the Library of Congress.

The map used for the endpapers by Pvt. Boyd C. Mutschler was obtained in an online auction. It was one of 12,000 published and distributed to the men of the First Armored Division as a souvenir of the unit's participation in the 1941 Louisiana and Carolina Maneuvers.

The frontispiece depicts a hill covered with 2,000 draftees awaiting assignment at Fort Lewis Washington, March 1941.

ENDPAPERS

"Wherein the 1st Armored Division solved important problems pertaining to war." Decorations and text by Pvt. Boyd C. Mutschler. Map drawn and published by 16th Engineers. Reproduction Unit 1st Armored Division, Fort Know, KY. Mutschler who hailed from Evansville, Indiana, was a draftee who drew the map showing the movements of his unit through the Louisiana and Carolina maneuvers. Mutschler would eventually spend thirty months in overseas combat zones with his division in both North Africa and Italy where he was among those who took part in the Anzio landing.

BIBLIOGRAPHY

Adams, John A. *General Jacob Devers: World War II's Forgotten Four Star*. Bloomington: Indiana University Press, 2015.

Ambrose, Stephen E. *Eisenhower*. 2 vols. New York: Simon and Schuster, 1983–84.

———. *The Supreme Commander: The War Years of General Dwight D. Eisenhower*. 1970. Reprint. Jackson: University Press of Mississippi, 1999.

Astor, Gerald. *The Greatest War: Americans in Combat 1941–1945*. Novato, Calif.: Presidio, 1999.

Banks, Herbert C. *1st Cavalry Division: A Spur Ride Through the 20th Century*. Limited ed. Paducah, Ky.: Turner Publishing, 2002.

Barbier, Mary Kathryn. "George C. Marshall and the 1940 Louisiana Maneuvers." *Louisiana History: Journal of the Louisiana Historical Association* 44, no. 4 (2003): 389–410.

Barrett, Claire. "Rejected!" *MHQ: Quarterly Journal of Military History* (Summer 2017): 17ff.

Bearden, Bob. *To D-Day and Back: Adventures with the 507th Parachute Infantry Regiment and Life as a World War II POW*. Saint Paul, Minn.: Zenith Press, 2007.

Bennett, Donald V. *Honor Untarnished: A West Point Graduate's Memoir of World War II*. New York: Forge Books, 2004.

Bercuson, David, and Holger H. Herwig. *One Christmas in Washington: The Secret Meeting Between Roosevelt and Churchill That Changed the World*. Woodstock, N.Y.: Overlook Press, 2006.

Berg, A. Scott. *Lindbergh*. New York: G. P. Putnam's Sons, 1998.

Bergerud, Eric. *Touched with Fire—The Land War in the South Pacific*. New York: Viking, 1966.

Beschloss, Michael. *The Conquerors: Roosevelt, Truman and the Destruction of Hitler's Germany 1941–1945*. New York: Simon and Schuster, 2002.

Bland, Larry I. "George C. Marshall and the Education of Army Leaders." *Military Review* 68 (1988): 27–37.

Blumenson, Martin. *Mark Clark: The Last of the Great World War II Commanders*. New York: Congdon and Weed, 1991.

———. *Patton: The Man Behind the Legend, 1885–1945*. New York: William Morrow and Company, 1985.

———. *The Patton Papers, 1940–1945*. 2 vols. Boston: Houghton Mifflin, 1975.

Bogle, Lori Lyn. *The Pentagon's Battle for the American Mind: The Early Cold War*. College Station: Texas A&M University Press, 2004.

Bracey, J. H., and A. Meier. "Allies or Adversaries?: The NAACP, A. Philip Randolph and the 1941 March on Washington." *Georgia Historical Quarterly* 75, no. 1 (Spring 1991): 1–17.

Bradley, Omar N., and Clay Blair. *A General's Life: An Autobiography*. New York: Simon and Schuster, 1983.

Brendon, Piers. *Ike: His Life and Times*. New York: Harper and Row, 1986.

Brinkley, David. *Washington Goes to War*. New York: Knopf, 1988.

Buckley, Gail Lumet. *American Patriots: The Story of Blacks in the Military from the Revolution to Desert Storm*. New York: Random House Trade Paperbacks, 2002.

Burk, Robert F. *Dwight D. Eisenhower: Hero and Politician*. Boston: Twayne Publishing, 1987.

Burlingame, Roger. *Don't Let Them Scare You: The Life and Times of Elmer Davis*. Philadelphia: Lippincott, 1961.

Burns, G. Frank, Kelly Sergio, and Rex Bennett. "Somewhere in Tennessee: The Cumberland in Wartime, 1940–1947." In *Rural Life and Culture in the Upper Cumberland*, edited by Michael E. Birdwell and W. Calvin Dickinson, 227–45. Lexington: University Press of Kentucky, 2004.

Calhoun, Mark. *General Lesley J. McNair: Unsung Architect of the U.S. Army*. Modern War Studies. Lawrence: University Press of Kansas, 2015.

Cameron, Robert S. *Mobility, Shock, and Firepower: The Emergence of the U.S. Army's Armor Branch, 1917–1945*. Washington, D.C.: Center of Military History, U.S. Army, 2008.

Cannon, Jimmy. *The Sergeant Says*. New York: A. A. Knopf, 1943.

Chambers, John W. *To Raise an Army: The Draft Comes to Modern America*. New York: Free Press, 1987.

Charman, Terry C. *Outbreak 1939: The World Goes to War*. London: Imperial War Museum/Virgin Books, 2010.

Childs, Marquis W. *I Write from Washington: An Interpretation and History of Washington since 1932*. New York: Harper and Brothers, 1942.

Clark, Grenville. *Memoirs of a Man: Grenville Clark*. Collected by Mary Clark Dimond. Edited by Norman Cousins and J. Garry Clifford. New York: Norton, 1975.

Clifford, J. Garry, and Samuel R. Spencer Jr. *The First Peacetime Draft*. Modern War Studies. Lawrence: University Press of Kansas, 1986.

Clifford, J. Garry, and Theodore A. Wilson, eds. *Presidents, Diplomats, and Other Mortals: Essays Honoring Robert H. Ferrell*. Columbia: University of Missouri Press, 2007.

Coffman, Edward M. *The Regulars: The American Army, 1898–1941*. Cambridge, Mass.: Belknap Press, 2004.

Collins, J. Lawton. *Lightning Joe: An Autobiography*. Baton Rouge: Louisiana State University Press, 1979.

Cooling, Benjamin Franklin. "The Arkansas Maneuvers, 1941." *Arkansas Historical Quarterly* 26, no. 2 (1967): 103–22.

———. "The Tennessee Maneuvers, June, 1941." *Tennessee Historical Quarterly* 24, no. 3 (1965): 265–80. http://www.jstor.org/stable/42622827.

Cray, Ed. *General of the Army: George C. Marshall, Soldier and Statesman*. New York: W. W. Norton, 1990.

Creamer, Robert W. *Baseball and Other Matters in 1941: A Celebration of the Best Baseball Season Ever—in the Year America Went to War*. Lincoln, Nebr.: Bison Books, 2000.

Dallek, Matthew. *Defenseless under the Night: The Roosevelt Years and the Origins of Homeland Security*. New York: Oxford University Press, 2016.

Daniels, Jonathan. *The Time Between the Wars*. New York: Doubleday, 1966.

D'Antoni, John G. "The Home Front: The Experience of Soldiers and Civilians in the Louisiana Maneuvers of 1940 and 1941" (2018). *University of New Orleans Theses and Dissertations*. Published online at https://scholarworks. uno.edu/cgi/viewcontent.

Davidson, Bill. "Desert Warfare: America Trains a New Kind of Army." *Yank*, September 23, 1942.

Davis, Kenneth S. *FDR: Into the Storm 1937–1940*. New York: Random House, 1993.

———. *FDR: The War President: 1940–1943.* New York: Random House, 2000.

Decker, Major Jeffrey W. "Logistics and Patton's Third Army: Lessons for Today's Logisticians." *Air and Space Power Journal* (March 20, 2003). Archived by Air University, https://www.airuniversity.af.edu/Portals/10/ASPJ/journals/Chronicles/decker.pdf.

Denton, Sally. *The Plots Against the President: FDR, a Nation in Crisis, and the Rise of the American Right.* New York: Bloomsbury Press, 2012.

DePastino, Todd. *Bill Mauldin: A Life up Front.* New York: W. W. Norton, 2008.

DeSilvio, David M. "The Influence of Domestic Politics on Foreign Policy in the Election of 1940." PhD diss., Wayne State University, 2008.

D'Este, Carlo. *Eisenhower: A Soldier's Life.* New York: Henry Holt, 2002.

———. *Patton: A Genius for War.* New York: Harper Perennial, 1996.

Dionne, E. J., Kayla Meltzer Drogosz, and Robert E. Litan. *United We Serve: National Service and the Future of Citizenship.* Washington, D.C.: Brookings Institution Press, 2003.

Dunne, Gerald T. *Grenville Clark: Public Citizen.* New York: Farrar, Straus and Giroux, 1986.

Dunn, Susan. *1940: FDR, Willkie, Lindbergh, Hitler—the Election amid the Storm.* New Haven, Conn.: Yale University Press, 2014.

Dzwonchyk, Wayne M. *A Brief History of the U.S. Army in World War II: The U.S. Army Campaigns of World War II.* Washington, D.C.: Center of Military History, U.S. Army, 1992.

Edwards, Michael. "Dress Rehearsal for War." *America in WWII* (August 2012): 34ff.

Eisenhower, Dwight D. *At Ease: Stories I Tell to Friends.* Garden City, N.Y.: Doubleday, 1948.

———. *Crusade in Europe: A Personal Account of World War II.* Garden City, N.Y.: Doubleday, 1948.

———. *Crusade in Europe: A Personal Account of World War II.* Baltimore: Johns Hopkins University Press, 1997.

———. *In Review: Pictures I've Kept; A Concise Pictorial Autobiography.* Garden City, N.Y.: Doubleday, 1969.

Eisenhower, John S. D. *General Ike: A Personal Reminiscence.* New York: Free Press, 2003.

Eisenhower, Susan. *Mrs. Ike: Memories and Reflections on the Life of Mamie Eisenhower.* New York: Farrar, Strauss and Giroux, 1996.

Eliot, Thomas H. "Did We Almost Lose the Army?" *New York Times*, August 12, 1991.

Essame, H. *Patton as Military Commander*. Conshohocken, Pa.: Combined Publishing, 1974.

Faber, Harold. *Soldier and Statesman: General George C. Marshall*. New York: Ariel Books, 1964.

Farago, Ladislas. *Patton: Ordeal and Triumph*. New York: Ivan Obolensky, 1970.

Flake, Dennis Edward. "Ike Reborn." *America in WWII* (June 2017): 12ff.

Flynn, George Q. *Conscription and Democracy: The Draft in France, Great Britain, and the United States*. Westport, Conn.: Greenwood Press, 2002.

———. *The Draft, 1940–1973*. Lawrence: University Press of Kansas, 1993.

Forty, George. *The Armies of George S. Patton*. London: Arms and Armour, 1996.

———. *Patton's Third Army at War*. 2nd ed. Havertown, Pa.: Casemate, 2015.

Fosdick, Roger Barry. "A Call to Arms: The American Enlisted Soldier in World War II." PhD diss., Claremont Graduate University, 1985.

Frye, William. *Marshall: Citizen Soldier*. Indianapolis: Bobbs-Merrill, 1947.

Fuller, Robert Paul. *Last Shots for Patton's Third Army*. Portland, Maine: New England Transportation Research, 2003.

Fullerton, Dan C. "Bright Prospects, Bleak Realities: The U.S. Army's Interwar Modernization Program for the Coming of the Second World War." PhD diss., Wichita State University, 2006.

Gabel, Christopher R. "George Catlett Marshall." In *Generals of the Army: Marshall, MacArthur, Eisenhower, Arnold, Bradley*, edited by James H. Willbanks, 55. Lexington: University Press of Kentucky, 2013.

———. "The 1941 Maneuvers: What Did They Really Accomplish?" *Army History* (April 1990): 5–7.

———. *Seek, Strike, and Destroy: U.S. Army Tank Destroyer Doctrine in World War II*. Leavenworth Papers 12. Fort Leavenworth, Kans.: Combat Studies Institute, U.S. Army Command and General Staff College, 1986.

———. *The U.S. Army GHQ Maneuvers of 1941*. Commemorative ed. Washington, D.C.: Center of Military History, U.S. Army, 1991.

Gerard, Philip. *Secret Soldiers: The Story of World War II's Heroic Army of Deception*. New York: Dutton, 2002.

Gillie, Mildred Hanson. *Forging the Thunderbolt: A History of the Development of the Armored Force.* Harrisburg, Pa.: Military Service Publishing, 1947.

Goodwin, Doris Kearns. *No Ordinary Time: Franklin and Eleanor Roosevelt; The Home Front in World War II.* New York: Simon and Schuster, 1995.

Gorin, Lewis Jefferson Jr. *Patriotism Prepaid.* Philadelphia and London: J. B. Lippincott Company, 1936.

Green, Constance McLaughlin. *The Secret City: A History of Race Relations in the Nation's Capital.* Princeton, N.J.: Princeton University Press, 1967.

Greenfield, Kent Roberts, Robert R. Palmer, and Bell I. Wiley. *The Army Ground Forces: The Organization of Ground Combat Troops.* Washington, D.C.: Center of Military History, U.S. Army, 1987.

Gregory, Ross. *America 1941: A Nation at the Crossroads.* New York: Free Press, 1989.

Griffith, Robert Jr. *Men Wanted for the U.S. Army: America's Experience with an All-Volunteer Army Between the World Wars.* Westport, Conn.: Praeger, 1982.

Groom, Winston. *1942: The Year That Tried Men's Souls.* New York: Grove Press, 2006.

————. *The Generals: Patton, MacArthur, Marshall, and the Winning of World War II.* Washington, D.C.: National Geographic, 2015.

Gullan, Harold I. "Expectations of Infamy: Roosevelt and Marshall Prepare for War, 1938–41." *Presidential Studies Quarterly* 28, no. 3 (1998): 510.

Hamilton, Nigel. *JFK: Reckless Youth.* New York: Random House, 1992.

Hammel, Eric M. *How America Saved the World: The Untold Story of U.S. Preparedness between the World Wars.* Minneapolis: Zenith Press, 2009.

Harris, Mark. *Five Came Back: A Story of Hollywood and the Second World War.* New York: Penguin Press 2015.

Hart, Scott. *Washington at War, 1941–1945.* Englewood Cliffs, N.J.: Prentice-Hall, 1970.

Heller, Charles E. "The U.S. Army, the Civilian Conservation Corps, and Leadership for World War II, 1933–1942." *Armed Forces and Society* 36, no. 3 (August 2009): 439–53.

Hershey, Lewis B. *Selective Service in Wartime: Second Report of the Director of Selective Service, 1941–42.* Washington, D.C.: Government Printing Office, 1943.

Hill, Jim Dan. *The Minute Man in Peace and War: A History of the National Guard.* Harrisburg, Pa.: Stackpole, 1964.

Hirshson, Stanley. *General Patton: A Soldier's Life*. New York: Harper Perennial, 2003.

Hobbs, Joseph Patrick, ed. *Dear General: Eisenhower's Wartime Letters to Marshall*. Baltimore: Johns Hopkins University Press, 1999.

Hodgson, Godfrey. *The Colonel: The Life and Wars of Henry Stimson, 1867–1950*. New York: Knopf, 1990.

Hoffman, Jon T., ed. *A History of Innovation: U.S. Army Adaptation in War and Peace*. Washington, D.C.: Center of Military History, U.S. Army, 2009.

Holland, James. *The Allies Strike Back, 1941–1943*. The War in the West, vol. 2. New York: Atlantic Monthly Press, 2017.

———. *Big Week: Smashing the Luftwaffe, February 1944*. New York: Atlantic Monthly Press, 2018.

Holt, Daniel D., ed. *Eisenhower: The Prewar Diaries and Selected Papers, 1905–1941*. Baltimore: Johns Hopkins University Press, 1998.

Holzimmer, Kevin C. *General Walter Krueger: Unsung Hero of the Pacific War*. Modern War Studies. Lawrence: University Press of Kansas, 2007.

Hope, Bob, as told to Pete Martin. *The Last Christmas Show*. Garden City, N.Y.: Doubleday, 1974.

Houston, Donald E. *Hell on Wheels: The 2d Armored Division*. San Rafael, Calif.: Presidio Press, 1977.

Hymel, Kevin M. "Red River Kids at War." *America in WWII* (August 2017): 18ff.

Isbell, Terry. "The Battle of the Bayous: The Louisiana Maneuvers, 1940, Natchitoches Parish La.," *Old Natchitoches Parish* 2, 1–2.

James, Rawn Jr. *The Double V: How Wars, Protest, and Harry Truman Desegregated America's Military*. New York: Bloomsbury Press, 2013.

Jeffers, H. Paul. *Taking Command: General J. Lawton Collins from Guadalcanal to Utah Beach and Victory in Europe*. New York: New American Library, 2009.

Jowett, Garth, ed. *Readings in Propaganda and Persuasion: New and Classic Essays*. Thousand Oaks, Calif.: Sage Publications, 2006.

Kaiser, David. *No End Save Victory: How FDR Led the Nation into War*. New York: Basic Books, 2014.

Karsten, Peter. "The US Citizen-Soldier's Past, Present, and Likely Future." *Parameters: The US Army War College Quarterly* (Summer 2001): 61–73.

Kendall, Park. *Gone with the Draft: Love Letters of a Trainee*. New York: Grosset and Dunlap, 1941.

Kennedy, David M., ed. *The Library of Congress World War II Companion*. New York: Simon and Schuster, 2007.

Kennedy, J. W. *Patton's Desert Training Center*. Fort Meyer, Va.: Council on America's Military Past, 1982.

Kennett, Lee. *G.I.: The American Soldier in World War II*. New York: Scribner's, 1987.

Ketchum, Richard M. *The Borrowed Years, 1938–1941: America on the Way to War*. New York: Random House, 1989.

Kimball, Penn T. "The Veterans of Future Wars: Princeton's Greatest Political Movement Started Just 30 Years Ago." *Princeton Alumni Weekly* (April 19, 1966): 12.

King, Martin, Michael Collins, and David Hilborn. *The Fighting 30th Division: They Called Them Roosevelt's SS*. Philadelphia and Oxford: Casemate, 2015.

Klein, Maury. *A Call to Arms: Mobilizing America for World War II*. New York: Bloomsbury Press, 2013.

Klingaman, William K. *1941: Our Lives in a World on the Edge*. New York: HarperCollins, 1988.

Korda, Michael. *Ike: An American Hero*. New York: Harper, 2007.

Krebs, Ronald R. *Fighting for Rights: Military Service and the Politics of Citizenship*. Cornell Studies in Security Affairs. Ithaca, N.Y.: Cornell University Press, 2006.

Kreidberg, Marvin A., and Merton G. Henry. *History of Military Mobilization in the United States Army, 1775–1945*. Washington, D.C.: Government Printing Office, 1955.

Kryder, Daniel. *Divided Arsenal: Race and the American State During World War II*. Cambridge: Cambridge University Press, 2000.

Lamb, Christopher J. "Leadership and Operational Art in World War II: The Case for General Lesley J. McNair." *Joint Force Quarterly* (January 2017): 120ff.

Lande, D. A. *I Was with Patton: First-Person Accounts of WWII in George S. Patton's Command*. Saint Paul, Minn.: MBI Publishing, 2002.

Lanning, Michael Lee. *The African-American Soldier: From Crispus Attucks to Colin Powell*. Secaucus, N.J.: Citadel, 1997.

Larrabee, Eric. *Commander in Chief—Franklin Delano Roosevelt, His Lieutenants, and Their War*. New York: Harper and Row, 1987.

Leckie, Robert. *Delivered From Evil—The Saga of World War II*. New York: Harper and Row, 1987.

Love, Edmund G. *The 27th Infantry Division in World War II*. Nashville, Tenn.: Battery, 1982 (reprint of original 1949 edition).

Lukacs, John. *June 1941: Hitler and Stalin*. New Haven, Conn.: Yale University Press, 2007.

Manchester, William. *American Caesar: Douglas Macarthur, 1880–1964*. Boston: Little, Brown, 1978.

———. *The Last Lion: Winston Spencer Churchill*. Boston: Little, Brown, 1983–2012.

Marshall, George C. *The Papers of George Catlett Marshall*. Edited by Larry I. Bland and Sharon Ritenour Stevens. 3 vols. Baltimore: Johns Hopkins University Press, 1983–2012.

Marshall, Katherine Tupper. *Together: Annals of an Army Wife*. New York: Tupper and Love, 1946.

Marshall, S. L. A. "How Is the Army Organized to Fight the War?" In *America Organizes to Win the War*, edited by Erling M. Hunt. New York: Harcourt Brace Jovanovich, 1942.

Martin, Ralph G. *The GI War, 1941–1945*. New York: Avon, 1968.

Mayhall, Van R. *Cranking Up a Fine War: A Louisiana Soldier from Boot Camp to General's Aide*. Austin, Tex.: ByrenLee Press, 1999.

Mcintosh, Phyllis. "The Corps of Conservation." *National Parks* (September–October 2001): 23.

McLean, Evalyn Walsh, with Boyden Sparkes. *Father Struck It Rich*. Boston: Little, Brown, 1936.

McMillin, Woody. *In the Presence of Soldiers: The 2nd Army Maneuvers and Other World War II Activity in Tennessee*. Nashville, Tenn.: Horton Heights Press, 2010.

Miller, Francis Trevelyan. *Eisenhower: Man and Soldier*. Philadelphia: John C. Winston, 1944.

Miller, Merle. *Ike the Soldier: As They Knew Him*. New York: Putnam, 1987.

Millett, Alan R., and Peter Maslowski. *For the Common Defense: A Military History of the United States of America*. New York: Simon and Schuster, 1994.

Morelock, Jerry D. *Generals of the Bulge: Leadership in the U.S. Army's Greatest Battle*. Mechanicsburg, Pa.: Stackpole Books, 2015.

Morningstar, James Kelly. *Patton's Way: A Radical Theory of War*. Annapolis, Md.: Naval Institute Press, 2017.

Mosley, Leonard. *Lindbergh: A Biography*. Garden City, N.Y.: Doubleday, 1976.

———. *Marshall: Hero for Our Times*. New York: Hearst Books, 1982.

Moyer, William R. "The 1994 Louisiana Maneuvers: Is Back to the Future What Our Army Needs?" Fort Leavenworth, Kans.: School of Advanced Military Studies, U.S. Army Command and General Staff College, 1992. www.dtic.mil/dtic/tr/fulltext/u2/a254158.pdf.

Murray, George Edwin Patrick. "The Louisiana Maneuvers: Practice for War." *Louisiana History* 13, no. 2 (Spring 1972): 117–38.

———. "The Louisiana Maneuvers, Practice for War." Master's thesis. Kansas State University, 1972.

Nelsen, John T. II. *General George C. Marshall: Strategic Leadership and the Challenges of Reconstituting the Army, 1939–41*. Carlisle Barracks, Pa.: Strategic Studies Institute, 1993.

Nelson, Donald M. *Arsenal of Democracy: The Story of American War Production*. New York: Harcourt Brace, 1946.

Newland, Samuel J. "Blitzkrieg in Retrospect." *Military Review* (July–August 2004): 86ff.

Ohl, John Kennedy. *Minuteman: The Military Career of General Robert S. Beightler*. Boulder, Colo.: Lynne Rienner, 2001.

Olson, Lynne. *Those Angry Days: Roosevelt, Lindbergh, and America's Fight Over World War II, 1939–1941*. New York: Random House Trade Paperbacks, 2014.

Osgood, Charles. *Kilroy Was Here: The Best American Humor from World War II*. New York: Hachette Books, 1989.

Ossad, Steven L., and Don R. Marsh. *Major General Maurice Rose: World War II's Greatest Forgotten Commander*. New York: Taylor Trade Publishing, 2003.

Patton, George S. *War as I Knew It*. With a new introduction by Rick Atkinson. Boston: Houghton Mifflin Co., 1978; 1995.

Payne, Robert. *The Marshall Story: A Biography*. New York: Prentice-Hall, 1951.

Perkins, Norris H., and Michael E. Rogers. *Roll Again Second Armored: Prelude to Fame 1940–1943*. Surrey, England: Kristall Productions, 1988.

Perret, Geoffrey. *Eisenhower*. New York: Random House, 1999.

———. *There's a War to Be Won: The United States Army in World War II*. New York: Random House, 1991.

Perry, Mark. "The Louisiana Maneuvers: 1940–41." *Military History* (November 2018).

———. *The Most Dangerous Man in America: The Making of Douglas MacArthur*. New York: Basic Books, 2015.

———. *Partners in Command: George Marshall and Dwight Eisenhower in War and Peace*. New York: Penguin Books, 2008.

Persico, Joseph E. "The Day When We Almost Lost the Army," *American Heritage* 62, no. 1 (Spring 2012): 38–45.

———. *Roosevelt's Centurions: FDR and the Commanders He Led to Victory in World War II*. New York: Random House, 2013.

Phillips, Cabell. *From the Crash to the Blitz, 1929–1939*. New York: Fordham University Press, 2000.

Pogue, Forrest C. *George C. Marshall*. 4 vols. New York: Viking, 1963–87. This is the standard against which all work on Marshall is judged. The series includes: *Education of a General, 1880–1939* (1963); *Ordeal and Hope, 1939–1942* (1966); *Organizer of Victory, 1943–1945* (1973); and *Statesman, 1945–1959* (1989).

Porter, David L. *The Seventy-Sixth Congress and World War II, 1939–1940*. Columbia: University of Missouri Press, 1979.

Ricks, Thomas E. *The Generals: American Military Command from World War II to Today*. New York: Penguin Books, 2013.

Roll, David. L. *George Marshall—Defender of the Republic*. New York: Dutton Caliber, 2019.

Rosengren, John. "Hank Greenberg: Superstar and Scapegoat." *Michigan History* 98, no. 5 (2014): 22ff.

Russell, Major General Henry Dozier. *The Purge of the Thirtieth Division*. Annapolis, Md.: Naval Institute Press, 2014.

St. John, Phillip A. *Second Armored Division History: Hell on Wheels*. Paducah, Ky.: Turner Publishing, 1991.

Sansone, Sgt. Leonard. *The Wolf*. New York: United Publishers, 1945.

Schroth, Raymond A. *The American Journey of Eric Sevareid*. South Royalton, Vt.: Steerforth Press, 1995.

Sevareid, Eric. *Eric Sevareid Papers, 1909–1993*. MSS39495. Manuscript Division, Library of Congress, Washington, D.C. http://hdl.loc.gov/loc.mss/eadmss.ms001003.

———. *Not So Wild a Dream*. New York: Atheneum Books, 1978.

Shachtman, Tom. *The Phony War, 1939–1940*. New York: Harper and Row, 1982.

Sloan, Bill. *Their Backs Against the Sea: The Battle of Saipan and the Largest Banzai Attack of World War II*. New York: Da Capo Press, 2017.

Smith, Gene. *The Dark Summer: An Intimate History of the Events That Led to World War II*. New York: Collier Books, 1989.

———. "The Seventeenth Largest Army." *American Heritage* 43, no. 8 (December 1992): 98ff.

Smith, Jean Edward. *Lucius D. Clay: An American Life*. New York: Henry Holt, 1990.

Smith, Starr. *Jimmy Stewart: Bomber Pilot*. Minneapolis: Zenith Press, 2006.

Snyder, Marty. *My Friend Ike*. New York: Frederick Fell, 1956.

Spinney, Robert G. *World War II in Nashville: Transformation of the Homefront*. Knoxville: University of Tennessee Press, 1998.

Stimson, Henry L., and McGeorge Bundy. *On Active Service in Peace and War*. 2 vols. New York: Harper and Brothers, 1948.

Stoler, Mark A. *George C. Marshall*. Twentieth Century American Biography Series. New York: Twayne, 1989.

Truscott, Lucian King. *The Twilight of the U.S. Cavalry: Life in the Old Army, 1917–1942*. Edited by Lucian K. Truscott III. With a foreword by Edward M. Coffman. Lawrence: University Press of Kansas, 1989.

Tuchman, Barbara Wertheim. *Stilwell and the American Experience in China, 1911–45*. New York: Macmillan, 1971.

Van-Ellis, Mark D. "Homegrown War Games." *World War II* 33, no. 3 (October 2018): 28.

Vogel, Victor. *Soldiers of the Old Army*. Texas A&M University Military History, 15. College Station, Tex.: Texas A&M University Press, 1990.

Walker, Fred L. *From Texas to Rome: A General's Journal*. Dallas: Taylor Publishing, 1969.

Wapshott, Nicholas. *The Sphinx: Franklin Roosevelt, the Isolationists, and the Road to World War II*. New York: W. W. Norton and Company, 2014.

Washburn, Patrick S. *A Question of Sedition: The Federal Government's Investigation of the Black Press during World War II*. New York: Oxford University Press, 1986.

Watson, Mark Skinner. *Chief of Staff: Prewar Plans and Preparations*. U.S. Army in World War II. Washington, D.C.: Historical Division, Department of the Army, 1950.

Weigley, Russell F. *The American Way of War: A History of United States Military Strategy and Policy*. Bloomington: Indiana University Press, 1977.

———. *History of the United States Army*. New York: Macmillan, 1967.

Weintraub, Stanley. *Pearl Harbor Christmas: A World at War, December 1941*. Cambridge, Mass.: Da Capo Press, 2013.

Westbrook, Stephen D. "The Railey Report and Army Morale, 1941." *Military Review* 60 (June 1980): 11–24.

White, Walter. *A Man Called White*. New York: Arno Press, 1969.

Whitlock, Flint. *The Rock of Anzio: From Sicily to Dachau, a History of the U.S. 45th Infantry Division*. New York: Basic Books, 2005.

Williamson, Porter B. *General Patton's Principles for Life and Leadership*. 5th ed. Tucson, Ariz.: Management and Systems Consultants, 2009.

Wolfe, Don M., ed. *The Purple Testament*. Garden City, N.Y.: Doubleday, 1947.

Womer, Jack, and Stephen C. DeVito. *Fighting With the Filthy Thirteen*. Philadelphia: Casemate, 2012.

Wortman, Marc. *1941: Fighting the Shadow War: A Divided America in a World at War*. New York: Atlantic Monthly Press, 2016.

Yarrison, James L. *The Modern Louisiana Maneuvers*. Center of Military History, U.S. Army, 1999.

Periodicals and news services (with names of reporters whose work was especially important to the author)

Arkansas Gazette

Army Laughs

Associated Press/AP (Rice Yahner, Gladwin Hill)

Baltimore Afro-American (Ollie Stewart)

Baltimore Sun (Mark S. Watson)

Beaumont Journal, Texas (Ralph Martin)

Boston Globe

Brooklyn Eagle

Chicago Defender

Chicago Tribune (Captain C. C. Corpening)

Christian Science Monitor (Joseph C. Harsch)

Collier's

Evening Star, Washington, D.C. (John H. Cline)

Hartford (Conn.) Courant (William J. Clew)

International News Service/INS (James L. Kilgallen)

Life

Miami Herald

NEA Newspaper Enterprise Association (Peter Edson)

New York Amsterdam News

New York Herald Tribune (Lewis B. Sebring Jr., John O'Reilly)

New York Times (Hanson W. Baldwin)

Newsweek

Our Army

Plain Dealer, Cleveland, Ohio (Roelif Loveland)

Reader's Digest

Shreveport Times (Don Ewing)

Tennessean (Randolph Tucker)

Time

Times-Picayune, New Orleans (A. S. Waller)

United Press/UP (Richard C. Hottelet, Leon Kay)

Washington Post (Edward T. Folliard, Marshall Andrews)

Yank

NOTES

PREFACE

1. Gerald T. Dunne, *Grenville Clark: Public Citizen* (New York: Farrar Straus and Giroux, 1986), 120. Dunne cites a letter to W. H. Sheehan of November 14, 1966.

CHAPTER 1

1. Richard Moe, *Roosevelt's Second Act: The Election of 1940 and the Politics of War*, Pivotal Moments in American History (New York: Oxford University Press, 2013), 11.
2. Price Day, "Marshall: Soldier's Soldier," *Sun Magazine (Baltimore Sun)*, October 3, 1943, 1; Nicolaus Mills, *Winning the Peace: The Marshall Plan and America's Coming of Age as a Superpower* (Hoboken, N.J.: Wiley, 2008), 57.
3. Leonard Mosley, *Marshall: Hero for Our Times* (New York: Hearst Books, 1982), 127–28.
4. Thomas Parrish, *Roosevelt and Marshall: Partners in Politics and War* (New York: Morrow, 1989), 97.
5. Ibid., 97–98. See also Ed Cray, *General of the Army: George C. Marshall, Soldier and Statesman* (New York: W. W. Norton, 1990), 139; and Harold I. Gullan, "Expectations of Infamy: Roosevelt and Marshall Prepare for War, 1938–41," *Presidential Studies Quarterly* 28, no. 3 (1998): 510.
6. Forrest C. Pogue, *George C. Marshall*, vol. 1, *Education of a General, 1880–1939* (New York: Viking, 1963), 181, 189.
7. George C. Marshall, "Profiting by War Experiences," *The Infantry Journal Reader*, ed. Joseph I. Greene (Garden City, N.Y.: 1943), 344; originally published in *Infantry Journal* 18 (1921): 34–37.
8. *Evening Star*, September 1, 1939, 22.
9. Forrest C. Pogue, *George C. Marshall*, vol. 2, *Ordeal and Hope, 1939–1942* (New York: Viking, 1966), 2.
10. Franklin D. Roosevelt, "Fireside Chat on the War in Europe," September 3, 1939, WWII Multimedia Timeline, 1939–41, History on the Net, http://www .historyonthenet.com/authentichistory/1939-1945/1-war/1-39-41/19390903_ FDR_Fireside_Chat_on_War_in_Europe.htm.
11. Gene Smith, *The Dark Summer: An Intimate History of the Events That Led to World War II* (New York: Collier Books, 1989), 277.
12. Tom Shachtman, *The Phony War, 1939–1940* (New York: Harper and Row, 1982), 75.

13. Mark Skinner Watson, *Chief of Staff: Prewar Plans and Preparations, U.S. Army in World War II* (Washington, D.C.: Historical Division, Department of the Army, 1950), 280; Andrew Cohen and Beth Heinsohn, *The Department of Defense, Know Your Government* (New York: Chelsea House, 1990), 49.

14. "Enlistments Lagging in Army Reserve," *New York Times*, March 26, 1939, 57.

15. Peyton C. March, *The Nation at War* (Garden City, N.Y.: Doubleday, 1932), 341.

16. U.S. Congress, Senate Hearings on the War Department Appropriations Bill, 1935, 74th Congress, first session, February 27, 1935, 7.

17. Watson, *Chief of Staff*, 25.

18. Carlo D'Este, *Patton: A Genius for War* (New York: Harper Perennial, 1996), 393.

19. Dwight D. Eisenhower, *At Ease: Stories I Tell to Friends* (Garden City, N.Y.: Doubleday, 1967), 173.

20. Mildred Hanson Gillie, *Forging the Thunderbolt: A History of the Development of the Armored Force* (Harrisburg, Pa.: Military Service Publishing, 1947), 32.

21. Smith, *The Dark Summer*, 147.

22. Robert Griffith Jr., *Men Wanted for the U.S. Army: America's Experience with an All-Volunteer Army Between the World Wars* (Westport, Conn.: Praeger, 1982), 201.

23. Memo to Brigadier General Thomas S. Hammond, commander of the Illinois National Guard's 66th Infantry Brigade, with headquarters in Chicago, April 13, 1934, *The Papers of George Catlett Marshall*, ed. Larry I. Bland and Sharon Ritenour Stevens (Lexington, Va.: George C. Marshall Foundation, 1981–), electronic version, based on *The Papers of George Catlett Marshall*, vol. 1, *"The Soldierly Spirit," December 1880–June 1939* (Baltimore and London: Johns Hopkins University Press, 1981), 425–28.

24. Gene Smith, "The Seventeenth Largest Army," *American Heritage* 43, no. 8 (December 1992): 98.

25. Victor Vogel, *Soldiers of the Old Army*, Texas A&M University Military History 15 (College Station, Tex.: Texas A&M University Press, 1990), 64.

26. Griffith, *Men Wanted for the U.S. Army*, 15.

27. Vogel, *Soldiers of the Old Army*, 64–66.

28. U.S. Senate Committee on Military Affairs, National Defense Hearings on HR 3791, 76th Congress, first session, testimony of February 21, 1939, 286.

29. Herbert Molloy Mason Jr., *The United States Air Force: A Turbulent History* (New York: Mason/Charter, 1976), 136.

30. Russell F. Weigley, *The American Way of War: A History of United States Military Strategy and Policy* (Bloomington: Indiana University Press, 1977), 402; *Biennial Reports of the Chief of Staff of the United States Army to the Secretary of War, July 1, 1939–June 30, 1945* (Washington, D.C.: Center of Military History, U.S. Army, 1996), 3.

31. L. C. Speers, "Our New Army Chief," *New York Times Magazine*, May 14, 1939, 17; *The Papers of George Catlett Marshall*, vol. 2, *"We Cannot Delay," July 1, 1939–December 6, 1941*, ed. Larry I. Bland, Sharon R. Ritenour, and Clarence E. Wunderlin Jr. (Baltimore: Johns Hopkins University Press, 1986), 59; Gullan, "Expectations of Infamy," 510.

32. J. Gilbert Norris, "17,000 Troops Moving Today on Manassas: 1,200 Trucks to Roll Through Washington before Night Falls; Guardsmen Start for Bull Run Army; Vanguard in Manassas Area; Thousands More Expected Today," *Washington Post*, August 5, 1939, 1.

33. John G. Norris, "1939 Maneuvers Will Contrast Strangely with Those Held on Same Ground in 1904: Battle of '63 Refought to Discover Mistakes Equipment, Forces Quite Different from Mechanized Army in Field Today; Cavalry Most Important; Then Capital Society Went to See the Big Show Staff Set up Huge Circus Tent Where They Entertained Visitors from Washington, Foreign Diplomats," *Washington Post*, July 30, 1939, A7.

34. John G. Norris, "Capital Safe," *Washington Post*, August 18, 1939, 1.

35. "Hot Weather Notes," *Brooklyn Eagle*, August 20, 1939, 20.

36. AP "Plattsburg Battle Ends in a Draw," *Ithaca Journal*, August 25, 1939, 2.

37. Hanson W. Baldwin, "Maneuvers End with Troops Mired," *New York Times*, August 25, 1939, 3; AP, "Manassas Marked Army Deficiencies, Staff Chief Says," *Washington Post*, August 29, 1939, 15.

38. *Springfield Republican*, July 18, 1939, 8.

39. N. T. Kenny, "Army Admits War Games Showed Deficiency," *Baltimore Sun*, August 29, 1939, 20.

40. Ibid.; Thomas Johnson, NEA/AP, "Army Is Being Remodeled Rapidly after Revelation at Army Day Last Year," *Greensboro (N.C.) Record*, April 6, 1940, 1. This article was syndicated to scores of newspapers and served to alert a large number of Americans to the problems of a deficient army.

41. "Sen. Lodge Says U.S. Must Keep Out of War," *Boston Globe*, August 31, 1939, 15.

42. Pogue, *Ordeal and Hope*, 90.

43. "Our Preparedness Efforts," *Brooklyn Eagle*, September 26, 1939, 10.

44. Christopher Capozzola, *Uncle Sam Wants You: World War I and the Making of the Modern American Citizen* (New York: Oxford University Press, 2008), 33. Capozzola notes that Selective Service forms had a notation on their lower left-hand corners instructing draft board officials: "If person is of African descent, tear off this corner." By war's end, 2.3 million registration forms were missing a corner.

45. Rawn James Jr., *The Double V: How Wars, Protest, and Harry Truman Desegregated America's Military* (New York: Bloomsbury Press, 2013), 49.

46. Patrick S. Washburn, *A Question of Sedition: The Federal Government's Investigation of the Black Press during World War II* (New York: Oxford University Press, 1986), 34.

47. John L. Newby II, "The Fight for the Right to Fight and the Forgotten Negro Protest Movement: The History of Executive Order 9981 and Its Effect upon *Brown v. Board of Education* and Beyond," *Texas Journal on Civil Liberties and Civil Rights* 10, no. 1 (2004), 64.

48. Robert M. Citino, *The Path to Blitzkrieg: Doctrine and Training in the German Army, 1920–1939* (Boulder, Colo.: Lynne Rienner, 1999), 1ff.

49. UP, "Polish Cavalry Committed Suicide In Hopeless Charge," *Miami Herald*, September 23, 1939, 3. Alex Zakrzewski, "Debunking the Myth of the Polish

Cavalry," *Toronto Star*, June 1, 2017. (This piece, one of the best ever written on the subject, was inspired by Jim Cramer, host of the CNBC show *Mad Money*, who belittled the marketing strategy of the struggling Macy's department store in dealing with a host of problems, comparing its efforts to that of the Polish army during the 1939 German invasion: "Macy's is like the Polish army in World War II—it tried to field cavalry against German tanks and it did not end well.")

50. John T. Nelsen II, *General George C. Marshall: Strategic Leadership and the Challenges of Reconstituting the Army, 1939–41* (Carlisle Barracks, Pa.: Strategic Studies Institute, 1993), 16, http://www.questia.com/read/118804876/general-george-c-marshall-strategic-leadership.

51. Christopher R. Gabel, *The U.S. Army GHQ Maneuvers of 1941*, commemorative ed. (Washington, D.C.: Center of Military History, U.S. Army, 1991), 10.

52. Commander Peter C. DeMane, "George C. Marshall: The Forgotten Master Strategist," National War College, Washington, D.C., http://www.dtic.mil/dtic/tr/fulltext/u2/a441648.pdf.

53. The term *blitzkrieg* first became popular during the 1939 Polish invasion. Its first use in the American press appears to have been in an article in the September 12, 1938, edition of the *Baltimore Sun*, entitled "Vision of 'Blitzkrieg': Does Peace Reside in Germany's Forfeiture of Plan for 'Lightning Attack?'"

54. Nelsen, *General George C. Marshall: Strategic Leadership*, 14.

55. Charles E. Heller, "The U.S. Army, the Civilian Conservation Corps, and Leadership for World War II, 1933–1942," *Armed Forces and Society* 36, no. 3 (August 2009): 439–53; Marvin A. Kreidberg and Merton G. Henry, *History of Military Mobilization in the United States Army, 1775–1945* (Washington, D.C.: Government Printing Office, 1955), 554–55.

CHAPTER 2

1. Watson, *Chief of Staff*, 31.

2. Cabell Phillips, *From the Crash to the Blitz, 1929–1939* (New York: Fordham University Press, 2000), 124, 127.

3. W. W. Waters, *B.E.F. The Whole Story of the Bonus Army* (New York: AMS Press, 1970, reprint of 1933 edition), 16–17.

4. The major source for this account is based on a work coauthored by the author: Paul Dickson and Thomas B. Allen, *The Bonus Army: An American Epic* (New York: Walker Books, 2006).

5. Constance McLaughlin Green, *The Secret City: A History of Race Relations in the Nation's Capital* (Princeton, N.J.: Princeton University Press, 1967), 220.

6. Eisenhower, Dwight D., *At Ease: Stories I Tell to Friends* (Garden City, N.Y.: Doubleday, 1948), 217.

7. Ibid., 217; Mosley, *Marshall: Hero for Our Times*, 107.

8. Dickson and Allen, *The Bonus Army*, 193.

9. David Burner, *Herbert Hoover: A Public Life* (New York: Knopf, 1979), 312.

10. AP, "Army to Cut $50 Million in Fiscal Year 1933," *Charlotte Observer*, June 18, 1933, 13.

11. Mark Perry, *The Most Dangerous Man in America: The Making of Douglas Mac-Arthur* (New York: Basic Books, 2015), 9.

12. George C. Marshall to Germain Seligman, March 29, 1933, in *The Papers of George C. Marshall*, vol. 1, *The Soldierly Spirit*, 392.

13. Griffith, *Men Wanted for the U.S. Army*, 154.

14. Christopher M. Hill, "The All-Voluntary Army: Historical Challenges," *Military Review* 80, no. 3 (2000).

15. Kelly McMichael Scott, "FDR, Lewis Douglas, and the Raw Deal," *Historian* (Fall 2000).

16. Arthur Krock, "Revolt Against Veterans' Cuts Comes to the Surface," *New York Times*, June 1, 1933, 18.

17. Franklin D. Roosevelt Library, President's Personal File # 95, Representative Virginia E. Jenckes to Stephen Early, May 17, 1933, with enclosure of letter from Carl A. Sanderson, contact officer, Disabled American Veterans, Sebring, Ohio, May 15, 1993.

18. *Washington Post*, July 1, 1933, 3; Jennifer D. Keene, *Doughboys, the Great War, and the Remaking of America* (Baltimore, Md.: Johns Hopkins University Press, 2003), 19.

19. *The Public Papers and Addresses of Franklin D. Roosevelt*, vol. 2, *The Year of Crisis, 1933* (New York: Russell and Russell), 99.

20. Dickson and Allen, *Bonus Army*, 216.

21. *Washington Daily News*, May 22, 1933; Dickson and Allen, *Bonus Army*, 216; Keene, *Doughboys*, 201.

22. Kreidberg and Henry, *History of Military Mobilization*, 554–55.

23. Perry, *Most Dangerous Man in America*, 10.

24. Ibid., 8.

25. Oscar Baradinsky, "Military Propaganda in the CCC," *Panorama: A Monthly Survey of People and Ideas* (July 1934): 10. Baradinsky owned the Alicat Bookstore in Yonkers, N.Y., in a building that my father inherited from my grandparents. Baradinsky, who changed his name to Baron at some point, had a great influence on the author as a child. His widow, Florenz Baron, gave me a copy of the *Panorama* cited here.

26. AP, *Kansas City Star*, February 19, 1935, 2.

27. Ray Tucker, "Washington Whirligig," *Macon Telegraph*, August 5, 1935, 4.

28. Omar N. Bradley and Clay Blair, *A General's Life: An Autobiography* (New York: Simon and Schuster, 1983), 72.

29. Katherine Tupper Marshall, *Together: Annals of an Army Wife* (New York: Tupper and Love, 1946), 13.

30. George C. Marshall to Leo A. Farrell, March 26, 1938, Papers of George C. Marshall, 586–87; Herbert Mitgang, "A Soldier Who Supported New Deal Social Change," *New York Times*, July 18, 1990, C17.

31. Mosley, *Marshall: Hero for Our Times*, 105.

32. Marshall, *Together*, 13.

33. Ibid., 5.

34. Memo to Brigadier General Thomas S. Hammond, commander of the Illinois National Guard's 66th Infantry Brigade, April 13, 1934, *The Papers of George Catlett Marshall*, vol. 1, "*The Soldierly Spirit*," 425–28.

35. William Frye, *Marshall: Citizen Soldier* (Indianapolis: Bobbs-Merrill, 1947), 223; The most recent biography of Marshall by David L. Roll devotes only a single paragraph to Marshall's CCC experience.

36. Halstead to Marshall, May 26, 1933 (G. C. Marshall Papers [Fort Screven]), *The Papers of George Catlett Marshall*, vol. 1, "The Soldierly Spirit,"), 392–93.

37. "French Guests to Visit Camp," *The Charleston* (S.C.) *Evening Post*, August 26, 1933, 2.; J. V. Nielsen Jr., "Staff Officer at Dedication of Camp Layfayette, *Charleston* (S.C.) *Evening Post*, September 14, 1933, 1.

38. William Manchester, *American Caesar: Douglas MacArthur, 1880–1964* (Boston: Little, Brown, 1978), 157.

39. William Frye, *Marshall: Citizen Soldier* (Indianapolis: Bobbs-Merrill, 1947), 225. Marshall, *Together*, 18.

40. Editor's note, *GCM Papers*, 513: and Malin Craig to George C. Marshall, December 1, 1936, *GCM Papers*, 516–17.

41. Marshall, *Together*, 28–30.

42. GCM Papers, 1: 586. See also, Larry I. Bland, "George C. Marshall and the Education of Army leaders," *Military Review* 68 (1988): 29.

43. Christopher R. Gabel, "George Catlett Marshall," in *Generals of the Army: Marshall, MacArthur, Eisenhower, Arnold, Bradley*, ed. James H. Willbanks (Lexington: University Press of Kentucky, 2013), 35; Jack Kenny, "Doug MacArthur Is the Man," *New American*, September 8, 2014; George C. Marshall to Charles P. Summerall, June 1, 1933, *GCM Papers*, 396; George C. Marshall to John J. Pershing, July 11, 1933, *GCM Papers*, 398; and J. Garry Clifford and Samuel R. Spencer Jr., *The First Peacetime Draft* (Lawrence: University Press of Kansas, 1986), 101.

44. Letter to Major General Roy Keehn, quoted in William Frye, *Marshall: Citizen Soldier* (Indianapolis: Bobbs-Merrill, 1947), 239. GCM Papers, vol. 1, "The Soldierly Spirit," *December 1880–June 1939* (Baltimore and London: Johns Hopkins University Press, 1981), 525–28.

45. Cartoon published in June 1, 1938, issue of the newsletter; cited in Bland, "George C. Marshall and the Education of Army Leaders," 27–37.

46. Perry, *Most Dangerous Man in America*, 209.

47. Pogue, *Education of a General*, 276; David L. Roll, *George Marshall Defender of the Republic* (New York: Dutton Caliber, 2019), 103.

48. Stephen E. Ambrose, "Good Idea to Revive Civilian Conservation Corps," *Times-Picayune*, May 26, 1992.

CHAPTER 3

1. George Gallup, "Rearmament Gains Popularity, *Richmond (Va.) Times-Dispatch*, December 28, 1938, 20.

2. *Newsweek*, September 20, 1941, 15.

3. Wayne S. Cole, *Senator Gerald P. Nye and American Foreign Relations* (Minneapolis: University of Minnesota Press, 1962), 128–30.

4. Leonard Mosley, *Lindbergh: A Biography* (New York: Doubleday, 1976), 25; Charles Lindbergh, "Aviation, Geography, and Race," *Reader's Digest*, November 1939.

5. Edwin Black, "The Horrifying American Roots of Nazi Eugenics," History News Network, September 2003, http://hnn.us/article/1796.

6. John G. Norris, "For the First Time U.S. Organizes an Army Prepared for Action on Short Notice: Plan Five Reorganized Divisions Expansion in Line with Recommendations Recently of Gen. Pershing," *Washington Post*, October 8, 1939, A7.

7. Donald M. Nelson, *Arsenal of Democracy: The Story of American War Production* (New York: Harcourt Brace, 1946), 46.

8. Ibid., 46.

9. "Woodring Stresses the US Need of Army 100% Efficient," *Washington Post*, December 28, 1939, 1. "New Army Rifle Held Equal of Three Springfields," *Chicago Tribune*, September 22, 1939, 12.

10. John Grover, AP, "Try Out Lessons of Europe's War," *Omaha World Herald*, May 5, 1940, 13.

11. Frederick Palmer, North American Newspaper Alliance, "Long War or Quick Peace Is the Issue," Cleveland *Plain Dealer*, October 9, 1939, 5.

12. Walter Lippmann, "The Coming Piece," as syndicated in *Evansville Courier and Press*, October 29, 1939, 7.

13. Watson, *Chief of Staff*, 104.

14. Mary E. Murphy, *The British War Economy, 1939–1943* (New York: Professional and Technical Press, 1943), 329.

15. AP, "Col. Lindbergh Sees No 'Justification' on Either Side in War," *Evening Star*, February 20, 1940, 2. Clifford and Spencer, *First Peacetime Draft*, 8.

16. "Real, Phony War Finds George Snoring Peacefully," *New York Herald Tribune*, European ed., February 12, 1940, 3.

17. James C. Schneider, *Should America Go to War?: The Debate over Foreign Policy in Chicago, 1939–1941* (Chapel Hill: University of North Carolina Press, 1989), 21; House Appropriations Committee, Hearings on HR 9209, 76th Congress, third session, Washington, D.C., 1943.

18. John G. Norris, "Army Funds Cut, Alaska Base Denied," *Washington Post*, April 4, 1940, 1.

19. Elbridge Colby, *Army Talk* (Princeton, N.J.: Princeton University Press, 1942), 130, 182. Colby points out that the British once used the term *sham fight* instead of *sham battle*.

20. AP, "Louisiana Gets Army Maneuvers, Overton Says," *Biloxi (Miss.) Daily Herald*, February 7, 1940, 1; J. R. Triplet, AP, "U.S. Army Peacefully Prepares for Largest Peacetime Show," *Atlanta Constitution*, March 10, 1940, 10A.

21. Terry Isbell, "The Battle of the Bayous: The Louisiana Maneuvers, 1940, Natchitoches Parish La.," *Old Natchitoches Parish* 2, 1–2, http://files.usgwarchives.net/la/natchitoches/military/maneuver.txt.

22. AP, "36,000 to Pass Through Mississippi to War Games," *Baton Rouge Advocate*, March 22, 1940, 15.

23. Hadley Cantril and Mildred Strunk, *Public Opinion, 1935–1946* (Princeton, N.J.: Princeton University Press, 1951), 970–71.

24. Katherine Marshall, *Together*, 62.

25. Clifford and Spencer, *First Peacetime Draft*, 8; Nick Smart, *British Strategy and Politics during the Phony War: Before the Balloon Went Up* (Westport, Conn.: Praeger, 2003), 6; "Army Fund Report Cuts It 67 Million: Total Is Put at $785,999,094 in Revision Offered to House by Committee Plane Demand;

A Factor Foreign War Market Held to Raise Capacity Here—Base in Alaska Given Up: $103,710,000 for Equipment Extensive Training Is Asked," *New York Times*, April 4, 1940, 12.

26. Smart, *British Strategy and Politics during the Phony War*, 6.

27. AP, "'New 'Government' Set Up at Oslo," *Bellingham (Wash.) Herald*, April 9, 1940, 1.

28. John G. Norris, "The War Is On!" *Washington Post*, April 14, 1940, L11; "Gen. Marshall Plans Army's Biggest Maneuvers," *Washington Post*, April 28, 1940, 5.

29. "Heavy Guns Rout in Georgia Battle," *New York Times*, April 19, 1940, 6.

30. "Big Battle Expected in Maneuvers Today," *Columbus (Ga.) Daily Enquirer*, May 5, 1940, 1.

31. "Attachés Barred and Our War Games," *New York Times*, April 25, 1940, 6.

32. Henry N. Dorris, "Wargame to Test Blitzkrieg Method," *New York Times*, May 23, 1940, 10.

33. "Civilians to Aid in Army Games," *New Orleans States*, April 17, 1940, 13.

34. "Army Corps Moves 600 Miles in Six Days," *New York Times*, May 12, 1940, 17.

35. AP, "Invading Army," *Baton Rouge Advocate*, May 10, 1940, 12.

36. AP, "Red Army Wins in Swift Drive in Texas Forest," *Chicago Tribune*, May 10, 1940, 10.

37. AP, "Motorized U.S. Troops Score in War Games," *Atlanta Constitution*, May 11, 1940, 7.

38. Charles F. Speare, NANA, "Latest Nazi Move Rouses Wall Street," *Omaha World Herald*, May 12, 1940, 43.

39. UP, *New York Times*, May 19, 1940, 5.

40. "First Year of Defense Effort Spotlights Vitality of Nation," *Newsweek*, May 19, 1941, 35ff.

41. T. A. Price, "War Maneuvers' Bombing Day Shows Alarming Inadequacy of Army's Strengths in Planes," *Dallas Morning News*, May 24, 1940, 7.

42. Mark Perry, "The Louisiana Maneuvers: 1940–41," *Military History* (November 2018).

43. AP, "Army Officers in War Games Draw Censure," *New York Herald Tribune*, May 28, 1940, 13.

44. UP, "Lieut. General Leroy C. Lutes," *Marietta (Ga.) Journal*, January 8, 1946, 4.

45. "Billions for Defense," *Time*, May 27, 1940.

46. Westbrook Pegler, "Scattered Army," *Washington Post*, May 22, 1940, 9.

47. Price, "War Maneuvers' Bombing Day."

48. "Lodge for Army of 750,000," *New York Times*, May 21, 1940, 1; *Senator Lodge of Massachusetts Speaking on Condition and Needs of the Army*, 76th Congress, third session, *Congressional Record* (vol. 86, pt. 6, 76th Cong., 3rd sess., 6130–39, 6877).

49. Pogue, *Ordeal and Hope*, 90.

50. Mary Kathryn Barbier, "George C. Marshall and the 1940 Louisiana Maneuvers," *Louisiana History: Journal of the Louisiana Historical Association* 44, no. 4 (2003): 410.

51. "New Orleans Host to 1000 Race Soldiers," *Chicago Defender*, May 18, 1940, 6.

52. Henry N. Dorris, "Army Tests of Men on Reserve of Food," *New York Times*, May 10, 1940, 10; Paul Dickson, *Chow: A Cook's Tour of Military Food* (New York: Plume, 1978), 49.

53. Ralph McGill, "One Word More," *Atlanta Constitution*, May 12, 1940, 10.

54. Clinton K. Murray, Lynn L. Horvath, Charles D. Ericsson, and Christoph Hatz, "An Approach to Prevention of Infectious Diseases during Military Deployments," *Clinical Infectious Diseases* 44, no. 3 (February 1, 2007), 424–30; "Army Games Prove 'Health Defenses' Good," *Atlanta Constitution*, May 31, 1940, 15.

55. "Billions for Defense," *Time*, May 27, 1940.

56. Dickson and Allen, *Bonus Army*, 36, 329; "A Cavalry Major Evicts Veteran Who Saved His Life in Battle," *New York Times*, July 30, 1932, "Army Major Forced to Throw Out Vet Who Saved His Life in World War," *Washington Daily News*, July 30, 1932.

57. "Heroes: Battle of Washington," *Time*, August 8, 1932, http://content.time.com/time/subscriber/article/0,33009,744107,00.html.

58. Wayne M. Dzwonchyk, *A Brief History of the US Army in World War II: The US Army Campaigns of World War II* (Washington, D.C.: Center of Military History, U.S. Army, 1992), 5.

59. "Senate Committee Votes 2-Ocean Navy: Group Unanimously Approves $5,008,169,277 Supplemental Bill for Defense" *New York Times*, August 20, 1940, 7; "First Year of Defense Effort Spotlights Vitality of Nation," *Newsweek*, May 19, 1941, 35ff.

60. American Institute of Public Opinion, George Gallup, *Richmond (Va.) Times-Dispatch*, June 2, 1940, 54.

61. M. H. Gillie, *Forging the Thunderbolt: History of the U.S. Army's Armored Forces, 1917–45* (Mechanicsburg, Pa.: Stackpole Books, 2006), 170; "The Army in Georgia," *Atlanta Constitution*, July 30, 1940, 9.

62. Nelson, *Arsenal of Democracy*, 41.

63. *Founding Families: Digital Editions of the Papers of the Winthrops and the Adamses*, ed. C. James Taylor, Massachusetts Historical Society, 2017, http://www.masshist.org/apde2/.

64. Hoagland, William, *The Whiskey Rebellion: George Washington, Alexander Hamilton, and the Frontier Rebels Who Challenged America's Newfound Sovereignty* (New York, Scribner, 2006), 217.

65. Daniel Webster, "Daniel Webster on the Draft: Text of a Speech Delivered in Congress, December 9, 1814," Books and Publications, 131, https://digicom.bpl.lib.me.us/books_pubs/131.

66. "Draft Riots," *Columbia Encyclopedia*, 6th ed. (New York: Columbia University Press, 2017); John S. Brown, "The Draft," *Army*, August 2007.

67. David R. Henderson, "From 'Porous' to 'Ruthless' Conscription, 1776–1917," *Independent Review* 14, no. 4; S. M. Lee, Twenty-Slave Law (2012, May 31). In Encyclopedia Virginia. Retrieved from http://www.EncyclopediaVirginia.org/Twenty-Slave_Law.

68. Peter Karsten, "The US Citizen-Soldier's Past, Present, and Likely Future," *Parameters: The US Army War College Quarterly* (Summer 2001): 61–73.

CHAPTER 4

1. "Future Veterans, Unite!" *Daily Princetonian*, March 14, 1936, 2, copy in Seeley G. Mudd Library, Princeton University, Princeton, N.J.
2. "Future Veterans Said to Total 6,000," *New York Times*, March 24, 1936, 45. The senator was David A. Reed of Pennsylvania.
3. "Future Veterans Bow to Criticism," *New York Times*, March 21, 1936, 19.
4. "Future Wars Bonus Drive Called 'Crazy,'" *Washington Post*, March 18, 1936, x–17.
5. "House Hears Future Veterans Denounced for Unpatriotism," *Washington Post*, April 2, 1936, 9.
6. Oswald Garrison Villiard, "Issues and Men," *Nation*, April 18, 1936, 450.
7. "Future Veterans Amuse First Lady," *Washington Post*, April 3, 1936, 88.
8. "Columbia Seniors Cool to New Deal," *New York Times*, March 25, 1936, 26.
9. "Lobbies for Bonus in College Recess," *New York Times*, April 2, 1936, 23.
10. "Legion's Depot for Veterans of Future Smacks of Nursery," *Washington Post*, April 25, 1936, 17. The vets got on the radio with the grand opening of the first aid station and sang the ditty:

   > Let's be wise, let's be prudent
   > Sings the modern college student
   > We will never fight the foe
   > Unless we're paid before we go.

11. Harry Haller, "A Jest That Stirred a Nation," *Baltimore Sun*, May 3, 1936, SM3.
12. The *New York Times* was especially troubled about how to characterize the Veterans of Future Wars, finally creating the term *serio-satirical* to describe the group. ("Youth Asks a Program," *New York Times*, June 28, 1936, 16.)
13. "The Financial Bookshelf," *Wall Street Journal*, May 4, 1936, 3. According to a review in the *Princeton Alumni Weekly*, Gorin's book was also accepted by the university's Politics Department as his senior thesis, suggesting an academic motive as well. Read today, the book is well crafted and loaded with factual arguments, such as pointing out that the last payment for a Revolutionary War pension was made in 1905. The book also has the least useful but most engaging index this reader has ever encountered. Sample entries:

   > Calvin Coolidge, stifles smile, 48.
   > Foreigners, how to annoy them, 23.

14. "New Peace Plan Urged," *New York Times*, June 1, 1936, 6.
15. Religious News Service, "The Week in Religion," *Lexington Leader*, November 11, 1939, 2.
16. "MacLeish Assails the Cynics," *Baltimore Sun*, May 24, 1940, 1; "M'Leish Finds U.S. Morally Unready," *New York Times*, May 24, 1940, 4.
17. "Students at Yale Against Allied Aid," *New York Times*, May 26, 1940, 12.
18. John G. Clifford, "Grenville Clark and the Origins of Selective Service," *Review of Politics* 35, no. 1 (January 1973): 17–40; Dunne, *Grenville Clark*, 122–23.
19. Watson, *Chief of Staff*, 189; the meeting of May 22, 1940, was reported in the *New York Times*, May 23, 1940, 1.

20. George Q. Flynn, *The Draft, 1940–1973* (Lawrence: University Press of Kansas, 1993), 11.
21. *New York Times*, May 26, 1940, 12; Godfrey Hodgson, *The Colonel: The Life and Wars of Henry Stimson, 1867–1950* (New York: Knopf, 1990), 222–23.
22. Lynne Olson, *Those Angry Days: Roosevelt, Lindbergh, and America's Fight Over World War II, 1939–1941* (New York: Random House Trade Paperbacks, 2014), 209. Many accounts have been written of the push to sell the draft to the American people, but Olson seems to be the first to have discovered the role of professional public relations in marshaling public support for the draft. Boone's role in promoting the World's Fair had been totally successful, but his name was seldom mentioned, although he was honored on the fair's last day in 1940.
23. Dunne, *Grenville Clark*, 129.
24. Kenneth S. Davis, *FDR—Into the Storm:1937–1939* (New York: Random House, 1993), 570.
25. Dunne, *Grenville Clark*, 124.
26. Larry I. Bland, ed., *The Papers of George Catlett Marshall*, vol. 2 (Baltimore: Johns Hopkins University Press, 1986), 263.
27. John T. Nelsen II, *General George C. Marshall: Strategic Leadership and the Challenges of Reconstituting the Army, 1939–41* (Carlisle Barracks, Pa.: Strategic Studies Institute, 1993).
28. The original copy of FDR's letter to Woodring is in possession of the Shapell Manuscript Foundation and can be viewed at http://www.shapell.org/manuscript/fdr-fires-isolationist-secretary-of-war-woodring. In the letter, Roosevelt offers Woodring the position of governor of Puerto Rico in return for his service to the country, an offer that is refused. Albert A. Blum, "Birth and Death of the M-Day Plan," in *American Civil-Military Decisions*, ed. Harold Stein (University of Alabama Press, 1963), 71.
29. Kreidberg and Henry, *History of Military Mobilization*, 578.
30. Henry L. Stimson and McGeorge Bundy, *On Active Service in Peace and War*, vol. 2 (New York: Harper and Brothers, 1948), 323–24; Hodgson, *The Colonel*, 216–17.
31. David L. Roll, *George Marshall Defender of the Republic* (New York: Dutton Caliber, 2019), 140.
32. Susan Dunn, *1940: FDR, Willkie, Lindbergh, Hitler—the Election Amid the Storm* (New Haven, Conn.: Yale University Press, 2014); Olson, *Those Angry Days*, 206.
33. John J. Pershing to Marshall Sheppard, July 3, 1940, Sen. 76A-E1, Box 116, Legislative Division, National Archives from David L. Porter, *The Seventy-Sixth Congress and World War II, 1939–1940* (Columbia: University of Missouri Press, 1979), 134.
34. "Conscription Is American," *Evening Star*, July 4, 1940, 6.
35. Griffith, *Men Wanted for the U.S. Army*, 193.
36. Letter to the editor, *Sacramento Bee*, August 17, 1940, 28.
37. Chesley Manly, "Charges Slush Fund Raising to Promote Draft," *Chicago Tribune*, August 7, 1940, 1.
38. Ibid., also various accounts including: William E. Coffey, "Isolationism and Pacifism: Senator Rush D. Holt and American Foreign Policy," *West Virginia*

History 51 (1992): 1–14; AP, "'Liar' and 'Rat' Epithets Used in Senate Row," *Arkansas Gazette*, August 9, 1940, 3. Verbatim account in *Congressional Record*, 76th Congress, third session, 1940, vol. 86, pt. 9, 9921–23, 9923–25, 9938–39, 9978–81.

39. David L. Porter, *The Seventy-Sixth Congress and World War II, 1939–1940* (Columbia: University of Missouri Press, 1979), 144; "Barroom Brawl," *San Francisco Chronicle*, August 11, 1940, 19. "Adler Gives Reply," *Chicago Tribune*, August 7, 1940, 2.

40. "In 'Imminent Peril'?" *Columbus (Ohio) Dispatch*, August 12, 1940, 4.

41. Charles Hurd, "Need of Men Vital," *New York Times*, August 3, 1940, 1.

42. "Senators Planning Bipartisan Block to Fight Draft," *Evening Star*, August 3, 1940, 1; *New York Times*, August 7, 1940, 2.

43. *New York Times*, August 18, 1940; *New York Herald Tribune*, August 27, 1940.

44. John Roy Carlson (pseudonym for Arthur Derounian), *Under Cover: My Four Years in the Nazi Underworld of America* (New York: E. P. Dutton, 1943), 128–29.

45. Clifford and Spencer, *First Peacetime Draft*, 175; "Mothers Hang Pepper Effigy on Capitol Hill," *Chicago Tribune*, August 22, 1940, 6.

46. C. P. Trussell, "Savage Attack Launched Against Draft Bill as House Debate Opens: Police Eject Heckler for 'Fascism,'" *Baltimore Sun*, September 4, 1940, 2.

47. AP, "Fistfight Marks Debate in House over Draft Bill," *New York Herald Tribune*, September 5, 1940, 1.

48. Emmet Crozier, "Wilkie Opposes Draft Delay," *New York Herald Tribune*, September 11, 1940, 1.

49. UP, "Roosevelt's Off Tonight to See N.Y. War Game," *Binghamton (N.Y.) Press and Sun-Bulletin*, August 10, 1940, 4.

50. Marshall Andrews, "Army Has Man Power But Lacks Tools of War," *Washington Post*, September 1, 1940, A9; Bryan Thompson, "The Town of De Kalb and the August 1940 War Maneuvers," available online at http://www.dekalbnyhistorian.org/LocalHistoryArticles/1940WarManeuvers/warmaneuvers.html.

51. Hanson W. Baldwin, "All of Army Found in Need of Training," *New York Times*, September 9, 1940, 1.

52. Christopher Gabel, *The U.S. Army GHQ Maneuvers* 13.

53. Franklin D. Roosevelt, "Executive Order 8530 Calling out the National Guard," August 31, 1940, online by Gerhard Peters and John T. Woolley, *The American Presidency Project*, http://www.presidency.ucsb.edu/ws/?pid=16000.

54. David M. DeSilvio, "The Influence of Domestic Politics on Foreign Policy in the Election of 1940," PhD diss., Wayne State University, 2008, 218.

55. In the Senate, 40 Democrats and 7 Republicans voted in favor; in the House vote, 186 Democrats and 46 Republicans were in favor; 32 Democrats, 88 Republicans, and 4 others against.

56. Earl Rickard, "Marshall Builds the U.S. Army," Warfare History Network, warfarehistorynetwork.com/daily/wwii/marshall-builds-the-u-s-army.

57. *GCM Papers*, 308–312.

58. Rosenman, *Working with Roosevelt* (New York: Harper, 1952), 225.

59. George Gallup, "American Youth Speaks Up," *Reader's Digest*, October 1940, 51–56.
60. "Students Support Draft," *Baltimore Sun*, October 11, 1940, 13.
61. Peter Karsten, "The US Citizen-Soldier's Past, Present, and Likely Future," *Parameters: US Army War College Quarterly* (Summer 2001): 61–73.
62. The meeting was held at 11:30 a.m., Franklin Roosevelt Day by Day, Pare Lorentz Center, FDR Presidential Library, September 27, 1940, http://www.fdrlibrary.marist.edu/daybyday/daylog/september-27th-1940/. Walter White, "Conference at White House, Friday, September 27, 11:35 A.M.," Arthur B. Spingarn Papers, Library of Congress.
63. Walter White, *A Man Called White* (New York: Arno Press, 1969), 191. There are several other versions of Knox's comments, for example: "We have a factor in the Navy that is not so in the Army, and that is that these men live aboard ship. And in our history, we don't take Negroes into a ship's company," from Blanche Wiesen Cook, *Eleanor Roosevelt, Volume 3: The War Years and After, 1939–1962* (New York: Viking, 2016), 340.
64. Morris J. MacGregor Jr., *Integration of the Armed Forces, 1940–1965* (Washington, D.C.: Center of Military History, U.S. Army, 1981), 15–16.
65. White, *A Man Called White*, 186–87.
66. MacGregor, *Integration*, 19.
67. "The Problem," *Time*, October 28, 1940.
68. Leon Hardwick, "Segregation in the Army," *Washington Post*, October 23, 1940, 10. This was a letter to the editor.
69. James A. Hagarty, "Third Term a Peril, Willkie Declares," *New York Times*, September 12, 1940, 1.
70. MacGregor, *Integration*, 19.
71. White, *A Man Called White*, 188.

Chapter 5

1. AP, "U.S. Prints 700,000 Blanks for Army Draft," *Chicago Tribune*, June 16, 1940, 5.
2. AP, "Seminole Indians Agreed to Register for a Draft," *Baltimore Sun*, October 17, 1940, 4; AP, "Indian Chief Defies Draft," *Arkansas Gazette*, October 17, 1940, 3; AP "Senator Calls Draft Program Unnecessary," *Omaha World-Herald*, October 17, 1940, 1.
3. "Registration of 4700 Members of University Runs off Smoothly," *Harvard Crimson*, October 17, 1940, 1.
4. "Draft Draws Large Crowds: Early Turnout Heavy as Local Eligibles Rush to Sign," *New York Amsterdam News*, October 1940, 1.
5. AP, "World War Vet Who Was in Marines at 13 Must Sign for Draft," *Chicago Tribune*, October 15, 1940.
6. "Hollywood Heroes Answer Call," *New York Times*, October 17, 1940, 13.
7. "Joe Louis Leads Negro Sports Stars in Draft," *New York Amsterdam News*, October 26, 1940, 19: UP, "Control," *News and Observer*, October 17, 1940, 10.
8. "Ulysses of Trojan War Fame Had Nothing on Martin," *Wall Street Journal*, October 17, 1940, 1; "Nation's Notables Answer Call; Three Rockefellers Are Included," *New York Times*, October 17, 1940, 13.

9. "Doctors and Nurses Register 400 Men in 11 Hospitals," *Evening Star*, October 16, 1940, 8.

10. "Procedure Smooth," *New York Times*, October 17, 1940, 1; "Boro Signs 190,000 in Draft Rush," *Brooklyn Daily Eagle*, October 16, 1940, 1.

11. "Objectors to Service Advised to Register," *New York Times*, October 7, 1940, 9.

12. UP, "Draft Board Head Takes His Life," *Riverside (Calif.) Daily Press*, October 17, 1940, 2.

13. Author interview with Ed Bearss, Arlington, Virginia, July 19, 2017.

14. Franklin D. Roosevelt, "Radio Address for the Drawing under the Selective Service Act of 1940," October 29, 1940.

15. Flynn, *The Draft*, 21.

16. "First Draftee's Number Drawn as He and Fiancée Shop," *Washington Post*, October 30, 1940, 21.

17. Franklin D. Roosevelt, "Campaign Address at Boston, Massachusetts," October 30, 1940, online by Gerhard Peters and John T. Woolley, *The American Presidency Project*, http://www.presidency.ucsb.edu/ws/?pid=15887.

18. "Draft Lottery a Tedious Job; Goes All Night Long," *Chicago Tribune*, October 30, 1940, 9; Clifford and Spencer, *First Peacetime Draft*, 3.

19. George Thorpe, "Skilled Workers Least Likely to Be Called," *Washington Post*, August 26, 1940, 1.

20. C. P. Trussell, "Draft Form Asks Confidendial Data," *Baltimore Sun*, October 4, 1940, 24.

21. "Army Will Take Reds, Bundsmen in Draft Call," *Chicago Tribune*, October 9, 1940, 6.

22. Paul W. Ward, "Army Asks Bar on 'Young Bums,'" *Baltimore Sun*, October 23, 1940, 14.

23. AP, "Gorin in US Reserves," *Times-Picayune*, November 2, 1940, 18.

24. "National Affairs: Timetable," *Time*, December 16, 1940.

25. "Draft Delay," *Newsweek*, September 2, 1940, 20; "Marriage Rate Boosts Realty," *Seattle Times*, November 17, 1940, 40.

26. See Charles E. Heller, "The U.S. Army, the Civilian Conservation Corps, and Leadership for World War II, 1933–1942," *Armed Forces and Society* 36, no. 3 (August 2009): 439–53; Heller studied this development in this work, in which he noted: "Yet given its impact on mobilization, the CCC has never received recognition for its contributions to the war effort. The individuals previously involved with the CCC assisted in the mobilization training, manning, and leading of new units as the citizen Army expanded."

27. AP, "Military Drill Is Ordered for CCC Men," *Washington Post*, August 7, 1941, 1.

28. Lyle M. Spencer, "What Do You Mean . . . A Year out of Your Life," *This Week*, December 8, 1940, 3.

29. "Draft Machine Has Surprises," *Baltimore Sun*, November 15, 1940, 30.

30. Lee Kennett, *G.I.: The American Soldier in World War II* (Norman: University of Oklahoma Press, 1997), 29.

31. AP, "US Army's Number One Conscript Is Jobless Plumber's Helper," *Miami Herald*, November 19, 1940, 1.

32. AP, "Army to Get First Conscripts Today," *Baltimore Sun*, November 18, 1940, 11.

33. "20 P.C. of Draftees Sent Home," *Boston Herald*, November 19, 1940, 1.

34. "Draft Rejections Here Mount to 25 Percent," *Boston Globe*, November 20, 1940, 11.

35. "Errors in Tests Given Selectees," *Baltimore Sun*, November 28, 1940, 28.

36. "Government to Aid Rejected Draftees," *Augusta (Ga.) Chronicle*, November 11, 1940, 1.

37. Kennett, *G.I.*, 27.

38. Robert Dallek, *An Unfinished Life: John F. Kennedy, 1917–1963* (New York: Little, Brown, 2003). The *Stanford Daily* put JFK's picture on its front page, and the story got national play; "Envoy Kennedy's Son Gets Early Draft Number" was the headline in the *Chicago Tribune*.

39. Marc Schulman, "Navy Service," History Central, Multieducator Inc., 1996–2019, http://www.historycentral.com/JFK/bio/Navy.html.

40. INS, "Jimmy Stewart Just 'Slats' to Soldiers after Induction," *Washington Post*, March 23, 1941, 1; Claire Barrett, "Rejected!" *MHQ: Quarterly Journal of Military History* (Summer 2017): 17ff.

41. Jimmie Fidler, column, *San Francisco Examiner*, April 4, 1941, 6.

42. Robert W. Creamer, *Baseball and Other Matters in 1941: A Celebration of the Best Baseball Season Ever—in the Year America Went to War* (Lincoln, Nebr.: Bison Books, 2000), 121–22.

43. Todd DePastino, *Bill Mauldin: A Life up Front* (New York: W. W. Norton, 2008), 7–8, 47–48.

44. "Physical Tests for Draft Show Gain in Health," *Chicago Tribune*, January 1, 1941, A7.

45. "Wonder Bread," *Wilson Quarterly* 36, no. 2 (2012): 65ff.

46. John W. W. Sullivan, "White Bread to Contain More Vitamins," Cleveland *Plain-Dealer*, February 17, 1941, 6.

47. James Rorty, quoted in Howard E. Wilson, Nelle E. Bowman, and Allen Y. King, *This America: Our Land, Our People, Our Faith, Our Defense* (New York: American Book Company, 1942), 89.

48. Bradley and Blair, *A General's Life*, 106–8.

49. William F. Ogburn, "Effects of the Draft on the Rest of Us," *New York Times Magazine*, February 23, 1941, 3, 26.

50. Lewis S. Hershey, *Selective Service in Peacetime, the National Director's First Report to the President 1940–41* (Washington, D.C.: Government Printing Office, 1942, 129.

51. Gallup Poll, *Washington Post*, December 28, 1940, 7.

52. David L. Levine, letter to the editor, *Washington Post*, January 14, 1941, 6.

53. Wesley S. Griswold, "When Conscription Struck Americans Funny," *Hartford (Conn.) Courant*, January 5, 1941, SM3.

54. "Radio Address Delivered by President Roosevelt from Washington, December 29, 1940," Mount Holyoke College, https://www.mtholyoke.edu/acad/intrel/WorldWar2/arsenal.htm.

55. "Buick Will Make Airplane Engines," *New York Times*, January 3, 1941, 8.

CHAPTER 6

1. Donald E. Houston, *Hell on Wheels: The 2d Armored Division* (Novato, Calif.: Presidio Press, 1995), 40.
2. Martin Blumenson, *The Patton Papers, 1940–1945* (Boston: Houghton Mifflin, 1975), 16.
3. AP, "Visiting Newsmen See Armored Division Work," *Columbus (Ga.) Daily Enquirer*, November 26, 1940, 7.
4. D'Este, *Patton: A Genius for War*, 384; "Panzer Unit Wins Praise—Best in World General Declares," *Miami Herald*, December 15, 1940, 26.
5. AP, "Army Providing for Recreation," *Greensboro (N.C.) Record*, December 13, 1940, 17.
6. Stanley Hirshson, *General Patton: A Soldier's Life* (New York: Harper Perennial, 2003), 236–37.
7. Nelson M. Shepard, "Army Aims to Keep Men Happy and in Field and Cantonment," *Evening Star*, October 13, 1940, 27; "Wide Social Life Mapped for Army," *New York Times*, October 13, 1938, 7.
8. *GCM Papers*, 459–61.
9. Marshall Andrews, "Food, Housing of D.C. Guard Pose Problem," *Washington Post*, November 28, 1940, 9.
10. Robert Bruce Sligh, "Plowshares into Swords: The Decision to Mobilize the National Guard in 1940," PhD diss., Texas A&M University, 1990, 168–70.
11. "25 Camps Delayed; Inductions Wait," *New York Times*, December 13, 1940, 17.
12. Watson, *Chief of Staff*, 196; S. B. Hays et al., *Preventive Medicine in WWII*, vol. 4, *Communicable Diseases, Transmitted Chiefly Through Respiratory and Alimentary Tracts* (Washington, D.C.: Office of the Surgeon General, 1958), 116, http://history.amedd.army.mil/booksdocs/wwii/PM4/CH04.Influenza.htm.
13. "Mobilization 1940," *National Guard* (September 1980, 12–17); Flint Whitlock, *The Rock of Anzio: From Sicily to Dachau; A History of the U.S. 45th Infantry Division* (New York: Basic Books, 2005), 22.
14. DePastino, *Bill Mauldin*, 48–49.
15. "Finishing Touches to Job Now Being Added," *The State* (Columbia, S.C.), January 4, 1941, 2.
16. *GCM Papers*, To Major General Frederic H. Smith, November 7, 347.
17. *GCM Papers*, 359.
18. "Guards Fight Flu in Tents as Draftees Get Barracks," *Seattle Times*, December 6, 1940, 14.
19. Bradley and Blair, *A General's Life*, 91.
20. Ibid.
21. Pogue, *Ordeal and Hope*, 119.
22. Edward G. Maxwell, "Conditioning the Draft Army," *Baltimore Sun*, October 6, 1940, M1.
23. "Our New Army," *Collier's Weekly*, June 14, 1941, 38, http://www.unz.org/Pub/Colliers-1941jun14.
24. Pogue, *Ordeal and Hope*, 113; Forrest C. Pogue, *George C. Marshall: Interviews and Reminiscences*, rev. ed. (Lexington, Va.: George C. Marshall Research Foundation, 1991), February 15, 1957, interview with General Marshall, tape 16-M.

25. Arthur Bartlett, "Best Outfit in the Army," *Parade*, July, 6, 1941, 46.
26. "Chief of Staff Places Morale Six to One above Materiel," *Christian Science Monitor*, February 26, 1941, 8.
27. *Life*, July 7, 1941, 95.
28. Charles Hurd, "Army Recreation Solved by General," *New York Times*, July 14, 1941, 8.
29. Richard Sassman, "Bob Hope and the Road to G.I. Joe,"*America in World War II*, magazine accessed online at http://www.americainwwii.com/articles/bob-hope-and-the-road-to-gi-joe/." John Hunneman, "It All Began at March Field," *San Diego Times-Union-Tribune*, July 2, 2003.
30. Alison McLean, "This Month in History: February Anniversaries Momentous or Merely Memorable," *Smithsonian*, February 2011, 16.
31. "NBC Stars Play for Soldiers," *Fresno Bee*, July 27, 1941, 27.
32. "Comedy Capers in Khaki," *Newsweek*, February 10, 1941, 62; *Newsweek*, June 9, 1941, 56.
33. "Roosevelt Pays Tribute to Joe Palooka's Creator," *Baton Rouge Advocate*, June 19, 1941, 6.
34. John G. Norris, "Author Marshall Brings Out a Bestseller on Army Life," *Washington Post*, February 9,1941.
35. War Department, *FM 21-100 Basic Field Manual: Soldier's Handbook* (Washington, D.C.: Government Printing Office, 1941), 239.
36. "Army Slang Novelties from the United States," *Manchester (England) Guardian*, February 22, 1941, 4.
37. AP, "New Army Praised by Gen. Marshall," *Baltimore Sun*, March 30, 1941, 10.
38. Ibid.
39. GCM Papers, Also, *New York Times*, June 16, 1941, 8.
40. William Klingaman, *1941: Our Lives in a World on the Edge* (New York: Harper-Collins, 1988).
41. Pogue, *Ordeal and Hope*, 113.
42. Director of Selective Service, *Selective Service In Wartime: Second Report of the Director of Selective Service, 1941–42* (Washington, D.C.: Director of Selective Service, 1942), 283.
43. "Boys at Fort Bragg in High Spirits," *Baltimore Afro-American*, February 15, 1941, 5.
44. "Whites Have Rifles, Colored None, at Dix: *Afro* Reporters Find Camp Dix, N.J., a Beehive of Activity; Barracks Going up for 372nd Infantry; White Troops Only Get Guns for Ft. Dix Drills," *Baltimore Afro-American*, March 8, 1941, 3.
45. "One Negro out of 60,000 Hired in Aircraft Industry, Report Reveals: Jim Crow Rampant in Coast Plants," *Atlanta Daily World*, September 19, 1940, 1.
46. "10,000 Should March on D.C., Says Randolph," *Baltimore Afro-American*, January 25, 1941, 3.
47. Gail Lumet Buckley, *American Patriots: The Story of Blacks in the Military from the Revolution to Desert Storm* (New York: Random House Trade Paperbacks, 2002), 270.
48. AP, "Randolph in Appeal to F.D.R. on Bias: R.R. Brotherhood Chief Cites War Emergency as Time for Action," *Chicago Defender* (natl. ed.), April 12, 1941, 9;

A. Philip Randolph, "Why F.D.R. Won't End Defense Jim Crow," *Baltimore Afro-American*, April 12, 1941.

49. Michael Lee Lanning, *The African-American Soldier: From Crispus Attucks to Colin Powell* (Secaucus, N.J.: Citadel, 1997), 169.

50. Documentation for this march, including a copy of one of the pledge forms can viewed on the web page of the Franklin D. Roosevelt Library at https://fdrlibrary .tumblr.com/post/59599151265/1941-plans-for-a-march-on-washington-a -precursor.

51. A. Philip Randolph to NAACP Secretary Walter White, March 18, 1941, NAACP Records, Manuscript Division, Library of Congress (088.00.00), courtesy of the A. Philip Randolph Institute, Digital ID # na0088.

52. This dialogue from Randolph's recollection of a Lyndon Baines Johnson Library transcript of the conversation that appeared in Jessie-Lynne Kerr, "THE DAY FREEDOM MARCHED Those who took part in historic event still have vivid memories of that day," *Florida Times-Union*, August 28, 2003, A-1.

53. Walter White, *A Man Called White* (New York: Arno Press, 1969), 192; David M. Kennedy, *Freedom from Fear* (New York: Oxford University Press, 2004), 342.

54. Editorial, "Crusade for Democracy," *Chicago Defender*, June 28, 1941, 14. Beth Tompkins Bates, *Pullman Porters and the Rise of Protest Politics in Black America, 1925–1945* (Chapel Hill: University of North Carolina Press, 2001), 161.

55. Ulysses Lee, *The Employment of Negro Troops*, United States Army in World War II (Washington, D.C.: Center of Military History, U.S. Army, reprinted. 2000; first printed 1966, CMH Pub 11-4); "Believes Fort Benning Soldier was Killed," *Atlanta Daily World*, April 24, 1941, 1; "Youth Congress Demands Probe of Ga. 'Lynching,'" *Baltimore Afro-American*, April 26, 1941, 1; "Ask F.D.R. to Probe Death of Ft. Benning Soldier: Killing Is Called Act of a Mob," *Atlanta Daily World*, April 27, 1941, 1.

CHAPTER 7

1. Thomas E. Ricks, *The Generals: American Military Command from World War II to Today* (New York: Penguin Books, 2013), 32–33.

2. Pogue, *Ordeal and Hope*, 85.

3. Benjamin Franklin Cooling, "The Tennessee Maneuvers, June, 1941," *Tennessee Historical Quarterly* 24, no. 3 (1965): www.jstor.org/stable/42622827.

4. "Panzer Division Will Enter Maneuvers for the First Such Field Test in Our History," *New York Times*, May 25, 1941, 8.

5. Woody McMillin, *In the Presence of Soldiers: The 2nd Army Maneuvers and Other World War II Activity in Tennessee* (Nashville, Tenn.: Horton Heights Press, 2010), 27.

6. Blumenson, *Patton Papers, 1940–1945*, 33.

7. In the great scheme of things, the pin story meant little, but the fact that some version of the story appeared in many of the nation's 2,400 daily newspapers suggested the degree to which the press saw the events in Tennessee as newsworthy. Two examples: Lee Carson, "Great Safety Pins! The Army Nearly Loses an All-Out Battle," *Washington Post*, June 2, 1941, 7; "Crisis Averted as Safety Pins Reach U.S. Army," *State* (Columbia, S.C.), June 2, 1941, 12.

8. McMillin, *In the Presence of Soldiers*, 55.

9. Randolph Tucker, "'Hell on Wheels' Division Poised for Sweep Into State in First Crucial Defense Test," *The Tennessean* (Nashville), June 15, 1941, 4.

10. AP, "30th Ready for Start of Games," *State*, June 2, 1941, 1.

11. AP, Rice Yahner, "U.S. Training Men to Fight Against Tanks," *San Diego Union*, July 13, 1941, 62.

12. Norris H. Perkins and Michael E. Rogers, *Roll Again Second Armored: Prelude to Fame 1940–1943* (Surrey, England: Kristall Productions, 1988). McMillin, *In the Presence of Soldiers*, 47. Houston, *Hell on Wheels*, 65.

13. Hilton H. Railey, "Tries Fear Tactic in Tennessee War," *New York Times*, June 17, 1941, 14.

14. AP, "Armored Unit Takes a Beating in Tennessee Maneuvers," *Washington Post*, June 18, 1941, 9.

15. UP, "Important Week Ahead for Army," *Charleston News and Courier*, June 22, 1941, 6; AP, "Care for Property Handicaps Tanks in Practice War," *Evening Star*, June 18, 1941, 13.

16. "Force of 70,000 Play at War in First U.S. Test of Tanks," *Newsweek*, June 30, 1941, 28.

17. Perkins and Rogers, 57.

18. Randolph Tucker, "Armored Outfit Annihilates Fifth Division, Proving Blitz Power, Giving Natives Grim Show," *Tennessean*, June 21, 1941, 1.

19. G. Frank Burns, Kelly Sergio, and Rex Bennett, "Somewhere in Tennessee: The Cumberland in Wartime, 1940–1947," in *Rural Life and Culture in the Upper Cumberland*, ed. Michael E. Birdwell and W. Calvin Dickinson (Lexington: University Press of Kentucky, 2004), 229–30.

20. UP, Henry McLemore, "By Henry McLemore," *Evansville (Ill.) Courier and Press*, June 24, 1941, 6.

21. AP, Jerry T. Baulch, "Hank Greenberg 'Killed! Tanks Complete 2-Day Job in Seven Hours," *Tennessean*, June 24, 1941, 1.

22. AP, Rice Yahner, "U.S. Training Men to Fight Against Tanks," *San Diego Union*, July 13, 1941, 62.

23. Ibid.

24. Paul F. Gorman, The Secret of Future Victories, IDA Paper 13-2653 (Washington, D.C.: Institute for Defense Analyses, 1992), https://archive.li/jM9s8#selection-501.0-573.23.

25. Norris H. Perkins and Michael E. Rogers, *Roll Again Second Armored: Prelude to Fame 1940–1943* (Surrey, England: Kristall Productions, 1988), 43.

26. AP, Rice Yahner, "Mechanized Warfare Is Bringing Generals Back to Front Lines," *Tennessean*, June 21, 1941, 3. Patton would use this line about spaghetti often and it would end up being one of his most oft-quoted aphorisms, sometimes appearing in collections of quotes about leadership.

27. *Life*, Defense Issue, July 7, 1941, 74–89.

28. Blumenson, *The Patton Papers, 1940–1945*, 39.

29. Ibid., 41.

30. "A $25 Maneuver," *Detroit Times*, July 8, 1941, 3.

31. AP, *New York Times*, May 10, 1941, 12.

32. Doug Davis, "Historian, WWII Vets Recall TN Maneuvers," Murfreesboro, Tenn. (July 30, 2011).
33. UP, "Anti-Tank Units Formed," *Evening Post*, July 4, 1941, 7.
34. Bill Cunningham, "New Army Gets the Works in Maneuvers," syndicated from the *Boston Herald* in *Washington Post*, June 20, 1941, 12.
35. Lewis B. Sebring Jr., "Speed of Training and Arming of New Troops Exceeds Hopes," *New York Herald Tribune*, July 6, 1941, A-1.
36. Ibid.
37. Norris H. Perkins and Michael E. Rogers, *Roll Again Second Armored: Prelude to Fame 1940–1943* (Surrey, England: Kristall Productions, 1988), 47.
38. AP, Rice Yahner, "Army Builds New Division for Defense Against Tanks," *Evening Star*, July 13, 1941, 33.
39. Ibid., 32.
40. This point is made eloquently in Cooling, "The Tennessee Maneuvers, June 1941"; Cooling reports that the advantage of these aircraft was little noted at the time.
41. Creamer, *Baseball and Other Matters in 1941*, 276–77. The "yoo-hoo" incident occurred during Joe DiMaggio's 56-consecutive-game hitting streak, which to this day is recalled as one of the great moments in American sports history. Creamer's book celebrates 1941 as the best baseball season ever.
42. William M. Christie, *1941: The America That Went to War* (New York: Carrel Books, 2016).
43. AP, "Army Asks Lear for His Side of the Yoo-Hoo Story," *Chicago Tribune*, July 11, 1941, 7.
44. "Yoo-Hooing Soldiers Defended; General Lear Criticized in House," *Washington Post*, July 10, 1941, 1.
45. "Capitol Hill 'Generals' Consolidate in Assault on Yoo-hoo March," *Christian Science Monitor*, July 11, 1941, 11. Undersecretary of War Robert Patterson announced that the Army was not going to release Lear's side of the story, as to do so would create a new "hullaballoo," which would leave little time for anything else. This implied that there was more to the story or, as retired colonel Benjamin H. Pope put it in a letter published in the *San Francisco Chronicle*: "Anyone who knows Ben Lear or the military service knows that there undoubtedly was much more than a 'Yoo hoo' involved in that matter, but the whole truth must not be published as it would spoil a swell story." Benjamin H. Pope, "Smearing the Army Uniform," *San Francisco Chronicle*, July 7, 1941, 12.
46. Mark M. Boatner III, *Biographical Dictionary of World War II* (Novato, Calif.: Presidio Press, 1999), 308, in his entry on Lear calls the "yoo-hoo" incident a "major career setback." AP, Rice Yahner, "Generals Lear and Krueger, Both Former Privates, Match Wits in New War Games," *Evansville Courier*, August 18, 1941, 3.
47. "Sites Raised in Arms Output as FDR Calls for More Speed," *Newsweek*, May 12, 1941, 38.
48. *Biennial Reports of the Chief of Staff of the United States Army to the Secretary of War, July 1, 1939–June 30, 1945* (Washington, D.C.: Center of Military History, U.S. Army, 1996), 13.

CHAPTER 8

1. "FDR Message on Army Issue Spotlights Perils Facing U.S.," *Newsweek*, July 28, 1941, 11.

2. This impending struggle was, according to Marshall biographer Forrest Pogue, a major reason the Ben Lear "yoo-hoo" affair had been "magnified out of all proper proportion." Others suggested that the level of congressional outrage over the incident had been fueled by the belief that draftees and their parents needed an extra reason to have the term of service end after a year.

3. FDR Message 12; "Ignore Draft Opponents until Soldiers Speak Up," *Socialist Call*, August 2, 1941, 2.

4. Carson McCullers, *Reflections in a Golden Eye* (Boston: Mariner Books, 2000), 1.

5. David Lawrence, "Need Is Shown for Extending Draft Service," *Christian Science Monitor*, July 16, 1941, 7.

6. "Charity Begins at Home," *New York Daily News*, June 4, 1941, 6: This item is also cited in Lee, *Employment of Negro Troops*, 65.

7. Eric Sevareid, *Not So Wild a Dream* (New York: Atheneum Books, 1978), 201.

8. Burton K. Wheeler, "Unity for Peace," speech delivered in the Senate, March 20, 1941, *Vital Speeches of the Day*, vol. 7, 446–48.

9. Henry L. Stimson and McGeorge Bundy, *On Active Service in Peace and War*, vol. 2 (New York: Harper and Brothers, 1948), 378–80.

10. Alford T. Hearne, "A Soldier's Letter," *San Francisco Chronicle*, July 25, 1941, 4.

11. "Wheeler Goes Too Far Says Roosevelt," *Washington Post*, July 26, 1941, 1; "Stimson Absolves Wheeler on Cards," *Baltimore Sun*, July 30, 1941, 1.

12. "Heated Protests in Senate Debate," *Charleston News and Courier*, July 29, 1941, 2.

13. AP, "Wheeler Admits Sending Cards; Near Treason, Stimson Asserts," *Hanover (Pa.) Daily Sun*, July 24, 1941, 1.

14. Dorothy Thompson, "Unexplainable B. K. Wheeler," *San Francisco Chronicle*, July 31, 1941, 12.

15. Henry McLemore, *Oregonian* (Portland, Oreg.), July 29, 1941, 10.

16. "Many Selects Going AWOL, Wheeler Says," *Washington Post*, July 21, 1941, 1.

17. Stimson and Bundy, *On Active Service*, vol. 2, 378; "Apology to Senator Wheeler, After the Smear What?" *Social Justice*, August 11, 1941, 5.

18. William S. Neil, "Rejects Compromise," *Detroit Times*, July 24, 1941, 1.

19. Two sources claim the OHIO movement was staged by the isolationists, but neither offers sourcing for the assertion: Ted Morgan, *FDR: A Biography* (Simon and Schuster: New York, 1985), 598; Mosley, *Marshall: Hero for Our Times*, 147.

20. Franklin D. Roosevelt, "Message to Congress on Extending the One-Year Service Limit for Draftees," July 21, 1941, White House news release, Washington, D.C., July 21, 1941, https://www.ibiblio.org/pha/timeline/410721awp.html.

21. Joseph E. Persico, "The Day When We Almost Lost the Army," *American Heritage* 62, no. 1 (Spring 2012): https://www.americanheritage.com/content/day-when-we-almost-lost-army.

22. George Gallup, "Public Split on Draft Act," *Miami Herald*, August 6, 1941, 5.

23. "*Life* Reporter Finds Many Gripes Have Lowered Army Morale," *Life*, August 18, 1941, 17–18.

24. "Problem of Morale," *Time*, August 18, 1941, 35–36. Discussion of the articles appears in Marshall's letter to Bernard Baruch of August 19, 1941, which can be accessed at https://www.marshallfoundation.org/library/digital-archive/to-bernard-m-baruch-9/.

25. Anthony H. Leviero, "Will Toss Stones in Grenade Drill," *New York Times*, November 18, 1940, 10; Leviero, "First Tests Show the 27th Is Bright," *New York Times*, December 8, 1940, 14.

26. Captain M. M. Corpening, "New York's 27th Termed Best in Army Exercises," *Chicago Tribune*, June 8, 1941, 2.

27. Lance Morrow, "*Time* Runs Out: Henry Luce and His Empire Belonged to Another Country, Another Era," *City Journal* (N.Y.), February 9, 2018, https://www.city-journal.org/html/time-runs-out-15716.html.

28. "Rayburn Opposes Amendment to Keep Selects beyond Year," *Washington Post*, July 10, 1941, 10; "Gen. Marshall, Stimson Talk with Rayburn," *Washington Post*, July 12, 1941, 2.

29. William S. White, *Rayburn* (Austin: Texas Monthly Press, 1977), 265–66; *Congressional Record*, House, 1941, vol. 87, 6938–39; Robert Dallek, *Lone Star Rising: Lyndon Johnson and His Times, 1908–1960* (New York: Oxford University Press, 1991), 227.

30. J. Garry Clifford and Theodore A. Wilson, eds., *Presidents, Diplomats, and Other Mortals: Essays Honoring Robert H. Ferrell* (Columbia: University of Missouri Press, 2007), 209. This account is based on an oral history of Manesco at the National Archives.

31. Paul Saunders, "The Speaker and the Draft," *American History*, August 2001, 43–46; Joseph Persico, "The Day We Almost Lost the Army," *Roosevelt's Centurions: FDR and the Commanders He Led to Victory in World War II* (New York: Random House, 2013), 10–12.

32. C. P. Trussell, "2½ Draft Passes House by 203–202 Vote: Scene Drama Packed," *Baltimore Sun*, August 13, 1941, 1.

33. David Lawrence, "Draft Vote Political Gamble," *Evening Star*, August 14, 1941, 12; Editorial, "203 to 202," *St. Louis Post-Dispatch*, August 13, 1941.

34. Watson, *Chief of Staff*, 231.

35. The Nazi statement that was carried by the Associated Press alleged that "a certain clique in the United States" was inciting to war. AP, "Nazi Pleased by 203, 202 Vote on U.S. Army Term," *Marshfield-News Herald*, August 14, 1941, 1.

36. Gladstone Williams, "A Majority of One," *Atlanta Constitution*, August 19, 1941, 4.

37. "25 Soldiers Unburden Themselves on Army Morale," Washington, D.C., *Sunday Star*, August 24, 1941, 2.

38. Robert E. Sherwood, *Roosevelt and Hopkins: An Intimate History* (New York: Harper, 1948), 366; "President Signs Draft Extension Act," *Evening Star*, August 18, 1941; David Stafford, *Roosevelt and Churchill: Men of Secrets* (Woodstock, New York: Overlook Hardcover, 2000), 69.

39. Hilton H. Railey, "Infantry Holds Up under Swift Blow," *New York Times*, June 18, 1941, 15.

40. Philip Gerard, *Secret Soldiers: The Story of World War II's Heroic Army of Deception* (New York: Dutton, 2002), 38–40. Railey's article "'Close-up' of Life in Officers' Camp: Candidates [sic] Gives Moving Picture of His Tests and Tribulations, but Decides They Are Well Worth While" appeared in the *New York Times* on September 29, 1918, 39. According to Railey, he turned down the offer to become Hitler's public relations man for a number of reasons but mainly because of Hitler's persecution of Jews.

41. *The Papers of George Catlett Marshall*, ed. Larry I. Bland, Sharon Ritenour Stevens, and Clarence E. Wunderlin Jr. (Lexington, Va.: George C. Marshall Foundation, 1981–). Electronic version based on *The Papers of George Catlett Marshall*, vol. 2, *"We Cannot Delay," July 1, 1939–December 6, 1941* (Baltimore and London: Johns Hopkins University Press, 1986), 591–92.

42. Marshall interview, January 22, 1957, online at: https://marshallfoundation .org/library/digital-archive/to-bernard-m-baruch-9/.

43. UP, "Morale of Army Varies with That of People, Says Gen. Lear, Answering Charge It Is Low," *New York Times*, August 19, 1941, 23.

44. AP, "Dateline Denver," August 20, *Baltimore Sun*, August 21, 1941, 1.

45. AP, "Draft Army to Serve Average of 18 Months," *Rockford (Ill.) Morning Star*, August 20, 1941, 1.

46. C. P. Trussell, "Army Morale Is Cause of Wide Concern," *Baltimore Sun*, August 24, 1941, 1, *Baltimore Sun*, August 21, 1941, 1.

47. Lee Kennett, *G.I.: The American Soldier in World War II* (New York: Scribner's, 1987), 68.

48. Joseph W. Ryan, *Samuel Stouffer and the GI Survey: Sociologists and Soldiers during the Second World War* (Knoxville: University of Tennessee Press, 2013), 38.

49. Lori Lyn Bogle, *The Pentagon's Battle for the American Mind: The Early Cold War* (College Station, Tex.: Texas A&M University Press, 2004), 42; Gerard, *Secret Soldiers*, 39.

50. *Ibid*, 42.

51. Stimson and Bundy: *On Active Service*, vol. 2, 379.

52. Sevareid, *Not So Wild a Dream*, 202–3.

53. "Army Morale," *Hartford Courant*, September 5, 1941, 12.

54. Charley Cherokee, "National Grapevine," *Chicago Defender*, September 13, 1941, 13.

55. Mosley, *Marshall: Hero for Our Times*, 45–46. This contains a vivid account of Marshall and the Plattsburg camp.

56. Joseph R. Fischer, "Omar Nelson Bradley," in *Generals of the Army: Marshall, MacArthur, Eisenhower, Arnold, Bradley*, ed. James H. Willbanks (Lexington: University Press of Kentucky, 2013), 186.

57. General Frederick J. Kroesen, "Officer Candidate School: An Introduction," *Army*, November 2017.

58. Geoffrey Perret, *There's a War to Be Won: The United States Army in World War II* (New York: Random House, 1991), 114–15.

59. GCM Papers, Bradley to Marshall, July 26, 1941, 490–91.

CHAPTER 9

1. Sam H. Jones, "The Governor's View," *Times-Picayune*, August 3, 1941, 21.

2. "Army to Stage World's Biggest Mock Battle," *New York Herald Tribune*, May 8, 1941, 3.

3. AP, "Producers and Army Confer on Movies," *Christian Science Monitor*, July 14, 1941, 10; "Army Public Relations Sells Job Here," *Los Angeles Times*, July 14, 1941, 3.

4. AP, "U.S. Is Procuring Half of Louisiana for Maneuvers," *Washington Post*, May 6, 1941, 37.

5. Pogue, *Ordeal and Hope*, 89.

6. AP, "US Army Chief Discloses Plan for United Military," *Christian Science Monitor*, June 24, 1941, 3.

7. John Thompson, "Drill Draftees Day and Night to Finish Training," *Chicago Tribune*, July 2, 1941, 20.

8. AP, "General Krueger Asserts Cavalry Isn't Making Most of Mobility," *Baltimore Sun*, July 23, 1941, 12.

9. John L. Mortimer, "Lack of Equipment," reprinted from *Houston Press*, *Baltimore Sun*, June 16, 1941, 10.

10. Meigs O. Frost, "War Game Menu Is Being Planned for 300,000 Men," *Times-Picayune*, July 11, 1941, 3; "Feeding Maneuver Armies to Represent One of Greatest Problems of Quartermaster," *Baton Rouge Advocate*, August 3, 1941, 3.

11. AP, "Bread for Big War Games 'Cured' to Last for 2 Weeks," *New York Times*, July 30, 1941, 9.

12. Major Frank L. Nelson, "Rollin' Fourth at Benning is Fightingest Division," *Columbus (Ga.) Daily Enquirer*, November 5, 1941, 24.

13. "Lands Furnished for Army Maneuvers," *Columbus (Ga.) Daily Enquirer*, July 28, 1941, 6.

14. Gabel, *U.S. Army GHQ Maneuvers of 1941*, 58.

15. The biggest push came on August 7, when 60 Louisiana State Troopers, Army MPs, and public health officials swept through the Lake Charles area under the motto "Vice is Out," shutting down honky-tonks, juke joints, gambling dens, and houses of prostitution. At the end of the day, $160,000 in gambling equipment had been confiscated and destroyed; AP, "Trailer Girls to Be Kept Moving," *Arkansas Gazette*, August 8, 1941, 12.

16. "Red Light District Blacked Out after 95 Years in City," *Corpus Christi Caller-Times*, August 8, 1941, 2.

17. AP, "Maneuvers Delay Opening of Schools," *Los Angeles Times*, August 15, 1941, 5.

18. "Maneuvers to Put 1,000 Planes Aloft," *Baltimore Sun*, August 1, 1941, 9.

19. UP, "Army Demands 'Realism' on Wargame Prisoners," *New York Times*, August 9, 1941, 6.

20. Isbell, "Battle of the Bayous," 4.

21. AP, "Troops in the Maneuver to Be 'Guinea Pigs' for Malaria Tests," *Chicago Tribune*, July 23, 1941, 1.

22. "Louisiana Acts to Guard Health of Army in Games," *Tampa Tribune*, August 12, 1941, 11.

23. Edward Montague Kirby and Jack W. Harris, *Star-Spangled Radio* (Chicago: Ziff-Davis, 1948), 16.

24. "Times-Herald to be with Co. L. At Army Maneuveurs," *Times-Herald*, August 12, 1941, 1.

25. Ralph Martin, "Big Guns of Newswriting World Gather at Camp Polk—Army Covers Nothing Up," *Beaumont (Tex.) Journal*, August 29, 1941, 7.

26. Gabel, *U.S. Army GHQ Maneuvers of 1941*, 58.

27. William J. Clew, "Troops Camp Second Night in Florida," *Hartford Courant*, July 26, 1941, 2; Clew, "Connecticut Troops Travel along Gulf Coast," *Hartford Courant*, July 31, 1941, 5.

28. "Jones Warns Against Fifth Columnists at Maneuvers," *Baton Rouge Advocate*, July 30, 1941, 6.

29. Susan Eisenhower, *Mrs. Ike: Memories and Reflections on the Life of Mamie Eisenhower* (New York: Farrar, Straus and Giroux, 1996), 173.

30. Carlo D'Este, *Eisenhower: A Soldier's Life* (New York: Henry Holt, 2002), 211.

31. John Thompson, "Military Boom Hits Quiet Dixie City with a Bang," *Chicago Tribune*, June 29, 1941, 11.

32. Ollie Stewart, "Selby Men Want to Be Transferred," *Baltimore Afro-American*, August 2, 1941, 1.

33. "A Protector of Democracy Asks Some Protection," *Chicago Defender*, August 23, 1941, 1.

34. "Fear Grips 1,000 Soldiers in Arkansas for War Maneuvers," *Atlanta Daily World*, August 20, 1941, 1.

35. "Making 'Goat' of 5 Soldiers, NAACP Claims," *Atlanta Daily World*, October 7, 1941, 1.

36. "Race Troops Get Welcome in Arkansas," *Chicago Defender*, September 6, 1941, 1.

37. Charley Cherokee, "Frankenstein," *Chicago Defender*, August 30, 1941, 15.

38. Corporal Jay. A. Brown, "Our Military Might," *Atlanta Daily World*, August 19, 1941, 6.

39. "Secretary Stimson," *Time*, August 25, 1941.

40. Henry Stimson, "Address to Selectees: You Will Not Falter—You Cannot Fail," August 15, 1941, *Vital Speeches of the Day*, vol. 7, 685–88, http://www.ibiblio.org/pha/policy/1941/1941-08-15b.html; Stimson and Bundy, *On Active Service*, vol. 2, 379.

41. William J. Clew, "New Army's Test Seen in Next Six Weeks," *Hartford Courant*, August 17, 1941, 4.

42. Major R. A. Griffin, "Political Fiction Peps Up War Games in South," *Life*, September 1, 1941, 31–35. In the following issue of the magazine, Griffin objected to the magazine's use of his name in publishing the war game scenario. *Life's* rebuttal was that a press release issued by the Second Army was fair game.

43. "Army Rescues 75,000 Men Trapped in the Arkansas Maneuvers," *Atlanta Constitution*, August 26, 1941, 4.

44. "140 Miles of 'Hell on Wheels' to Roll Through City This Week," *Shreveport Times*, August 10, 1941, 13.

45. Lewis B. Sebring, "2nd Field Army on Move to Start Vast War Games," *New York Herald Tribune*, August 12, 1941, 9.

46. "Sham Battle Rages in Junction City," *Arkansas Gazette*, September 7, 1941, 9.
47. Kevin M. Hymel, "Red River Kids at War," *America in WWII*, August 2017, 18ff.
48. See *Baton Rouge Advocate*, September 1, 1941, 10.
49. "Motion Pictures to Be Provided State Soldiers," *Times-Picayune*, September 3, 1941, 6.
50. "Landing Boats Used," *Christian Science Monitor*, August 19, 1941.
51. UP, "Mythical Foe Lands on Coast," *Los Angeles Times*, August 12, 1941, 7; "We're 'Invaded,' but Don't Faint!" *Los Angeles Times*, August 14, 1941, A-4.
52. "Assembly Day for 6th Corps," *Boston Globe*, August 26, 1941, 8.
53. Eric Coster, "Fourth Army Morale Lauded by General Dewitt, *San Francisco Examiner*, August 23, 1941, 7.

CHAPTER 10

1. "Army Officers Age Limits Fixed," *Washington Post*, September 5, 1941, 1.
2. AP, "170 Officers Affected by Army Purge," *Baltimore Sun*, September 13, 1941, 3; Wayne S. Cole, *Charles A. Lindbergh and the Battle Against American Intervention in World War II*, 173.
3. "Army: The Baffle of Louisiana," *Time*, September 29, 1941.
4. Watson, *Chief of Staff*, 242.
5. The full text of FDR's speech can be found at http://www.fdrlibrary.marist .edu/_resources/images/msf/msf01443. AP, "Trio Pushing for War, Says Lindbergh," *Baltimore Sun*, September 12, 1941, 1.
6. A. Scott Berg, *Lindbergh* (New York: G. P. Putnam's Sons, 1998), 427.
7. "America First Leader Critical for Attack on Jews," *Baltimore Sun*, September 14, 1941, 16; Walter Winchell's column of September 22, 1941, cited in *Durham (N.C.) Sun*, 4.
8. "Lindbergh Hits Below the Belt," *Kansas City Times*, September 13, 1941, 22.
9. Ansel E. Talbert, "Grasshopper Planes Win Maneuvers Role," *New York Herald Tribune*, August 10, 1941, A14.
10. Joseph C. Harsch, "Army Begins Test of Force," *Christian Science Monitor*, September 15, 1941, 1.
11. Perkins and Rogers, *Roll Again*, 61.
12. Ibid. 57.
13. D. A. Lande, *I Was with Patton: First-Person Accounts of World War II in George S. Patton's Command* (Saint Paul: MBI Publishing Co., 2002), 17; "Maneuvers May Be Army's Last," *Monroe (La.) Morning World*, 117.
14. Radio station WSM out of Nashville had a mobile crew of six men on the job. WLW out of Cincinnati, which fed 25 midwestern stations, had the audacity to send two women to cover the games. The women were allowed to witness prebattle tank demonstrations and dive-bomber attacks. But as the games were about to begin, they were sent home by authorities and replaced by male reporters.
15. Roelif Loveland, "Half Million Poised for War Games," Cleveland *Plain Dealer*, September 15, 1941, 1.
16. Lewis B. Sebring Jr., "2d Army Moves across River to Meet 3d in Test," *New York Herald Tribune*, September 16, 1941, 1.

17. "Big Maneuvers Test U.S. Army," *Life*, October 6, 1941, 38.
18. Perkins and Rogers, *Roll Again*, 61.
19. AP, Jerry T. Baulch, "Second Army Sweeps Across Red River in La. Maneuvers," *Columbia (S.C.) Record*, September 15, 1941, 18.
20. Ladislas Farago, *Patton: Ordeal and Triumph* (New York: Dell, 1970), 160–61.
21. Captain M. M. Corpening, "Regiment Walks into Ambush in Louisiana 'War,'" *Chicago Tribune*, September 17, 1941.
22. "Maneuvers over the Mike," *Newsweek*, September 29, 1941, 63; AP, "War Games Move toward Major Clash," *Dallas Morning News*, September 17, 1941, 8.
23. International News Service, James L. Kilgallen, *Detroit News*, September 17, 1941, 2; Joseph C. Harsch, "Army Springs New Strategy in War Games," *Christian Science Monitor*, September 20, 1941, 1.
24. "Pressure Groups Hampering Army Building, Marshall Says," *Milwaukee Journal Sentinel*, September 16, 1941, 11; *The Papers of George Catlett Marshall*, ed. Larry I. Bland, Sharon Ritenour Stevens, and Clarence E. Wunderlin Jr. (Lexington, Va.: George C. Marshall Foundation, 1981–). Electronic version based on *The Papers of George Catlett Marshall*, vol. 2, *"We Cannot Delay," July 1, 1939–December 6, 1941* (Baltimore and London: Johns Hopkins University Press, 1986), 606–12.
25. "Legion's Aristocracy Dines in State; Celebrities Shine and Dressy Affair," *Milwaukee Journal Sentinel*, September 16, 1941, 11.
26. John O'Reilly, "Paratroopers Get First Workout in Louisiana Army Maneuvers," *New York Herald Tribune*, September 18, 1941, 19; Hanson W. Baldwin, "Chutists' Drop into War Game," *New York Times*, September 18, 1941, 15.
27. Joseph C. Harsch, "Army Springs New Strategy in War Games," *Christian Science Monitor*, September 20, 1941, 1.
28. John O'Reilly, "With the Third Army," and Lewis B. Sebring Jr., "2d Army Opens First Big Drive of Maneuvers," both from *New York Herald Tribune*, September 19, 1941, 6.
29. Hanson Baldwin, "Invaders Crush 'Reds' in South: First Phase of Maneuvers in Louisiana Ends in Retreat of Smaller Units Defending," *New York Times*, September 20, 1941, 13; Lewis B. Sebring Jr., "Armored 2d Army Hurled Back, Gen. Lear Forced to Flee Again," *New York Herald Tribune*, September 20, 1941, 1A.
30. UP, Leon Kay, "Confused Second Army Lays Down Weapons," *Miami Herald*, September 20, 1941, 2.
31. Murray, "The Louisiana Maneuvers," 25.
32. UP, Richard Hottelet, "Swamps Stop Heavy Machines and Snipers Do the Rest," *Evansville (Ill.) Press*, September 20, 1941, 1.
33. AP, "Tanks Need Support," *State Times Advocate* (Baton Rouge, La.), September 20, 1941, 1.
34. Piers Brendon, *Ike: His Life and Times* (New York: Harper and Row, 1986), 74.
35. John S. D. Eisenhower, *General Ike: A Personal Reminiscence* (New York: Free Press, 2003), 76.
36. Thaddeus Holt, "The Final Scrimmage," MHQ: Quarterly Journal of Military History 4, no. 2 (Winter 1992): http://www.historynet.com/relax-its-only-a-maneuver.htm/. Holt noted that Sevareid recalled many years later that

"many of his colleagues were at least as interested in personal strategies as in military ones, notably how to get a drink amid the patchwork of wet, dry, and in-between counties and parishes that made up the 1941 South."

37. Joseph C. Harsch, *At the Hinge of History: A Reporter's Story* (Athens: University of Georgia Press, 1993), 67.

38. Merle Miller, *Ike the Soldier: As They Knew Him* (New York: Putnam, 1987), 327. Eisenhower learned about these comments made by Krueger in a letter from Jones, mailed on March 7, 1945, when Eisenhower understood that troops under his command and led by his friend Courtney Hodges crossed the Rhine.

39. Robert S. Allen and Drew Pearson, "Washington Merry-Go-Round," *Lexington Leader*, October 2, 1941.

40. Notes from Pogue interview with General Krueger, conducted on November 7, 1957, in San Antonio; quoted here with written permission of the George C. Marshall Foundation.

41. Jerry D. Morelock, "'I'm Going to Command the Whole Shebang'" (*American History*, August 2015, 38ff); H. Paul Jeffers, *Taking Command: General J. Lawton Collins from Guadalcanal to Utah Beach and Victory in Europe* (New York: New American Library, 2009); Dwight D. Eisenhower, *In Review: Pictures I've Kept; A Concise Pictorial Autobiography* (Garden City, N.Y.: Doubleday, 1969), 39.

    Morelock wrote: "As chief of staff for one of those commanders, General Walter Krueger of the Third Army, Ike ran the 1941 Louisiana Maneuvers, an unprecedented exercise in simulated combat for nearly a half million troops. That success earned him promotion to brigadier general and cemented his reputation Army-wide, particularly with Marshall who had become Army chief of staff in 1939." In 1990, the U.S. Army's Center of Military History published a brochure on Eisenhower's military career, as a remembrance of the 100th anniversary of his birth, which referred to Ike's role in the maneuvers: "Third Army decisively defeated Lt. Gen. Ben Lear's opposing Second Army in wide-ranging war games that got national publicity, and in which Eisenhower was credited with devising Third Army's plan of battle." The brochure also melodramatically says of Eisenhower: "In 1941, this remarkable soldier was nearing the end of an undistinguished military career that had afforded him few opportunities to demonstrate his leadership."

42. Kevin C. Holzimmer, *General Walter Krueger: Unsung Hero of the Pacific War*, Modern War Studies (Lawrence: University Press of Kansas, 2007), 89.

43. "Marty Snyder, Restaurateur, Eisenhower's Mess Sergeant," obituary, *New York Times*, July 2, 1974, 38; Marty Snyder, *My Friend Ike* (New York: Frederick Fell, 1956), 31.

44. "Legislators Fly to War Maneuvers," *Arkansas Gazette*, September 17, 1941, 6.

45. "Senate Passes 2nd Lend-Lease Bill, 59–13," *Washington Post*, October 24, 1941, 1.

46. W. H. Lawrence, "Dynamo of Democracy's Arsenal," *New York Times*, August 24, 1941, 115.

47. "U.S. Makes Too Few Planes Because It Made No Plans," *Washington Post*, August 25, 1941; Franklin D. Roosevelt, radio address, delivered Labor Day, September 1, 1941, *Vital Speeches of the Day*, vol. 7, 706–7.

48. John O'Reilly, "3rd Army Resting," *New York Herald Tribune*, September 21, 1941, 18.

49. UP, Richard C. Hottelet, "Live Bombing of Shreveport Is Due Today," *Beaumont (Tex.) Journal*, September 22, 1942, 4.

50. Pogue, *Ordeal and Hope*, 89.

51. Lewis B. Sebring Jr., "2d Army Shifts Tactics as Mud Gums up Roads," *New York Herald Tribune*, September 26, 1941, 8.

52. AP, "Parachute Troops Conduct Air Raid," *Baltimore Sun*, September 27, 1941, 4; Mark S. Watson, "Watson Finds Army Morale Improved by Maneuvers: Spirits Which Sagged in Camp Routines Revive by Interesting Louisiana War Games," *Baltimore Sun*, September 30, 1940, 1.

53. AP, "Paratroops Hit 'Reds' in Rear," *San Diego Union*, September 27, 1941, 5.

54. Eisenhower, *At Ease: Stories I Tell to Friends*, 218.

55. Gabel, *U.S. Army GHQ Maneuvers of 1941*, 60.

56. Norris and Rogers, *Roll Again*, 66.

57. Jerry T. Baulch, "War Games a Success; Troops Ready to Leave," *Baton Rouge Advocate*, September 29, 1929, 1.

58. Lewis B. Sebring Jr., "Inferior Force Saves Shreveport from Capture as War Games End," *New York Herald Tribune*, September 29, 1941, 1A; AP, Jerry T. Baulch, "Armistice Ends War after Fight for Shreveport," *Times-Picayune*, September 29, 1941, 1; Hanson W. Baldwin, "War Games Over: Blues Near Goal," *New York Times*, September 29, 1941, 8.

59. Don M. Ewing, "Night March in Louisiana Beat Germans at the Bulge," *Shreveport Times*, March 2, 1945, 2.

60. AP, "Six More Deaths Bring Maneuver Total to 94," *Evening Star* (Washington, D.C.), October 3, 1941, 17; AP, "236 Deaths Seen for Maneuvers—119 Are Expected in Louisiana Games," *Baton Rouge Advocate*, September 11, 1941, 2.

61. "First Lap," *San Francisco Chronicle*, October 5, 1941, 21.

62. "Two-Way Homing Pigeons to Be Used in Army's Louisiana War Maneuvers," *Richmond (Va.) Times-Dispatch*, September 7, 1941, 7.

63. AP, "Indians to Act as Signal Corps Using Own Tongue Over Radio," *Dallas Morning News*, August 21, 1941, 2; "Indian Dialects in Army," *Baltimore Sun*, August 31, 1941, 5.

64. "Radio Announcer Is Gassed," *Tampa Times*, September 25, 1941, 9.

65. Ralph Martin, "Hang Out Wash on Front Line," *Knoxville News-Sentinel*, September 21, 1941, 37.

66. *Evening Star* (Washington, D.C.), November 9, 1941, 5.

67. Murray, "The Louisiana Maneuvers," 14.

68. Herbert C. Banks, *1st Cavalry Division: A Spur Ride through the 20th Century*, limited ed. (Paducah, Ky.: Turner Publishing, 2002); Rickey Robertson, "Horse Tales of the U.S. Cavalry in Louisiana 1941," *West Central's Best*, November 18, 2016, http://www.westcentralsbest.com/life/features/horse-tales-of-the-u-s-cavalry-in-louisiana/article_335df1a4-a5d7-11e6-ad26-5f86631210f2.html.

69. Jerry T. Baulch, "War Games a Success; Troops Ready to Leave," *Baton Rouge Advocate*, September 29, 1929, 1.

70. Mark S. Watson, "Watson Finds Army Morale Improved by Maneuvers: Spirits Which Sagged in Camp Routines Revive By Interesting Louisiana War Games," *Baltimore Sun*, September 30, 1941, 1.

71. Ibid.

72. John H. Cline, "Morale of Third Army Appears Based on Zest for Soldier Life," *Evening Star*, September 20, 1941, 3; Cline, "Army Life Irks Homesick Yank, But He Ranks High in Morale," *Evening Star*, September 22, 1941, 3.

73. Donald V. Bennett, *Honor Untarnished: A West Point Graduate's Memoir of World War II* (New York: Forge Books, 2004), 75; Elizabeth M. Collins, "Patton 'Bested' at the Battle of Bermuda Bridge," U.S. Army, https://www.army.mil/article/26400.

74. *Newsweek*, September 21, 1941, 31.

75. AP, "Lodge Advocates 'Specialist' Army,'" *Christian Science Monitor*, October 6, 1941; AP, "Senator Long Back from Louisiana War Games, Urges New Army Policy," *Christian Science Monitor*, October 7, 1941, 2.

76. NEA, Ralph Martin, "Dictionary Takes a Licking as 'Dog Faces' and 'Glamor Boys' Give Army New Slang," *Columbus (Ga.) Daily Enquirer*, August 31, 1941, 18; Bess Stevenson, "Made in Louisiana: Smart Army, Lasting Impressions and Picturesque Slang," *Fort Worth Star-Telegram*, September 12, 1941, 10; Robert S. Allen and Drew Pearson, Washington Merry-Go-Round, *Washington Post*, October 1, 1941, "Popular Expression in the New Citizen Army, 'Situation normal, everything snafoo.'"

77. James Marlow, "Morale of Army Highly Improved in Maneuvers," *Times-Picayune*, October 5, 1941, 16.

78. "Troops Saw Little Action in Louisiana Army Maneuvers," *Norfolk Journal and Guide*, October 11, 1941, 1.

79. DePastino, *Bill Mauldin*, 71; Bill Mauldin, *The Brass Ring: A Sort of Memoir* (New York: W. W. Norton, 1971), 109.

80. DePastino says this cartoon originally appeared in the *Oklahoma City Times*, September 13, 1941.

CHAPTER 11

1. Merle Miller, *Ike the Soldier: As They Knew Him* (New York: Putnam, 1987), 329. Miller interviewed Clark for his book and quoted Clark's recollection directly from that interview. When Merle Miller retold this story in his book, he commented: "Some days it was as if they were still at West Point."

2. Susan Eisenhower, *Mrs. Ike*, 172.

3. Ty Seidule, "The Reformer: Eisenhower in the Interwar Years," originally published in French as "Eisenhower dans les entre-deux-guerres," De Gaulle et les jeunes turcs dans les armées occidentals," *Actes Academi* Collection, ed. Francois Cochet (Paris: Broché, 2008).

4. *The Papers of George Catlett Marshall*, ed. Larry I. Bland, Sharon Ritenour Stevens, and Clarence E. Wunderlin Jr. (Lexington, Va.: George C. Marshall Foundation, 1981–). *We Cannot Delay," July 1, 1939–December 6, 1941* (Baltimore and London: Johns Hopkins University Press, 1986), 619–22.

5. AP, "Gen. McNair Calls for Replacement of 'Weak' Officers," *Evening Star* (Washington, D.C.), September 30, 1941, 2.

6. Hanson W. Baldwin, "War Games Bare Laxity in Discipline," *New York Times*, October 1, 1941, 4.
7. "General Payne Is Relieved of Command," *Hartford Courant*, October 4, 1941, 1.
8. Stimson and Bundy, *On Active Service*, vol. 2, 351.
9. James J. Cooke, *Pershing and His Generals: Command and Staff in the AEF* (Westport, Conn.: Praeger, 1997), 67; Merwin H. Browne, "Army Moving to Get Streamlined Command," *Sun Magazine*, November 2, 1941, SM13.
10. "Army Replaces Many Combat Officers; Hundreds More to Go," *Washington Post*, October 15, 1941, 1.
11. Pogue, *Ordeal and Hope*, 93.
12. Letter from Marshall to General Hugh Drum, October 27, 1941, George C. Marshall Papers, Pentagon Office Collection, Selected Materials, George C. Marshall Research Library, Lexington, Va.
13. Gene R. Casey, "3 Colonels Relieved for Age; Juniors Get Chance," *Boston Globe*, October 6, 1941, 1.
14. "Reports Powell Relieved of Post," *New York Times*, October 9, 1941, 12.
15. Richard W. Stewart, "The Red Bull Division: The Training and Initial Engagements of the 34th Infantry Division, 1941–43," *Army History* (Winter 1993): 4.
16. "Morale up to People," *Kansas City Star*, October 6, 1941, 6.
17. Pogue, *Ordeal and Hope*, 100.
18. John J. Pershing Papers, General Correspondence, Library of Congress, Washington, D.C.
19. *GCM Papers*, 396: *"We Cannot Delay," July 1, 1939-December 6, 1941*, 648–49.
20. *New York Times*, October 16, 1941, 11.
21. Richard L. Stokes, "Historic Role of the National Guard Feeds under Merger Method," *Kansas City Star*, November 11, 1941, 16.
22. Quotation directly from Pogue, *Ordeal and Hope*, 100.
23. Ricks, *The Generals*, 35.
24. Drew Pearson and Robert S. Allen, "Washington Merry-Go-Round," *Washington Post*, October 22, 1941; Arthur C. Wimer, "Zone Stand Undisclosed by Maloney," *Hartford Courant*, October 26, 1941, 2.
25. H. G. Wells, NANA, "Wells Urges More Army Efficiency," *Hartford Courant*, November 16, 1941, C8.
26. Mark S. Watson, "New Type of Army Forming as Guard Fades," *Baltimore Sun*, November 12, 1941, 1. These new Replacement Training Centers where new men were to be trained did not even exist until March 1941. The name was kept through World War II, and later, as casualties mounted overseas, the word *replacement* took on added relevance.
27. Paul Mallon, "News behind the News," *Greensboro (N.C.) Record*, November 29, 1941, 6.

CHAPTER 12

1. Damon Runyon, "War Games Are Befuddling," *Columbus (Ohio) Dispatch*, September 19, 1941, 23.
2. John Mason Potter, "Army Horse Gives Hoss-Laff to Critics during

Maneuvers," *Boston Globe*, October 24, 1941, 20; Mark S. Watson, "Cavalrymen Glum at Prospect of Horse vs. Motor Maneuvers," *Baltimore Sun*, October 30, 1941, 13.

3. Eric Sevareid Papers, 1909–1993, MSS39495, Manuscript Division, Box 1: D1 Reel 5, script for CBS Radio broadcast, November 18, 1941, Library of Congress, Washington, D.C.

4. Houston, *Hell on Wheels: The 2d Armored Division* (San Rafael, Calif.: Presidio Press, 1986, 1977), 91.

5. "Noted Names Found on Roster of the Twenty-Sixth Infantry," *Baltimore Sun*, October 15, 1941, 24.

6. Don Whitehead, "Diary of a Correspondent at the Carolina Maneuvers," *Springfield Republican*, November 7, 1941, 6.

7. Felix R. McKnight, "U.S. Army Morale Is Ready for Conflict," *Dallas Morning News*, October 29, 1941, 4.

8. Edward T. Folliard, "Selectees Renege on Threats to Go Over the Hill—Too Busy!" *Washington Post*, November 6, 1941, 1; Joseph C. Harsch, "Problems of Army Morale: Aims and Appreciation," *Christian Science Monitor*, September 30, 1941, 1. One of the rare later references to the OHIO movement would come in 1948, when a *Washington Post* editorial argued against allowing Communists to participate in the draft: "It would be folly to attribute such moves as the 'over the hill in October' campaign of 1941 or the premature demobilization clamor of 1945–6 solely to the Communists. But certainly they were quick to capitalize on soldier demoralization and twist it to their ends." This assertion was published without any proof. The exact origin of the OHIO movement is still unknown.

9. *The Papers of George Catlett Marshall*, ed. Larry I. Bland, Sharon Ritenour Stevens, and Clarence E. Wunderlin Jr. (Lexington, Va.: George C. Marshall Foundation, 1981–). *"We Cannot Delay," July 1, 1939–December 6, 1941* (Baltimore and London: Johns Hopkins University Press, 1986), 667–668.

10. "U.S.O.'s Agents Blaze Comfort Trail for Army," *New York Herald Tribune*, October 5, 1941, 33.

11. "Soldier's Soul Not First Thing to Go After," *Dallas Morning News*, October 10, 1941, 1.

12. Donald Houston, *Hell on Wheels: The 2d Armored Division* (Novato, Calif.: Presidio Press, 1995). *Times-Picayune*, November 18, 1941, 2. Other newspapers citing this story: *Miami Herald*, November 23, 1941, 48; Harold W. Carlisle, *Columbus (Ohio) Dispatch*, November 25, 1941, 17. This led to a new round of articles and headlines, such as: "Head of Carolina Maneuvers Admits Gen. Drum's Capture," "General Nabbed in Maneuvers and Three-Star Capture."

13. Thaddeus Holt, "The Final Scrimmage," MHQ: Quarterly Journal of Military History 4, no. 2 (Winter 1992): http://www.historynet.com/relax-its-only-a -maneuver.htm/.

14. Gabel, *U.S. Army GHQ Maneuvers of 1941*, 148.

15. Marshall Andrews, "Tank Methods in War Games Ruled Sound," *Washington Post*, November 25, 1941, 34.

16. Photo caption, *Stanford (Calif.) Daily Advocate*, November 19, 1941, 5; Van R. Mayhall, *Cranking Up a Fine War: A Louisiana Soldier from Boot Camp to General's Aide* (Austin, Tex.: ByrenLee Press, 1999), 23.

17. Perkins and Rogers, *Roll Again*, 82.

18. Lewis B. Sebring Jr., "Troops in Field Feast Today on Army Turkeys," *New York Herald Tribune*, November 23, 1941, 19.

19. N. T. Kenny, "Troops in Carolinas Prepare for Final Week of Maneuvers," *Baltimore Sun*, November 23, 1941, 20.

20. "Enough Gasoline for Trip to Sun in Autos for Carolina Maneuvers," *Christian Science Monitor*, October 17, 1941, 8.

21. AP, "Four Soldiers Burned to Death in Carolina," *Daily Herald* (Arlington Heights, Illinois), November 10, 1941, 10, Major Jeffrey W. Decker, "Logistics and Patton's Third Army: Lessons for Today's Logistician," *Air and Space Power Journal*, published online, March 20, 2003; archived by Air University, https://www.airuniversity.af.edu/Portals/10/ASPJ/journals/Chronicles/decker.pdf.

22. "Died for Country," *Miami Herald*, November 25, 1941, 7.

23. Eric Sevareid Papers, Box 1: D1 Reel 5, radio script; UP, "Lodge Suggests U.S. Infantry Ride in Future," *Greenville (S.C.) News*, November 27, 1941, 6.

24. Walter Lippmann, "Notes on the Carolina Maneuvers," *Washington Post*, November 20, 1941, 15.

25. Frederick Palmer, NANA, "Carolina Maneuvers Show Our Army Has Improved," *Evansville (Ill.) Courier and Press*, November 25, 1941, 6.

26. AP, "Parachutists Make Effective Attack in Carolina Battle Maneuvers," *Springfield (Mass.) Republican*, November 27, 1941, 1.

27. C. Lincoln Christensen, "The 1941 Carolina Maneuvers Found America Unprepared for a World Conflict," *World War II* 16, no. 6 (February 2002).

28. AP, Rice Yahner, "Fourth Corps Jammed into Large Funnel," *Greenville (S.C.) News*, November 28, 1941, 1.

29. AP, A. F. Littlejohn, "Bitter Mock War Wages in Carolinas," *Sacramento Bee*, November 28, 1941, 6; AP, A. F. Littlejohn, "'Cease Firing' Order Issued for War Games, *Greenville (S.C.) News*, November 29, 1941, 1.

30. David B. Christensen, "The 1941 Carolina Maneuvers, "Light Tank M3 Stuart," *Tank Encyclopedia*, November 28, 2014, http://www.tanks-encyclopedia .com/ww2/US/M3_stuart.php.

31. Pogue, *Ordeal and Hope*, 208; GCM Papers, Interviews and Reminiscences for Forrest C. Pogue, "Tape 18—Marshall Plan; lessons of World War I; reforming the Infantry School, 1927–32, Patton," 547, George C. Marshall Research Foundation: http://marshallfoundation.org/library/digital-archive/tape-18-marshall-plan-lessons-world-war-reforming-infantry-school-1927-32-patton/.

32. Ladislas Farago, *Patton: Ordeal and Triumph* (New York: Ivan Obolensky, 1963), 163–65; D'Este, *Patton: Genius for War*, 395–96.

33. W. W. Chaplin, INS, "Maneuvers Pave Roads with Gold," *Detroit Times*, November 29, 1941, 20.

34. "No Lost Battalions," *Augusta (Ga.) Chronicle*, November 28, 1941, 6. The popular romantic and largely fictional notion of a lost battalion wandering for

days behind enemy lines and finally fighting its way back to safety was now seen as a reason for rebuke and a display of stupidity. As the editorial cited above put it, "His ability to read maps and keep from getting lost is just another of the reasons why the American soldier is the best in the world."

35. Mary Hornaday, "Morale on the Home Front," *Christian Science Monitor*, November 27, 1941, 13.

36. Sevareid, *Not So Wild a Dream*, 203.

37. Eric Sevareid Papers, Box 1: D1 Reel 5, script for his CBS Radio broadcast, November 26, 1941.

38. "Next: Airports That Can Be Built in Only Two Days," *Repository*, December 12, 1941, 22; Richard K. Smith, "Marston Mat," *Air Force* April 1989, 104ff.

39. Larry Munnikuysen, "Early Army Respirators," *Journal of the Company of Military Historians* 58, no. 3 (Fall 2006): 1.

40. AP, "Maneuvers Show American Troops Not Ready for Warfare, McNair Declares," *Greensboro (N.C.) Daily News*, December 1, 1941, 1.

41. Thaddeus Holt, "The Final Scrimmage," MHQ: Quarterly Journal of Military History 4, no. 2 (Winter 1992): http://www.historynet.com/relax-its-only-a-maneuver.htm/.

42. Jack Womer and Stephen C. DeVito, *Fighting with the Filthy Thirteen* (Philadelphia: Casemate, 2012), 55.

43. Ibid., 57.

44. "Toughen in Field—with Grin and Camera," *Kansas City Star*, September 21, 1941.

45. The map was produced by Private Boyd C. Mutschler and titled "The Grand Maneuvers of 1941 Where the First Armored Division Solved Important Problems Pertaining to War"; *Army Laughs*, December 1941; cover.

46. Park Kendall, *Gone with the Draft: Love Letters of a Trainee* (New York: Grosset and Dunlap, 1941), 107.

47. Jack Stinnett, "Army Humor Goes on and on Forever," *Repository*, September 9, 1941, 4.

48. May Tinée, "Training Camp Comedy Year's Funniest Film," *Chicago Tribune*, December 8, 1941, 25.

49. Garth Jowett, ed., *Readings in Propaganda and Persuasion: New and Classic Essays* (Thousand Oaks, Calif.: Sage Publications, 2006), 17.

50. Mark Harris, *Five Came Back: A Story of Hollywood and the Second World War* (New York: Penguin Press, 2014), 113.

51. Cole, *Senator Gerald P. Nye*, 186.

52. UP, "Wilke Blasts Senators," *San Francisco Chronicle*, September 11, 1941.

53. "Santa Visits Army Early—800,000 to Get Yule Furloughs," *Washington Post*, November 21, 1941, 13.

54. Merle Miller, "The Red One," *Yank*, May 25, 1945, 2–5. This interview was given when Bloom's unit was fighting in Germany. General Roosevelt had died the previous summer in France. Merle Miller went on to become a major writer and compiler of best-selling biographies of Harry Truman, Lyndon Johnson, and Dwight D. Eisenhower.

55. Houston, *Hell on Wheels*, 1995, 101.

56. Omar Bradley, *A General's Life: An Autobiography* (New York: Simon and Schuster, 1983), 99.

57. "Devens Negro Unit Not to Take Part in N.C. Maneuvers," *Boston Globe*, October 3, 1941, 16; "First Army Goes South with All Units Except Crack Negro Outfit," *New York Amsterdam News*, October 11, 1941, 1.

58. Ollie Stewart, "366th Has 134 Colored Officers," *Baltimore Afro-American*, September 13, 1941, 1; "Bar Race Troops from War Games," *Chicago Defender*, October 11, 1941, 1.

CHAPTER 13

1. "Topics of Sermons That Will Be Heard in the Churches of the City Tomorrow," *New York Times*, December 6, 1941, 11. A Gallup poll released the previous week concluded that for most Americans, Sunday was a time of spiritual escape—of peace and comfort away from the storms of life.

2. S. L. Price, "The Second World War Kicks Off: December 7 1941 Redskins Versus Eagles on Pearl Harbor Day," *Sports Illustrated*, November 29, 1999.

3. "U.S. at War! Japan Bombs Hawaii, Manila," *Washington Post Extra*, December 7, 1941, 1.

4. K. D. Richardson, *Reflections of Pearl Harbor: An Oral History of December 7, 1941* (Westport, Conn.: Praeger, 2005), 149.

5. Jay G. Hayden, NANA, "Peace Means Revolution for Japan," *Evening Star* (Washington, D.C.), December 12, 1941, 14.

6. Marc Wortman, *1941: Fighting the Shadow War; A Divided America in a World at War* (New York: Atlantic Monthly Press, 2016), 226.

7. Katherine Marshall, *Together*, 99.

8. Roger Burlingame, *Don't Let Them Scare You: The Life and Times of Elmer Davis* (Philadelphia: Lippincott, 1961), 179.

9. Jonathan Daniels, *The Time Between the Wars* (New York: Doubleday, 1966), 338.

10. Mauldin, *Brass Ring*, 113; Starr Smith, *Jimmy Stewart: Bomber Pilot* (Saint Paul, Minneapolis, Minn.: Zenith Press, 2006), 15; Carl M. Cannon, "When Jimmy Stewart Went to War," *Real Clear Politics*, December 8, 2015, https://www.realclearpolitics.com/articles/2015/12/08/when_jimmy_stewart_went_to_war_128972.html.

11. Andrew A. Rooney, *My War* (New York: Public Affairs, 2000), 28; Nigel Hamilton, *JFK, Reckless Youth* (New York: Random House, 1992), 424–25.

12. Hank Greenberg, with Ira Berkow, *The Story of My Life* (Chicago: Ivan Dee Publishers, 2001), 142; UP, "Hank Greenberg to Re-Enter Army," *Knoxville News-Sentinel*, December 10, 1941, 13.

13. Harrison E. Salisbury, *A Journey for Our Times: A Memoir* (New York: Harper and Row, 1983), 152.

14. Dwight D. Eisenhower, *Crusade in Europe: A Personal Account of World War II* (Garden City, N.Y.: Doubleday, 1948), 13–14.

15. Ruth Ellen Patton Totten, *The Button Box: A Daughter's Loving Memoir of Mrs. George S. Patton*, ed. James Patton Totten (Columbia, Mo.: University of Missouri Press, 2005), 323.

16. Percy L. Greaves and Bettina B. Greaves, *Pearl Harbor: The Seeds and Fruits of Infamy* (Auburn, Ala.: Ludwig von Mises Institute, 2010), 242; Dunne, *Grenville Clark*, 136.

17. Stimson and Bundy, *On Active Service*, vol. 2, 394; Hodgson, *The Colonel*, 242–43.

18. Bradley and Blair, *A General's Life*, 103.

19. Burlingame, *Don't Let Them Scare You*, 180.

20. Sevareid, *Not So Wild a Dream*, 205.

21. A myth, which persisted over time, was that these names were listed in a "little black book" that Marshall stowed in his desk. The myth was repeated in many histories and biographies; even Marshall's official biographer, Dr. Forrest C. Pogue, referenced it in the second volume of the biography. Pogue later came to realize that the little black book did not exist—at least not on paper in notebook form. The official site of the Marshall Foundation contains this explanation: "Those familiar with Marshall know that he had an incredible memory and could vividly recall past experiences and people he had met. Marshall's uncanny ability to remember details made it possible for him to keep a list of officers he was considering entirely in his mind rather than recording it in a 'little black book.' When asked about Marshall's 'little black book' Foundation staff explain that no physical 'little black book' existed and that if Marshall had kept a 'little black book' it would have only existed in his mind." "Marshall Myths: Marshall's 'Little Black Book,'" posted by "Jeffrey," December 11, 2015, George C. Marshall Foundation, https://www.marshallfoundation.org/blog/marshall-myths-marshalls-little-black-book/.

22. Hanson W. Baldwin, "The Making of the American Officer," *New York Times Magazine*, December 7, 1941, SM3.

23. Major William R. Keast, "Provision of Enlisted Replacements," Army Ground Forces, study no. 7 (Washington, D.C: Historical Section, Army Ground Forces, 1946), 1–4, https://history.army.mil/books/agf/AGF007/index.htm.

24. Lewis B. Hershey, *Selective Service in Wartime: Second Report of the Director of Selective Service, 1941–42* (Washington, D.C.: Government Printing Office, 1943), 26–27.

25. "Company, Workers Redeem Ford War Legacy; Giant Willow Run Plant Helped to Build the 'Arsenal of Democracy,'" *Automotive News*, June 15, 2003, 10.

26. Marquis W. Childs, *I Write from Washington: An Interpretation and History of Washington Since 1932* (New York: Harper and Brothers, 1942), 242.

27. E. B. Henderson, "Negro Fliers," *Washington Post*, December 7, 1941, B-6; Alan M. Osur, *Blacks in the Army Air Forces during World War II: The Problems of Race Relations*, Special Studies/Office of Air Force History, United States Air Force (Honolulu, Hawaii: University Press of the Pacific, 2005), 24.

28. Memo, "CofAC for G-3, 31 May 40, sub: Employment of Negro Personnel in Air Corps Units, G-3/6541Gen527," quoted in MacGregor, *Integration of the Armed Forces*, chap. 2.

29. Patrick S. Washburn, *A Question of Sedition: The Federal Government's Investigation of the Black Press during World War II* (New York: Oxford University Press, 1986), 57; George C. Marshall, "41.12.08 Address to the Conference of Negro Newspaper Editors," December 8, 1941, George C. Marshall

Foundation, www.marshallfoundation.org/library/41-12-08-address-to-the
-conference-of-negro-newspaper-editors.

30. Householder's exact words were invoked during the 21st-century debates on
gays in the military, when those who opposed gays argued that the Army was
not a sociological experiment.

31. Remarks of Colonel E. R. Householder at the Conference of Negro Newspaper
Representatives, Munitions Building, Washington, D.C., December 8, 1941,
National Archives and Records Administration, Records of the Office of the
Assistant Secretary of War (OASW) 1916–47, 107.

32. Neil A. Wynn, *The Afro-American and the Second World War*, 2nd ed. (New York:
Holmes and Meier, 1993), 24.

33. Charley Cherokee, "National Grapevine," *Chicago Defender*, December 20,
1941, 13.

34. "Newsmen Score War Department Policy," *Chicago Defender*, December 13,
1941, 1.

35. History, Art and Archives, U.S. House of Representatives, "Rankin, Jeannette," https://history.house.gov/People/Listing/R/RANKIN,-Jeannette
-(R000055)/.

36. UP, "Nye Says U.S. Provoked Quarrel," *Knoxville News Sentinel*, December 8,
1941, 2; Childs, *I Write from Washington*, 244.

37. Ronnie Dugger, *The Politician: The Life and Times of Lyndon Johnson; The Drive
for Power, from the Frontier to Master of the Senate* (New York: W. W. Norton,
1982), 239; Margaret Truman, *Harry S. Truman* (New York: Avon Books,
1978), 148.

38. "The Nation Mobilizes," *New York Times*, December 14, 1941, E2.

39. AP, "Volunteers Swamp Recruiting Offices Throughout Nation," *Evening Star*
(Washington, D.C.), December 9, 1941, 5; AP, "Feller Enlists in Navy after
Spending Day with Gene Tunney," *Evening Star*, December 12, 1941, 20; Wil-
liam B. Mead, *Even the Browns* (Chicago: Contemporary Books, 1978), 32.

40. Stimson and Bundy, *On Active Service*, vol. 2 , 395.

CHAPTER 14

1. Dwight D. Eisenhower, *At Ease: Stories I Tell to Friends*, 249; diary entry of
January 4, 1942, in The Eisenhower Diaries, ed. Robert H. Ferrell (New York:
W. W. Norton, 1981), 40.

2. Joseph P. Hobbs, *Dear General—Eisenhower's Wartime Letters to Marshall* (Baltimore: Johns Hopkins University Press, 1999), 1.

3. Mark Perry, *Partners in Command: George Marshall and Dwight Eisenhower in
War and Peace* (New York: Penguin Press, 2007), 12–13; David L. Roll, *George
Marshall Defender of the Republic* (New York: Dutton Caliber, 2019), 195.

4. Dan Majors, "Christmas 1941: With World at War, Churchill Joins FDR for
Washington Yule," *Pittsburgh Post-Gazette*, December 25, 2011.

5. Stanley Weintraub, *Pearl Harbor Christmas: A World at War, December 1941*
(Cambridge, Mass.: Da Capo Press, 2012), 33; David Bercuson and Holger
H. Herwig, *One Christmas in Washington: The Secret Meeting Between Roos-
evelt and Churchill That Changed the World* (Woodstock, N.Y.: Overlook Press,

2006), 112; http://www.bbc.co.uk/history/ww2peopleswar/timeline/factfiles/nonflash/a1140346.shtml.

6. Edmund G. Love, *The 27th Infantry Division in World War II* (Nashville, Tenn.: Battery, 1982), 16.

7. "O Little Town of Bethlehem," *Christian Reader*, November 2000, 66.

8. Stanley W. Weintraub, *15 Stars* (New York: Free Press, 2007), 35.

9. Letter to Pershing, January 13, 1942, Blumenson, *Patton Papers, 1940–1945*, 47.

10. Love, *The 27th Infantry Division in World War II*, 16. The New York State Military Museum maintains a complete history of the 27th in World War II: dmna.ny.gov/historic/reghist/wwii/infantry/27thInfDiv/27thInfDivMain.htm.

11. AP, "Louisiana Hands in Bill for Road Damage by Army," *Chicago Tribune*, January 1, 1942, 19. Several books, including Carlo D'Este's biography of Patton *(Patton: A Genius for War)*, and several internet sites devoted to the Desert Training Center claim that Patton delivered a speech to his staff in January in which he said: "The war in Europe is over for us. England will probably fall this year. Our first chance to get at the enemy will be in North Africa. We cannot train troops to fight in the desert of North Africa by training in the swamps of Georgia. I sent a report to Washington requesting a desert training center in California. The California desert can kill quicker than the enemy. We will lose a lot of men from the heat, but training will save hundreds of lives when we get into combat. I want every officer and section to start planning on moving all our troops by rail to California." This quotation is suspect and is possibly a function of poor memory on the part of the author. The books and web pages that contain the quote either do not reference the source or attribute it to Porter B. Williamson, *General Patton's Principles for Life and Leadership*, 5th ed. (Tucson, Ariz.: Management and Systems Consultants, 1979), 30. Williamson did serve with Patton and presents a number of quotations that he attributes to Patton. Neither this particular thought about Britain nor the bizarre suggestion that Patton predicted its fall before the end of 1942 appears in Patton's papers or in any other source. To openly predict the fall of Great Britain while Churchill was still in the United States would have been a major issue in the eyes of many, including Marshall, Stimson, and Roosevelt.

12. Letter of March 13, 1942, to General Jacob Devers, Blumenson, *Patton Papers, 1940–1945*, 60.

13. "Army to Train Air Infantry and Desert Fighter Forces," *Washington Post*, March 28, 1942, 3; "Army to Train Troops in Rugged West," *Chicago Tribune*, March 28, 1942, 7; "Desert Corps Is Organized," *Columbia (S.C.) Record*, April 1, 1942, 2. The Army press release said in part: "The region is known for its healthful climate and many nationally known resorts are nearby." The actual number of citizens one could find in this neighborhood could be counted on one's fingers. In fact, when he went west to map out the area in which he would train his men, Patton traveled for four days without encountering another human being. Before the end of his press conference, Stimson said that the area in question was nothing at all like the place the Army had described in a "slightly lyrical" press release issued the day before, which made it sound a little like

Palm Beach. Even though Palm Springs was then about an hour drive from the spot, Stimson actually mentioned Palm Beach, Florida.

14. Gladwin Hill, "Desert Troops Train in California's 'Little Libya,'" *Christian Science Monitor*, May 7, 1942, 13. Hill would later become one of the best-known reporters of the *New York Times*, where he worked for 44 years.

15. GCM Papers, *"The Right Man for the Job," December 7, 1941–May 31, 1943*, 165; see also "Marshall and the *Stars and Stripes*," posted by "csonnier," April 21, 2017, George C. Marshall Foundation, https://www.marshallfoundation. org/blog/marshall-stars-stripes; John J. Pershing, *My Experiences in the World War*, 2 vols. (New York: Frederick A. Stokes Company, 1931, vol. 1), 318.

16. AP, John A. Moroso III, "Convoy Beats Subs, 'Pushes Periscopes Down' on Crossing," *Richmond (Va.) Times-Dispatch*, May 19, 1942, 1.

17. See *Chicago Tribune*, May 19, 1942, 1.

18. "Allies Put on Big 'War' in Northern Ireland," *New York Times*, July 10, 1942, 4; "Ernie Pyle 'Going Places,'" *Evansville (Ill.) Press*, August 10, 1942, 6.

19. Cray, *General of the Army*, 135.

20. Blumenson, *Patton Papers, 1940–1945*, 61.

21. Gene Amole, "Recent Heat Wave Can't Compare to Sauna of '42," *Rocky Mountain News* (Denver, Colo.), July 23, 1998, 6A.

22. Weldon F. Heald, "With Patton on Desert Maneuvers," *Desert*, July 1960, 6–7ff. Deaths were reported in: George W. Howard, "The Desert Training Center/California-Arizona Maneuver Area," *Journal of Arizona History* 26, no. 3 (Autumn 1985): 273–94. The death toll from dehydration was not known at the time and became public only well after the war. Howard's primary source was Roger W. Hubbard's "An Analysis of Current Doctrine in Use for the Prevention and Treatment of Heat Casualties Resulting from Operation in the Heat," U.S. Army Research Institute of Environmental Medicine, October 1978. There are references on the World Wide Web that as many as 200 died at the Desert Training Center, but this resulted from an improper reading of the Heald article, which says the Army had files on 198 soldiers who died from heatstroke in the United States.

23. Hubert Essame, *Patton: A Study in Command* (New York: Scribner, 1974), 39.

24. Bill Davidson, "Desert Warfare: America Trains a New Kind of Army," *Yank*, September 23, 1942, 5.

25. "Historic California Posts, Camps, Stations and Airfields: California/Arizona Maneuver Area (Desert Training Center)," State Military Museums, California Military Department, updated June 23, 2017, http://www.militarymuseum.org/ CAMA.html.

26. UP, "U.S. Armored Corps Ends Training in California," *Greensboro (N.C.) Daily News*, May 7, 1942.

27. John S. Lynch, *Patton's Desert Training Center* (Fort Myer, Va.: Council on America's Military Past, 1986), 17–22.

28. AP, William F. Boni, "Army to Test New K-2 Ration Kit in Desert," *Washington Post*, August 29, 1942, B5.

29. AP, William F. Boni, "California Desert Toughens Fighting Men for Uncle Sam," *Baltimore Sun*, August 24, 1942, 2.

30. UP, William C. Fayette, "Heat Fails to Down Tank Corps at Indio," *Riverside (Calif.) Daily Press*, August 25, 1942, 7.

31. Hershey, *Selective Service in Wartime: Second Report*, 293.

32. James G. Thompson, letter to the editor, *Pittsburgh Courier*, January 31, 1942; reprinted April 11, 1942, 5.

33. Albert D. Hughes, "Pilots, Pilots, Pilots—Yet More Are Needed," *Christian Science Monitor*, May 15, 1942, 13.

34. Dean McGowen, "Joe Louis, 66, Heavyweight King Who Reigned 12 Years, Is Dead," *New York Times*, April 13, 1981.

35. Official Navy History site: https://www.history.navy.mil/research/histories/biographies-list/bios-m/miller-doris.html.

36. Buckley, *American Patriots*, 275.

37. Dwight D. Eisenhower, *Eisenhower's Own Story of the War: The Complete Report by the Supreme Commander, General Dwight D. Eisenhower, on the War in Europe from the Day of Invasion to the Day of Victory* (New York: Arco Publishing, 1946), 1.

38. Robert E. Sherwood, *Roosevelt and Hopkins: An Intimate History*, rev. ed. (New York: Harper, 1948), 615. Sherwood wrote of the decision: "Roosevelt . . . insisted that the decision had been made and must be carried through with expedition and vigor."

39. Orr Kelly, *Meeting the Fox: The Allied Invasion of Africa, from Operation Torch to Kasserine Pass to Victory in Tunisia* (New York: Wiley, 2002), 12.

40. James Holland, *The Allies Strike Back, 1941–1943*, The War in the West, vol. 2 (New York: Atlantic Monthly Press, 2017), 279.

41. Blumenson, *Patton Papers, 1940–1945*, 82–83.

42. "Army to Stress Task Forces in New Maneuvers," *Chicago Tribune*, May 15, 1942, 7.

43. AP, "Tanks Undergo Extensive Tests," *Baton Rouge State Times Advocate*, September 10, 1942, 16.

44. Hanson W. Baldwin, "Third Army Troops Win High Praise," *New York Times*, August 20, 1942, 12.

45. Meredith Hindley, *Destination Casablanca: Exile, Espionage, and the Battle for North Africa in World War II* (New York: PublicAffairs, 2017), 215.

46. Eric Ethier, "Into Africa," *America in WWII*, December 2007, 28ff; Blumenson, *Patton Papers, 1940–1945*, 108.

47. "World: A Misunderstanding Ends," *Time*, November 23, 1942.

48. AP, Don Whitehead, "Might of U.S. Forces Seen after First Year in this War," *Richmond (Va.) Times-Dispatch*, December 6, 1942, 1.

49. AP, "394 Jap Ships Lost in Pacific War to 86 American Vessels," *Evening Star*, December 7, 1942, 3; UP, "Repair Crews Share Glory With Pearl Harbor Heroes," *San Diego Union*, December 7, 1942, 22.

50. Hershey, *Selective Service in Wartime: Second Report*, 10–19.

51. Marshall Andrews, "American Soldier Now Ready, Willing, Able: The U.S. Army Measures Up to Global War," *Washington Post*, December 6, 1942, B-3.

52. Keith Huxen, "The Battle of Kasserine Pass," February 5, 2018, National World War II Museum: https://www.nationalww2museum.org/war/articles/battle-kasserine-pass. Huxen serves as the senior director of research and history

in the Institute for the Study of War and Democracy at the museum in New Orleans.

53. UP, "U.S. Army Will Quit High Desert Camps," *Sacramento Bee*, April 29, 1944, 21; AP, "Soldiers Lost in Desert, 3 Die," *Fort Worth Star-Telegram*, July 28, 1943, 9.

54. Woody McMillin, *In the Presence of Soldiers: The 2nd Army Maneuvers and Other World War II Activity in Tennessee* (Nashville, Tenn.: Horton Heights Press, 2010), 426.

55. E. W. Baker, "U.S. Army Will Permit Press to Witness Louisiana Maneuvers," *Pittsburgh Courier*, May 1, 1943, 14.

56. "Officer Praises 442nd Team for Spirit, Efficiency in Italy," *Minidoka Irrigator*, October 7, 1944, 1. This story was well distributed; the reference here is from a weekly newspaper published at the Minidoka War Relocation Center in Hunt, Idaho.

57. Bob Bearden, *To D-Day and Back: Adventures with the 507th Parachute Infantry Regiment and Life as a World War II POW* (Saint Paul, Minn.: Zenith Press, 2007), 48.

58. "Herb Caen, "It's News to Me," *San Francisco Chronicle*, November 15, 1943, 7.

59. Love, *The 27th Infantry Division in World War II*, 13.

60. Mark Perry, "The Greatest War Games," *Military History* (February–March 2009).

61. "Fund-raiser Recalls Patton's Feast," *Times-Picayune*, July 29, 2001.

62. Sue Odom Oliver, "Witness to Live War Games," *America in WWII*, October, 2012, 4.

63. Robert Strunsky and Paul M. Hollister, eds., *From D-Day through Victory in Europe: The Eye-Witness Story as Told by War Correspondents on the Air* (New York: Columbia Broadcasting System, 1945), 249.

CHAPTER 15

1. Mark Skinner Watson, *Chief of Staff: Prewar Plans and Preparations*. U.S. Army in World War II. Washington, D.C.: Historical Division, Department of the Army, 1950, 192.

2. Fischer, "Omar Nelson Bradley," 186; Bradley and Blair, *A General's Life*, 97.

3. John Wagner, "In Memoriam: General John W. Vessey, Jr., USA," *Joint Force Quarterly* (April 2017).

4. "Lesson of the Marshall Era," *Life*, November 2, 1959, 26.

5. Mark Clark, "Remarks on CCC by General Mark Clark, the Citadel, Charleston, S.C., October 31, 1980," in the *National Association of Civilian Conservation Corps Alumni (NACCCA) Chapter 5 News-Bulletin* (Seattle), December 2000.

6. Perret, *There's a War to Be Won*, 463.

7. Frank Capra, *The Name above the Title* (New York: Macmillan, 1971), 327.

8. Perret, *There's a War to Be Won*, 473; see also "Marshall and the *Why We Fight* Films," posted by "csonnier," October 26, 2018 (originally published November 28, 2014), George C. Marshall Foundation, https://www.marshallfoundation.org/blog/marshall-and-the-why-we-fight-films/.

9. Princeton website on VFW, https://etcweb.princeton.edu/CampusWWW/Companion/veterams_future_wars.html.

10. Dwight D. Eisenhower, *Crusade in Europe: A Personal Account of World War II* (Baltimore: Johns Hopkins University Press, 1997), 11–12.

11. NEA, Ernie Deane, "The Way It Seems to Me," *Mexia (Tex.) Daily News*, June 5, 1952, 1.

12. Pogue, *Ordeal and Hope*, 89.

13. H. Paul Jeffers, *Taking Command: General J. Lawton Collins From Guadalcanal to Utah Beach and Victory in Europe* (New York: Dutton Calibre, 2009).

14. Don M. Ewing, "Night March in Louisiana Beat Germans at the Bulge," *Shreveport Times*, March 2, 1945, 2.

15. AP, Don M. Ewing, "Patton Trick of 1941 Aids Him in Belgium," *Columbia (S.C.) Record*, March 3, 1945, 14. "Patton's Nocturnal Dashes on Maneuvers Are Paying Off Now," *Fort Worth Star-Telegram*, March 4, 1945, 2.

16. John Andrew Prime, "Christmas a Bittersweet Time for Shreveporter," *Shreveport Times*, December 25, 2002, B5. After a long career as a journalist, Ewing died in 1978 at age 83.

17. Kenneth Macksey, *Tank Warfare: A History of Tanks in Battle* (London: Rupert Hart–Davis, 1971), 134.

18. "Lessons Learned from Louisiana War Maneuvers," *Arkansas Gazette*, October 4, 1941, 4.

19. UP, Leon Kay, "Tank Attack Can Be Routed," *Charleston (S.C.) Evening Post*, September 20, 1941, 14.

20. George Edwin Patrick Murray, "The Louisiana Maneuvers, September, 1941: Practice for War," master's thesis, Kansas State University, 1972, 41.

21. Christopher R. Gabel, "The 1941 Maneuvers: What Did They Really Accomplish?" *Army History*, April 1990, 5–7.

22. "William T. Piper, Who Developed the Cub, Dead," *New York Times*, January 17, 1970, 31.

23. Murray, 36.

24. Keith Matheny, "Special Report: Battle Ready," *Desert Sun*, [Palm Springs, Calif.], November 11, 2007, A-1.

25. "Lt. Gen. McNair Killed in Action in U.S. Offensive in Normandy," *New York Herald Tribune*, July 28, 1944, 1A.

26. "'Yoo-Hoos' for Lear as He Leaves Ship," *New York Times*, July 20, 1945, 24. Some of the Lear obituaries seemed to be written in order to bring humiliation to Lear's life via the "yoo-hoo" incident rather than give proper weight to his role in World War II. A particularly sad and one-sided example came in a UPI obituary published in the *Washington Post* (November 2, 1966, B-5), which devoted ten paragraphs to the "yoo-hoo" incident and one sentence to WWII.

27. Barbara Wertheim Tuchman, *Stilwell and the American Experience in China, 1911–45* (New York: Macmillan, 1971), 241.

28. Walter Krueger, *From Down Under to Nippon: The Story of the 6th Army in World War II* (Washington, D.C.: Government Printing Office, 1953), 5.

29. Interview with Forrest Pogue, June 28, 1962, cited in Ricks, *The Generals*, 34.

30. U.S. Senate Featured Biography: Henry Cabot Lodge Jr.: https://www.senate .gov/artandhistory/history/common/generic/Featured_Bio_LodgeHenry CabotJr.htm.

31. Ed Holden, "Cabot Lodge Is Bringing Own Peace to UN," *New York Daily News*, December 28, 1952, 56.

32. Gerard, *Secret Soldiers*, 1.

33. "First Draftee Low on Points," *Springfield (Mass.) Republican*, May 17, 1945, 13.

34. Buckley, *American Patriots*, 275.

35. Obituary for Dr. Norris H. Perkins II from the *Oregonian* from Genealogy Bank.com, https://www.genealogybank.com/doc/obituaries/obit/1274EC6396094BE0-1274EC6396094BE0.

36. "Marty Snyder, Restaurateur, Eisenhower's Mess Sergeant," obituary, *New York Times*, July 2, 1974, 38: Marty Snyder, *My Friend Ike* (New York: Frederick Fell, 1956), 98.

37. See Jack Womer and Stephen C. DeVito, *Fighting with the Filthy Thirteen*, (Philadelphia: Casemate, 2012); see also Leo Shane III, "'Filthy Thirteen' Veterans Recount Their Antics during WWII," *Stars and Stripes*, November 10, 2008, https://www.stripes.com/news/filthy-thirteen-veterans-recount-their-antics-during-wwii-1.85075.

38. James Holland, *Big Week: Smashing the Luftwaffe, February 1944* (New York: Atlantic Monthly, 2018), 343–44; Warren E. Thompson, "Mr. Stewart goes to Vietnam," *Vietnam*, August 2009, 39. Stewart died in 1997 at age 89.

39. Stephen Plotkin, "Sixty Years Later, the Story of PT-109 Still Captivates," *Prologue* 35, no. 2 (Summer 2003). The official U.S. Navy report on the sinking of *PT-109* was written by Lieutenant (later supreme court justice) Byron White.

40. "Joe and Hank Put 'Em on the Line," *Our Army*, April 1942, 8.

41. Sam Greene, "Hank Breaks in Again with a Bang," *Sporting News*, July 5, 1945, 2.

42. Richard Sassaman, "Bob Hope and the Road to GI Joe," *America in World War II*, October 2007, http://www.americainwwii.com/articles/bob-hope-and-the-road-to-gi-joe/.

43. John Steinbeck, "Steinbeck Says Bob Hope Rates Recognition for Service in the War," *New York Herald Tribune*, July 26, 1943. This article was syndicated to a number of other newspapers, giving it extra impact.

44. Patrick J. Dickson, "Cartoonist Bill Mauldin, Friend of GIs as Creator of 'Willie and Joe,' Dies at 81," *Stars and Stripes*, January 23, 2003, 1.

45. From "Marshall and the *Stars and Stripes*," April 21, 2017, George C. Marshall Foundation, https://www.marshallfoundation.org/blog/marshall-stars-stripes.

46. Sergeant Leonard Sansone, *The Wolf* (New York: United Publishers, 1945), iii.

47. Perret, *There's a War to Be Won*, 467; 1; Gabel, "George Catlett Marshall," 55.

48. The isolationists driven from Congress by voters were Bennett Champ Clark of Missouri, Gerald P. Nye of North Dakota, Burton K. Wheeler of Montana, Henrick Shipstead of Minnesota, and Hamilton Fish Jr. of New York. Leonard Mosley, *Lindbergh: A Biography* (Garden City, N.Y.: Doubleday, 1976), 339; Burlingame, *Don't Let Them Scare You*, 180.

49. Frank McNaughton, "Sam Rayburn: Speaker of the House," *Time*, September 27, 1943.

50. Thomas H. Eliot, "Did We Almost Lose the Army?" *New York Times*, August 12, 1991, A-15; James V. Symington, "The Vote That Saved the Army in the Days after Pearl Harbor," *New York Times*, September 1, 1991, E10. Symington, who was a member of the House for many years, was Wadsworth's grandson and presumably the source of Marshall's remark.

51. George Q. Flynn, *Conscription and Democracy: The Draft in France, Great Britain, and the United States* (Westport, Conn.: Greenwood Press, 2002), 230; Flynn, *The Draft*, 49–50. This error was even made by many important historians after the war, including Samuel Eliot Morison and Barbara Tuchman and Robert Caro. (Thomas H. Eliot; To the Editor, The American Historical Review, Volume 90, Issue 1, 1 February 1985, Pages 271–272; (*The Oxford History of the American People*, 999) (*The March of Folly*, 31), Robert A. Caro, A Path to Power Vol. I *the Years of Lyndon Johnson* (New York: Alfred A. Knopf, 1982), 595.)

52. Senate, Hearings before the Committee on Armed Services, *Universal Military Training*, 80th Cong., 2d sess., July 26, 1948, 688.

53. Margaret Dornfeld, *The Turning Tide: From the Desegregation of the Armed Forces to the Montgomery Bus Boycott (1948–1956)* (New York: Chelsea House, 1995), 20.

54. Republican Party Platforms, "Republican Party Platform of 1948," June 21, 1948, online by Gerhard Peters and John T. Woolley, *The American Presidency Project*, https://www.presidency.ucsb.edu/node/273392.

55. "Crisis in the Making," *Newsweek*, June 7, 1948, 28–29.

56. Democratic Party Platforms, "1948 Democratic Party Platform," July 12, 1948, online by Gerhard Peters and John T. Woolley, *The American Presidency Project*, https://www.presidency.ucsb.edu/node/273225.

57. "Grandstand Play," Cleveland *Plain Dealer*, July 28, 1948, 8.

58. Richard M. Dalfiume, *Desegregation of the U.S. Armed Forces: Fighting on Two Fronts, 1939–1953* (Columbia: University of Missouri Press, 1969), 173.

59. AP, "Bill Would Allow Services Volunteer Segregation Choice," *Columbus (Ga.) Daily Enquirer*, July 30, 1938, 1.

60. "Mr. Randolph Takes a Walk," *Baltimore Afro-American*, August 18, 1948, 4.

61. Drew Pearson and Robert S. Allen, "Washington Merry-Go-Round," *Miami Herald*, August 3, 1948, 6.

62. Hanson W. Baldwin, "Segregation in the Army," *New York Times*, August 8, 1948, 51; Walter C. White, letter to the editor, *New York Times*, August 17, 1948, 30.

63. President's Committee on Equality of Treatment and Opportunity in the Armed Services, *Freedom to Serve: Equality of Treatment and Opportunity in the Armed Services* (Washington, D.C.: Government Printing Office, 1950), 64; online at Harry S. Truman Presidential Library and Museum, https://www.trumanlibrary.org/civilrights/freeserv.htm.

64. Sara Neufeld, "'The Highest Standard of Democracy': Truman's Order Changed the Face of Military Leaders," *Virginian Pilot*, July 26, 1998.

65. UP, "M'Arthur Assails 'Jim Crow' in Army," *New York Times*, May 28, 1951, 3.

66. National Association for the Advancement of Colored People, *1953 Annual Report*, 38.

67. "Val Washington's 'Report to President Eisenhower,'" *Pittsburgh Courier*, August 20, 1955, 21.

68. See Alex Macaulay, "The Modern Citadel," presented at Citadel History Symposium: Marching Through Time, April 20, 2006, http://www.citadel .edu/root/history-symposium/88-info/info-home/history/2396-the-modern -period; "Gen. Mark Clark Wants Jim Crow Army?" *Chicago Defender*, May 12, 1956, 9.

69. A recording and transcript of Randolph's address can be accessed at https:// www.jacksonville.com/article/20130820/NEWS/801247969.

ACKNOWLEDGMENTS

1. Samuel Eliot Morison, *History of United States Naval Operations in World War II, Vol. II: Operations in North African Waters, October 1942–June 1943* (Boston: Little Brown and Co., 1957), 28. A full account of Clarke's remarkable career appears in his Wikipedia entry, https://en.wikipedia.org/wiki/William_P.O._Clarke.

INDEX

Abbott, Bud, 136, 273, 335
Adler, Julius Ochs, 80–81, 87–88
Adler, Mortimer J., 79
African Americans. *See also* NAACP
    as aviators, 287–88
    Brown v. Board of Education (1954), 348
    at Camp Shelby, 201, 278
    CCC and, 26–27, 35
    Double V (desegregation progress, mid-1942), 305–7, 341–42
    early integrated Army units, 128
    Executive Order 8802, 146
    Louisiana maneuvers and, 61, 201–3, 239–40
    March on Washington, 145–46, 348
    93rd "all-colored" division, 313
    94th Engineers, 201–2
    segregation of soldiers, historical perspective, 16–18
    Selective Service and desegregation, 341–49
    Selective Service and draft of, 96–99, 102, 143–47, 170, 187
    Tuskegee experiments on, 62
    Twenty-Slave Law (1862), 70
    USO camps for, 134
African theater (World War II)
    battle of Kasserine Pass, 312–13
    "Little Libya" maneuvers in California, 297–99, 302–5, 313, 323, 328
    Marshall-Stimson invasion plan, 296
    Operation Torch, 37, 308–13
Alaska, vulnerability of, 51
Aldington, Richard, 78
Alexander, John G., 89
Allen, Henry, 239
Allen, Robert S., 225, 237, 248
Ameche, Don, 102
America First Committee (AFC), 45, 83, 140–41, 170–74, 211–13
America (Jesuit magazine), 77

American Caesar (Manchester), 39
American Civil Liberties Union (ACLU), 104
American Expeditionary Force, 79
American Independence League, 77
American Institute of Public Opinion, 65–66
American Legion, 43, 55, 76, 219
American Medical Association, 118
American Military Command from World War II to Today (Ricks), 329
American Revolution, African American soldiers in, 16
American Youth Congress, 96
"America's Interest in Britain's Fleet" (Stimson), 84
Amsterdam News (Harlem), 99, 102, 103, 313
Andrews, M. Frank, 12, 63, 64
Andrews, Marshall, 92, 312
Andrews Sisters, 136
Angelo, Joe, 64
Arkansas Gazette, 206
Arkansas maneuvers, 205–7
Army, 1–22. *See also* Army Air Corps; deaths during peacetime; maneuvers and field exercises; morale; National Guard; population statistics; Second Armored Division; weapons and equipment; *individual names of camps and forts; individual names of leaders; individual names of units*
    African American soldiers segregated in (1939), 16–18 (*See also* African Americans)
    Army Corps of Engineers, 23
    Bureau of Army Public Relations inception, 191
    compensation of soldiers, 8–11, 89, 126, 138 (*See also* Civilian Conservation Corps)

Army, (*continued*)
  cooperation with other branches of
    military by, 192–93
  discipline problems, 1 32, 130, 154,
    185–86, 196–97, 235–36, 242–43
  "G.I. Joe" and G.I. Bill of Rights, 337
  lack of preparedness (1939), 4–11
  marriage by soldiers, 10, 31, 37, 118–19
  Marshall appointed chief of staff, 1–4,
    6–9, 11, 12, 15–16, 20–22
  Provisional Tank Brigade inception,
    64–65
  Replacement Training Centers, 249
  Reserve, 5, 29, 75, 110, 141–42, 244–50
  Roosevelt's and Marshall's build-up of
    (*See* Louisiana maneuvers)
  Stars and Stripes, 116, 299–300, 333, 338–39
  triangular *vs.* square divisions of, 20–22,
    49, 54, 236
  uniforms and hats of, 122, 160–61, 213
  Woodring on isolationism, 19–20
Army Air Corps
  African American aviators, 287–88
  conspicuous absence of (1939), 15
  Japanese submarine sunk by, 295
  lack of funding, 11–12, 15, 17–18
  Louisiana maneuvers and, 50, 52, 59,
    214–15, 314
  officer purge and, 209
  parachute troops/paratroopers of, 59,
    220–21, 229–30, 267, 273
  training budget cuts, 29
  Tuskegee Institute, 287, 306
Army Laughs (magazine), 271
Army Relief Society, 306
Arnold, Henry H. "Hap," 268, 287
"Assistance to the Far East" (Eisenhower),
  294
Associated Negro Press, 102
Associated Press
  on Desert Training Center, 299, 304
  on jeeps, 311
  on maneuver training, 56, 161, 223, 232,
    268
  on military disinformation, 219
  on morale, 300
  on "Phoney War," 52
  on Selective Service, 91, 108, 184
  on "shoot-on-sight" speech (Roosevelt),
    211–13
  on "Yoo-hoo!" incident, 165–66

At Ease (radio show), 315
Atlanta Constitution, 62, 85, 181
Atlanta Daily World, 203
Atlantic (magazine), 48

Baer, Buddy, 306
Baker, George, 272
Baker, Newton, 71
Baldwin, Hanson W., 222, 233, 243, 285,
  309, 331, 345–46
Baltimore Afro-American, 144–45, 201, 345
Baltimore Sun, 15, 113, 120, 180, 184, 210,
  237, 317–18, 331
Bamberger, Louis, 213
Bankhead, William B., 177
Baradinsky, Oscar, 34
Barbier, Mary Katherine, 61
Barrow, Joseph Louis, 102–3
Baruch, Bernard, 183
Baton Rouge Advocate, 200
"battle" of Tennessee. *See* Tennessee
  maneuvers
Baugh, Sammy "Slingin'," 102, 279
Baulch, Jerry, 158, 232
BBC, 211–13
Bearden, Bob, 314
Bearss, Edwin C., 105
Belgium, invasion of, 65, 80
Bell, Mildred C., 106
Bell, Robert, 106
Bennett, Donald V., 238
Benning, Fort. *See* Fort Benning
Benning method, 189
Bergen, Edgar, 135
Berlin, Irving, 296
Berman, B. H., 74
Billings, LeMoyne "Lem," 282
Bloom, Max, 276
Boni, William F., 304–5
"Bonus Army" protests, 24–33, 64
"Boogie Woogie Bugle Boy" (song), 136,
  273
Boone, Perley, 81, 85, 86
Boston Globe, 277
Boston Herald, 113
Bradley, Mary, 283
Bradley, Omar
  on Army expansion, 130–31
  CCC and, 23, 35–36, 41, 42
  on OCS, 242, 318
  on Patton, 277

Pearl Harbor attack and, 283–84, 285
Selective Service and, 118, 189, 345–46
Brees, Herbert J., 58–59
Breger, Dave, 272, 337
Brotherhood of Sleeping Car Porters, 97–99
Browder, Earl, 140
Brown, J. A., 203
Brown v. Board of Education (1954), 348
Buck Privates (film), 136, 273
Buick Motor Company, 121
Bulge, battle of the, 323–24, 333
Bullitt, William, 1
Bull Run (Manassas) maneuvers (1939), 12–16, 149
Burke, Edward R., 84–85
Burke-Wadsworth bill (Selective Training and Service Act of 1940), 84–86, 96. *See also* Selective Service System
Burley, Dan, 313
Burlingame, Roger, 284
Burner, David, 28
Butler, Smedley, 44
Byrd, Richard E., 182
Byrnes, James, 82

Caen, Herb, 314
California
    "Little Libya" maneuvers in, 297–99, 302–5, 313, 323, 328
    maneuvers and exercises (1941) in, 207–8
Camp Lafayette, 38–39
Camp Murray, 130
Camp Newspaper Service (CNS), 339
Camp Shelby, 132, 201, 278
Canada, World War II entrance of, 19
Caniff, Milt, 339
Capra, Frank, 274, 320–21
Capstaff, Albert, 134–35
Carcamo, Cindy, 327
Carolinas maneuvers (1941), 251–78
    African Americans serving in, 277–78
    discharge of older draftees following, 276–77
    extension of service and, 168
    first phase of, 256–62
    G.I. culture resulting from, 271–75, 337–39
    officer purge and, 245, 247–48
    preparation for, 149, 251–55

public opinion and press coverage of, 266–69
    review of, 269–70
    second phase of, 262–63
    USO and, 255–56
    weapons used for, 264–65
cartoons and cartoonists, 41, 117, 120, 127, 136–37, 240, 337–39
Casablanca, Operation Torch and, 310
Castle, William, 140–41
Caught in the Draft (film), 135, 273
CBS, 5, 94, 170, 198, 216, 281. *See also* Sevareid, Eric
CCC. *See* Civilian Conservation Corps (CCC, "Tree Army")
celebrity draftees/enlistees, 102–3, 114–17, 158, 161, 287–88, 306, 333–35, 338. *See also individual names*
Chaffee, Adna R., Jr., 63, 64, 66, 151
Chamberlain, Neville, 52, 56
Chaney, Lon, Jr., 102
Chaplains of Future Wars, 74
Chaplin, Charlie, 274
Cherokee, Charley, 187, 203, 288
Chicago Daily News, 84
Chicago Defender, 61, 146, 187, 202, 203, 288, 348
Chicago Tribune, 87–88, 140, 176, 193, 198, 273
Childs, Marquis, 286, 289
China, Japan invasion of, 47, 88
Christensen, C. Lincoln, 264
Christian Science Monitor, 79, 215, 225, 266
Churchill, Winston, 301, 307
    Atlantic Charter and, 178, 182
    on Marshall's legacy, 319
    on Nazi propaganda, 19
    as prime minister, 56
Citadel, 348
Citizens' Military Training Camps (CMTC), 29, 79–80, 188
Civilian Conservation Corps (CCC, "Tree Army"), 23–42
    "Bonus Army" protests and, 24–33, 64
    CCC graduates and draft, 110–11
    criticism of, 34
    inception of, 23–24
    legacy of, 319–20
    Marshall and, 23, 27–28, 30, 36–43
    older veterans and recruits as members of, 32–36
    USO camps built by, 134

civilians. *See also* Civilian Conservation
	Corps (CCC, "Tree Army"); United
	Services Organizations (USO)
	Civilian Volunteer Effort (CVE), 83
	Louisiana maneuvers and, 55, 201
	Marshall on civilian defense force, 254–55
	morale of, 266–67
	native hospitality by, 161–62, 200
	volunteer chaplains, 139
	"Yoo-hoo!" incident and, 165–66, 328
civil rights movement. *See* African
	Americans
Civil War, 70
Clark, Bennett Champ, 246–47
Clark, D. Worth, 89
Clark, Grenville
	Clark Plan, 79–88, 91, 93, 94
	draft extension and, 174, 182, 188
	legacy of, 317
	NAACP Legal and Educational Defense
		Fund and, 348–49
	Pearl Harbor attack and, 283
Clark, Mark W., 214, 226, 241, 284, 318,
	319, 347–48
Cleveland Plain Dealer, 344
Clew, William J., 204–5
Cline, John H., 237–38
Coast Guard, 306
codetalkers, 234
Cohen, William, 349
Cohn, Harry, 275
Cohn, Jack, 275
college students, activism of. *See*
	isolationism
Collins, J. Lawton, 226, 284, 323
Colmer, William M., 51
Colonna, Jerry, 135
communism
	Communist Party USA, 140, 307
	Peace Mobilization Society, 90
	Red-baiting, 75
Congregation Rodeph Sholom, 279
Congress. *See also individual names of*
	representatives; individual names of
	senators
	Army expansion and, 132
	CCC and, 24–27, 29–31, 33, 35, 42
	draft extension and, 169, 174–75,
		177–81, 340–41
	isolationism of, 20, 339–40 (*See also*
		isolationism)

Lodge as only active duty member of,
	238
on Louisiana maneuvers, 50, 52, 54, 57,
	59, 65–67, 192–93
National Defense Act (1920), 85
on officer purge, 246
on Phoney War, 47
on popular culture depictions of Army,
	274–75
on prostitution, 196–97
Removal Board of, 210
resolution of war, 289–92
Selective Service desegregation and,
	344–45
Selective Service legislation of, 84–96
	(*See also* Selective Service System)
War of 1812 and, 69
war production expenditures,
	227–28
Congress of American Mothers, 89–90
Connolly, John, 289–90
conscientious objectors (COs), 77, 104,
	109–10
Coolidge, Calvin, 24–25
Cooper, Gary, 333
Cornwallis, Lord, 251
Corpening, C. C., 199
Correspondents of Future Wars, 74
Costello, Lou, 136, 273, 335
Coughlin, Charles, 45, 173
Cowen, Ruth, 266
Cox, Edward E., 90
Craig, Malin, 1, 7, 39, 210, 242
Creamer, Robert, 164–65
Crisis (NAACP magazine), 17–18, 313
Crosby, Bing, 296
Crusade in Europe, The (Eisenhower), 313,
	321
Cunningham, Bill, 162

Daily Princetonian (Princeton University),
	72–73
Dallas Morning News, 59–60, 254–55
Daly, John, 199, 234–35, 281, 331
Davis, Benjamin O., Sr., 99
Davis, Elmer, 284
Davis, Kenneth S., 82
D-Day
	National D-Day Museum, 315, 317
	preparation and events of, 205, 307–8,
		314–15, 327, 333–34, 337

deaths during peacetime
draft extension and low morale, 176
lynching on Army base, 147
during maneuvers and exercises, 59, 164, 217, 233, 260, 263
maneuvers and planning for, 196
World War I veterans' benefits and, 31–32
Dellinger, David, 104
Denmark, invasion of, 52
desertion rumor, "Over the Hill in October" (OHIO), 173–77, 181–87, 243, 255, 271–72
Desert Training Center (California), 297–99, 302–5, 313, 323, 328
D'Este, Carlo, 6–7, 249
Devers, Jacob L., 284
Dewey, Thomas, 343
DeWitt, John L., 248
DiMaggio, Joe, 103, 335
Dirksen, Everett, 165–66, 289
Dirty Dozen, The (film), 333
Disabled American Veterans, 31
Dix, John, 127
Dorris, Henry N., 54
Dos Passos, John, 78
Double V, 305–7, 341–42
Douglas, Lewis W., 30–31
draft extension. *See* Selective Service System, extension of service
Drew University, 74
Drum, Hugh
career ambition of, 2, 329
Carolinas maneuvers and, 252, 256–58, 260, 262–63, 265
First Army role of, 174
officer purge and, 245, 248
Pearl Harbor attack and, 283, 284
Plattsburg exercises/maneuvers, 13–16, 60, 91–94
Dworshak, Henry C., 89

Earhart, Amelia, 182–83
Early, Stephen, 98, 295
Economy Act (1933), 31
Edgar Bergen and Charlie McCarthy Show (radio show), 135–36
Edison, Charles, 84
Edison, Thomas, 84
Eichelberger, Robert L., 284
81st Infantry Division, 304

Eisenhower, Dwight D. "Ike"
on armored divisions of Army, 7
CCC and, 27, 33
characterization and image of, 224–27, 241–42
The Crusade in Europe, 313, 321
D-Day and, 307–8
desegregation of Selective Service, 347–49
leadership legacy of, 318, 328, 330–34
Louisiana maneuvers (1941) role and impact of, 201, 321–25
MacArthur and, 27
Mauldin and, 338
North Africa invasion and, 308
Pearl Harbor attack and, 282–84
as president, 330, 334, 347
on Pyle's death, 138
victory speech (May 8, 1945), 316
War Plans Division appointment, 293–94, 297
Eisenhower, John, 224, 226
Eisenhower, Susan, 241
Eliot, George Fielding, 199
Emrick, Stanley D., 56–57
Ennis, Skinnay, 135
eugenics, 44–45, 118–19
European theater (World War II)
Atlantic Charter, 178, 182
battle of the Bulge, 323–24, 333
blitzkrieg, 21–22
Churchill on "Europe first," 294–96
D-Day, 205, 307–8, 314–15, 327, 333–34, 337
Dunkirk battle, 65
German invasions (*See* Germany)
Lend-Lease Act (1941), 141, 214, 227
Marshall Plan and, 319
McNair on tank use in, 258
Northern Ireland maneuvers, 299–302
as "Phoney War," 47–52
Soviet Union invasion of Finland, 45
V-E (Victory in Europe) Day, 341
Evening Star (Washington, D.C.), 86, 103, 125, 237
Ewing, Don M., 233, 324–25
Executive Order 8530, 93
Executive Order 8802, 146
Executive Order 9981, 341–47

"Fall in line—Fall in line" (song), 74
Fechner, Robert, 41

Federal Bureau of Investigation (FBI), 54
Feller, Bob, 103, 290–91
Ferguson, Homer, 265
Fidler, Jimmie, 115
"Filthy Thirteen," 333
Finland, invasion of, 45
Fischer, Joseph R., 189
Fish, Hamilton, Jr., 89–91, 340
Fisher, Ham, 136–37
Five Came Back (Harris), 274
Flexner, Stuart Berg, 337
FM 21-100 Basic Field Manual (Marshall),
    137–38
Folliard, Edward T., 270
Fonda, Henry, 102
food. *See* health and nutrition
Ford, Gerald, 331
Ford, Henry, 141, 340
Forrest, Nathan Bedford, 222
Fort Benning, 122–24, 147, 189, 276–77.
    See also Second Armored Division
Fort Dix, 127, 176
Fortune (magazine), 177
442nd Infantry Regiment, 314
France
    CCC visit by, 38–39
    Dunkirk battle, 65
    German invasion of, 56
    Maginot Line, 47
    McNair on massed guns in, 258
    "Phoney War" and, 47, 48
    World War I and African American
        soldiers in, 17
    World War II entrance by, 4–5
Freedom to Serve (President's Committee
    on Equality of Treatment and
    Opportunity in the Armed Services),
    346
Fresno Bee, 136
Frye, William, 39, 41
Fuller, Claude, 75

Gabel, Christopher R., 21, 58, 93, 326
Gallup, George and Gallup Polls
    on draft extension, 175
    on Roosevelt, 65–66
    on Selective Service, 77–78, 95, 96,
        101–2, 120, 311
    on World War I, 43
Gandhi, Mahatma, 342
Garand M-1 rifles, 46, 121, 194, 227, 298

Garroway, Dave, 331
General Electric, 121
General Motors, 109
Gerard, Philip, 332
Germany
    Belgium invaded by, 80
    Congress members as Nazi
        sympathizers, 89
    declaration of war against U.S., 291–92
    Denmark invaded by, 52
    France invaded by, 56
    Hitler-Stalin non-aggression pact, 22, 90
    Hitler Youth Movement, 34
    Holocaust, 109, 172
    Nazi propaganda, 18–19, 254, 320
    Nuremberg trials, 340
    Poland invaded by, 1–7, 11–12, 16,
        18–22, 42–47
    Rommel's Afrika Korps, 311 (*See also*
        Operation Torch)
    Russia invaded by, 169, 250, 293
    Siegfried Line, 47
    U.S. Navy attacked by, 250
    USS *Greer* attacked by, 210–11
Gerow, Leonard J., 297
Gerry, Elbridge, 67–68
Ghost Army (23rd Headquarters Special
    Troops), 331–32
G.I. Army. *See* Army
G.I. Bill of Rights, 337
G.I.: The American Soldier in World War II
    (Kennett), 185
Gibson, Josh, 103
Gillem, Alvan C., Jr., 63
Gold Star Mothers of Veterans of Future
    Wars (Home Fire Division), 73, 75
Goldwyn, Sam, 275
Gone with the Draft (Kendall), 272
Gorin, Lewis J., Jr., 72, 75, 76, 108, 321
Grant, U. S., 264
Great Britain
    bombing of London, 102
    Dunkirk battle, 65
    on "Europe first," 294–96
    Lend-Lease Act (1941), 141, 214, 227
    Lindbergh on, and reaction to, 212–13
    "Phoney War" and, 48
    Revolutionary War, 68–69
    weapons supplied to, 82–84
    Wells on officer purge for, 249
    World War II entrance by, 4–5

Great Dictator, The (film), 274
Great Guns (film), 273
Greeley, John A., 218
Green, Constance McLaughlin, 27
Greenberg, Hank, 103, 116, 158, 161, 184, 276, 282, 335
"Green Light Letter" (Roosevelt), 291
Griffin, R. A., 205
Griswold, Oscar W., 252, 256, 260, 262–63
Gropman, Alan, 346
Gruenther, Alfred M., 225, 318, 330
Gurney, Chandler, 246

Hall, Felix, 147
Halstead, Laurence, 38
Hamilton, Alexander, 68
Hammond, Thomas S., 8
Hardwick, Leon, 99
Hardy, Oliver, 273
Harper's magazine, 118
Harris, Mark, 274
Harrison, West A., 277
Harsch, Joseph C., 215, 225
Hartford Courant, 187, 200, 204, 243
Harvard Crimson (Harvard University), 49
Hastie, William H., 99
Hayden, Jay G., 280
Heald, Weldon F., 302–3
health and nutrition
    Army medical personnel, 249–50
    during Carolinas maneuvers, 259
    CCC and, 35–37, 40
    C rations, 61
    of draftees, 112–14, 117–18
    K rations, 304
    Louisiana maneuvers and, 194–95, 198, 207, 226, 235
    Patton's "desert stove" and water plan, 302–3
    prostitution and, 130, 132, 196–97, 235–36
    segregation and, 97–99
    during Tennessee maneuvers, 152, 162–64
    Tuskegee experiments, 62
Hearne, Alford T., 171
Hearst, William Randolph, 75
Hemingway, Ernest, 78
Henle, Raymond Z., 295
Herr, John, 7
Hersey, John, 334

Hershey, Lewis B., 94, 286
Herzberg, Richard A., 138
Hill, Gladwin, 299
Hill, T. Arnold, 97
Hitler, Adolf. *See also* Germany
    Capra on, 320
    on eugenics, 44–45
    The Great Dictator (film), 274
    Hitler-Stalin non-aggression pact, 22, 90
    Nazi propaganda of, 18–19, 254, 320
    "Phoney War" and, 52
    Selective Service and public opinion about, 108, 169, 170, 172, 183
    U.S. election (1940) and, 85
    U.S. isolationism and, 321
Hodges, Courtney H., 284
Hoffman, Clare E., 89
Holland, James, 308
Holman, Rufus, 88
Holt, Rush Dew, 86–88, 101
Home Fire Division (Gold Star Mothers of Veterans of Future Wars), 73, 75
Hong Kong, fall to Japan by, 296
Hooper, Vincent, 216
Hoover, Herbert, 26, 27, 28, 30, 83, 171
Hope, Bob, 106, 134–36, 220, 273, 335–37
Hopkins, Harry, 3
Hormel, Jay C., 141
Hornaday, Mary, 266
horse cavalry (1939–1941), 7, 15, 18–19, 21, 63–64, 66, 193–94, 218, 236, 251–52, 269
Hottelet, Richard C., 199, 223, 229, 331
Householder, Eugene, 287–88
Houston, Donald E., 277
Houston Press, 194
Hurley, Patrick J., 27
Hutchins, Robert, 177
Huxen, Keith, 312
Hymel, Gary, 207
Hymel, Gene, 207

I Hear America Talking (Flexner), 337
Inouye, Daniel, 314
International News Service, 266
Ismay, Hastings, 301
isolationism
    college students' protests, 72–79
    draft extension protest and sabotage/ treason accusations, 170–74
    early Army expansion and, 140–41

isolationism, (*continued*)
  Louisiana maneuvers and, 43–47, 65
  public/activists' opinions changed about,
    210–13, 270, 321, 339–40
  Republican Party isolationists *vs.*
    interventionists, 85
  war resolution and, 289
  Woodring on, 19–20, 46
Italy, declaration of war by, 291–92
It Can't Happen Here (Lewis), 172

Jackson, William P., 10
Japan
  Alaska as vulnerable to, 51
  China invasion by, 47, 88
  escalation of tension with, 250, 265
  Hong Kong's fall to, 296
  Pearl Harbor attack by, 279–92
  U.S. merchant ships sunk by, 311
  West Coast planned attack by, 295
Japanese Americans
  442nd Infantry Regiment, 314
  Pearl Harbor attack and suspicion of,
    281
Jeffers, H. Paul, 323
Jehovah's Witnesses
  as concentration camp victims, 109
  as conscientious objectors, 104–5, 109
Jewish Welfare Board, 134, 212
Jim Crow laws. *See* African Americans
Jimmy Stewart (Smith), 115
Joe Palooka (comic strip), 136–37
Johnson, Campbell C., 99
Johnson, Hiram, 172
Johnson, Louis A., 19–20, 83
Johnson, Lyndon B., 177–78, 180–81,
    289–90, 331
Jones, Sam H., 191, 200–201
Jonkman, Bartel J., 89
Journal of the American Medical Association,
    117

Kansas City Star, 271
Kansas City Times, 213
Kasserine Pass, battle of, 312–13
Kay, Leon, 199, 216–17, 222
Kendall, Park, 272
Kennedy, John F., 49, 103, 114, 282, 330,
    331, 334, 338
Kennedy, Joseph, Jr., 103
Kennedy, Joseph P., Sr., 49, 171

Kennett, Lee, 185
"KILROY WAS HERE," 337
King, Martin Luther, Jr., 348
Kirk, Alan, 114
Knox, Frank, 84–85, 97–98, 280
Knox, Henry, 68
Knudsen, William, 109
Knutson, Harold, 89
Korean War, 346
Krock, Arthur, 31
Krueger, Walter
  Lear and, 166
  legacy of, 329–30
  Louisiana maneuvers and, 194, 200–201,
    213, 216–17, 220–26, 231, 232, 309,
    313, 324–25
  officer purge and, 243, 249
  Pearl Harbor attack and, 284
Kyser, Kay, 102

La Guardia, Fiorello, 104, 281
Landis, Kenesaw Mountain, 290–91
Landon, Alf, 66, 84
Langford, Frances, 135, 336
Latzko, Andreas, 78
Laurel, Stan, 273
Laux, Herbert, 147
Lawrence, David, 169–70, 180
Lawton, John Edward, 112–13, 332
Lear, Ben
  draft extension and, 176, 183–84
  legacy of, 328
  Louisiana maneuvers and, 200, 213–14,
    217–23, 230–32, 237
  officer purge and, 246–47, 248
  Pearl Harbor attack and, 284
  Tennessee maneuvers and, 151
  "Yoo-hoo!" incident and, 164–66, 328
Lee, Henry, 68
Lend-Lease Act (1941), 141, 214, 227
Leviero, Anthony H., 176
Lewis, Sinclair, 172
Libya. *See* African theater (World War II)
Life (magazine), 160–62, 175–77, 181–83,
    185–86, 205, 217
Lincoln, Abraham, 70, 127, 338
Lindbergh, Charles
  Allen on, 237
  America First Committee and, 140
  anti-Semitism of, 211–13
  draft extension and, 171, 173

as Nazi sympathizer, 11, 44, 48
on Nuremberg trials, 340
plane of, 264
Linderman, Harold C., 112–13
Lindley, Allen L., 86
Lippmann, Walter, 47–48, 96, 261
Lloyd, Harold, 106
Lodge, Henry Cabot, Jr., 15, 60, 238–39,
   260–61, 330–31
Lodge, Henry Cabot (grandfather), 60
Loomis, Don, 115
Los Angeles Times, 208
Louis, Joe, 102–3, 306
Louisiana maneuvers (1940), 43–71
   African American participation in, 61
   communication used for, 219, 222,
      233–34
   draft and, 67–71
   equipment tested in, 62
   injuries and deaths from, 59
   isolationism and, 43–47, 65
   Marshall's plans for, 49–54
   military funding increase and, 65–67
   Nazi *vs.* U.S. weaponry, 45–46
   officer promotion and, 241–42
   officer purge and, 242–50
   Patton and increased armored force,
      63–65
   phases of, 55–61
   "Phoney War" and, 47–52
   subsequent exercises, 91–93
Louisiana maneuvers (1941), 190–208,
   209–40
   Arkansas maneuvers as preparation for,
      205–7
   change in public opinion prior to,
      210–13
   draft extension and morale, 203–5
   Eisenhower on impact of, 321–25
   extension of service and, 168
   KOTMK (Red Army) and ALMAT
      (Blue Army), defined, 205, 213
   legacy of, 314–16
   New England exercises and, 208
   officer purge and, 209–10
   officers and leadership legacy and,
      328–31
   Phase I, 217–28
   Phase II, 229–33
   planning and logistics for, 190–201
   preparation for, 149, 213–17

racial hostility and, 201–3
results of, 233–40
scholarly examination of, 325–26
Second and Third Armies' role in, 191
weapon/equipment legacy of, 326–27
West Coast exercises and, 207–8
Louisiana maneuvers (1942), 309
Louisiana maneuvers (1944), 313
Love, Edmund, 315
Luce, Henry R., 160, 177
Lutes, Roy, 327

MacArthur, Douglas
   as Army Chief of Staff, 6
   CCC and, 23, 27–29, 32–35, 39, 41
   on desegregation, 346–47
   officer purge and, 242
   personal relationship with Eisenhower,
      27
   racism of, 240
MacGregor, Morris J., 98
MacLeish, Archibald, 78–79
Maginot, André, 47
Magruder, Bruce, 63
Major, E. M., 114
"Making of the American Officer, The"
   (Baldwin), 285
Manasco, Carter, 178
Manassas (Bull Run) maneuvers (1939),
   12–16, 149
Manchester, William, 39
Manchester Guardian (Great Britain), 139
maneuvers and field exercises. *See also*
      Louisiana maneuvers; Tennessee
      maneuvers
   land rights acquired for, 51, 150, 196
   "Little Libya" maneuvers in California,
      297–99, 302–5, 313, 323, 328
   Manassas maneuvers, 12–16, 149
   in 1944, 313–14
   Northern Ireland maneuvers, 299–302
   Plattsburg exercise/maneuvers, 13–16,
      60, 91–94
   review of all 1941 maneuvers, 269–70
   umpire role for, 56, 63, 149–50, 159–60,
      215–16, 230–31
March, Peyton C., 6
March of Time (newsreel company), 76
March on Washington, 145–46, 348
March on Washington, Randolph on,
   144–46

Marine Corps
  African Americans in, 306
  population size (1939), 5
Marshall, George C.
  on African American soldiers, 240
  African theater strategy, 296
  on arms production, 109
  Carolinas maneuvers and, 256, 261,
    265–66, 274, 278
  CCC and, 23, 27–28, 30, 36–43
  chief of staff appointment, 1–4, 6–9, 11,
    12, 15–16, 20–22
  on civilian defense force, 254–55
  draft extension and, 168–69, 170,
    173–78, 182–84, 186–89
  Eisenhower appointed to War Plans
    Division, 293–94
  "Europe first" strategy, 295
  FM 21-100 Basic Field Manual, 137–38
  legacy of, 317–19, 320, 322–23, 326,
    327–30, 339–41
  Louisiana maneuvers (1940) and, 49–54,
    57, 60–63, 65, 67
  Louisiana maneuvers (1941) and, 190,
    192–93, 197, 207, 219–21, 227, 229,
    230, 232, 234, 236
  Marshall Plan, 319
  Morale Division established by, 124–28,
    131–37, 139–40 (*See also* morale)
  Officer Candidate School (OCS),
    188–89, 242, 285, 312, 318
  officer promotions and, 241–42
  officer purge and, 209–10, 239, 242–50,
    312, 318
  Pearl Harbor attack and response by,
    280–81, 284–88
  Roosevelt's personal relationship with,
    3–4
  on Selective Service debate and passage,
    81–82, 84, 91–98
  speeches and radio addresses by, 129–30,
    139–40
  Stars and Stripes, 299–300
  Tennessee maneuvers and, 148–49, 166,
    167
  on "time of peril," 142
Marshall, George Preston, 279
Marshall, Katherine Tupper, 36–40, 51, 281
Marston Mat, 268, 327
Martin, Edward, 247–48

Martin, Joseph W., Jr., 89
Martin, Ralph, 239
Martin, William McChesney, Jr., 103,
  115–16
Mauldin, Bill, 116–17, 127–28, 240, 272,
  281, 338
Maverick, Maury, 75, 76
Mayer, Louis B., 275
McCormack, John, 178
McCullers, Carson, 169
McFarlane, William D., 74
McGill, Ralph, 62
McLemore, Henry, 158, 173
McMillin, Woody, 153, 162
McNair, Lesley J.
  Carolinas maneuvers and, 257–58, 263,
    265, 268, 269
  Desert Training Center and, 298
  as General Headquarters chief of staff,
    131
  legacy of, 328
  Louisiana maneuvers and, 192, 222,
    232–34, 236, 325
  officer purge and, 209, 210, 242, 246
McNaughton, Frank, 340
meals. *See* health and nutrition
Mencken, H. L., 131
Meredith, Burgess, 199
Merry-Go-Round (syndicated newspaper
  column), 225
Mexican-American War (1846–1848), 69
Miami Herald, 19, 260
military training. *See* Louisiana maneuvers;
  Selective Service System
Militia Act (1792), 68
Miller, Doris "Dorie," 306–7, 332
Miller, Merle H., 212–13
Miller, Samuel, 104–5
Millis, Walter, 78
Minton, Sherman, 87, 181
Molotov, Vyacheslav, 22
Monroe, James, 69
Montgomery, Bernard, 265
morale
  Army Morale Division, 124–28, 131–37,
    139–40
  civilian morale, 266–67
  draft extension and low morale, 173–77,
    181–87, 203–5
  G.I. culture and, 271–75, 337–39

Louisiana maneuvers (1941) and
protection of, 200
officer purge and, 209–10, 242–50
"Over the Hill in October" (OHIO)
and, 173–77, 181–87, 243, 255,
271–72
Stars and Stripes, 116, 299–300, 333,
338–39
during Tennessee maneuvers, 162–64
Morelock, Jerry, 328
Morgenthau, Henry, Jr., 83
Morrow, George, 165
Mortimer, John L., 194
Mosley, Leonard, 2
Motion Picture Producers and Distributors
of America, 275
M-1 rifles, 46, 121, 194, 227, 298
Muldrow, Hal L., 127
Murray, George Edwin Patrick, 326, 327
Murrow, Edward R., 5, 331
Mussolini, Benito, 321
Mutual Broadcasting Network, 211–13,
216

NAACP (National Association for the
Advancement of Colored People)
on Air Corps, 17–18
Crisis, 17–18, 313
Legal and Educational Defense Fund,
348–49
on Louisiana maneuvers (1941), 203
March on Washington proposed by,
145–46, 348
on 93rd, 313–14
on Selective Service and segregation,
97–99
Selective Service desegregation and,
343–49
Napoleon, 133
National D-Day Museum (National World
War II Museum), 315, 317
National Defense Act (1920), 85
National Emergency Committee, 81
National Guard
Army proportion represented by, 141
CCC and, 29
draft of (1940), 93
federalization of, 126–28
Louisiana maneuvers and, 54
officer purge in, 243–50

Plattsburg exercises/maneuvers, 13–16,
60, 91–94
training (1939), 5
National Jewish Welfare Board, 134, 212
National Negro Publishers Association,
287
Native Americans
codetalkers, 234
early integrated Army units, 128
Seminole Indians and draft, 101
Navy
African Americans in, 306
cooperation with other branches of
military by, 192–93
expansion of (1940), 65
German U-boats attacks on, 250
Kennedy and, 334
Knox as secretary of, 84–85, 97–98
Louisiana maneuvers and, 50, 214–15
Pacific theater, 308
Pearl Harbor attack and enlistment in,
290–91
segregation in, 97–99
Navy Relief Society, 306
NBC Radio, 83–84, 129–30, 216, 254–55,
336
Negro Youth Congress, 147
Nelson, Donald M., 46
New England, Louisiana maneuvers (1941)
and exercises in, 208
New Masses, 90
Newsweek, 15, 136, 169
New York Daily News, 199, 261
New York Herald Tribune, 171, 213, 217,
223, 228–29, 336–37
New York Times
Adler and, 80–81, 87–88
Baldwin's legacy and, 331
Lippman and, 47–48, 96
on Louisiana maneuvers, 228, 233, 309
on morale, 125
on Pearl Harbor, 285
on "Phoney War," 52
on Plattsburg exercises, 92, 94
Railey's legacy and, 331–32
on Selective Service, 103–4, 170, 171,
182, 185, 341, 345
on Tennessee maneuvers, 151, 156
on war-related industries, 12
New York Tribune, 96

93rd "all-colored" division, 313
94th Engineers, 201–2
Nixon, Richard M., 331
Norrell, William F., 166
Norris, John G., 45
North American Aviation, 121
North American Newspaper Alliance
   (NANA), 56
Northern Ireland maneuvers, 299–302
Norway, invasion of, 52
"Not My People's War" (Wright), 90
Nutter, Charles, 199
Nye, Gerald, 44, 89, 220, 275, 289, 339–40

officers
   Citadel and desegregation, 348
   Louisiana maneuvers and leadership
      legacy, 328–31
   non-commissioned, and CCC, 34
   non-commissioned, in Louisiana
      maneuvers, 58
   Officer Candidate School (OCS),
      188–89, 242, 285, 312, 318
   promotions (1939), 7–8
   promotions (1941), 241–42
   purge of, 209–10, 239, 242–50, 312, 318
   tested by Tennessee maneuvers, 148–50,
      157–59
Oliver, James C., 89
Oliver, Robert T., 321
101st Airborne Division, 323–24, 333
Operation Torch, 37, 308–13
Oppenheimer, Adurm, 102
O'Reilly, John, 222, 228
Our Army (magazine), 335
"Our Military Might" (Brown), 203
"Over the Hill in October" (OHIO),
   173–77, 181–87, 243, 255, 271–72
Overton, John Holmes, Sr., 50

Pacific theater (World War II). *See also*
   Japan; Pearl Harbor attack
   "Assistance to the Far East"
      (Eisenhower), 294
   Hong Kong's fall to Japan, 296
   Lindbergh on, 44
   U.S. victories (1942), 311
   V-J (Victory over Japan) Day, 341
Palmer, Frederick, 261–62
Panorama (Boston periodical), 34
Parachute Battalion (film), 273

Parran, Thomas, Jr., 62
Patch, Alexander M., 284
Patman, Wright, 25–26
Patriotism Prepaid (Gorin), 76
Patterson, Robert, 92, 121, 145, 209
Patton, Beatrice, 283
Patton, George S.
   "Battle of Bermuda Bridge" incident,
      238
   battle of the Bulge and, 323–24, 333
   Carolinas maneuvers and, 252–53, 256,
      257, 263, 264, 265–66, 276–77
   CCC and "Bonus Army," 27, 28, 64
   characterization and image of, 122–23,
      153–54, 157, 160–62
   death of, 323, 324–25
   Drum's career ambition and, 2
   leadership legacy of, 323–25
   legacy of, 318, 323–25, 331, 332, 338
   "Little Libya" maneuvers in California,
      297–99, 302–5, 313, 323, 328
   Louisiana maneuvers (1940) and, 63–64,
      66
   Louisiana maneuvers (1941) and, 191,
      206, 214–18, 222, 224, 229, 231–33,
      235, 238
   Operation Torch, 37, 308–11
   Pacific theater planning and victories,
      297–99, 302–4, 308–11, 313, 315
   Pearl Harbor attack and, 283, 284
   tank brigades established by, 66, 122–24
      (*See also* Second Armored Division)
   Tennessee maneuvers and, 151–61
Payne, Morris B., 243
Peace Mobilization Society, 90
Pearl Harbor attack, 279–92
   African Americans at, 306–7
   Army expansion success and, 311–12
   Japanese Americans as under suspicion,
      281
   Marshall's response to, 280–81, 284–88
   news of, 279–84
   resolution of war, 289–92
   Roosevelt's address about, 288–89
Pearson, Drew, 225, 248
Peck, James L. H., 18
Pegler, Westbrook, 59
Pepper, Claude, 90, 228
Pepsodent Show, The (radio show), 134
Perkins, Norris H., 157, 159, 163, 215, 218,
   231–32, 259, 332

Perret, Geoffrey, 189, 320
Perry, Mark, 294
Pershing, John J. "Black Jack"
  on African Americans in combat, 17
  CCC and, 40
  Marshall's appointment to chief of staff,
    1–3
  on military training, 85–86
  on officer purge, 246–47
  Pancho Villa raid by, 126
  Patton's correspondence with, 297
  on *Stars and Stripes*, 299
  World War I and, 244
"Phoney War," 47–52
Piper, William, 326–27
Piper Cub, 164, 215, 268, 327
Pittsburgh Courier, 17, 305, 306–7, 346
Plattsburg exercises/maneuvers, 13–16, 60,
  91–94
Plattsburg Plan, 79, 188–89
Plotkin, Stephen, 334–35
Pogue, Forrest C., 131, 244, 265
Poland, invasion of, 1–7, 11–12, 16, 18–22,
  42–47
population statistics
  Army (1939), 5
  Army inductions (July 1941), 169
  Army (October 1941), 249
  Army volunteers *vs.* draftees, 317
  Army (World War I), 6
  Marine Corps (1939), 5
  United States population (1940), 100
Prelude to War (documentary), 320
President's Committee on Equality of
  Treatment and Opportunity in the
  Armed Services, 346
press coverage. *See* public opinion and
  press coverage; *individual names of
  journalists*; *individual names of media
  outlets*
Price, T. A., 59–60
Princeton University, 72–77, 321
"Profiting by War Experiences" (Marshall),
  3
Providence Sunday Journal, 100–101
Provisional Tank Brigade, 64–65
public opinion and press coverage. *See
  also* isolationism; *individual names of
  journalists*; *individual names of media
  outlets*
  air mail used for dispatches, 237

Army's Distinguished Service Medal
  awarded to Palmer, 261–62
Bureau of Army Public Relations
  inception, 191
Capra's training films/documentaries,
  274, 320–21
  of Carolinas maneuvers, 266–69
cartoons and cartoonists, 41, 117, 120,
  127, 136–37, 240, 272, 337–39
change in opinion toward war (1941),
  210–13
civilian morale, 266–67
Gallup Polls, 43, 65–66, 77–78, 95, 96,
  101–2, 120, 175, 311
G.I. culture and, 271–75, 337–39
on Louisiana maneuvers, 56, 191, 198,
  206
Louisiana maneuvers (1941) and legacy
  of journalists, 331–32
Nazi propaganda, 18–19, 254, 320
newspaper circulation (1941), 152
Patton on, 123–24
Pearl Harbor attack news, 279–84
purposeful military disinformation, 219,
  222, 331–32
Pyle and, 138, 301
risks to journalists covering military, 234
on Selective Service, 72–79, 95–97
on Tennessee maneuvers, 153–56, 160–62
women reporters, 266–67
Pyle, Ernie, 138, 301

Quisling, Vidkun, 52

race and racism. *See* African Americans
Railey, Hilton Howell, 156, 182–87,
  331–32
"Railey Report," 182–87
Randolph, A. Philip, 97–98, 144–46,
  342–49
Rankin, Jeannette, 289
Rayburn, Sam, 91, 177–80, 340
R-Day (October 16, 1940), 100–105
Reader's Digest, 95
Reflections in a Golden Eye (McCullers), 169
Remarque, Erich Maria, 78
Reminiscences (MacArthur), 27
Reserve Army
  enlistment term, 141–42
  officer purge and, 244–50
  Reserve Officers Corps leadership, 110

Reserve Army, (*continued*)
  ROTC, 29, 75
  term of commitment, 142
  training (1939), 5
Revolutionary War, 68–69
Richardson, Robert C., 191–92
Ricks, Thomas E., 329
Ridgway, Matthew, 148
Riggs, Thomas, Jr., 75, 270
Rise and Fall of the Third Reich, The (Shirer), 331
Road to War (Millis), 78
Roberts, Stanley, 347
Robinson, Elsie, 26
Rockefeller, David, 103
Rockefeller, John D., III, 103
Rockefeller, Laurance, 103
Rockefeller, Winthrop, 103, 115, 253
Rockwell, Norman, 276, 338
Roll, David L., 41, 84, 294
Roll Again Second Armored (Perkins), 332
Rommel, Erwin, 265, 309, 311, 312
Rooney, Andy, 116, 282, 338
Roosevelt, Eleanor, 32, 75, 77, 96, 145, 294
Roosevelt, Franklin, Jr., 103
Roosevelt, Franklin D., 307–8
  appointed chief of staff by, 1–4, 6–9, 11, 12, 15–16, 20–22
  on arms production, 120–21
  Army expansion and, 126, 136–37, 141, 144–46
  Atlantic Charter and, 178, 182
  CCC and, 23, 28–32, 34, 37, 40
  Drum and, 329
  election of (1936), 66
  election of (1940), 108
  "Europe first" policy, 294–96
  Executive Order 8530, 93
  Executive Order 8802, 146
  G.I. Bill of Rights and, 337
  "Green Light Letter," 291
  legacy of, 317
  Lindbergh and, 212–13, 340
  Louisiana maneuvers and, 57, 65, 67, 192–93, 203, 211–12, 228
  New Deal of, 23–24
  1940 election of, 95–97
  officer promotions and, 241
  Pearl Harbor attack and, 283, 287–91
  "Phoney War" and, 45–47
  as secretary of Navy, 192–93

Selective Service and, 77, 78, 80–85, 88–89, 91, 95–99, 100, 105–9
Selective Service and draft extension, 169–72, 174–75, 176, 178, 182, 185
"shoot-on-sight" speech, 211–13
Roosevelt, John, 103, 107
Roosevelt, Quentin, 253
Roosevelt, Theodore, 84, 253
Roosevelt, Theodore, Jr., 253, 276
Rosenman, Samuel, 95, 340
Runyon, Damon, 251
Rutherford, Albert G., 178
Ryder, Gene, 199

Sacramento Bee, 86
Salisbury, Harrison, 221, 282
San Francisco Chronicle, 88, 314
Sansone, Leonard, 339
Santa Anna, Antonio López de, 70
Saturday Evening Post, 199, 276
Scott, Charles L., 223
Scott, Winfield, 69
Seattle Times, 130
Sebring, Lewis B., 162–63, 217, 229, 232
Second Armored Division
  additional tank destroyer battalions called for, 162
  in Carolinas maneuvers, 252, 268, 269, 277
  inception of tank brigades in, 64–66
  in Louisiana maneuvers (1941), 215, 217, 224, 229, 238
  Patton appointed commander of, 66, 122–24
  Provisional Tank Brigade and, 64–66
  Roll Again Second Armored (Perkins), 332
  in Tennessee maneuvers, 151–62
Segal, Bernard, 256
Seidule, Ty, 242
Selective Service System, 79–99, 100–121
  African Americans and disproportionate draft, 143, 305
  CCC graduates and, 110–11
  celebrity draftees/enlistees, 102–3, 114–17, 158, 161, 287–88, 306, 333–35, 338
  Clark Plan and, 79–88, 91, 93, 94
  college students' protests against, 72–79
  conscientious objectors (COs), 77, 104, 109–10
  desegregation of, 341–49

desertion rumor, "Over the Hill in
October" (OHIO), 173–77, 181–87,
243, 255, 271–72
draft boards and classification, 107–9
draft number system of, 105–7, 111–12
enlistment term, 141–42
fears about draft, 118–19
Fish amendment proposal for, 89–91
health and nutrition of draftees, 117–18
historical perspective of draft, 67–71
impact of, 340–41
legacy of selected draftees, 332–33
Marshall on passage of Burke-
Wadsworth, 94–95
Marshall on "Selective Service Army,"
139–40
Navy as volunteer system (1941), 250
Pearl Harbor attack and expansion of,
285–86
Plattsburg exercises and, 91–94
public opinion and 1940 election, 95–97
R-Day (October 16, 1940), 100–105
rejection and negative malingering,
113–14
Roosevelt on "muster," 81, 105–6
segregation of African American
soldiers, 96–99
Selective Service Act (1917), 71
Selective Training and Service Act of
1940 (Burke-Wadsworth bill), 84–86,
96
success of (1942), 311–12
volunteer draftees and, 111–13
World War I draft and, 71
Selective Service System, extension of
service, 168–89
Congress on, 169, 174–75, 177–81,
340–41
discharges permitted, 184–85
Louisiana maneuvers (1941) and, 203–5
morale and, 173–77, 181–87
need for, 168–70
Officer Candidate School inception and,
188–89
protest and sabotage/treason accusation,
170–74
Sevareid, Eric
on Carolinas maneuvers, 252, 260–61,
267
on draft extension, 170, 186
legacy of, 331

on Louisiana maneuvers, 199, 225, 234
on Pearl Harbor attack, 284, 285
Sherman, William, 251
Sherrod, Robert, 224–25
Sherwood, Robert E., 182, 307
Shirer, William L., 199, 331
Short, Dewey Jackson, 179–80
Shreveport Times, 233, 240, 324
Silverstone, Murray, 275
Simon, Abe, 306
Simpson, William Hood, 284
Slocum, Bill, 199, 267
Smith, Frederic H., 128
Smith, Gerald L. K., 45
Smith, Starr, 115
Smith, William A., 277
Snow, Edgar, 199
Snyder, Marty, 226–27, 332
Social Justice (magazine), 173
Soldiers of the Old Army (Vogel), 10
Somers, Andrew L., 179
Soviet Union
German invasion of Russia, 169, 250,
293
Hitler-Stalin non-aggression pact, 22,
90
invasion of Finland by, 45
McNair on tank use in, 258
Truman on, 342
Spanish-American War, 31, 84
Speare, Charles F., 56
"Spirit of '41, The" (CBS radio broadcasts),
199
spirituality
chaplains and, 139
USO and, 256
war discussion in houses of worship,
279
Springfield (Mass.) Republican, 181
St. Louis Post Dispatch, 180
Stalin, Joseph, 22, 90, 169, 308
Starke, Alex, 37
Stars and Stripes (Army), 116, 299–300, 333,
338–39
Steinbeck, John, 336–37
Stephenson, Bess, 239
Stewart, James (Jimmy), 102, 114–15,
281–82, 333–34
Stewart, Ollie, 201, 277–78
Stilwell, Joseph W. "Vinegar Joe," 42, 62,
329

Stimson, Henry
  African theater strategy of, 296, 298–99
  Army expansion and, 122, 130, 133, 136,
      142
  Carolinas maneuvers and, 254, 266, 269
  draft extension and, 170–73, 177, 186,
      188–89
  Drum and, 329
  on G.I. culture, 339
  legacy of, 317, 319
  Lodge and, 330
  Louisiana maneuvers (1941) and,
      192–93, 197, 204, 230
  officer promotion/purge and, 241, 244,
      247, 290–10
  Pearl Harbor attack and, 280, 283, 292
  Selective Service and, 106, 109
  Selective Service debate and passage,
      83–85, 97–98
  Tennessee maneuvers and, 158, 159,
      162
  "Yoo-hoo!" incident and, 166
Stinnett, Jack, 272
Stuart, J. E. B., 222
Stuart, R. Douglas, Jr., 140
Sulzberger, Arthur Hays, 182, 185
Sweeney, Martin L., 91

Taft, Robert A., 86, 141, 169, 330
Taft, William Howard, 83
tank brigades. *See* Second Armored
      Division
Taylor, Millicent, 79
Taylor, Robert, 102
Taylor, Zachary, 197
"Ten little registrants standing in a line"
      (rhyme), 119
Tennessean (Nashville), 153–54, 157, 158
Tennessee maneuvers, 148–67
  army expansion and, 167
  morale and conditions during, 162–64
  in 1944, 313
  preparation for, 150, 152–53
  press coverage of, 153–56, 160–62
  "Railey Report," 182–87
  Second Armored Division's role in,
      151–62
  for testing officers, 148–50, 157–59
  27th Infantry Division, 127, 176
  "Yoo-hoo!" incident and, 165–66, 328

terminology
  bivouac, 154
  books about, 272
  dog face, 338
  Double V, 305–7
  FM 21-100 Basic Field Manual (Marshall)
      on, 138
  G.I., 138
  muster *vs.* draft (or conscription), 81, 105–6
  peacetime *vs.* time of peril, 142
  phony/phoney, 47
  race, 61
  shakedown, 126
  SNAFU and slang used in Louisiana
      maneuvers (1941), 239
  streamlined, 21
That Hamilton Woman (film), 274
Third Army Aircraft Warning Service, 55
This Week (newspaper supplement), 111
Thomas, Norman, 34
Thompson, Dorothy, 96, 172
Thompson, John, 193
366th Infantry, 277
Thurmond, Strom, 345
Time (magazine)
  on draft extension, 176–77, 183
  Eisenhower and, 224
  on Louisiana maneuvers, 59, 204
  on officer purge, 210
  on Operation Torch, 310
  on segregation, 98–99
  on Selective Service, 340
  on weapons manufacturing, 109
Times Herald (Port Huron, Michigan), 199
Tinée, May, 273
training programs. *See* Civilian
      Conservation Corps (CCC, "Tree
      Army"); maneuvers and field exercises
"Treasury Raid" (protest), 77
"Tree Army." *See* Civilian Conservation
      Corps (CCC, "Tree Army")
Trinity College (Connecticut), 139–40
Truman, Harry S.
  on desegregation, 342–46, 349
  draft extension and, 181
  Executive Order 9981 (Truman's
      desegregation order), 341–47
  Marshall Plan and, 319
  on officer purge, 246
  Pearl Harbor attack and, 290

Truman, Ralph Emerson, 246–47
Truscott, Lucian K., 284
Trussell, C. P., 184–85
Tuchman, Barbara, 329
Tucker, Ray, 35
Tunisia, Operation Torch and, 37, 308–13
Tunney, Gene, 291
Turner, John C., 321
Tuskegee experiments, 62
Tuskegee Institute, 287, 306
23rd Headquarters Special Troops (Ghost Army), 331–32
Twenty-Slave Law (1862), 70
27th Infantry Division
  Japanese submarine intercepted by, 295
  Louisiana maneuvers (1941), 222, 237
  Pearl Harbor attack and, 291
  Tennessee maneuvers, 127, 176

Ulio, James, 133
"Unexplainable B. K. Wheeler, The" (Thompson), 172
Union Theological Seminary, 104
United Press, 156, 216–17, 223, 228–29
United Services Organizations (USO), 134–37, 207, 255–56, 335–37
University of Maryland, 96
Urban League, 97–99, 144–46
U.S. Department of War. *See also* Stimson, Henry
  on arms production, 121
  Eisenhower in War Plans Division, 293–94
  isolationism of, 19–20
  on racial tension, 203
  on segregation, 98
  Woodring's resignation, 82–83
  on "Yoo-hoo!" incident, 166–67, 328
USS *Greer*, 210–11
USS *Kearny*, 250
USS *PT-109*, 334
USS *Reuben James*, 250
USS *West Virginia*, 306–7

Vandenberg, Arthur, 88
Van Zandt, James E., 74
Vassar College, 73
Vessey, John W., Jr., 318
Veterans Administration, 43
Veterans of Foreign Wars, 15
Veterans of Future Wars, 72–79, 270, 321

V-E (Victory in Europe) Day, 341
Vincent, Beverly M., 91
V-J (Victory over Japan) Day, 341
Vogel, Victor, 10–11

Wadsworth, James Wolcott, 84–85, 174–75, 177–78, 340–41
Walk in the Sun, A (film), 315
Wall Street Journal, 76, 103
war correspondents. *See* public opinion and press coverage
War Is a Racket (Butler), 44
War of 1812, 69
Washington, George, 68–69
Washington, Val, 347
Washington Post
  on Army reorganization, 45
  on Carolinas maneuvers, 254
  on *FM 21-100 Basic Field Manual* (Marshall), 137–38
  on isolationism, 270, 321
  on Louisiana maneuvers, 228
  on Northern Ireland maneuvers, 301
  on Officer Candidate Schools, 312
  on Plattsburg exercises, 92
  on segregation, 99
  on Tennessee maneuvers, 156
Washington Whirligig (syndicated column, Tucker), 35
Waters, Walter W., 25–26
Watson, Mark Skinner, 48, 236, 237, 317, 331
Watson, Tom, 199
Wayne, John, 102
weapons and equipment. *See also* maneuvers and field exercises; Second Armored Division
  aircraft, 164, 214–15, 268, 327
  autogiros, 197
  for communication, 62, 219, 222, 233–34, 303, 327
  dust respirators, 268
  fuel for maneuvers, 195–96, 259–60
  Garand M-1 rifles, 46, 121, 194, 227, 298
  Hitler's Panzer divisions, 5, 18–19, 45–46, 63
  horse cavalry (1939–1941), 7, 15, 18–19, 21, 63–64, 66, 193–94, 218, 236, 251–52, 269
  inadequate supply, 11

weapons and equipment, (*continued*)
jeeps, 304, 311
lack of preparedness (1939), 7, 11–12
Lend-Lease Act (1941) and, 141, 214, 227
Louisiana maneuvers and, 46, 59–62, 66, 326–27
manufacturing, 67, 109, 120–21, 227–28, 286
Marston Mat, 268, 327
race and disproportionate assignment of, 144
tank attacks and air superiority, 223
Woodring's resignation and, 82–83
Webster, Daniel, 69
Weigley, Russell, 12
Weil, Granger, 199
Wells, H. G., 249
Wheeler, Burton K., 141, 169, 170–73, 237, 340
While England Slept (Kennedy), 114
Whiskey Rebellion (1794), 68
White, Walter, 97, 98, 99, 145–46, 345–46, 348
"White Christmas" (Berlin), 296
Whitehead, Don, 311
Why We Fight (film series), 320
Wilkins, George Hubert, 302
Wilkins, Roy, 313
Williams, Gladstone, 181
Willkie, Wendell, 88–89, 91, 99, 108, 275
Wilson, Charles, 347
Wilson, Woodrow, 16, 74, 283
Wolf, The (cartoon, Sansone), 339
Women's Army Auxiliary Corps, 306

Womer, Jack, 269–70, 333
Wonder Bread, 118
Woodring, Harry Hines, 19–20, 39, 46–47, 82–83, 88–89
Word Study (Herzberg), 138
World War I
African American soldiers in, 17
"Bonus Army" and veterans of, 24–33, 64 (*See also* Civilian Conservation Corps (CCC, "Tree Army"))
draft during, 71, 117
MacLeish on post-World War I writers, 78–79
Marshall's role in, 3
Meuse-Argonne campaign, 304
Patton's role in, 63
Pershing and, 244
Plattsburg Plan and, 79, 188–89
public opinion about, 43
Wilson and, 74
World War II. *See* African theater; Army; Congress; European theater; Marshall, George C.; Pacific theater; Selective Service System
Wright, Richard, 90
Wynn, Neil A., 288

Yahner, Rice, 154–55, 163, 263
Yale University, 79–80, 83
Yank (magazine), 303, 337
Yeldell, B. O., 196
"Yoo-hoo!" incident, 165–66, 328
Young, Charles, 16–17

Zorina, Vera, 335
Zukor, Adolph, 275